W9-DJQ-995

DIRECTIONS 2

Advertising and Design in Canada

DIRECTIONS 89

CORPORATE SPONSORS

ART DIRECTORS CLUB
OF TORONTO

BLUMER LEVON LTD.

CANON CANADA INC.

COMMODORE AMIGA
OF COMMODORE BUSINESS
MACHINES LIMITED

EMPRESS GRAPHICS INC.

HEIDELBERG CANADA

MATTHEWS INGHAM AND LAKE INC.

PROVINCIAL PAPERS
A DIVISION OF
ABITIBI-PRICE INC.

STUDIO CENTRE

TECHNI PROCESS LIMITED

AWARDS PRESENTATION

FORD OF CANADA LIMITED

THE GLOBE AND MAIL

THE ART DIRECTORS CLUB OF TORONTO

PRESIDENT

HEATHER COOPER

BOARD OF DIRECTORS

HEATHER COOPER, CHAIRPERSON
DIETER KAUFMANN, VICE PRESIDENT
STUART ASH
BERT BELL
THEO DIMSON
LOUIS FISHAUF
GEORGES HAROUTIUN
TERRY ILES
KEN RODMELL

EXECUTIVE COMMITTEE

HEATHER COOPER, PRESIDENT
WALTER AUGUSTOWITSCH
SKIP DEAN
CHRISTINE DOWNS
TERESA FERNANDES
ARNOLD KELLY
LISA MILLER
MARIA MURRAY
JIM WIDEMAN
BARBARA WOOLLEY
VERN ZIMMERMAN

ADMINISTRATIVE STAFF

DAWN COONEY
LINDA VOPNI
VIRGINIA WICKSTROM

*A very special thanks to Linda Vopni and Virginia Wickstrom.
Without their expertise and labours the judging weekend, the
show and this book would have been virtually impossible.*

CREDITS

*A publication of Applied Arts Inc.
20 Holly Street, Suite 208
Toronto, Ontario, Canada M4S 3B1
Telephone (416) 488-1163*

ART DIRECTOR
GEORGES HAROUTIUN

EDITOR
PETER GIFFIN

DESIGNERS
BONITA BOCANEGRA-COLLINS
GARY DARAKJIAN

CONTRIBUTING PHOTOGRAPHERS
BERT BELL
VINCENT NOGUCHI
MYRON ZABOL

CONTROLLER/OFFICE MANAGER
RITA HAROUTIUN

DISTRIBUTION/CIRCULATION MANAGER
JANET HAMER

PRODUCTION
M.A.G. GRAPHICS INC.

PAGE LAYOUTS
LIGHTSPEED COLOUR LAYOUT SYSTEM

TYPESETTING
TECHNI PROCESS LIMITED

COLOUR SEPARATIONS
EMPRESS GRAPHICS INC.

PRINTING
MATTHEWS INGHAM AND LAKE INC.

PAPER
BASKERVILLE GLOSS 80 LB.
MANUFACTURED BY PROVINCIAL PAPERS,
A DIVISION OF ABITIBI-PRICE INC.

DISTRIBUTED BY
CANADA
FIREFLY BOOKS LIMITED
*3520 PHARMACY AVENUE
UNIT 1C, SCARBOROUGH,
ONTARIO, CANADA M1W 2T8*

WORLDWIDE
ROCKPORT PUBLISHERS
*5 SMITH STREET
ROCKPORT, MASS.
U.S.A. 01966*

*Applied Arts has tried its best to ensure that all the credits in this publication are correct.
However, if a mistake has been made, we extend our apologies.*

PUBLISHED BY APPLIED ARTS INC.

PRESIDENT
GEORGES HAROUTIUN

*All rights reserved, Reproduction of any part of this book is strictly forbidden. All transparencies
and/or illustrations reproduced in this book have been accepted on the condition that they are
reproduced with the knowledge and prior consent of the photographer and/or illustrator
concerned and no resposibility is accepted by the Publigher or Printer for any infringement of
copyright or otherwise arising out of publication thereof.*

*COPYRIGHT 1989
APPLIED ARTS INC.*

ISBN 0-921940-02-5
ISSN 0840-8769

*All Arts are one, howe'er
distributed they stand;
Verse, tone, shape, color, form,
are fingers on one hand.*

-WILLIAM W. STORY
(1819-1895)

HEATHER COOPER, PRESIDENT

ALLAN KAZMER

A PASSION FOR ADVERTISING

The day after our selection committee had unanimously voted Allan Kazmer the 1989 winner of the Les Usherwood Award for a lifetime of excellence in the field of communication arts, I happened to be having lunch with Barbara Dunne, a friend who had been the account director on Christie Brown during the time which Allan did some of his best work. I asked if she could think of one word to describe him, and without hesitation she said, "Passion."

I didn't realize how right she was until I got back to the agency and looked it up in the dictionary. One definition explains that passion is "any emotion or feeling as love, desire, anger, hate, fear, grief, joy, hope, etc., especially when of a compelling nature." Allan has never approached the art of communication in a clinical or calculated way; he's always done it with passion.

It is the reason Allan has done some of the very best creative work this country has seen over the last 20 years and continues to lead the way.

I was fortunate to be Allan's creative partner for a number of years and can tell you that working with somebody who is as passionate about his work as Allan is not always easy. But the results are invariably rewarding.

This is the first time the Les Usherwood Award has been given to a copywriter. I cannot think of a more deserving recipient.

Brian Harrod
Executive Vice-President and
Creative Director,
Harrod & Mirlin

Photo by BERT BELL

RITZ

To fight private label, we suggested that Christie put the name "Ritz" right on the cracker. The ad makes big news of little news in a gracious and whimsical manner.

READ THIS AD TO YOUR DOG

Involve the pet owner. Involve the pet. Have fun. We've got to take ourselves less seriously.

HOLLAND CHEESE

This was Brian Harrod's headline and layout. All I did was add the blurb on the bottom that came straight out of research. Thanks partner.

TWO MAJOR EVENTS

Of all the VW ads I've been a part of, this is perhaps my favourite. Perhaps.

SALADA MORNING MARMALADE

As I recall, we actually recommended that the client change their packaging to a good old Mason jar.

THE RITZ RIDDLE

Up until now, you couldn't tell whether this was the frontside of a Ritz cracker or the backside of a Ritz cracker. Even worse, you couldn't tell whether this was the front or the back of one of the many pretend Ritz's. Fortunately for us all, Mr. Christie has taken steps to clarify the Ritz riddle. This is indeed the back of a real Ritz and once you turn the page you'll know why.

THE RITZ RIDDLE RESOLVED

Right now, Ritz and only Ritz has the word Ritz right on the Ritz. So now you can stop people from slipping you a pretend Ritz when what you really want is a real Ritz. And too, now you'll never confuse the reverse side of a Ritz from the front side of a Ritz. Our thanks to Mr. Christie for resolving the Ritz riddle.

Read this ad to your dog.

Dear (Dog's name). Good news. The next time I go shopping, I'm going to take this coupon (tear off coupon and show to dog) and buy you a great taste treat.

You know that nice Ken-L Ration Burger you like so much. Well now you have a choice. (Show dog picture of food in ad.) This is Ken-L Ration Burger with Liver Flavoured Chunks. ▪▪▪ (Point to liver flavoured chunks shown above.) See those dark brown chunks. That's the liver taste. (Look dog directly in eyes.) And it's actually better for you than fresh liver. Because it gives you all the protein, vitamins and minerals you need. (If dog is wagging his tail, take coupon and go directly to store. If dog pretends to be nonchalant, redeem coupon on your next shopping trip. Pat dog and say:) You're a good dog, (Dog's name). And (Your name) loves you.

Ken-L Ration Burger with Liver Flavoured Chunks.

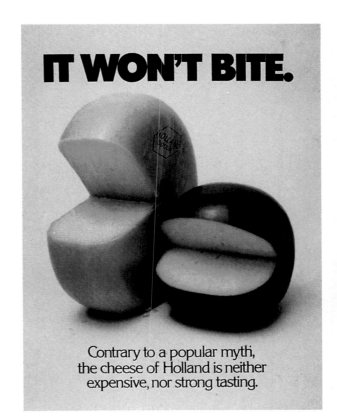

IT WON'T BITE.

Contrary to a popular myth, the cheese of Holland is neither expensive, nor strong tasting.

Two major events in the history of locomotion.

In the beginning we all walked. And for centuries, foot-power was basically it. Then some clever person invented the wheel. So we really started to get around. But oxen-power and horse-power had their limitations. After all, oxen and horses had to eat. And had to sleep.

So somebody invented the automobile. Which was a pretty neat idea. Except you had to be rich to buy one. And rich to operate one. Then along came Volkswagen, the "people wagon". Finally, a car people could afford to buy. And afford to run.

Who will ever forget the VW Beetle. It was revolutionary in design and durability. And just about everybody could afford one.

And how about Rabbit. Finally, sophisticated engineering came to a sub-compact car. The front-wheel drive Rabbit was destined to become the most copied car in its class. However, copies are just that. Copies.

Then the Jetta appears. A car in a class by itself. A German engineered sports sedan, yes. Expensive to buy, no. In summary, along came Volkswagen. And the rest is history.

VOLKSWAGEN

How can we make our marmalade more homemade?

Change our jar?

Wouldn't help a bit. We already use thick-cut chunks of the best tropical oranges, lemons and grapefruit. Slow simmer them in small batch kettles, using our own special recipe. And call it Shirriff 'Good Morning' Marmalade. We could change our jar and label, but the taste would remain the same. Homemade.

SALADA/SHIRRIFF QUALITY FOODS

JAC COVERDALE
**Founder and Creative Director,
Clarity Coverdale Rueff Advertising**

Before founding the Minneapolis-based agency in 1979, Jac Coverdale worked as an account executive and art director at Associates & Larranaga, Grey Advertising and Carmichael Lynch. Some of CCR's current accounts are the City of Minneapolis, the National YMCA and Northwestern National Life Insurance.

MARK FENSKE
**Creative Director,
Wieden & Kennedy**

Mark Fenske works on a variety of accounts at the Los Angeles office of Wieden & Kennedy, including Nike, Pepe Jeans, Speedo Swimsuits, Gallo and Paramount Pictures. He is also an instructor at the Art Center College of Design in Pasadena.

DAVID LUBARS
**Executive Vice-President/
Creative Director,
Leonard Monohan Lubars
& Partners**

Prior to becoming a partner at LML&P in Providence, Rhode Island last year, David Lubars had worked at Chiat/Day in Los Angeles, creating ads for Apple Computers and Pizza Hut and heading the creative group responsible for the Yamaha Motor Corporation and truck division of Nissan Motors U.S.A.

KERRY GRAHAM
**Senior Vice-President/
Associate Creative Director
Hill, Holliday,Connors, Cosmopolus**

Kerry Graham has helped create advertising for such clients as Royal Crown Cola, United Jersey Banks, Labatt's USA, Jordan Marsh Company and Centrust Savings Bank. Before joining the Boston agency last year, he had an award-winning career at the Atlanta office of J. Walter Thompson.

SUSAN FITZGERALD
**Senior Art Director
Chiat/Day/Mojo**

Susan Fitzgerald has helped create advertising for IBM, Chemical Bank, Napa Naturals, Domaine Chandon and Sara Lee. Before joining the New York-based agency, she worked at Lord Einstein O'Neill, Hal Riney & Partners, Fitzgerald and Mead and Hoefer, Dieterich + Brown.

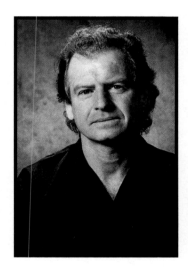

SEYMON OSTILLY
**Vice-President/
Associate Creative Director
Lord Einstein O'Neill**

Originally born and raised in South Africa, for the past 12 years Seymon Ostilly has lived and worked in New York, putting his creative energies into such accounts as IBM, Contel, Elizabeth Arden, *The Wall Street Journal, The New Yorker* and Wrangler. He has won numerous awards.

BOB CIANO
Art Director,
Travel & Leisure

During the past 20 years, Bob Ciano has held 12 jobs at various publications, including *Life, The New York Times* and *Esquire*. At this rate, the New York-based art director predicts that he will run out of magazines to work at in another 12 years.

RUDY HOGLUND
Art Director, Time

Rudy Hoglund has been art director of *Time* magazine since 1980 and was recipient of the 1986 National Magazine Award for design. He has worked in the past with Milton Glaser and Walter Bernard, and assisted Bernard in his redesign of *Time* in 1977.

MELLISA TARDIFF
Art Director,
Town & Country

Before becoming art director at *Town & Country* magazine in 1979, Melissa Tardiff worked as a graphic designer with New York's Metropolitan Transportation Authority. She currently teaches magazine design at the School of Visual Arts and is past president of the Society of Publication Designers.

NEIL SHAKERY
Partner,
Pentagram Design

Formerly the art director of *Psychology Today* and *Saturday Review* and associate art director of the original *Look* magazine, Neil Shakery works at the San Francisco office of Pentagram. He has designed prototypes and editorial formats for various American and Canadian magazines.

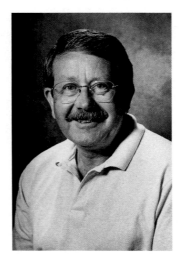

JAMES CROSS
Founder, Cross Associates

The Los Angeles and San Francisco
offices of Cross Associates do a range of
design work for blue-chip corporations,
including annual reports, corporate
identity programs and marketing
communications. James Cross is the
international president of the Alliance
Graphique Internationale.

TRACEY SHIFFMAN
**Partner, Tracey Shiffman
Roland Young Design Group**

With a distinguished reputation in the
Los Angeles design community, Tracey
Shiffman works for such clients as the
Museum of Contemporary Art, Los
Angeles; the Getty Center for Education
in the Arts; Capitol Records; Pacific
Arts Video; and Otis Parsons School of
Design.

The business of

Commodore Amiga 2000
68000 CPU, 16/32 bit, 1 MB Ram

Commodore Amiga 2000 HD
68000 CPU, 16/32 bit, 1 MB Ram,
40 MB Autoboot hard disk

®Commodore and Commodore Amiga are
 trademarks of Commodore Business Machines Limited.
®MS-DOS is a trade mark of Microsoft Corporation.

All photos of judges by
MYRON ZABOL

LYLE METZDORF
President, Lyle Metzdorf, Inc.

Before forming his own design firm and
advertising agency in New York City,
Lyle Metzdorf was, among other things,
editor of *Graphis* magazine and chairman
and creative director of Metzdorf
Advertising, one of the largest
independently owned ad agencies in
southwest United States.

WILLIAM DRENTTEL
President, Drenttel Doyle Partners

Recent clients of William Drenttel's
New York-based design firm and
advertising agency include Olympia &
York, The World Financial Center, Liz
Claiborne, *Spy* magazine and J&B
Scotch. Before founding the business,
Drenttel was a senior vice-president at
Saatchi & Saatchi Advertising.

being creative

raphic arts, illustration, music, video production,
ublishing, and scores of other creatively driven
ompanies have already discovered that the Amiga®
000, 2000 HD, and the new 2500 are invaluable
reative tools of the trade. To date, Commodore®
as sold over one million Amigas worldwide. The
eason for this success is obvious. For the cost of
n Amiga you simply can't find another computer
nat delivers what Amiga can.
  Amiga is recognized as a world leader in micro-
omputer graphics technology. With the power and
peed to generate and use a tremendous range of
raphics. But Amigas' benefits don't stop there. By
dding an optional bridgecard, Amiga will also run
1S-DOS® (AT or XT) programs. And Amiga is the
nly computer in its price range that gives you the
bility to run both types of programs simultaneously
nrough it's multi-tasking capability.
  So, if your business relies on creativity, take a look
t the future. Take a look at the Amiga 2000, 2000 HD
r the 2500. And find out why only Amiga
nakes it possible.

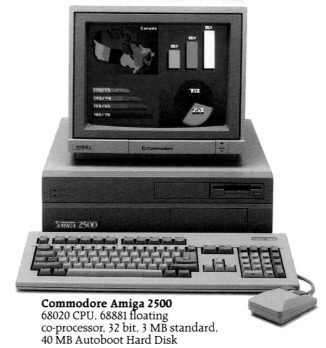

Commodore Amiga 2500
68020 CPU, 68881 floating
co-processor, 32 bit, 3 MB standard,
40 MB Autoboot Hard Disk

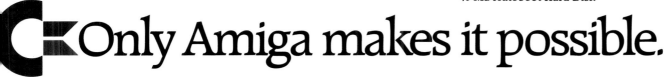

C= Only Amiga makes it possible.

A FEW THINGS YOU SHOULD KNOW ABOUT THE ART DIRECTORS CLUB OF TORONTO

(AND WHY AN ESSENTIAL INGREDIENT IS MISSING)

- The ADCT is a non-profit organization which depends on the hard work of a few dedicated volunteers.

- The ADCT exists to promote creativity and excellence in our business and to inspire young practitioners to reach for the stars.

- The ADCT produces an annual book that serves as a valuable record of the best work done in this country.

- The ADCT promotes, organizes, produces and hosts a show that attracts 2,000 people annually, raising the visibility and stature of what we do.

- The ADCT spreads recognition around. In the past five years, some 250 companies have received awards for their work.

- The ADCT awards are respected. Why else would Canada's best send in 2,295 entries in 1989?

- The ADCT avoids the incestuousness that plagues some shows. By bringing in high profile international judges, your work is treated fairly and without self-interest.

- The ADCT brings in guest speakers who are leaders in the field – Helmut Krone and George Lois, for example.

- The ADCT has been going since 1948 – there's no show quite like the old show.

- The ADCT has about 365 members, a surprisingly small number to support all the efforts needed to help make our profession better – the essential ingredient that's missing is *you*.

The Art Directors Club of Toronto

Join the Club

For more information call or write: The Art Directors Club of Toronto, 945 Mt. Pleasant Road, Toronto, Ontario M4P 2L7. (416) 483-1400.

Color has 41% more stopping power.

Sale up to 41% off

Sale up to 41% off

Color increases readership by 41%.

If you have a message to get across, you can increase the chances of it being seen just by using color. But you can improve the odds even more when your message has been copied on Canon's Color Laser Copier. Colors reproduce with such remarkable clarity, that in many cases you'd be hard pressed to tell the photocopy from the original. And digital technology allows you to make your work even more eye-catching.

Among other things, this marvel of technology can combine words and pictures, enlarge and reduce with exacting precision, manipulate artwork, change one color to

Copy from film

another and add color to black and white originals. The result can be a colorful message that begs to be read.

So if you're looking for an area in which to outshine the competition, try using the color copier that has no competition. To arrange for a demonstration, see your nearest Canon NP copier dealer, or call 1-800-387-1241.

Stretch and condense

Canon
COLOR LASER COPIER

The computer dealer that's also known for its off-screen performances.

As well as showing the design community how to do a better job on the critically acclaimed Apple® Macintosh™, Blumer-LeVon has also been selling traditional art supplies for years.

Which means we've naturally set the stage for better service.

Take our delivery system for example.

Because we know that time is of the essence in your business, our trucks are on the road not once, but two times daily delivering all the hardware, software and other supplies you'll need. Packages are inspected beforehand to guarantee that you get everything you order and that everything's working up to spec.

We'll even let you know if we're out of something before the order arrives so you can make alternate arrangements. A small detail maybe. But being able to take care of things like this can mean a big deal to your business.

To find out more about our services on computer systems and courses, give us a call.

Because if you want to be a screen star, it pays to go with someone who has already distinguished themselves in a supporting role.

Blumer-LeVon
WE SPEAK YOUR LANGUAGE

Authorized Dealer

25 Prince Andrew Place, Don Mills, Ontario M3C 2H2 (416) 444-8431

Apple, the Apple logo and Macintosh are trademarks of Apple Computer Inc.

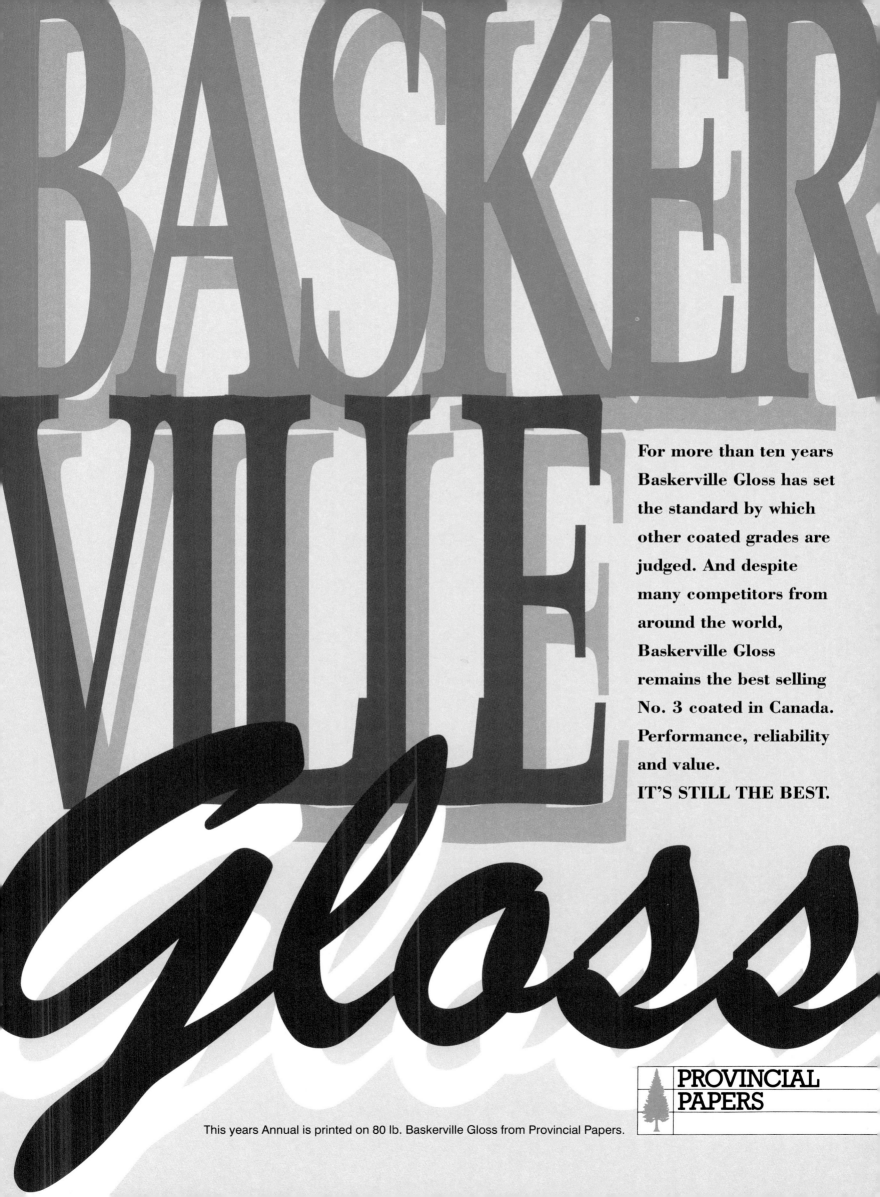

BASKERVILLE *Gloss*

For more than ten years Baskerville Gloss has set the standard by which other coated grades are judged. And despite many competitors from around the world, Baskerville Gloss remains the best selling No. 3 coated in Canada. Performance, reliability and value. **IT'S STILL THE BEST.**

PROVINCIAL PAPERS

This years Annual is printed on 80 lb. Baskerville Gloss from Provincial Papers.

Typography from A to Z.

Photography: Jerry Manco

Techni Process Limited Two Stewart Street Toronto Canada (416) 363 2493

Let's face it. Your reputation is riding on every job you do.

We know...

EMPRESS GRAPHICS INC.

175 MIDWEST ROAD, SCARBOROUGH, ONTARIO, CANADA. M1P 3A7 TEL. (416) 751-0980 FAX (416) 288-9935

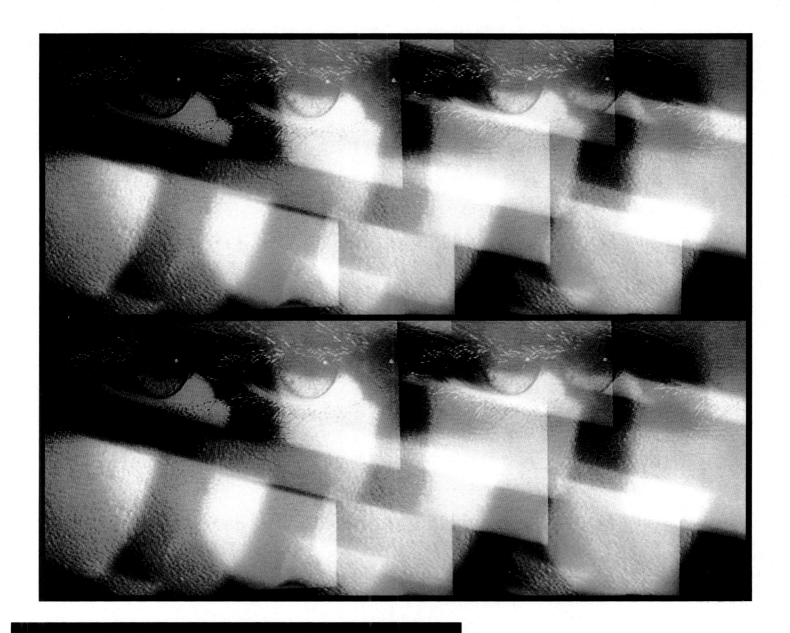

This image isn't worth the paper it's printed on.

THAT'S EASY TO UNDERSTAND WHEN YOU CONSIDER IT WAS CREATED ON VIDEO. AND NO MATTER WHAT KIND OF PAPER THIS IMAGE IS TRANSFERED TO, IT WILL NEVER BE AS IMPACTFUL AS THE ORIGINAL TAPE VERSION. STUDIO CENTRE UNDERSTANDS THIS AND OUR FACILITIES IN TORONTO REPRESENT OUR COMMITMENT TO THE INDUSTRY.

AT STUDIO CENTRE YOU'LL FIND THE LEADING MANUFACTURERS OF VIDEO EQUIPMENT. AND THIS STARTS WITH THE MOST SOPHISTICATED OF VIDEO CAMERAS AND PROJECTION SYSTEMS TO THE SMALLEST OF GRIP EQUIPMENT AND ACCESSORIES. WHICH MEANS, IF YOU'RE LOOKING FOR A COMPLETE SELECTION OF SONY INDUSTRIAL AND COMMERCIAL VIDEO PRODUCTS INCLUDING CAMERAS, TAPE MACHINES AND DISPLAY DEVICES, YOU'LL FIND THEM AT STUDIO CENTRE. IT ALSO MEANS YOU'LL FIND PROFESSIONAL VIDEO AND AUDIO TAPE IN THE SAME LOCATION. AND WHEN IT COMES TO LIGHTING, YOU CAN PLUG INTO DESISTI, LOWELL AND LTM ALL AT STUDIO CENTRE.

HOWEVER, WHAT MAKES STUDIO CENTRE WORTH LOOKING INTO, IS EVERYTHING WE SELL, WE RENT. AND THIS INCLUDES FULLY GRIDDED RENTAL STUDIOS WITH DRIVE-IN CAPABILITY.

SO WHEN IT COMES TO PUTTING YOUR NEXT IMAGE TO TAPE, CALL STUDIO CENTRE AT 391-5500 LOCALLY AND TOLL-FREE 1-800-668-9165. OR COME SEE IT LIVE AND IN PERSON AT 58 SCARSDALE ROAD IN TORONTO, ONTARIO M3B 2R7. IT'LL BE WORTH YOUR WHILE.

STUDIO CENTRE

STUDIO CENTRE IS A DIVISION OF QUEEN STREET CAMERA INC.

TITLE
MR. ROGER'S NEIGHBOURHOOD
ART DIRECTOR
JOHN FINN
WRITER
MIKE O'REILLY/ TOM GOUDIE
CREATIVE DIR.
MICHAEL GARRETT/ TERRY ILES
AGENCY
YOUNG & RUBICAM LTD.
CLIENT
FORD MOTOR COMPANY

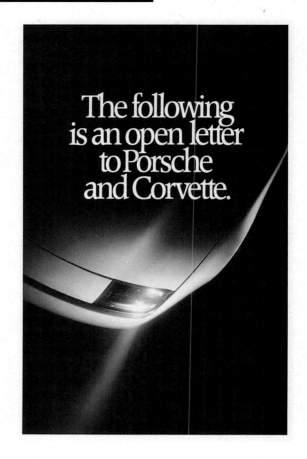

TITLE
Z
ART DIRECTOR
GEOFFREY B. ROCHE
WRITER
TERRY O'REILLY
DESIGNER
GEOFFREY B. ROCHE
CREATIVE DIR.
GEOFFREY B. ROCHE/ RICHARD HADDEN
PHOTOGRAPHER
BOB GRIGG
TYPOGRAPHER
WORD FOR WORD
AGENCY
CHIAT DAY ADVERTISING
CLIENT
NISSAN

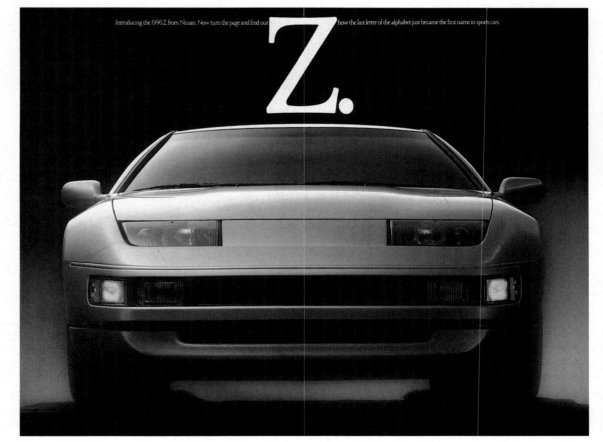

A thousand words on what we believe in.

Not all Torontonians have an excuse for being late this morning.

TITLE
SNOW AD
ART DIRECTOR
WOLFGANG HERTMANN
WRITER
JACK NEARY
CREATIVE DIR.
PETER LANYON
TYPOGRAPHER
CHARACTER COUNT
AGENCY
COSSETTE
CLIENT
PASSPORT

TITLE
A THOUSAND WORDS
ART DIRECTOR
GERRY MONSIER
WRITER
PETER LANYON
CREATIVE DIR.
PETER LANYON
PHOTOGRAPHER
MARK EMMERSON
TYPOGRAPHER
TYPSETTRA LTD.
AGENCY
COSSETTE
CLIENT
BANK OF BERMUDA

Deep in the mists of forgotten time lurks a mysterious legend. It was the Halstatt Era., 600 B.C. If Conan the Barbarian lived it was during this epoch.

The world was newer then. The mountain streams of Middle Europe ran clear. Wildflowers and aromatic herbs grew abundantly in the warm sun. Life was good.

It was a time of happy wars and sad songs and idyllic contentment. Time was told by the passing of nights not of days.

In fact partying, next to war, was the major sport. In these simpler times, long before the civilizing influences of the six pack and a bag of pretzels, the creation of beverages was an art as prized as the swordmakers.

One day, the legend has it down as Tuesday, October 7, 687 B.C., a certain Druid, Samoledt of the

Helveti Tribe, was sampling a batch of what the people farther east across the Urals now call "the stuff that's virtually unattainable unless you stand in line for 3 days." It was bland. Mind numbingly, boringly bland.

Then inspiration struck like Thor's thunderclap. "Why not infuse the liquid with precious herbs and botanicals?" Why not indeed.

A year passed. Well, almost a year. It was the Feast of Cornucopia. The Rising of the Harvest Moon. Football Season. The most auspicious time of the Druidic Calendar.

Samoledt rolled out the infused barrel. And, as well as inventing a new musical tradition, he began the legend that lives on as Alpenbitter.

Today Rittmeister's Alpenbitter is unique.

A tantalizingly delicate blending of Alpen grown herbs and botanicals and gentle sweetness.

A mysteriously refreshing taste when mixed with effervescent liquids. (cola, soda, gingerale.)

When you enjoy Alpenbitter in moderation you partake of a European tradition that has its heritage deep in the mists of forgotten time.

Available in 750 mL and 100 mL sizes.

Right now. At an LCBO store near you.

TASTE THE LEGEND.

TITLE
ANYONE WHO WANTS ALPENBITTER ...
ART DIRECTOR
RAYMOND LEE
WRITER
RODERICK MACKIN
CREATIVE DIR.
RAYMOND LEE
TYPOGRAPHER
HEAD PRIMETYPE BODY: PROTYPE
AGENCY
RAYMOND LEE & ASSOCIATES LTD.
CLIENT
RITTMEISTER OF CANADA INC.

TITLE
LESS GREEN TO BE IN THE PINK
ART DIRECTOR
JAAN ANDRE
WRITER
KEARNEY FREEMAN
CREATIVE DIR.
BRUCE McCALLUM
ILLUSTRATOR
GERRY SEVIER
TYPOGRAPHER
WORD FOR WORD
AGENCY
FCB/RONALDS-REYNOLDS
CLIENT
BERMUDA DEPARTMENT OF TOURISM
PRODUCTION MANAGER
JUNE MURRAY

Bermuda has long been renowned for its powder-pink beaches, buildings and flowers. Not to mention its crystalline, turquoise waters and azure skies.

And right now you can visit our pastel island in the sun for less than last year. Thanks to the stronger Canadian dollar.

While the exchange rate has dropped, Bermuda's attractions haven't. In a mere 2½ hours, you can touch down amidst our unrivalled scenic splendours. Where you'll soon discover our people are as warm and

inviting as our soft, sandy beaches.

Of course, some difficult decisions await you. What do you do first? Soak up a little of the island's British heritage over High Tea? Indulge in a little tennis, golf, horseback riding or gourmet dining? Or do you shop from a world of international merchandise, featuring prices that will warm your heart?

Whatever you do, pay Bermuda a visit soon. Besides saving money this year, you'll have an experience you'll treasure forever.

For a free Bermuda vacation kit, in Canada call 1-800-Bermuda, or send this coupon to: Bermuda Department of Tourism P.O. Box 4000, Station A, Mississauga, Ontario L5A 3W3

NAME

STREET _____ CITY

PROVINCE _____ POSTAL CODE

Bermuda Is You, Isn't It?

It Takes Less Green To Be In The Pink This Year.

HOW TO ENSURE THE OTHERS SURFACE FOR YOUR MEETING.

In today's business world, people have busy schedules. So gathering people from across the city, the country or around the world for a meeting in one place at one time is nearly impossible, unless you schedule regular TeleForum™ teleconferencing meetings. TeleForum allows you to meet more often to review budgets, for new product briefings, or to simply get the status on your projects.

You'll get the right people talking, every time, even when they're not in their own offices. Bell Canada's state-of-the-art digital technology makes TeleForum one of the most advanced systems of teleconferencing ever introduced. Voices sound natural so everyone can interject ideas, make suggestions and report on business, while excellent sound quality is always maintained. So keep your business

above water. Experience the TeleForum difference by calling a TeleForum sales consultant, at 1-800-561-6600 or dial "0" and book your calls with the TeleForum operator.

TeleForum.
THE EASY WAY TO MEET MORE OFTEN.

Bell
Nationwide Communications through Telecom Canada

™ Trademark Bell Canada.

TITLE
SURFACE
ART DIRECTOR
DARCY MALONEY
WRITER
MICHAEL CHAMBERLAIN
CREATIVE DIR.
BOB HAWTON
ILLUSTRATOR
RON BERG
TYPOGRAPHER
HUNTER BROWN/ MAX BROWN
AGENCY
McKIM ADVERTISING
CLIENT
BELL CANADA

TITLE
MOONS
ART DIRECTOR
DARCY MALONEY
WRITER
MICHAEL CHAMBERLAIN
CREATIVE DIR.
BOB HAWTON
ILLUSTRATOR
RON BERG
TYPOGRAPHER
HUNTER BROWN/ MAX BROWN
AGENCY
McKIM ADVERTISING
CLIENT
BELL CANADA

TITLE
GROUND
ART DIRECTOR
DARCY MALONEY
WRITER
MICHAEL CHAMBERLAIN
CREATIVE DIR.
BOB HAWTON
ILLUSTRATOR
RON BERG
TYPOGRAPHER
MAX BROWN/ HUNTER BROWN
AGENCY
McKIM ADVERTISING
CLIENT
BELL CANADA

TITLE
**TEN THOUSAND
DOLLARS LIGHTER**
ART DIRECTOR
TIM O'CONNELL
WRITER
**LISA SHIMOTAKAHARA/
TIM O'CONNELL**
CREATIVE DIR.
GARY PROUK
PHOTOGRAPHER
TERRY COLLIER
TYPOGRAPHER
TYPSETTRA LTD.
AGENCY
**SCALI, McCABE, SLOVES
(CANADA) LTD.**
CLIENT
VOLVO CANADA LTD.
PRODUCTION MANAGER
RON SCOTT

TITLE
FIT A FAX
ART DIRECTOR
JOE AMARAL
WRITER
CHRIS DACYSHYN
CREATIVE DIR.
PETER LANYON
PHOTOGRAPHER
JOHN STEPHENS
TYPOGRAPHER
TYPE STUDIO
AGENCY
COSSETTE
CLIENT
PANASONIC

TITLE
**ON THE WAY TO
CALGARY, YOU'LL SEE
CHINA**
ART DIRECTOR
DAVE KELSO
WRITER
**BILL LOWER/
SHELLEY AMBROSE**
CREATIVE DIR.
**DAVE KELSO/
BILL LOWER**
PHOTOGRAPHER
RICHARD PICTON
TYPOGRAPHER
EKLIPSE
AGENCY
**J. WALTER THOMPSON
ADVERTISING**
CLIENT
WARDAIR CANADA LTD.

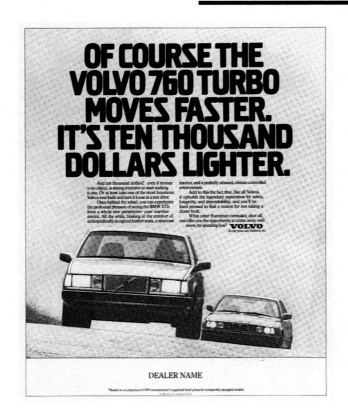

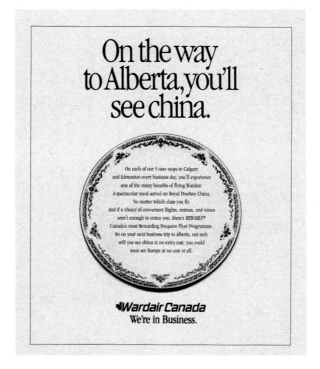

A
S I L V E R

TITLE
SURFACE
MOONS
GROUND
ART DIRECTOR
DARCY MALONEY
WRITER
MICHAEL CHAMBERLAIN
CREATIVE DIR.
BOB HAWTON
ILLUSTRATOR
RON BERG
TYPOGRAPHER
MAX BROWN/
HUNTER BROWN
AGENCY
McKIM ADVERTISING
CLIENT
BELL CANADA

How To Ensure The Others Surface For Your Meeting.

 In today's business world, people have busy schedules. So gathering people from across the city, the country or around the world for a meeting in one place at one time is nearly impossible, unless you schedule regular TeleForum™ teleconferencing meetings.

TeleForum allows you to meet more often to review budgets, for new product briefings, or to simply get the status on your projects.

You'll get the right people talking, every time, even when they're not in their own offices.

Bell Canada's state-of-the-art digital technology makes TeleForum one of the most advanced systems of teleconferencing ever introduced. Voices sound natural so everyone can interject ideas, make suggestions and report on business, while excellent sound quality is always maintained. So keep your business above water. Experience the TeleForum difference by calling a TeleForum sales consultant, at 1-800-561-6600 or dial "0" and book your calls with the TeleForum operator.

TELEFORUM.
THE EASY WAY TO MEET MORE OFTEN.

Bell
Nationwide Communications
through Telecom Canada

™ *Trademark Bell Canada.*

A
SILVER

TITLE
FUTURE
A THOUSAND WORDS
ART DIRECTOR
GERRY MONSIER
WRITER
PETER LANYON
CREATIVE DIR.
PETER LANYON
PHOTOGRAPHER
ANN SPURLING
TYPOGRAPHER
TYPSETTRA LTD.
AGENCY
COSSETTE
CLIENT
BANK OF BERMUDA

As the days get cooler, remember that Summer is only 2½ hours away—in Bermuda.

Instead of an overcoat, you could be slipping on a coat of suntan lotion on one of our sandy, pink beaches. Where temperatures still hover around the 75° mark through November.

In fact, with its gentle sun and warm breezes, Autumn is probably Bermuda's most inviting time of year. Ideal for all-day play on our countless, outdoor courts. Or golf on championship courses that are on a par with the world's best.

Or, if sightseeing warms your heart, you can always explore Bermuda's unique mix of lush, semi-tropical scenery and old-world British heritage.

When the sun does finally set, you'll discover Bermuda is equally enchanting under the stars. With glittering nightlife and dining that equals anything this side of the Atlantic.

For a few extra weeks of Summer, visit Bermuda this Fall. Your place in the sun awaits you.

For a free Bermuda vacation kit, in Canada call 1-800-Bermuda, or send this coupon to: Bermuda Department of Tourism, P.O. Box 4000, Station A, Mississauga, Ontario L5A 3W3

NAME

STREET   CITY

PROVINCE   POSTAL CODE

Bermuda Is You, Isn't It?

In Autumn You'll Find Everything Under The Sun In Bermuda.

Bermuda has long been renowned for its powder-pink beaches, buildings and flowers. Not to mention its crystalline, turquoise waters and azure skies.

And right now you can visit our pastel island in the sun for less than last year. Thanks to the stronger Canadian dollar.

While the exchange rate has dropped, Bermuda's attractions haven't. In a mere 2½ hours, you can touch down amidst our unrivalled scenic splendours. Where you'll soon discover our people are as warm and inviting as our soft, sandy beaches.

Of course, some difficult decisions await you. What do you do first? Soak up a little of the island's British heritage over High Tea? Indulge in a little tennis, golf, horseback riding or gourmet dining? Or do you shop from a world of international merchandise, featuring prices that will warm your heart?

Whatever you do, pay Bermuda a visit soon. Besides saving money this year, you'll have an experience you'll treasure forever.

For a free Bermuda vacation kit, in Canada call 1-800-Bermuda, or send this coupon to: Bermuda Department of Tourism P.O. Box 4000, Station A, Mississauga, Ontario L5A 3W3

NAME

STREET   CITY

PROVINCE   POSTAL CODE

Bermuda Is You, Isn't It?

It Takes Less Green To Be In The Pink This Year.

TITLE
EVERYTHING UNDER THE SUN
MORE BERMUDA
LESS GREEN TO BE IN THE PINK
ART DIRECTOR
JAAN ANDRE
WRITER
KEARNEY FREEMAN
CREATIVE DIR.
BRUCE McCALLUM
ILLUSTRATOR
GERRY SEVIER
TYPOGRAPHER
WORD FOR WORD
AGENCY
FCB/RONALDS-REYNOLDS
CLIENT
BERMUDA DEPARTMENT OF TOURISM
PRODUCTION MANAGER
JUNE MURRAY

TITLE
**FOR BUTTER OR
FOR WURST
FOR RICHER OR POURER
TO HALVE AND TO HOLD**
ART DIRECTOR
MATTHEW GYULAY
WRITER
**STEVE KOCH/
MATTHEW GYULAY**
CREATIVE DIR.
MACK CAPEL
PHOTOGRAPHER
MICHAEL LANT
AGENCY
SAFFER ADVERTISING
CLIENT
KITCHEN CONNECTION

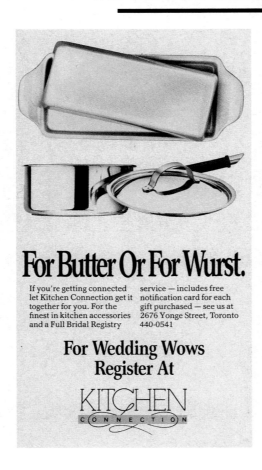

For Butter Or For Wurst.

If you're getting connected let Kitchen Connection get it together for you. For the finest in kitchen accessories and a Full Bridal Registry service — includes free notification card for each gift purchased — see us at 2676 Yonge Street, Toronto 440-0541

For Wedding Wows Register At

KITCHEN CONNECTION

For Richer Or For Pourer.

If you're getting connected let Kitchen Connection get it together for you. For the finest in kitchen accessories and a Full Bridal Registry service — includes free notification card for each gift purchased — see us at 2676 Yonge Street, Toronto 440-0541

For Wedding Wows Register At

KITCHEN CONNECTION

Now you don't have to give up your first born to own a sports car.

As a proud parent you expect to make certain sacrifices for your children. Your Hawaiian vacation for their higher education. Your new set of golf clubs for their new set of braces. Your really great sports car for a really sedate family sedan.

But there are times after all, when as a parent you just have to put your foot down. Which is exactly the idea behind the new Nissan Maxima.

Put your foot down and you'll discover its 3-litre, multi-port, fuel-injected V6. Churning out 181 lb-ft of torque, this modified Z-car engine propels the Maxima from 0-60 mph faster than a BMW 635CSi.* And the Maxima SE has sports car stopping power.

With standard 4-wheel disc brakes and our advanced "Anti-lock Braking System", for straighter, shorter stops, even on wet roads.

While on winding roads, a 4-wheel independent suspension with front and rear stabilizer bars gives you the kind of cornering you just don't find in a regular sedan.

And, on top of all that, we've given this sports car something else you'll appreciate: the unique ability to take care of itself.

Each and every Maxima comes with The Maxima Plus program. That means you'll have virtually no maintenance, parts or labour costs for a full 3 years or 60,000 kms.

See your Nissan dealer for additional details.

Of course, if you had a sports car with this much built-in performance and security, you'd want to take everyone you know for a ride. Now the great thing about our sports car is, you can take them four at a time.

The new Maxima. Think of it as the 4-Door Sports Car.

NISSAN

Built for the Human Race.

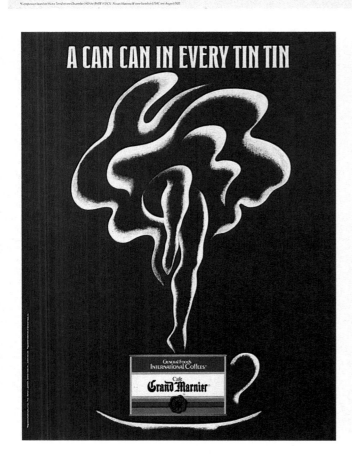

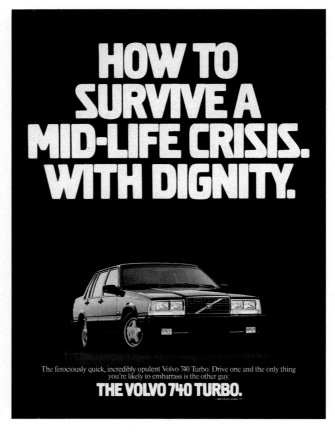

A
G O L D

TITLE
FIRST BORN
ART DIRECTOR
GEOFFREY B. ROCHE
WRITER
DICK SITTIG
DESIGNER
GEOFFREY B. ROCHE
CREATIVE DIR.
GEOFFREY B. ROCHE/ RICHARD HADDEN
PHOTOGRAPHER
DAVE LE BON
TYPOGRAPHER
WORD FOR WORD
AGENCY
CHIAT DAY ADVERTISING
CLIENT
NISSAN

A
S I L V E R

TITLE
CAN CAN
ART DIRECTOR
LEIF NIELSEN
WRITER
STEVE CONOVER
CREATIVE DIR.
RICK DAVIS
PHOTOGRAPHER
DESMOND MONTAQUE
AGENCY
YOUNG & RUBICAM LTD.
CLIENT
GENERAL FOODS INC.

TITLE
MID LIFE CRISIS
ART DIRECTOR
JOHN SPEAKMAN
WRITER
TERRY BELL
CREATIVE DIR.
GARY PROUK
PHOTOGRAPHER
TERRY COLLIER
TYPOGRAPHER
TYPSETTRA LTD.
AGENCY
SCALI, McCABE, SLOVES (CANADA) LTD.
CLIENT
VOLVO CANADA LTD.
PRODUCTION MANAGER
RON SCOTT

TITLE
BOOMERANG
ART DIRECTOR
PETER HOLMES
WRITER
**JAY SANKEY/
PETER HOLMES**
CREATIVE DIR.
PETER HOLMES
PHOTOGRAPHER
TIM SAUNDERS
TYPOGRAPHER
**COOPER & BEATTY,
LIMITED**
AGENCY
**FRANKLIN DALLAS
ADVERTISING INC.**
CLIENT
FORMICA CANADA
COLOUR SEPARATIONS
H & S RELIANCE

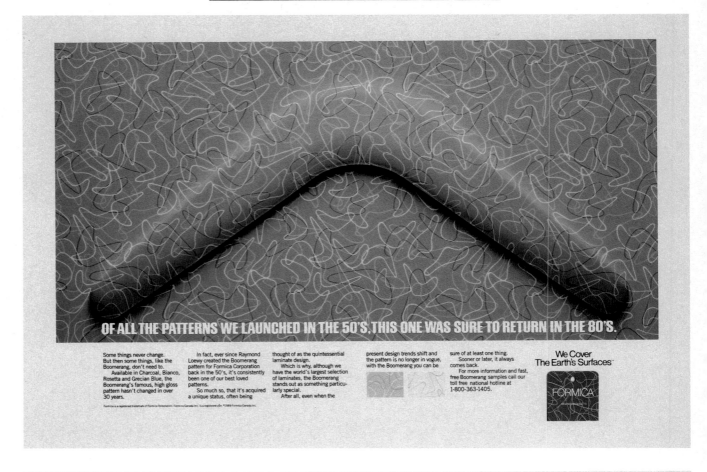

TITLE
SAND TEXTURE
ART DIRECTOR
PETER HOLMES
WRITER
**JAY SANKEY/
PETER HOLMES**
CREATIVE DIR.
PETER HOLMES
PHOTOGRAPHER
TIM SAUNDERS
TYPOGRAPHER
**COOPER & BEATTY,
LIMITED**
AGENCY
**FRANKLIN DALLAS
ADVERTISING INC.**
CLIENT
FORMICA CANADA
COLOUR SEPARATIONS
H & S RELIANCE

To create a better faucet we'll go to great lengths. And sometimes to great widths.

While exploring the countless design possibilities that one can pursue with a faucet, we inadvertently stumbled across a startling new possibility: "What can be done with the water?"

This question initiated a veritable outpouring of unconventional thinking, a by-product of which is unveiled here.

The Grand Masters series is a strikingly different faucet, crafted as it is from the finest corrosion-resistant solid brass.

It also includes all of the now classic Rubinet hallmarks of technical proficiency such as ceramic disc cartridges in place of washers, and controls which offer a mere quarter turn to full water acceleration.

But what distinguishes the Grand Masters series from other faucets, even from other Rubinet faucets, is of course the way in which it forms and delivers water.

This revolutionary design has been painstakingly produced in two distinct models, a lavatory faucet as shown here and a bathtub faucet with hand-held spray and fully retractable hose.

Both are available in a fashionable palette of enamel and metal finishes with accents of polished brass or chrome.

And, as with all Rubinet faucets, the Grand Masters is fully covered by an unprecedented five-year warranty.

The longest and most comprehensive of its kind.

Of course we fully realize a faucet which is so completely different from conventional design won't necessarily make a splash with everyone.

Only those with a capacity for unconventional thinking. A way of thinking which will be duly rewarded at your nearest authorized Rubinet dealer.

RUBINET

© 1988 Rubinet Brass Canada Limited.

TITLE
GREAT WIDTHS
ART DIRECTOR
PETER HOLMES
WRITER
PETER HOLMES/
MARK GREENBERG
PHOTOGRAPHER
PAT LACROIX
TYPOGRAPHER
THE COMPOSING ROOM
AT COOPER & BEATTY
AGENCY
FRANKLIN DALLAS
CLIENT
RUBINET BRASS
CANADA LTD.

One of few faucets that deserve to be placed on a pedestal.

In a world of parity products, it's a rarity for those cursed with above average expectations to find things worthy of their attention. Let alone their acclaim.

Yet these demanding individuals can take heart because there are a few exceptions.

Rubinet is a company that considers obsession and zealotry to be virtues. And it is this philosophy that has compelled us, once again, to create a completely new faucet category.

Ten is a faucet series quite unlike anything you've seen before or are likely to see again.

It is a product designed in an environment free of the usual cost constraints and time restrictions that so often circumvent brilliance.

And it's a consummate example of what can be achieved there.

Ten combines all of the classic Rubinet design and engineering advancements, including washerless ceramic disc cartridges and quarter-turn controls housed in meticulously tooled solid brass constructions.

And its sleek form is made all the more resplendent by lustrous finishes the likes of which faucets have never seen before.

White pearl, black pearl, matte black and brushed silver. All hand-finished and hand-polished with fitted accents of either polished chrome or 24 carat gold plate.

And as with all Rubinet faucets, Ten is not only backed by CSA approval, but by an unprecedented 5-year warranty. The longest and most comprehensive of its kind.

Naturally a faucet produced so contrary to standard production line practice has many virtues. However it also has one countermand.

Ten is only available in miniscule quantities, at your nearest authorized Rubinet dealer.

RUBINET

© 1988 Rubinet Brass Canada Limited.

TITLE
ON A PEDESTAL
ART DIRECTOR
PETER HOLMES
WRITER
PETER HOLMES
CREATIVE DIR.
PETER HOLMES
PHOTOGRAPHER
SHIN SUGINO
TYPOGRAPHER
THE COMPOSING ROOM
AT COOPER & BEATTY
AGENCY
FRANKLIN DALLAS
CLIENT
RUBINET BRASS
CANADA LTD.
COLOUR SEPARATION
BOMAC

TITLE
THREE YEARS
ART DIRECTOR
GEOFFREY B. ROCHE
WRITER
TERRY O'REILLY
DESIGNER
GEOFFREY B. ROCHE
CREATIVE DIR.
**RICHARD HADDEN/
GEOFFREY B. ROCHE**
PHOTOGRAPHER
DAVE LE BON
TYPOGRAPHER
CANADIAN COMPOSITION
AGENCY
CHIAT DAY ADVERTISING
CLIENT
NISSAN

Remove this car from the showroom and you'll get three years.

Who could blame you. After all, the Nissan Maxima is the pinnacle of refined luxury. With a Jekyll under that Hyde. Pure performance.

And every polished inch of that dual personality is covered by the Maxima Plus Program.

Which includes the bumper-to-bumper No-Nonsense Warranty for 3 years or 60,000 kilometres. And 6 years or 100,000 kilometres on the powertrain. But surprise. This coverage extends to the actual upkeep of the vehicle itself.

For 3 years or 60,000 kilometres, we shower your Maxima with free regular inspections. Down to such routine tasks as oil, filter and spark-plugs.

Tire rotations and pressure settings. Lubrication of doors and hinges.

There's more. A courtesy car is provided should your Maxima become disabled overnight. Towing is free to the nearest Nissan dealer. And the entire program is fully transferable to any future owners of the vehicle. So there are only three things we can't offer you by law. Gasoline, insurance and plates. And if that isn't reassuring enough, J.D. Power & Associates* surveyed new car owners and found the Maxima to be the "Most Trouble-Free New Car" on the road today. Visit your Nissan dealer and get away in a new Maxima. You'll automatically get three years. Of free labour. Not hard labour.

The Maxima Plus Program.

NISSAN

Built for the Human Race.

Drive away in a Maxima, and we'll throw the book at you. The Maxima Plus Program book.

A dual plenum intake system maximizes horsepower at all ranges.

The Maxima Brougham offers you entertainment to the tune of 4 self-equalizing Bose™ speakers.

ABS Brakes pull in the reins on the Maxima SE's horsepower.

Front and rear stabilizer bars offer you handling rarely found in a sedan.

Maxima SE. Voted "Best New Sedan Of the Year" by the Automobile Journalists Association of Canada.

The refined dash design offers maximum clarity and finger tip control.

The Maxima SE's rear spoiler slices through turbulent air.

High performance 15" cast alloy wheels help cool disk brakes.

The 5-speed transmission is perfectly computer-matched to the Maxima engine.

J.D. Power and Associates, 1989 New Car Initial Quality Survey.

TITLE
EVER WONDER
ART DIRECTOR
PETER HOLMES
WRITER
PETER HOLMES
CREATIVE DIR.
PETER HOLMES
PHOTOGRAPHER
SHIN SUGINO
TYPOGRAPHER
**THE COMPOSING ROOM
AT COOPER & BEATTY**
AGENCY
**FRANKLIN DALLAS
ADVERTISING INC.**
CLIENT
MIROLIN INDUSTRIES
COLOUR SEPARATIONS
H & S RELIANCE

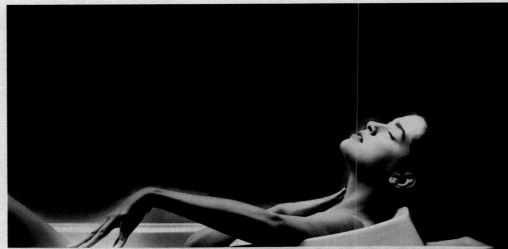

EVER WONDER WHY SOME PEOPLE CALL THEIR BATHROOM A RESTROOM?

Perhaps it was first introduced as a polite alternative by the genteel society.

But today, in this increasingly stressful world, the whirlpool has given the name true meaning.

The pioneering designers of the Mirocast Whirlpool believed that every bathroom should be a restroom.

That everybody should benefit from the rapturous effects of massaging jets placed in strategic, anatomical locations. That everybody should experience the departure of stress and tension while lying in an ergonomically designed cradle.

What they designed is just such a whirlpool.

The Mirocast Whirlpool series is quite unlike any other whirlpool. It offers sizes, shapes and an assortment of contemporary colours to suit every taste. And each one features the jets, motor and hardware that has garnered much critical acclaim for comfort, safety and reliability.

The best way to see these whirlpools is to visit an authorized Mirocast dealer.

Or visit a friend, with a restroom.

1989 Mirolin Industries Inc. Maxxone, Mirolin and Mirolin logo are registered trademarks of Mirolin Industries Inc. 200 Norseman Street, Toronto, Ontario.

Mirocast Whirlpools   ◆ Mirolin

BELLY LAUGHS.

Roseanne
Tonight at 9pm

CTV   CFCF 12

TITLE
BELLY LAUGHS
ART DIRECTOR
DAVID SHARPE
WRITER
GARY LENNOX
CREATIVE DIR.
**DAVID SHARPE/
MICHAEL PAUL**
AGENCY
SMW ADVERTISING
CLIENT
CTV

No big deal, unless you have a baby.

This small safety device is called the Child Seat Anchor, and it comes free with most new GM cars.

Your dealer installs it, then you attach it to the tether strap of your child's seat. The Anchor prevents your child's seat—and your child—from lurching forward in the event of an unavoidable sudden stop.

The Child Seat Anchor. A little something for your little one, from GM.

LOOK AT GM TODAY.

TITLE
**NO BIG DEAL, UNLESS
YOU HAVE A BABY**
ART DIRECTOR
MICHAEL WELSH
WRITER
BILL KEENAN
CREATIVE DIR.
BILL DURNAN
PHOTOGRAPHER
GEORGE SIMHONI
TYPOGRAPHER
TYPSETTRA LTD.
AGENCY
MacLAREN LINTAS INC.
CLIENT
**GENERAL MOTORS OF
CANADA**

TITLE
THE NEW VOLKSWAGEN SERVICE CENTRE
ART DIRECTOR
DUNCAN BRUCE
WRITER
MARTA CUTLER
CREATIVE DIR.
ALLAN KAZMER
PHOTOGRAPHER
GEORGE SIMHONI
TYPOGRAPHER
TYPSETTRA LTD.
AGENCY
DDB NEEDHAM WORLDWIDE ADVERTISING LTD.
CLIENT
VOLKSWAGEN CANADA LTD.

The new Volkswagen service centre.

It may not be quite as large as you were expecting.

And no, there isn't a Volkswagen sign out front.

But don't let that fool you for a second. This phone booth is actu-ally the nerve centre of our new Guaranteed Mobility service.

Should you ever have a problem with your '89 Volkswagen, one phone call is all it takes to bring help.

Any time of day or night.

If your battery fails, or your radiator springs a leak.

Even if your Volkswagen breaks down.

And if repairs take an unexpect-ted amount of time, we'll even arrange for overnight accommo-dation or lend you another car for up to 2 days.

Guaranteed Mobility comes as standard equipment on every '89 Volkswagen. And you're covered for the first 6 years (as long as you have repairs and annual scheduled main-tenance performed).

So next time you spot a phone booth, think of it as your personal hotline to Volkswagen.

You might even want to call us, just to say hello. For complete infor-mation, visit your nearest dealer.

Guaranteed Mobility

TITLE
JOIN THE VIRGIN OF THE MONTH CLUB
ART DIRECTOR
DUNCAN BRUCE
WRITER
LOUIS J. DELAMARTER
CREATIVE DIR.
ALLAN KAZMER
TYPOGRAPHER
TYPSETTRA LTD.
AGENCY
DDB NEEDHAM WORLDWIDE ADVERTISING LTD.
CLIENT
HARLEQUIN ENTERPRISES LTD.

TITLE
REMEMBER HOW HER EYES LIT UP
ART DIRECTOR
KATHRYN BERGMAN
WRITER
KAREN LEVENSON
CREATIVE DIR.
MICHAEL PAUL
AGENCY
SMW ADVERTISING
CLIENT
NIKON CANADA

Join
the virgin
of the month
club.

Harlequin Regency Romances™ have enjoyed a 55% to 75% net sell-through in the past.

Cash in on chaste debutantes being charmingly chased by libidinous Lords.

Every month Harlequin will be offering your customers two romantic romps through Regency England.

At the same time we'll be offering you a modern, hard-nosed opportunity to profit from Regency Romance sales. In the past Harlequin Regency Romances have enjoyed a 55% to 75% net sell-through.

So, place your standing order now for the romantic event of the season: Harlequin Regency Romances.™ Two per month starting this May.

Discover for yourself that chastity has its own rewards.

Harlequin Regency Romances™

Remember how her eyes lit up?

It's a crying shame when red-eye ruins a good shot.

That's why Nikon created the new Tele Touch 300.

It's the only camera that virtually eliminates red-eye.

Because it's the only camera that has the revolutionary new red-eye reduction flash.

The result: perfect flash photos. Everytime.

But great photos aren't the only thing you get with the Tele Touch 300. You get dual lenses. A choice of wide angle, for groups and landscapes, and medium telephoto, for perfect portraits.

Add to this Nikon's stylish, protective clam-shell design and you've got one of the slimmest dual lens cameras around. It'll fit anywhere, from pockets to pocketbooks. And, to top it off, the Tele Touch 300 is affordable.

So, if you don't want to see red again, see your authorized Nikon dealer, and ask for the Tele Touch 300. It's the one sure way to get perfect photos in a flash.

Nikon
We take the world's greatest pictures®

Nikon Canada Inc., 1366 Aerowood Drive, Mississauga, Ontario L4W 1C1 (416)625-9910

"PROBABLY THE BEST FASHION STATEMENT I CAN MAKE
IS THAT THIS SUIT IS FOUR YEARS OLD."
Cy Mann

"I've heard a lot of fashion statements since I entered the business over 40 years ago.

Right now, a statement I hear a lot is that fashion's an illusion.

I can't agree.

To my mind, fashion's a look and feel which results from skill, experience and an uncompromising dedication to fit.

That's always been our view at Mr. Mann. We want to make you look and feel good by creating a suit which suits you: a classic.

We put it together to last. And the fit must be perfect.

I can't remember the number of times we've done something like removing a sleeve and sewing it back just to rotate it 1/4-inch to make sure it drops perfectly clean and neat.

It's just one small example of how fastidious we can be about detail.

As far as styling is concerned, our Mr. Mann attitude is still traditional with just a hint of upbeat, contemporary flavour. Our body fit is relaxed with a slight emphasis on shoulder and chest.

Whatever your exact style preference, we guarantee you a garment which benefits from over four centuries of tailoring experience.

We offer people like Jack who makes only trousers; Frank who makes only coats and Joe who specializes in tuxedo facings and hand detail. They've all been at it for about four decades.

How much does it cost to put all our experience to work for you? Well, our two-piece custom-tailored suits start at $975. Custom shirts are from $120. Ready made shirts which we make in our custom work rooms are $90 and $110.

We also have some ready made blazers and slacks on hand, a wonderfully eclectic assemblage of accessories plus a unique selection of ties from around the world. Delivery on custom items is 30 days to five weeks.

Why not come see us and see how we suit you? I'm sure you'll end up both looking and feeling good about it. And making your own fashion statement. For years to come."

MR. MANN
TAILOR AND SHIRTMAKER

One Store Only.
41 Avenue Road, Toronto M5R 2G3 (416) 968-2022 9:30 – 6:00 Monday thru Saturday

We use Federal Express to ship anywhere in the world. Overnight to your door. Packaged beautifully. Ready for immediate wearing. You get one bill from Federal Express. No broker's needed.

TITLE
FASHION STATEMENT
ART DIRECTOR
GARY CARR
WRITER
DOUG LINTON
PHOTOGRAPHER
WESTSIDE STUDIOS
TYPOGRAPHER
STUDIOTYPE
AGENCY
AMBROSE CARR LINTON & KELLY
CLIENT
MR. MANN

It won't bite.

We promise. In fact, our new Sof-Touch Ultra won't bruise, or irritate your breasts in any way.

That's because every feature of the Sof-Touch Ultra is designed for comfort.

It's lightweight. So it won't tire your arms or cause fatigue the way manual pumps do. And it's battery operated. You're not restrained by cords or electric outlets. You can breast-pump wherever you breastfeed.

While most pumps are made with glass or hard plastic breast cups, the Sof-Touch Ultra is made of soft, flexible silicone. It gently molds to the breast preventing bruising and nipple soreness.

If that weren't enough, the Sof-Touch Ultra comes with a variety of nipple adapters so you customize the breast cup to suit your breast.

The easy-to-assemble parts come in a discreet, washable plastic carry-

all that fits easily into briefcases and most purses. Every piece is easy to clean and sterilize.

The Sof-Touch Ultra. It's the most comfortable way to breastfeed, next to baby.

Try Evenflo's plastic-free breast pads and breast creams, available wherever Evenflo products are sold.

evenflo
A Friend of The Family

Evenflo Juvenile Products Company, Division of Spalding & Evenflo Canada Inc., Brantford, Ont. N3T 5V7 (519) 751-1611
For a free copy of "The Nursing Experience" call toll free 1-800-265-0749, (8:30 am-4:30 pm Monday to Friday, Eastern Time).

TITLE
IT WON'T BITE
ART DIRECTOR
AUDREY MAYBERRY
WRITER
KAREN LEVENSON
CREATIVE DIR.
MICHAEL PAUL
AGENCY
SMW ADVERTISING
CLIENT
EVENFLO

TITLE
POP ART
ART DIRECTOR
COLIN PRIESTLEY
WRITER
BRENT PULFORD
CREATIVE DIR.
GRAY ABRAHAM
ILLUSTRATOR
DAVID CHESTNUT-WALLIS STUDIOS
TYPOGRAPHER
TYLER CLARKE
AGENCY
J. WALTER THOMPSON ADVERTISING
CLIENT
PEPSI-COLA CANADA LTD.

TITLE
SAVE YOUR BLOOD FOR THE RED CROSS
ART DIRECTOR
JAAN ANDRE
WRITER
KEARNEY FREEMAN
CREATIVE DIR.
BRUCE McCALLUM
ILLUSTRATOR
MIKE CARTER
TYPOGRAPHER
WORD FOR WORD
AGENCY
FCB/RONALDS-REYNOLDS
CLIENT
S.C. JOHNSON AND SON, LIMITED
PRODUCTION MANAGER
JUNE MURRAY

TITLE
MARCONI
ART DIRECTOR
CLARKE SMITH
WRITER
MIKE O'REILLY/ TOM GOUDIE
CREATIVE DIR.
RICK DAVIS
AGENCY
YOUNG & RUBICAM LTD.
CLIENT
OLAND BREWERIES

TITLE
SUNFLOWERS
ART DIRECTOR
RICK KEMP
WRITER
PETER LANYON
CREATIVE DIR.
PETER LANYON
TYPOGRAPHER
TYPE STUDIO
AGENCY
COSSETTE
CLIENT
GILBEY CANADA

TITLE
ONCE IN A...
THE NEW VOLKSWAGEN
SERVICE CENTRE
ART DIRECTOR
DUNCAN BRUCE
WRITER
MARTA CUTLER
CREATIVE DIR.
ALLAN KAZMER
PHOTOGRAPHER
TERRY COLLIER/
GEORGE SIMHONI
TYPOGRAPHER
TYPSETTRA LTD.
AGENCY
DDB NEEDHAM
WORLDWIDE
ADVERTISING
CLIENT
VOLKSWAGEN
CANADA INC.

Once in a...

On the very rare chance your Volkswagen breaks down, the blue moon will never see you standing alone.

Not with our new Guaranteed Mobility service. Should you ever have a problem with your '89 Volkswagen, one phone call is all it takes to bring help. Any time of day or night.

If your battery fails, or your radiator springs a leak. Even if your Volkswagen breaks down.

And if repairs take an unexpected amount of time, we'll even arrange for overnight accommodation or lend you another car for up to 2 days.

Guaranteed Mobility comes as standard equipment on every '89 Volkswagen.

And you're covered for the first 6 years (as long as you have repairs and annual scheduled maintenance performed by an authorized Volkswagen dealer).

The very best thing about Guaranteed Mobility is that you'll probably never need it.

But we'll always be there just the same. After all, you never know when a blue moon might appear.

For complete information, visit your nearest dealer.

Guaranteed Mobility

The new Volkswagen service centre.

It may not be quite as large as you were expecting.

And no, there isn't a Volkswagen sign out front.

But don't let that fool you for a second. This phone booth is actually the nerve centre of our new Guaranteed Mobility service.

Should you ever have a problem with your '89 Volkswagen, one phone call is all it takes to bring help. Any time of day or night.

If your battery fails, or your radiator springs a leak.

Even if your Volkswagen breaks down.

And if repairs take an unexpected amount of time, we'll even arrange for overnight accommodation or lend you another car for up to 2 days.

Guaranteed Mobility comes as standard equipment on every '89 Volkswagen. And you're covered for the first 6 years (as long as you have repairs and annual scheduled maintenance performed).

So next time you spot a phone booth, think of it as your personal hotline to Volkswagen.

You might even want to call us, just to say hello. For complete information, visit your nearest dealer.

Guaranteed Mobility

TITLE
**NATURAL
DURABLES
ENERGY**
ART DIRECTOR
RICHARD TALBOT
WRITER
ROBIN HEISEY
CREATIVE DIR.
LARRY GORDON
PHOTOGRAPHER
MICHAEL RIFELSON
TYPOGRAPHER
COMPOSING ROOM
AGENCY
SAATCHI & SAATCHI
CLIENT
**TOYOTA CANADA INC.
(NATIONAL)**
DIRECTOR , CREATIVE SERVICES
TERRY BELL

TOYOTA CAME TO CANADA FOR THE DURABLES.

If you go to Cambridge, Ontario, you'll find a picturesque community founded in the early 19th century. And you'll find Bill Zister. At a youthful 45, Bill is in fact one of the more experienced team members at Toyota's new Corolla plant in Cambridge. But, as it is with the nearby town he grew up in, Bill is finding that growing is something you never really finish doing. And neither is learning.

When he came to us, Bill was already a 1st class stationary engineer - he'd been in the field since he apprenticed with his uncle. And he'd seen a lot of progress. But when the Toyota plant went into production late last year, Bill saw something truly new. An enormous building, 83,000 square metres, but with the sense of quality you'd find in a small shop. And with over 600 team members - and growing - he still saw a community spirit like the one he grew up with. Now Bill is with us, learning Toyota ideas with names like Kaizen, Jidoka, and Takt-time. But Toyota is learning something far more interesting. We're learning about Bill.

TOYOTA

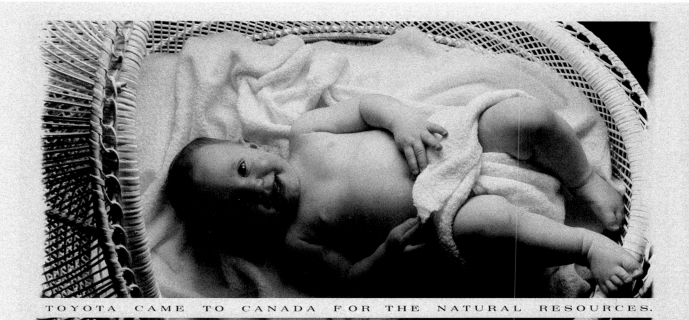

TOYOTA CAME TO CANADA FOR THE NATURAL RESOURCES.

With every new Canadian, our resources as a nation are expanded. Our future potential is enhanced. As Canadians, we can be forgiven an ardent fascination with the youth of Canada. Our country is young. Our history is being written with every new venture we undertake.

Now Toyota has brought a new venture to life in Canada. The Toyota manufacturing plant in Cambridge, Ontario is only the latest step in a long-standing commitment to Canada and Canadians. Over $400 million and hundreds of thousands of man-hours have been contributed.

Designed to build Toyota Corollas, it is a state-of-the-art production facility - an enterprise for our generation, and for those yet to come. What brought this investment to Canada? Our greatest resource: Our people. It is already apparent that in Canada, as in Japan, succeeding generations will find a sense of commitment with Toyota. Not only in Cambridge, but across the country.

TOYOTA

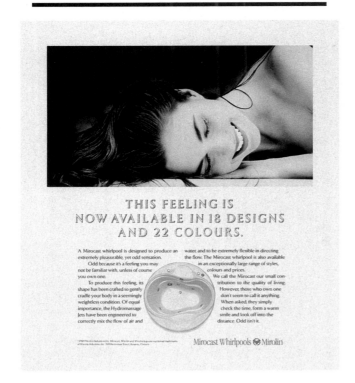

THIS FEELING IS NOW AVAILABLE IN 18 DESIGNS AND 22 COLOURS.

A Mirocast whirlpool is designed to produce an extremely pleasurable, yet odd sensation.

Odd because it's a feeling you may not be familiar with, unless of course you own one.

To produce this feeling, its shape has been crafted to gently cradle your body in a seemingly weightless condition. Of equal importance, the Hydromassage Jets have been engineered to correctly mix the flow of air and water, and to be extremely flexible in directing the flow. The Mirocast whirlpool is also available in an exceptionally large range of styles, colours and prices.

We call the Mirocast our small contribution to the quality of living. However, those who own one don't seem to call it anything. When asked, they simply check the time, form a warm smile and look off into the distance. Odd isn't it.

Mirocast Whirlpools ⬢ Mirolin

TITLE
THIS FEELING
EVER WONDER
ART DIRECTOR
PETER HOLMES
WRITER
PETER HOLMES
CREATIVE DIR.
PETER HOLMES
PHOTOGRAPHER
SHIN SUGINO
TYPOGRAPHER
THE COMPOSING ROOM
AGENCY
FRANKLIN DALLAS ADVERTISING INC.
CLIENT
MIROLIN INDUSTRIES
COLOUR SEPARATIONS
H & S RELIANCE

EVER WONDER WHY SOME PEOPLE CALL THEIR BATHROOM A RESTROOM?

Perhaps it was first introduced as a polite alternative by the genteel society.

But today, in this increasingly stressful world, the whirlpool has given the name true meaning.

The pioneering designers of the Mirocast Whirlpool believed that every bathroom should be a restroom.

That everybody should benefit from the rapturous effects of massaging jets placed in strategic, anatomical locations. That everybody should experience the departure of stress and tension while lying in an ergonomically designed cradle.

What they designed is just such a whirlpool.

The Mirocast Whirlpool series is quite unlike any other whirlpool. It offers sizes, shapes and an assortment of contemporary colours to suit every taste. And each one features the jets, motor and hardware that has garnered much critical acclaim for comfort, safety and reliability.

The best way to see these whirlpools is to visit an authorized Mirocast dealer.

Or visit a friend, with a restroom.

Mirocast Whirlpools   ⬢ Mirolin

TITLE
ON A PEDESTAL
STICK YOUR NECK OUT
GREAT WIDTHS
ART DIRECTOR
PETER HOLMES
WRITER
PETER HOLMES/
MARK GREENBERG
CREATIVE DIR.
PETER HOLMES
PHOTOGRAPHER
SHIN SUGINO/
PAT LACROIX
TYPOGRAPHER
THE COMPOSING ROOM
AT COOPER & BEATTY
AGENCY
FRANKLIN DALLAS
ADVERTISING INC.
CLIENT
RUBINET BRASS
CANADA LTD.
COLOUR SEPARATIONS
BOMAC

Sometimes you have to stick your neck out to design a superior kitchen faucet.

How can things progress beyond the ordinary unless someone first thinks beyond the ordinary?

This question presides as judge and jury over everyday life in the design offices of Rubinet. It's the question which summarily engenders such products as the Eliseo Kitchen faucet shown here.

The Eliseo incorporates two unique functions in one compact, single-lever faucet.

At once, it acts as a swivel-based faucet for typical tasks. But then with a pull-of-the-wrist and a flick-of-the-thumb, it's transformed into a hand-held spray with a fully-automatic retractable hose.

And although this seems like a lot to ask of one faucet, it incorporates these two functions without ignoring Rubinet's renowned commitment to aesthetic excellence.

The Eliseo is just one example in a line of Rubinet kitchen faucets, available in a palette of enamel and metal finishes.

Also available for you to view at your nearest authorized Rubinet dealer.

RUBINET

© 1989 Rubinet Brass (Canada) Limited

One of few faucets that deserve to be placed on a pedestal.

In a world of parity products, it's a rarity for those cursed with above average expectations to find things worthy of their attention. Let alone their acclaim.

Yet these demanding individuals can take heart because there are a few exceptions.

Rubinet is a company that considers obsession and zealotry to be virtues. And it is this philosophy that has compelled us, once again, to create a completely new faucet category.

Ten is a faucet series quite unlike anything you've seen before or are likely to see again.

It is a product designed in an environment free of the usual cost constraints and time restrictions that so often circumvent brilliance.

And it's a consummate example of what can be achieved there.

Ten combines all of the classic Rubinet design and engineering advancements, including washerless ceramic disc cartridges and quarter-turn controls housed in meticulously tooled solid brass constructions.

And its sleek form is made all the more resplendent by lustrous finishes the likes of which faucets have never seen before.

White pearl, black pearl, matte black and brushed silver. All hand-finished and hand-polished with fitted accents of either polished chrome or 24 carat gold plate.

And as with all Rubinet faucets, Ten is not only backed by CSA approval, but by an unprecedented 5-year warranty. The longest and most comprehensive of its kind.

Naturally a faucet produced so contrary to standard production line practice has many virtues. However it also has one countermand.

Ten is only available in miniscule quantities, at your nearest authorized Rubinet dealer.

RUBINET

© 1989 Rubinet Brass (Canada) Limited

In 1945, General Douglas MacArthur used his Duofold Parker Pen to end the war in the Pacific.

Since that time, the Parker Duofold has been instrumental in putting an end to many battles and skirmishes of a more intimate nature.

PARKER

THE DUOFOLD BALLPOINT COMES IN BLACK, MARBLED BLUE OR MAROON, AND A SELECTION OF POINT SIZES. A MATCHING FOUNTAIN PEN IS ALSO AVAILABLE. ALL PENS ARE HANDCRAFTED IN EUROPE.

Italian composer Giacomo Puccini wrote the opera La Bohême with a Parker Pen in 1896.

Parker Pens have been making words sing ever since.

PARKER

THE DUOFOLD FOUNTAIN PEN COMES IN BLACK, MARBLED BLUE OR MAROON, AND A SELECTION OF NIB SIZES. A MATCHING BALLPOINT IS ALSO AVAILABLE. ALL PENS ARE HANDCRAFTED IN EUROPE.

TITLE
IN 1945
ITALIAN COMPOSER
SIR ARTHUR
ART DIRECTOR
PETER DAY
WRITER
VIV TATE
CREATIVE DIR.
PETER DAY
TYPOGRAPHER
COMPOSING ROOM
AGENCY
DEACON DAY ADVERTISING
CLIENT
PARKER CANADA

TITLE
SUNFLOWERS
LIGHTNING
RAINBOW
ART DIRECTOR
RICK KEMP
WRITER
PETER LANYON
CREATIVE DIR.
PETER LANYON
PHOTOGRAPHER
STOCK/TOM IVES/
THE IMAGE BANK
TYPOGRAPHER
TYPE STUDIO
AGENCY
COSSETTE
CLIENT
GILBEY CANADA

GOLD

TITLE
PUNCH BACK
ART DIRECTOR
RANDY DIPLOCK
WRITER
RANDY DIPLOCK
CREATIVE DIR.
GARY PROUK
PHOTOGRAPHER
GEORGE SIMHONI
TYPOGRAPHER
TYPSETTRA LTD.
AGENCY
SCALI, McCABE, SLOVES (CANADA) LTD.
CLIENT
CANADIAN CHILDRENS FOUNDATION
PRODUCTION MANAGER
RON SCOTT

TITLE
IF THIS SPACE...
ART DIRECTOR
WINSTON LEE CHAN
WRITER
CURTIS DUFRESNE
CREATIVE DIR.
VERN JOHANSSON
TYPOGRAPHER
TYPSETTRA LTD.
AGENCY
AMBROSE CARR LINTON & KELLY
CLIENT
COMMUNITY ALCOHOL & DRUG SERVICES

TITLE
THE NEXT BEST THING
ART DIRECTOR
DIETER KAUFMANN/ DAVE MENEAR
WRITER
DIETER KAUFMANN/ DAVE MENEAR
CREATIVE DIR.
DIETER KAUFMANN
PHOTOGRAPHER
ADRIEN DUEY
AGENCY
ANDERSON ADVERTISING
CLIENT
THE KIDNEY FOUNDATION OF CANADA

SILVER

TITLE
BUSINESS, BUSINESS
ART DIRECTOR
DAVE KELSO
WRITER
BILL LOWER
CREATIVE DIR.
DAVE KELSO/
BILL LOWER
TYPOGRAPHER
EKLIPSE -
KIM CROFT
AGENCY
J. WALTER THOMPSON
ADVERTISING
CLIENT
TELEDYNE WATER PIK
CANADA

If you don't believe the advertising for Water Pik®, would you believe the research?

I earn my living writing advertising. And as I happily prepared to write this ad with a litany of cute expressions, catch phrases and the odd pun or two, you can imagine my horror when I was handed an oppressive stack of research results regarding the benefits of oral irrigation using a Water Pik Dental System.

Frankly, it's not something everyone wants to read about, let alone write about. Gingivitis. Pockets. Subgingival access. But if anyone understands the importance of these things, you do. And far better than I.

So, I had no alternative but to use this research. Now, I've done my best to make this material readable but I'm not making any promises. Yet as much as I hate to admit it, these findings seem to be far more compelling than any ad I could write.

The purpose of this comprehensive study was to demonstrate the benefit of Water Pik Oral Irrigation on gingival health by measuring effects on clinical parameters and marginal and subgingival microflora.

Treatment groups, adjunctive to normal oral hygiene were compared over six (6) months:

Group I   daily irrigation with 300 mL water, then 200 mL 0.06% Chlorhexidine
Group II daily irrigation with 500 mL of water
Group III twice-daily rinse with 0.12% CHX (positive control)
Group IV toothbrush (negative control)
Patients were randomly assigned and balanced by age and gender.

Enhancement of Gingival Health by Oral Irrigation with Chlorhexidine.
3-MONTH RESULTS
M.G. Newman, T. Flemmig, F. Doherty, et al. (UCLA School of Dentistry)

Study Summary: A double-blind study of 187 patients assessed the improvement of gingival health and reduction in disease-associated bacteria by oral irrigation. (Water Pik)

At 3 months compared to negative control, the group I) irrigating with 0.06% CHX had statistically significant (P≤0.01) reductions in GI (46.3%), GI Bleeding (53.7%), BOP (39.8%), plaque (50.9%) and pocket depth (5.9%). Water irrigation alone significantly reduced GI (30.0%), GI Bleeding (44.9%) and BOP (24.6%) but did not significantly reduce plaque (2.4%) or pocket depth (0.5%). Compared to positive rinse control, irrigation with 0.06% CHX was significantly better for GI (60.0%), GI Bleeding (88%), BOP (22%) and pocket depth, and also better for plaque and GI than water alone. CHX rinse was effective relative to negative control. Groups using CH had significant reduction in "Actinomyces; CHX irrigation group had significant reductions in Gram negative facultative rods.
Presented 1088 IADR.
Continental European Division.
Louvre, Belgium.
Results:
1. Despite minimal effect on supragingival plaque, water irrigation benefits are significant (compared to normal oral hygiene).

2. Irrigation delivery enhances the chemical effect of chlorhexidine over rinsing with it.
• Irrigating once per day with water then 0.06% chlorhexidine markedly enhanced improvement in gingival health.
• Irrigation with dilute chlorhexidine significantly reduced Actinomyces bacteria associated with gingivitis.

Chlorhexidine and Irrigation in Gingivitis: 6 months Correlative Clinical and Microbiological Findings.
6-MONTH RESULTS
T.F. Flemmig, M.G. Newman, S. Nachnani, et al. (UCLA, Los Angeles)

Study Summary: The objective was to evaluate the effect of irrigation with water or chlorhexidine (CHX) on gingival health and plaque microflora of 175 patients with naturally-occurring gingivitis. In this positive-negative controlled, examiner-blind study, 165 marginal/subgingival plaque samples were taken from 88 of the patients completing the 6 month trial. Microbiological analyses were performed using selective and non-selective culture methods.
Results: At 6 months, daily irrigation with water then 0.06% CHX (Group I) significantly reduced mean gingival inflammation by 42.5%. Bleeding on Probing by 35.4% and the total Colony-Forming Units of Gram negative anaerobic rods (P≤0.02) compared to toothbrush control. With 0.12% CHX rinse, mean gingival inflammation was reduced 24.1% and BOP by 15.0%. For both CHX irrigation and rinse groups, the Calculus Index was significantly increased while plaque was significantly reduced.

Daily water irrigation significantly reduced mean gingival inflammation by 23.1% and BOP by 24.0% at 6 months. There was no increase in supragingival plaque compared to Group IV.

In the small percentage of sites initially >4mm, GI was significantly reduced only by water irrigation (55.2%) and BOP by CHX irrigation (38.2%) when compared to toothbrush control.

In the following tables, for sites with initial pocket probing depth ≤4mm, GI and BOP were significantly reduced by all treatment groups. Group I irrigation was most effective in reducing BOP. (P≤0.05)

6 MONTH REDUCTION GINGIVAL INDEX		
Adjunctive to toothbrushing		
Group I CHX Irrigation	48.0%	
Group II Water Irrigation	28.0%	
Group III CHX Rinse	28.7%	
Group IV Toothbrush Control Comparison		

6 MONTH REDUCTION BLEEDING ON PROBING		
Adjunctive to toothbrushing		
Group I CHX Irrigation	38.6%	
Group II Water Irrigation	28.0%	
Group III CHX Rinse	15.9%	
Group IV Toothbrush Control Comparison		

Presented 3/18/89 AADR.
San Francisco.

Effects of 6 Month 0.06% Chlorhexidine Gluconate Irrigation on Plaque Microflora
6-MONTH RESULTS
S. Nachnani, M. Newman, T. Flemmig, et al. (UCLA School of Dentistry, Los Angeles)

Study Summary: This study documents the bacteriologic effects on marginal and subgingival plaque in gingivitis patients who participated in a 6-month, positive/negative controlled, examiner-blind study. Curette plaque samples from sites in each of the four test groups were characterized using selective and non-selective culturing methods.
Results: At baseline, all patients harboured plaque microflora typical of naturally-occurring gingivitis. Only at 3 months were Actinomyces significantly reduced by CHX irrigation and rinse; at 6 months no significant differences were apparent, but the numbers of Colony-Forming Units were reduced for both CHX rinse and irrigations groups.

All treatment groups reduced CFU and proportions of black pigmented Bacteroides at 6 months. Furthermore, CFU and percent of Gram negative anaerobic rods were significantly reduced at 6 months by irrigation with CHX.
At 6 months, the CFU of streptococci were similar for all four Groups.
Presented 3/19/89 AADR.
San Francisco.

Naturally, we think you should recommend the Water Pik Dental System to your patients. After all, the research shows the Water Pik Dental System to be effective in the enhancement of gingival health. Now we just have to see about the advertising.

For more information please write to: Teledyne Water Pik Canada, 82 Carrier Drive, Rexdale, Ontario, M9W 5R1.

Water Pik
DENTAL SYSTEMS

TITLE
SIWAK
ART DIRECTOR
DAVE MENEAR
WRITER
JANE CHAPMAN
CREATIVE DIR.
DIETER KAUFMANN
PHOTOGRAPHER
ADRIEN DUEY
AGENCY
ANDERSON ADVERTISING
CLIENT
LEEMING DIVISION -
PFIZER CANADA INC.

Introducing Plax. The greatest advance in home dental care since the *siwak*.

The age-old problem of plaque removal has a new solution. Plax. The only dental rinse designed specifically to remove plaque.

In hard-to-brush areas, the improvement over regular brushing was even more dramatic with Plax.
Formulated from trusted ingredients.
Plax is considered to be exceptionally safe even in "exaggerated use" circumstances. When test subjects greatly exceeded its recommended use, there were no signs of tissue sensitivity or damage to tooth enamel.

Plax encourages compliance.
Pleasant-tasting and convenient, Plax is easily incorporated into your patients' daily oral health care regimen.
For best results, patients should rinse with 1 tablespoon (15 mL) of Plax for 30 seconds before brushing with their regular dentifrice.
New Plax. The anti-plaque, pre-brushing rinse that is making dental history.

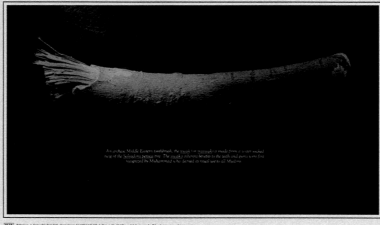

NEW!
Anti-Plaque
Pre-Brushing
Dental Rinse
Plax
■ Rinsing with PLAX then brushing normally removes up to 3 times more plaque than just brushing
■ Whitens teeth
Makes your mouth feel cleaner and look healthy

Checks Plaque Between Checkups.

AN IMITATION PART WON'T FOOL ANYONE.

We're not just splitting hairs. At first glance, you might not notice the important difference between a Motorcraft part and its imitators. But look again. The difference is obvious.
For one, only Motorcraft all-make parts measure up to our exact design specifications.
That means, we not only guarantee a precision fit, but promise a level of quality and durability that's second to none. And because of their availability, you'll never be left up in the
air waiting for the right part. All this adds up to one sizeable difference when it comes to
customer satisfaction.
So insist on genuine Motorcraft parts. They'll
make you look good.

Motorcraft
EXCEEDS THE NEED

TITLE
AN IMITATION PART
ART DIRECTOR
JOHN FINN
WRITER
**MIKE O'REILLY/
TOM GOUDIE**
CREATIVE DIR.
**MICHAEL GARRETT/
TERRY ILES**
AGENCY
YOUNG & RUBICAM
CLIENT
FORD MOTOR COMPANY

WITH FLUANXOL,
THE NEXT VOICE HE HEARS
CAN BE YOURS.

In order to reach the withdrawn, poorly
motivated schizophrenic you've got to break
through the depression and apathy.
Fluanxol can help.
Because the mood elevating properties of
Fluanxol are particularly suitable for increasing

alertness, cooperation and the desire for
social contact[23]
Fluanxol controls first rank psychotic
symptoms with proven efficacy.
And Fluanxol achieves these results with
little or no daytime sedation and a low

incidence of anticholinergic and cardio-
vascular effects[1]
What's more, 2 dosage formats: depot and
tablets, facilitate easy continuity of therapy.
FLUANXOL. It can put you within reach of
your withdrawn schizophrenic patient.

Fluanxol
Depot: flupenthixol decanoate 2%, IO%. Tablets: flupenthixol dihydrochloride 0.5mg, 3mg.
Antipsychotics
Distributed by:
Merrell Dow
†Trademark of H. Lundbeck & Co. A/S. Denmark

TITLE
**THE NEXT VOICE HE
HEARS**
ART DIRECTOR
DENNIS FORBES
WRITER
VICKI GRANT
CREATIVE DIR.
MICHAEL PAUL
AGENCY
SMW ADVERTISING
CLIENT
MERRELL DOW

TITLE
**FOR DISCUSSION
PURPOSES**
ART DIRECTOR
PETER BARRON
WRITER
PETER BARRON
CREATIVE DIR.
PETER BARRON
PHOTOGRAPHER
FRANK KITCHING
TYPOGRAPHER
TYPSETTRA LTD.
AGENCY
**J. WALTER THOMPSON
ADVERTISING**
CLIENT
**TOSHIBA OF CANADA
LTD.**

TITLE
HOLE IN THE HEAD
ART DIRECTOR
GERALD SCHOENHOFF
WRITER
THOMAS WEISNER
CREATIVE DIR.
**GERALD SCHOENHOFF/
THOMAS WEISNER**
TYPOGRAPHER
CANADIAN COMPOSITION
AGENCY
LUNCH PAIL
CLIENT
CANADIAN COMPOSITION

TITLE
44 TALL
ART DIRECTOR
KAREN PRINCE
WRITER
TERRY O'REILLY
CREATIVE DIR.
**GEOFFREY B. ROCHE/
RICHARD HADDEN**
TYPOGRAPHER
WORD FOR WORD
CLIENT
CHIAT DAY ADVERTISING
ARTIST
STUART FREEDMAN

THE CREATIVE SIDE

Right. Deep breath, loosen up the ol' brain...the ol' brain-a-reeni...the ol' brain-a-roony... el brain-ola. Hmmm...Ummm...Let's see. I spy with my little eye something that is...who made that mark on my wall? C'mon, let's go. Right. What's the idea, the *big* idea? Mmmm...Hmm, that's kinda funny. Yeah. Naa. Getting dark outside. Didn't have plans anyway. Days are getting longer, time is getting shorter. Better look at the ol' brief...the ol' brief-a-reeni...the ol' brief-a-roony...el brief-ola. Ummm...okay. Oh! What was that?...Jeez, I can't write that fast. Don't forget it. What was that idea? Oh perfect! Gone forever. Wait...that's right, that was it. Perfect! Nah, too similar to...Why did they have to come up with it? I hate that. This would be so good. I think I was born two years too late. Well, it's dark now. Is that guy mugging her or are they friends? Okay, let's see. Did I pay my phone bill? C'mon, concentrate. This is a toughy. Gotta stay loose. Keep the ol' brain loose. *"Me, me, me, me, me..."* Hmmm...Will I ever have another idea? What if by some fluke there is no idea for this? An idea just can't be thought of. It's no one's fault – it's just physics. Like a black hole waiting to materialize. Maybe I should take my vacation now. C'mon, this is a real opportunity to do some nice stuff. Wait a minute...Ha-ha. That's nice. Not quite that way. Hmmm...okay. I like that. No it's crap. Hmmm...Hangover doesn't help. Shouldn't have had those last six beers. Why do I have to be so damn social? *"La, la, la, la, la...Figaro, Figaro."* Okay. Right. I'm going to really start thinking. Is that a pimple? Am I getting a pimple? Oh man I can't believe it. I always thought when you were older that you weren't supposed to get pimples. Ripped off. Shut up! Sure is dark out. Look at that store sign. Lot of burned out bulbs...Look at that guy. If you just back up he could get out and you could both go. Gotta crack this, I'm not working another weekend. Hmmm... What? Not bad, wait a minute. WAIT. A. MINUTE. Oooooo...Yes that could work. Let me get this down. Yeah! Then we spin it off. That's great. *"Happy days are here again."* What an idea. Brilliant! This is the one. We could be talking a walk to the podium here. *"The hills are alive with the sound of music, la, la, la, la."* This is great! Ahhh...the world's a wonderful place. Thank you brain, ol' brain-a-roony. Thank you. Whew! Thought it wasn't going to come. What a relief. Thank you. I'm going to give all my money to charity. I'm going to be a good person. Ahhh...I can go home. Maybe even catch the news with Lloyd Robertson. Let me look at that again. Genius, sheer genius. I love this business. Couldn't see doing anything else. Give me 10 million dollars and I'd say "Keep it." Just give me this job...What an idea! Whew!...Jeez, is it getting light out?

THE 1989 MARKETING AWARDS
MARCH 2, HARBOUR CASTLE WESTIN

THE ACCOUNT SIDE

"Betty, do you have a lint brush?" I can't be late for this presentation. I'm always late. This day...what is it, everybody's gone nuts? Finally after six months we're going to present this thing. Pray the Creatives wear something reasonable. This could be the day we move the client one more inch. Hope they don't kick and scream too much. Gotta get that revision down to Media. Big guy upstairs, if you're listening, I need this one to go. I've worked too long and too hard. If the client makes one more change...Why do I have to carry the boom box...just doesn't look right. Okay, Creatives, I said I'd meet you at the elevators five minutes ago. Where's the U&A study? "Who's got the U&A study?" Oh...I've got it. Maybe I should be in Creative – make the big bucks. I could like coming in at 10:00 every day...getting taken out for lunch. I'll demand the brief, then ignore it anyway. God forbid a suit should have an idea. Some of us even do our own gardening. I love that first internal presentation. They're so sincere – predisposing me to strategic considerations that I predisposed them to four weeks ago. Can't forget that P&L for tomorrow. Things are going too smoothly. I must be forgetting something. I still can't believe I went through that entire meeting with mayonnaise on my cheek. This other thing is way behind schedule. How am I going to get everyone excited about it? I can't stand the thought of doing laundry tonight. If we can only sell this. I could use a month in L.A. about now. The beaches...dinners...even make it to the shoot a couple of times. Why doesn't anyone else bring money to shoots? 'Can you pick me up a toothbrush?' For God's sake. Acetates! Okay, they're here. C'mon guys, where are you? It's a good thing I told them the presentation was going to be last week – we'd never have been ready. Watch – the client will bring up that coupon promotion again. If I see another coupon promotion...I've gotta get a bigger account, get my billings up. If they only knew who works on their business. Someone who tapes Bugs Bunny every Saturday morning. I don't believe it. I thought I got that salt off my shoes. Think it's time for a store check...maybe Montreal. Couldn't believe that jerk last night. 'What do you do?' 'I'm an advertising Account Exec.' 'So you do the books?' I hate chapped lips. Finally. "Have you got everything?" – Have I got cab fare? They won't. – "All the props?" Can't have enough props. Client loves a show, gives them something to look at. I wish I could present. Look at this stuff: a shovel, an autographed glossy of Slim Whitman and a four foot plastic lobster. The client's going to eat this up.

THE 1989 MARKETING AWARDS
MARCH 2, HARBOUR CASTLE WESTIN

A

SILVER

TITLE
CREATIVE
ACCOUNT
CLIENT SIDE
ART DIRECTOR
MICHAEL WELSH
WRITER
BILL KEENAN
CREATIVE DIR.
BILL DURNAN
PHOTOGRAPHER
GREG CORBOLD ·
TDF ARTISTS
ILLUSTRATOR
H & S RELIANCE
TYPOGRAPHER
THE COMPOSING ROOM
AGENCY
MacLAREN LINTAS INC.
CLIENT
MARKETING AWARDS
PRODUCTION MANAGER
STEVE HOPKINS

TITLE
SHOOT THE BULL
BORROWED TIME
PRETTY PICTURE
ART DIRECTOR
MARIE POON/
DALE HENDERSON
WRITER
DALE HENDERSON
CREATIVE DIR.
DALE HENDERSON
PHOTOGRAPHER
JOHN MASTROMONACO/
DEBORAH SAMUEL/
SHIN SUGINO
AGENCY
HENDERSON & COMPANY
CLIENT
STUDIO CENTRE

Earn your living on borrowed time.

Not a pretty picture for 2¼ users.

TITLE
REVERE
POMPEII
KING RICHARD
ART DIRECTOR
TONY KERR
WRITER
BRUCE MacDONALD
CREATIVE DIR.
MARTY MYERS/
DENNIS BRUCE
PHOTOGRAPHER
BRADSHAW
PHOTOGRAPHY
TYPOGRAPHER
TYPSETTRA LTD.
AGENCY
MILLER MYERS BRUCE
DALLA COSTA
CLIENT
MEDIACOM INC.
IN HOUSE STUDIO
O'CONNELL STUDIO

Pompeii would have been ready.

Explosion of values? Bursting with stock?
Launching new product? Avert a sales catastrophy. Let them know
in advance with Mediacom Posters.

MEDIACOM
The Poster Network.

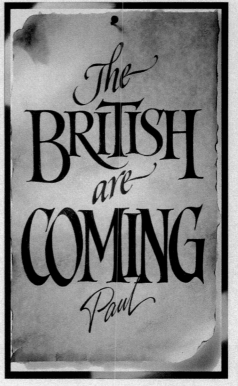

Revere would never have had to ride.

Indeed, Paul could have held his horses,
saved his voice and not spread the word, in the knowledge that Mediacom
Posters were busy alerting the citizens.

MEDIACOM
The Poster Network.

Puts colour in your cheeks.

Unwind.

GOLD

TITLE
**PUTS COLOUR IN
YOUR CHECKS
UNWIND
RED AND WHITE FOR
THE WINTER BLUES**
ART DIRECTOR
JIM BROWN
WRITER
BRAD MYERS

CREATIVE DIR.
KEITH RAVENSCROFT
ILLUSTRATOR
**THIERRY THOMPSON/
ROGER HILL**
AGENCY
OGILVY & MATHER
CLIENT
**THE CAMPBELL SOUP
CO., LTD.**

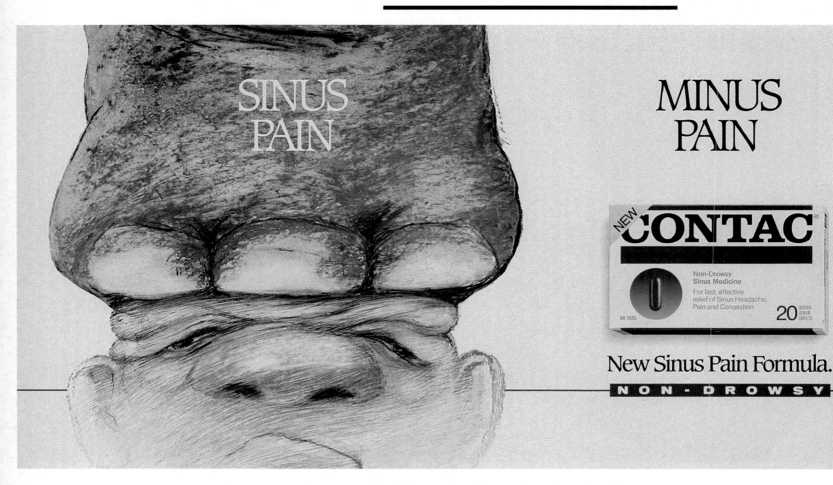

SINUS
PAIN

MINUS
PAIN

New Sinus Pain Formula.
NON-DROWSY

SILVER

TITLE
SINUS PAIN MINUS PAIN
ART DIRECTOR
CHARLES BONGERS
ILLUSTRATOR
JERZY KOLACZ/REACTOR
AGENCY
OGILVY & MATHER
CLIENT
CONTAC

SILVER

TITLE
CAN CAN
ART DIRECTOR
LEIF NIELSEN
EDITOR
STEVE CONOVER
CREATIVE DIR.
RICK DAVIS
PHOTOGRAPHER
DESMOND MONTAQUE
ILLUSTRATOR
LEIF NIELSEN
AGENCY
YOUNG & RUBICAM LTD.
CLIENT
GENERAL FOODS

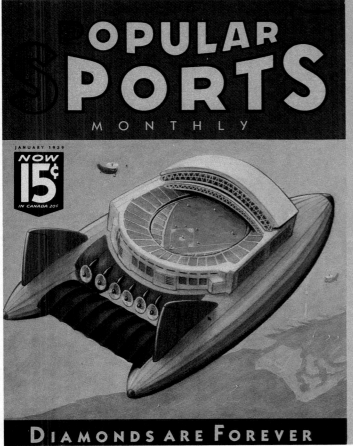

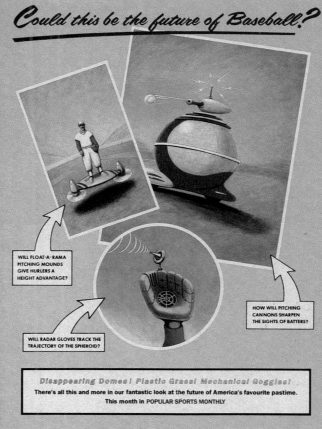

Could this be the future of Baseball?

WILL FLOAT-A-RAMA PITCHING MOUNDS GIVE HURLERS A HEIGHT ADVANTAGE?

WILL RADAR GLOVES TRACK THE TRAJECTORY OF THE SPHEROID?

HOW WILL PITCHING CANNONS SHARPEN THE SIGHTS OF BATTERS?

Disappearing Domes! Plastic Grass! Mechanical Goggles!
There's all this and more in our fantastic look at the future of America's favourite pastime.
This month in POPULAR SPORTS MONTHLY

A
SILVER

TITLE
SEASONS TICKETS BROCHURE
ART DIRECTOR
DEREK CHAPMAN
WRITER
JEFF BUTLER/ JOHN GEORGE
CREATIVE DIR.
DEREK CHAPMAN/ JEFF BUTLER
PHOTOGRAPHER
EKLIPSE STUDIOS
ILLUSTRATOR
EKLIPSE STUDIOS
TYPOGRAPHER
EKLIPSE STUDIOS
AGENCY
J. WALTER THOMPSON ADVERTISING
CLIENT
TORONTO BLUE JAYS BASEBALL CLUB

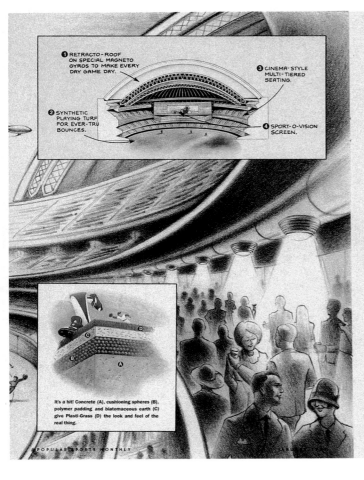

1 RETRACTO-ROOF ON SPECIAL MAGNETO GYROS TO MAKE EVERY DAY GAME DAY.

2 SYNTHETIC PLAYING TURF FOR EVER-TRU BOUNCES.

3 CINEMA-STYLE MULTI-TIERED SEATING.

4 SPORT-O-VISION SCREEN.

It's a hit! Concrete (A), cushioning spheres (B), polymer padding and biatomaceous earth (C) give Plasti-Grass (D) the look and feel of the real thing.

Root, Root, Root for the home screen!
Sport-O-Vision will play back those back to back homers.

This is the life! Hot dogs, beer and pretzels under the sun as the players take the field.

And what a field! The grass is all exactly the same colour and there's not a bad bounce or gopher hole out there. You look around to see the machine that trims this lawn, but don't bother. The field is made of plasti-grass, a turbo age compound that never needs watering or mowing!

You sit back in the luxury of your molded seat. The Blue Jay batter lays down a bunt – the third baseman charges, throws to first – a close play. Is he safe? Is he out? Look up at Sport-O-Vision – a huge movie screen that shows you the play again and again. He was out by a hair. "Kill the Ump!" you cry. But your voice is alone. The rest of the fans know that when Sport-O-Vision

was introduced in the 1950's, the screen showed the umpires were always right. So the men in blue stepped aside for the Electro-Age.

The magic of Sport-O-Vision also enables you to see the players up closer than ever before.

The classic baseball cap is there. But there's a new addition to ward off the glare from huge banks of Klieg lights that illuminate the field like a set from the talkies. The players are wearing shatter-resistant, tinted goggles that flip up and down for optimum vision.

Look there, at the batter! A bakelite cap protects him from errant pitches. And the boots. Look closely and you'll see the metal cleats have been replaced by pliable suction cups that give a better grip on the plasti-grass.

(Continued on page 8)

TITLE
WE NEED MORE THAN...
IT WILL TAKE PEOPLE
THE MOST POWERFUL
PEOPLE
ART DIRECTOR
DAVID KELSO
WRITER
BILL LOWER
DESIGNER
EKLIPSE STUDIOS
ILLUSTRATOR
HENRIK DRESCHER/
REACTOR
AGENCY
J. WALTER THOMPSON
ADVERTISING
CLIENT
UNITED WAY

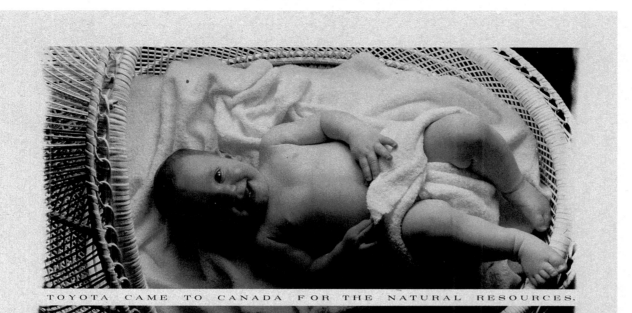

TOYOTA CAME TO CANADA FOR THE NATURAL RESOURCES.

With every new Canadian, our resources as a nation are expanded. Our future potential is enhanced. As Canadians, we can be forgiven an ardent fascination with the youth of Canada. Our country is young. Our history is being written with every new venture we undertake.

Now Toyota has brought a new venture to life in Canada. The Toyota manufacturing plant in Cambridge, Ontario is only the latest step in a long-standing commitment to Canada and Canadians. Over $400 million and hundreds of thousands of man-hours have been contributed.

Designed to build Toyota Corollas, it is a state-of-the-art production facility - an enterprise for our generation, and for those yet to come. What brought this investment to Canada? Our greatest resource: Our people. It is already apparent that in Canada, as in Japan, succeeding generations will find a sense of commitment with Toyota. Not only in Cambridge, but across the country.

TOYOTA

TITLE
**TOYOTA CAME TO
CANADA FOR THE
NATURAL RESOURCES**
ART DIRECTOR
RICHARD TALBOT
WRITER
ROBIN HEISEY
PHOTOGRAPHER
MICHAEL RAFELSON
AGENCY
**SAATCHI & SAATCHI
COMPTON HAYHURST**
CLIENT
TOYOTA

TOYOTA CAME TO CANADA FOR ITS ENERGY RESERVES.

With the opening of the new Corolla manufacturing plant in Cambridge, Ontario, Toyota has tapped into Canada's best energy resource: Our people. People who are helping to shape not only the future of Toyota, but the future of Canada itself.

At the Cambridge plant, new techniques in business and manufacturing are being perfected. Working with teammates from Japan and around the world, Canadians are learning Toyota concepts like Kaizen, or continuous improvement. And they're discovering something about themselves: that our Canadian craftsmanship is as good as any in the world. Already, a Canadian Corolla has won the prestigious Automobile Journalists' Association of Canada award for "The best vehicle built in Canada". By 1990, the Cambridge plant will be producing 50,000 Corollas a year, for sale throughout North America.

As one of the largest selling cars in history, the Corolla has an outstanding heritage. And so it is with Canadians. Our heritage of spirit and energy is our most valuable natural resource.

TOYOTA

TITLE
**TOYOTA CAME TO
CANADA FOR ITS
ENERGY RESERVES**
ART DIRECTOR
RICHARD TALBOT
WRITER
ROBIN HEISEY
PHOTOGRAPHER
MICHAEL RAFELSON
AGENCY
**SAATCHI & SAATCHI
COMPTON HAYHURST**
CLIENT
TOYOTA

TITLE
VOLKSWAGEN SERVICE CENTRE
ART DIRECTOR
DUNCAN BRUCE
WRITER
MARTA CUTLER
PHOTOGRAPHER
GEORGE SIMHONI
AGENCY
DDB NEEDHAM ADVERTISING
CLIENT
VOLKSWAGEN CANADA INC.

The new Volkswagen service centre.

It may not be quite as large as you were expecting.

And no, there isn't a Volkswagen sign out front.

But don't let that fool you for a second. This phone booth is actu-ally the nerve centre of our new Guaranteed Mobility service.

Should you ever have a problem with your '89 Volkswagen, one phone call is all it takes to bring help.

Any time of day or night.

If your battery fails, or your radiator springs a leak.

Even if your Volkswagen breaks down.

And if repairs take an unexpec-ted amount of time, we'll even arrange for overnight accommo-dation or lend you another car for up to 2 days.

Guaranteed Mobility comes as standard equipment on every '89 Volkswagen. And you're covered for the first 6 years (as long as you have repairs and annual scheduled main-tenance performed).

So next time you spot a phone booth, think of it as your personal hotline to Volkswagen.

You might even want to call us, just to say hello. For complete infor-mation, visit your nearest dealer.

VW Guaranteed Mobility

TITLE
THREE TIMES BLUER THAN BLUE
ART DIRECTOR
DIANNE EASTMAN
WRITER
IAN MIRLIN
PHOTOGRAPHER
VINCENT NOGUCHI
AGENCY
HARROD & MIRLIN
CLIENT
LEVI'S

Three times bluer than blue.

TRIPLE DARK DENIM

Levi's

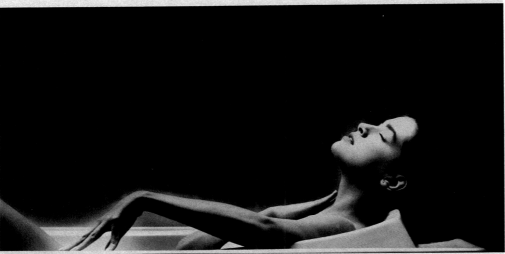

EVER WONDER
WHY SOME PEOPLE
CALL THEIR
BATHROOM
A RESTROOM?

Perhaps it was first introduced as a polite alternative by the genteel society.

But today, in this increasingly stressful world, the whirlpool has given the name true meaning.

The pioneering designers of the Mirocast Whirlpool believed that every bathroom should be a restroom.

That everybody should benefit from the rapturous effects of massaging jets placed in strategic, anatomical locations. That everybody should experience the departure of stress and tension while lying in an ergonomically designed cradle.

What they designed is just such a whirlpool.

The Mirocast Whirlpool series is quite unlike any other whirlpool. It offers sizes, shapes and an assortment of contemporary colours to suit every taste. And each one features the jets, motor and hardware that has garnered much critical acclaim for comfort, safety and reliability.

The best way to see these whirlpools is to visit an authorized Mirocast dealer.

Or visit a friend, with a restroom.

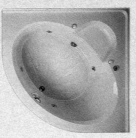

Mirocast Whirlpools ◆ Mirolin

TITLE
EVER WONDER
ART DIRECTOR
PETER HOLMES
WRITER
PETER HOLMES
CREATIVE DIR.
PETER HOLMES
PHOTOGRAPHER
SHIN SUGINO
TYPOGRAPHER
THE COMPOSING ROOM
AGENCY
FRANKLIN DALLAS ADVERTISING INC.
CLIENT
MIROLIN INDUSTRIES
COLOUR SEPARATIONS
H & S RELIANCE

THIS FEELING IS
NOW AVAILABLE IN 18 DESIGNS
AND 22 COLOURS.

A Mirocast whirlpool is designed to produce an extremely pleasurable, yet odd sensation.

Odd because it's a feeling you may not be familiar with, unless of course you own one.

To produce this feeling, its shape has been crafted to gently cradle your body in a seemingly weightless condition. Of equal importance, the Hydromassage Jets have been engineered to correctly mix the flow of air and water and to be extremely flexible in directing the flow. The Mirocast whirlpool is also available in an exceptionally large range of styles, colours and prices.

We call the Mirocast our small contribution to the quality of living. However, those who own one don't seem to call it anything. When asked, they simply check the time, form a warm smile and look off into the distance. Odd isn't it.

Mirocast Whirlpools ◆ Mirolin

TITLE
POP ART
ART DIRECTOR
COLIN PRIESTLY
WRITER
BRENT PULFORD
PHOTOGRAPHER
GEORGE SIMHONI
AGENCY
J. WALTER THOMPSON
CLIENT
PEPSI COLA CANADA LIMITED

TITLE
THIS FEELING
ART DIRECTOR
PETER HOLMES
WRITER
PETER HOLMES
CREATIVE DIR.
PETER HOLMES
PHOTOGRAPHER
SHIN SUGINO
TYPOGRAPHER
THE COMPOSING ROOM
AGENCY
FRANKLIN DALLAS ADVERTISING INC.
CLIENT
MIROLIN INDUSTRIES
COLOUR SEPARATIONS
H & S RELIANCE

A friend to the end.

LEVI'S

GOLD

TITLE
A FRIEND TO THE END
ART DIRECTOR
DIANNE EASTMAN
WRITER
GRAHAME ARNOULD
CREATIVE DIR.
**BRIAN HARROD/
IAN MIRLIN**
PHOTOGRAPHER
BERT BELL
AGENCY
HARROD & MIRLIN
CLIENT
LEVI STRAUSS

TITLE
**IF YOU'D RATHER BE
DRIVING...**
ART DIRECTOR
TIM O'CONNELL
WRITER
LISA SHIMOTAKAHARA
CREATIVE DIR.
GARY PROUK
TYPOGRAPHER
TYPSETTRA LTD.
AGENCY
**SCALI, McCABE, SLOVES
(CANADA) LTD.**
CLIENT
HERTZ CANADA LTD.
PRODUCTION MANAGER
MICHAEL PENNY

If you'd rather be driving, start walking.

We're just a few steps away at 39 Richmond Street West.

Can you really afford to rent from anyone else? **Hertz**

Hertz rents Fords and other fine cars.

New. But they'll improve.

The Earth Moved.

The Audi 200 quattro.

A
SILVER

TITLE
**NEW, BUT THEY'LL
IMPROVE**
ART DIRECTOR
DIANNE EASTMAN
WRITER
BILL DANIEL
CREATIVE DIR.
**BRIAN HARROD/
IAN MIRLIN**
PHOTOGRAPHER
BERT BELL
AGENCY
HARROD & MIRLIN
CLIENT
LEVI STRAUSS

TITLE
THE EARTH MOVED
ART DIRECTOR
HOWARD ALSTAD
WRITER
PHILIPPE GARNEAU
CREATIVE DIR.
ALLAN KAZMER
PHOTOGRAPHER
JOHN MASTROMONACO
AGENCY
**DDB NEEDHAM
WORLDWIDE
ADVERTISING LTD.**
CLIENT
**VOLKSWAGEN
CANADA INC.**

TITLE
SUNFLOWERS
ART DIRECTOR
RICK KEMP
WRITER
PETER LANYON
AGENCY
COSSETTE
CLIENT
GILBEY CANADA

SILVER

TITLE
CAN CAN
ART DIRECTOR
LEIF NIELSON
WRITER
STEVE CONOVER
CREATIVE DIR.
RICK DAVIS
PHOTOGRAPHER
DESMOND MONTAQUE
AGENCY
YOUNG & RUBICAM LTD.
CLIENT
GENERAL FOODS

SILVER

TITLE
FRESHLY SQUEEZED
ART DIRECTOR
DIANNE EASTMAN
WRITER
IAN MIRLIN
CREATIVE DIR.
BRIAN HARROD/
IAN MIRLIN
PHOTOGRAPHER
BERT BELL
AGENCY
HARROD & MIRLIN
CLIENT
EVIAN

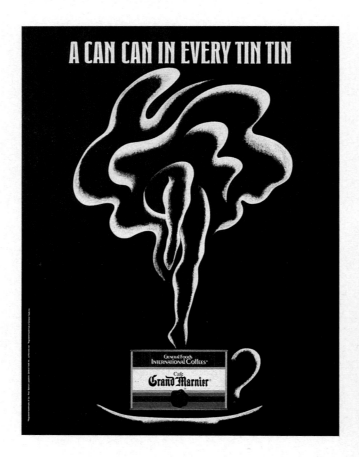

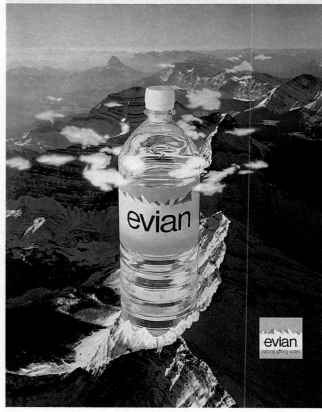

TITLE
RED AND WHITE FOR THE WINTER BLUES
ART DIRECTOR
JIM BROWN
WRITER
BRAD MYERS
CREATIVE DIR.
KEITH RAVENSCROFT
ILLUSTRATOR
ROGER HILL
AGENCY
OGILVY & MATHER
CLIENT
THE CAMPBELL SOUP CO. LTD.

TITLE
FACE OFF
ART DIRECTOR
MICHAEL EDWARDS
WRITER
MICHAEL deSOUZA
CREATIVE DIR.
MICHAEL EDWARDS
PHOTOGRAPHER
STANLEY WONG
TYPOGRAPHER
TYPSETTRA LTD.
AGENCY
FCB/RONALDS-REYNOLDS
CLIENT
MOLSON BREWERIES OF CANADA
PRODUCTION MANAGER
JUNE MURRAY

TITLE
IF YOU THINK YOU MIGHT HAVE BAD BREATH
ART DIRECTOR
STEPHANIE RICHMOND
WRITER
JOHN GEORGE
CREATIVE DIR.
GRAY ABRAHAM
PHOTOGRAPHER
KEN MULVENEY
AGENCY
J. WALTER THOMPSON ADVERTISING
CLIENT
ADAMS BRANDS INC. - A WARNER-LAMBERT CO.

Puts colour in your cheeks.

Unwind

TITLE
**PUTS COLOUR IN YOUR
CHEEKS**
ART DIRECTOR
JIM BROWN
WRITER
BRAD MYERS
CREATIVE DIR.
KEITH RAVENSCROFT
ILLUSTRATOR
THIERRY THOMPSON
AGENCY
OGILVY & MATHER
CLIENT
**THE CAMPBELL SOUP
CO. LTD.**

TITLE
UNWIND
ART DIRECTOR
JIM BROWN
WRITER
BRAD MYERS
CREATIVE DIR.
KEITH RAVENSCROFT
ILLUSTRATOR
ROGER HILL
AGENCY
OGILVY & MATHER
CLIENT
**THE CAMPBELL SOUP
CO. LTD.**

TITLE
HAVE A FIELD DAY
ART DIRECTOR
HOWARD ALSTAD
WRITER
PHILIPPE GARNEAU
CREATIVE DIR.
ALLAN KAZMER
ILLUSTRATOR
PAULA MUNCK
TYPOGRAPHER
TYPEWORKS LIMITED

AGENCY
**DDB NEEDHAM
WORLDWIDE
ADVERTISING LTD.**
CLIENT
**MERRELL DOW
PHARMACEUTICALS
(CANADA) INC.**

TITLE
NO STICK IN THE MUD
ART DIRECTOR
JAMES JUNG
WRITER
CLIVE DESMOND
CREATIVE DIR.
**BRIAN HARROD/
IAN MIRLIN**
PHOTOGRAPHER
BARRY JOHNSON
AGENCY
HARROD & MIRLIN
CLIENT
SUZUKI CANADA

Anyone who wants Alpenbitter raise your spea

Deep in the mists of forgotten time lurks a mysterious legend. It was the Halstatt Era., 600 B.C. If Conan the Barbarian lived it was during this epoch.

The world was newer then. The mountain streams of Middle Europe ran clear. Wildflowers and aromatic herbs grew abundantly in the warm sun. Life was good.

It was a time of happy wars and sad songs and idyllic contentment. Time was told by the passing of nights not of days.

In fact partying, next to war, was the major sport. In these simpler times, long before the civilizing influences of the six pack and a bag of pretzels, the creation of beverages was an art as prized as the swordmaker's.

One day, the legend has it down as Tuesday, October 7, 687 B.C., a certain Druid, Samoledt of the

Helveti Tribe, was sampling a batch of what the people farther east across the Urals now call "the stuff that's virtually unattainable unless you stand in line for 3 days." It was bland. Mind numbingly, boringly bland.

Then inspiration struck like Thor's thunderclap. "Why not infuse the liquid with precious herbs and botanicals?" Why not indeed.

A year passed. Well, almost a year. It was the Feast of Cornucopia. The Rising of the Harvest Moon. Football Season. The most auspicious time of the Druidic Calendar.

Samoledt rolled out the infused barrel. And, as well as inventing a new musical tradition, he began the legend that lives on as Alpenbitter.

Today Rittmeister's Alpenbitter is unique.

A tantalizingly delicate blending of Alpen grown herbs and botanicals and gentle sweetness.

A mysteriously refreshing taste when mixed with effervescent liquids.(cola, soda, gingerale.)

When you enjoy Alpenbitter in moderation you partake of a European tradition that has its heritage deep in the mists of forgotten time.

Available in 750 mL and 100 mL sizes.

Right now. At an LCBO store near you.

TASTE THE LEGEND.

TITLE
ANYONE WHO WANTS ALPENBITTER...
ART DIRECTOR
RAYMOND LEE
WRITER
RODERICK MACKIN
CREATIVE DIR.
RAYMOND LEE
TYPOGRAPHER
HEAD: PRIMETYPE
BODY: PROTYPE
AGENCY
RAYMOND LEE & ASSOCIATES LTD.

TITLE
SAY AHHH!
ART DIRECTOR
DIANNE EASTMAN
WRITER
BILL DANIEL/ DIANNE EASTMAN
CREATIVE DIR.
BRIAN HARROD/ IAN MIRLIN
PHOTOGRAPHER
KAREN PERLMUTTER
AGENCY
HARROD & MIRLIN
CLIENT
MEAD JOHNSON

TITLE
INNOCENT VICTIMS OF CRIME
ART DIRECTOR
CHRIS DICKSON
WRITER
CHRIS DICKSON
CREATIVE DIR.
MARTY MYERS/ DENNIS BRUCE
PHOTOGRAPHER
NIGEL DICKSON
AGENCY
MILLER MYERS BRUCE DALLA COSTA
CLIENT
MINISTRY OF THE ATTORNEY GENERAL
IN HOUSE STUDIO
O'CONNELL STUDIO

---

my doctor has a warm laugh.
my doctor has a cold stethoscope.
my doctor writes secret notes to my mom.
my doctor can see germs.
my doctor shows me pictures of my bones.
but I always have to show him how to say ahhh.

TEMPRA

When lives are torn apart by violent crime, who's there to help put the pieces back together?

The innocent victims of violent crime can have a difficult time putting their lives back together. The Ontario Government recognizes that medical costs, lost wages, and out-of-pocket expenses can add to the pain and suffering. The Criminal Injuries Compensation Board has been designed to help ease the burden and assist the victims financially, simply and compassionately.

For more information, contact: The Criminal Injuries Compensation Board, 439 University Avenue, 17th Floor, Toronto, Ontario, M5G 1Y8. Telephone (416) 965-4755.

THE CRIMINAL INJURIES COMPENSATION BOARD

**Puts colour
in your cheeks.**

Unwind.

GOLD

TITLE
UNWIND
**PUTS COLOUR IN YOUR
CHEEKS**
**RED AND WHITE FOR
THE WINTER BLUES**
ART DIRECTOR
JIM BROWN
WRITER
BRAD MYERS

CREATIVE DIR.
KEITH RAVENSCROFT
ILLUSTRATOR
**ROGER HILL/
THIERRY THOMPSON**
AGENCY
OGILVY & MATHER
CLIENT
**THE CAMPBELL SOUP
CO. LTD.**

SILVER

TITLE
**A FRIEND TO THE END
LOVE 'EM TO BITS
NEW BUT THEY'LL
IMPROVE**
ART DIRECTOR
DIANNE EASTMAN
WRITER
**BILL DANIEL/
GRAHAME ARNOULD/
IAN MIRLIN**

CREATIVE DIR.
**BRIAN HARROD/
IAN MIRLIN**
PHOTOGRAPHER
BERT BELL
AGENCY
HARROD & MIRLIN
CLIENT
LEVI STRAUSS

HOW TO REWIND AFTER WORK.

SUPER VHS VIDEOCASSETTE DECKS JVC

PLAY WITH A LOADED DECK.

SUPER VHS VIDEOCASSETTE DECKS JVC

TITLE
HOW TO REWIND AFTER WORK
NEW YEAR'S RESOLUTION
PLAY WITH A LOADED DECK
ART DIRECTOR
PETER HOLMES
WRITER
PETER HOLMES
CREATIVE DIR.
PETER HOLMES
PHOTOGRAPHER
TIM SAUNDERS
TYPOGRAPHER
COOPER & BEATTY, LIMITED
AGENCY
FRANKLIN DALLAS ADVERTISING INC.
CLIENT
JVC CANADA INC.
COLOUR SEPARATIONS
H & S RELIANCE

TITLE
HANDFUL
FEW SKINS
NOBODY
ART DIRECTOR
RICHARD CLEWES
WRITER
RICHARD CLEWES
PHOTOGRAPHER
PETER HUTCHINGS/
ROBERT MIZONO
TYPOGRAPHER
HUNTER BROWN
AGENCY
RICHARD CLEWES
CLIENT
BEACHCOMBER
PRINT PRODUCTION
GORD CATHMOIR

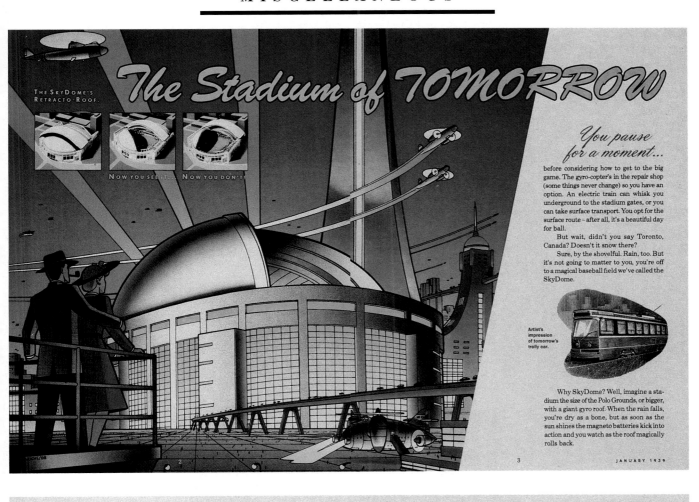

The Stadium of TOMORROW

THE SKYDOME'S RETRACTO-ROOF.

NOW YOU SEE IT... NOW YOU DON'T!

You pause for a moment...

before considering how to get to the big game. The gyro-copter's in the repair shop (some things never change) so you have an option. An electric train can whisk you underground to the stadium gates, or you can take surface transport. You opt for the surface route – after all, it's a beautiful day for ball.

But wait, didn't you say Toronto, Canada? Doesn't it snow there?

Sure, by the shovelful. Rain, too. But it's not going to matter to you, you're off to a magical baseball field we've called the SkyDome.

Artist's impression of tomorrow's trolly car.

Why SkyDome? Well, imagine a stadium the size of the Polo Grounds, or bigger, with a giant gyro roof. When the rain falls, you're dry as a bone, but as soon as the sun shines the magneto batteries kick into action and you watch as the roof magically rolls back.

3

JANUARY 1939

GOLD

TITLE
SEASON'S TICKETS BROCHURE
ART DIRECTOR
DEREK CHAPMAN
WRITER
JEFF BUTLER/ JOHN GEORGE
CREATIVE DIR.
DEREK CHAPMAN/ JEFF BUTLER
PHOTOGRAPHER
EKLIPSE STUDIOS
ILLUSTRATOR
EKLIPSE STUDIOS
TYPOGRAPHER
EKLIPSE STUDIOS
AGENCY
J. WALTER THOMPSON ADVERTISING
CLIENT
TORONTO BLUE JAYS BASEBALL CLUB

EQUIPPING THE FUTURE GENERATION of PLAYERS.

IT'S FUN to look at baseball years from now and speculate on every aspect of the game. But we at Popular Sports must admit that there's one area we are not equipped to speculate on – Fashion. What will the players be dressed like? We've asked Coco Canal, famed couturier, to sit in with Ted Brumwich, President of the American Fabrications Board and a ball fan in his own right.

Home (L) and Away (R) uniforms show the classic look in new wrinkle-no-more fabric.

POPULAR SPORTS: *Ted, how about fabrics of the future?*

TED BRUMWICH: Well even today some of our members are working on some pretty neat stuff. Fabrics that won't need ironing, plastics that will stretch but maintain their shape – probably of most interest to baseball will be some of the stain-resistants the DUDOW Chemical Co. is researching.

COCO CANAL: Zat is fantastique, Teddy! Because zen ze ballplayers won't have all zat dirt

when you see zem late in the game.

TED BRUMWICH: Well, I said stain resistant, Coco. I don't think we'll be able to keep out the grime from an aggressive slide into second.

COCO: And stretch plastics. So we could have a one piece uniform very snug, very fitting, because really, some of zose players have fantastic bodies.

POPULAR SPORTS: *A one piece suit, Ted, is that really possible?*

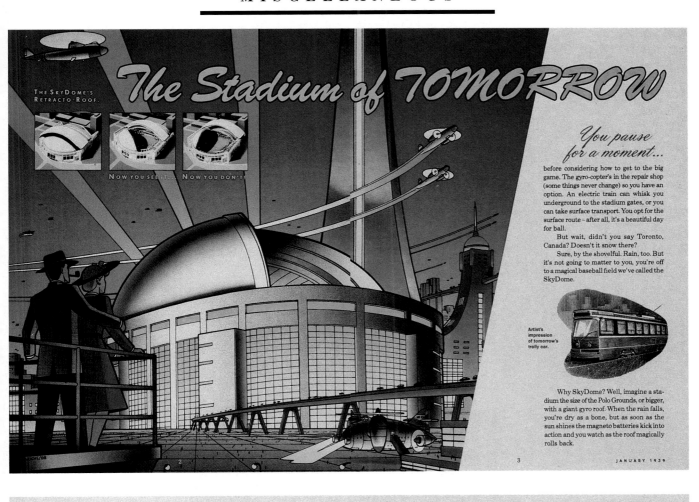

1989
1959
1939

Is this the glove of 1989? Our projections show the possible evolution of outfielding.

TED: Well, sure, I guess it's possible. But you have to remember you're dealing with a lot of tradition here. The current uniform is what the players and fans are used to...

COCO: And it really is quite functional.

TED: Sure, I mean, forgive me, Coco, but they're dressing for a ball game, not a ball.

COCO: Tee hee, Oh, zat's good.

SPORTS: *Coco – how about the markings?*

COCO: You know, I can never understand why zey don't have ze names of ze players on ze sweaters instead of ze numbers.

SPORTS: *Well, I think the umpires might have something to say about that.*

TED: Not to mention the program printers! But I could foresee a day where you'd have names and numbers.

SPORTS: *How about home and away uniforms, Ted. Any change?*

Micro-mechanics provide protection from the noon-day sun.

TED: Well, it's not really my domain, but we're seeing a lot more travel these days, and with some of the new airships you read about, I think you can see the day where players could be flying to faraway places to play.

SPORTS: *So the home uniforms will have the name of the team. But for away you want to see the name of the city.*

TED: Exactly.

Poly molecular compounds make for suction-cupped shoes.

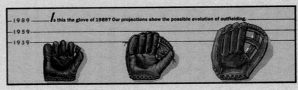

COCO: Well, baseball fashion is still fashion. And you know, zese new materials are very exciting from a designers' point of view. But zere have been new materials throughout the ages and I tell you what always happen. Zese designers go through ze trend, using ze material in wonderful new ways, new designs, but it always comes back to ze classics. So you use zese materials to make all new design, zen come back to making ze older, classic designs better.

SPORTS: *So we'll see a phase of modern designs but you think we'll eventually return to the basics — the button-front jersey, stockings and sanitaries, the knickerbocker trousers.*

COCO: It's a classic.

SPORTS: *How do you feel about that, Ted?*

TED: It's the way baseball's meant to be played.

A

SILVER

TITLE
McDONALD'S SUMMER CUPS
ART DIRECTOR
CARL W. JONES/ PAUL SYCH
CREATIVE DIR.
PAUL JOYCE
ILLUSTRATOR
RENE ZAMIC/ PAULA MUNCK/ JOE BIAFORE
AGENCY
VICKERS & BENSON ADVERTISING LTD.
DESIGN FIRM
REACTOR ART & DESIGN LTD./ MENTAL ART & DESIGN LTD.
CLIENT
McDONALD'S RESTAURANTS OF CANADA LTD.

A

SILVER

TITLE
DRINKS ARE FREE
ART DIRECTOR
DOMENIC SALLES
EDITOR
MIKE O'REILLY/ TOM GOUDIE
CREATIVE DIR.
RICK DAVIS
AGENCY
YOUNG & RUBICAM LTD.
CLIENT
SCOTT'S FOOD SERVICE

A

SILVER

TITLE
PORSCHE
ART DIRECTOR
GEOFFREY B. ROCHE
WRITER
TERRY O'REILLY
DESIGNER
GEOFFREY B. ROCHE
CREATIVE DIR.
GEOFFREY B. ROCHE/ RICHARD HADDEN
TYPOGRAPHER
CANADIAN COMPOSITION
AGENCY
CHIAT DAY ADVERTISING
CLIENT
NISSAN
ARTIST
STUART FREEDMAN

THE DRINKS ARE FREE.

Kentucky Fried Chicken

Porsche goes here.

To be inserted on rear-view mirror of 300Z.

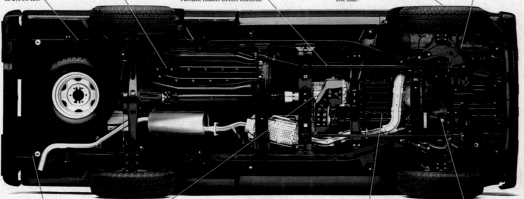

You can tell a lot about a Hardbody by its hard belly.

Semi-elliptical leaf springs let the Hardbody haul up to 2,000 lbs.

Skid plates under the fuel tank, engine and transfer case help ward off stumps and boulders.

The independent torsion bar suspension allows each wheel to deal with ruts and rocks without transferring the shock to the other wheel. Result, much better control.

Auto-locking front hubs let you shift into four-wheel drive without getting out of the cab.

The front stabilizer bar reduces body lean when you're taking turns at speed.

A welded ladder frame and box section design is about as strong a frame design as you can give a truck.

A two-speed transfer case gives you a choice of gear ranges. From stump-pulling low to street-cruising high.

NISSAN
Built for the Human Race.

The new optional electronic 4-speed overdrive automatic transmission has computer-controlled shift points that put it in the right gear for the situation.

Power-assisted rack-and-pinion steering makes the Hardbody as easy to handle off the road as on.

A
SILVER

TITLE
HARD BODY
ART DIRECTOR
KAREN PRINCE
WRITER
TERRY O'REILLY
CREATIVE DIR.
GEOFFREY B. ROCHE/
RICHARD HADDEN
TYPOGRAPHER
WORD FOR WORD
AGENCY
CHIAT DAY ADVERTISING
CLIENT
NISSAN

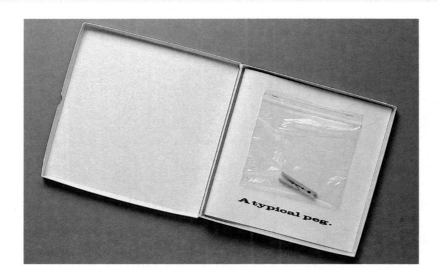

A
SILVER

TITLE
A TYPICAL PEG
ART DIRECTOR
RICHARD CLEWES
WRITER
RICHARD CLEWES
PHOTOGRAPHER
PETER HUTCHINGS
TYPOGRAPHER
ALPHA
AGENCY
RICHARD CLEWES
CLIENT
PETER HUTCHINGS
PRINT PRODUCTION
GORD CATHMOIR

TITLE
PERFORMANCE
ART DIRECTOR
GEOFFREY B. ROCHE
WRITER
TERRY O'REILLY
DESIGNER
GEOFFREY B. ROCHE
CREATIVE DIR.
RICHARD HADDEN/
GEOFFREY B. ROCHE
PHOTOGRAPHER
GARY McGUIRE
TYPOGRAPHER
CANADIAN COMPOSITION
AGENCY
CHIAT DAY ADVERTISING
CLIENT
NISSAN
ARTIST
STUART FREEDMAN

TITLE
ALPHABET
ART DIRECTOR
GEOFFREY B. ROCHE/
BRIAN HICKLING
WRITER
TERRY O'REILLY
DESIGNER
GEOFFREY B. ROCHE
CREATIVE DIR.
RICHARD HADDEN/
GEOFFREY B. ROCHE
PHOTOGRAPHER
TERRY COLLIER
TYPOGRAPHER
CANADIAN COMPOSITION
AGENCY
CHIAT DAY ADVERTISING
CLIENT
NISSAN
ARTIST
STUART FREEDMAN

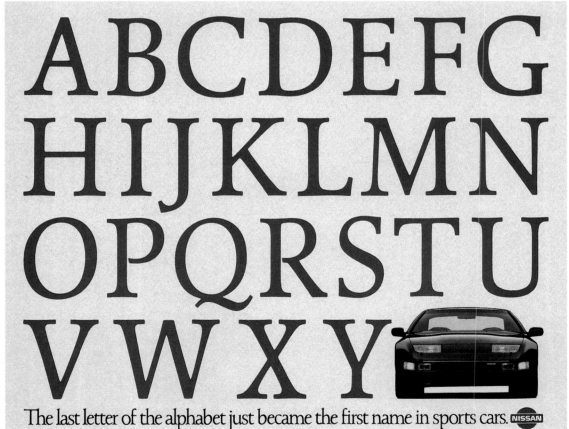

*Registered Trade Mark of Nabisco Brands Ltd © 1986 All Rights Reserved

TITLE
MICROWOVEN
ART DIRECTOR
BARRY CHEMEL
WRITER
KURT HAGAN
CREATIVE DIR.
STU EATON
ILLUSTRATOR
DESMOND MONTAGUE
AGENCY
FOSTER/McCANN-ERICKSON ADVERTISING
CLIENT
CHRISTIE BROWN & CO.
PRODUCTION
SANDRA REES

TITLE
BOOK OF FAUCETS
ART DIRECTOR
PETER HOLMES
WRITER
PETER HOLMES
CREATIVE DIR.
PETER HOLMES
PHOTOGRAPHER
DAVID EISENBERG
TYPOGRAPHER
THE COMPOSING ROOM
AGENCY
FRANKLIN DALLAS ADVERTISING INC.
CLIENT
RUBINET BRASS CANADA LTD.
SEPARATIONS
H & S RELIANCE
PRINTER
BRADBURY TAMBLYN BOORNE

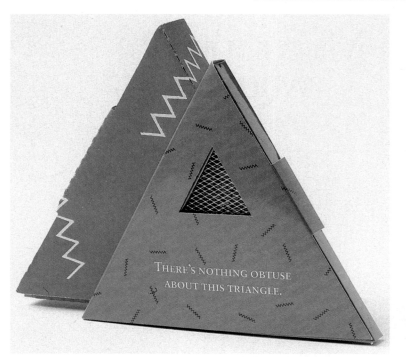

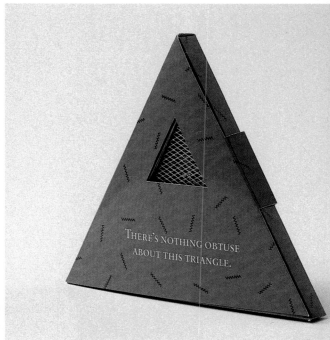

TITLE
**BASF FIBRES INC.
RICHMOND CARPET
DIRECT MAILER**
DESIGNER
CHRIS OLIVER
CREATIVE DIR.
BEV TUDHOPE
DESIGN FIRM
**TUDHOPE
ASSOCIATES INC.**
CLIENT
BASF FIBRES INC.
PRINTER
CAMPBELL GRAPHICS

TITLE
A TYPICAL NAIL
ART DIRECTOR
RICHARD CLEWES
WRITER
RICHARD CLEWES
PHOTOGRAPHER
PETER HUTCHINGS
TYPOGRAPHER
ALPHA
AGENCY
RICHARD CLEWES
CLIENT
PETER HUTCHINGS
PRINT PRODUCTION
GORD CATHMOIR

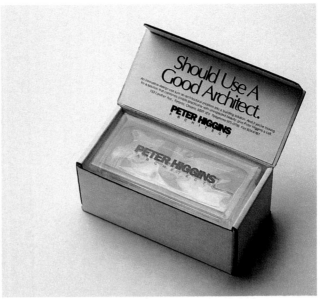

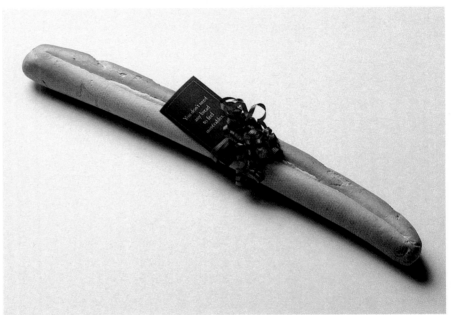

TITLE
GLASS BRICK
ART DIRECTOR
D. NILE
WRITER
BILL JAMES
AGENCY
THE JAMES GANG
CLIENT
PETER HIGGINS
ARTIST
FRANK JAMES

TITLE
BRYDON HARRIS DAVIDSON CORPORATE AWARENESS CAMPAIGN
ART DIRECTOR
JEFF EAMER/ SARAH RONCARELLI
WRITER
JEFF EAMER
CREATIVE DIR.
JEFF EAMER
ILLUSTRATOR
KIM MARTIN
TYPOGRAPHER
THE COMPOSING ROOM AT COOPER & BEATTY
AGENCY
BRYDON HARRIS DAVIDSON
CLIENT
BRYDON HARRIS DAVIDSON
PRODUCTION CO-ORDINATOR
PAT TURBACH

TITLE
BREAD
ART DIRECTOR
SHELLEY WILDEMAN
WRITER
PETER SELLERS
CREATIVE DIR.
JOHN BURGHARDT
AGENCY
BURGHARDT WOLOWICH CRUNKHORN
CLIENT
BURGHARDT WOLOWICH CRUNKHORN

ANNCR: Due to the explicit nature of the following, we will insert loud music over any strong language, nudity or sexual implications.

In the play called "What The Butler Saw," a psychiatrist asks a young lady to undress during...

SFX: "OH CANADA" (Loud, overplayed)

The doctor's wife walks in on them and says...

SFX: "OUR HOME AND NATIVE LAND"

Meanwhile, the doctor's wife is being black-mailed with photographs showing...

SFX: "TRUE PATRIOT LOVE"

The everyone exchanges clothes...

SFX: "WITH GLOWING HEARTS"

And then...

SFX: "WE SEE THEE RISE"

ANNCR: See "What The Butler Saw," by Joe Orton. One of the classic farces of modern British theatre. Now playing at the Bluma Apel Theatre. Presented by the Canadian Stage Company. For tickets call 366-7723.

"What The Butler Saw"

You'd be mad to miss it.

ANNCR: Mr. Thurston Swan, Theatrical Board of Censorship.

SWANSON: During the play, "What the Butler Saw," I counted 17 sexual references, blackmail involving compromising photographs, 4 instances of cross-dressing, 11 occasions of partial nudity, 2 pieces of suggestive lingerie, and a complete disregard for morally acceptable behaviour.

Then came scene two.

ANNCR: See "What The Butler Saw," the classic farce by Joe Orton. Presented by the Canadian Stage Company at the Bluma Apel Theatre. For tickets call 366-7723.

You'd be mad to miss it.

TITLE
OH CANADA
ART DIRECTOR
RANDY DIPLOCK
WRITER
TERRY O'REILLY
CREATIVE DIR.
DICK HADDEN
AGENCY
CHIAT DAY ADVERTISING
CLIENT
CANADIAN STAGE CO.
PRODUCTION COMP
AIR COMPANY
PRODUCTION PRODUCER
RICK SHURMAN
AGENCY PRODUCER
TERRY O'REILLY

TITLE
CENSOR
ART DIRECTOR
RANDY DIPLOCK
WRITER
TERRY O'REILLY
CREATIVE DIR.
DICK HADDEN
AGENCY
CHIAT DAY ADVERTISING
CLIENT
CANADIAN STAGE COMPANY
PRODUCTION COMP
AIR COMPANY
PRODUCTION PRODUCER
RICK SHURMAN
AGENCY PRODUCER
TERRY O'REILLY

SFX: BUZZER ALARM

FREDDY: (Groaning, muttering) Hmmm... morning already ...(Yawns) Get up and go to work ...Need breakfast ...(shuffling)... Down the stairs ...to the kitchen...

SFX: CUPBOARDS OPENING AND SHUTTING

...no, nothing interesting here, check the fridge...

SFX: FRIDGE DOOR OPENING. MAGICAL HARP MUSIC.

FREDDY: What the... Huh? Who are you?

FAIRY: Hi, Freddy. I'm the Breakfast Fairy. I'm here to shake up your breakfast.

FREDDY: Yeah, so why are you stirring that milkshake?

FAIRY: It's not a milkshake, silly. It's Carnation Instant Breakfast.

FREDDY: Looks like a milkshake to me ...All cold and frothy and creamy-smooth ...Chocolate, right?

FAIRY: Uh huh...

FREDDY: Hey, who *are* you anyway? I mean you're standing in *my* kitchen early in the morning in that blue off the shoulder number and you're trying to get me to drink a milkshake!

FAIRY: It's only *like* a milkshake, Freddy. Carnation Instant Breakfast IS breakfast... Taste it...

FREDDY: Mmmm... Delicious. But there's no way I'm drinking a milkshake for breakfast.

FAIRY: Relax, Freddy. Carnation Instant Breakfast is breakfast, made with the wholesome goodness of milk. C'mon, drink it.

FREDDY: Yeah, but my wife...

FAIRY: Freddy...

FREDDY: Oh, here goes ...Mmmmm... Mmmmm

FAIRY: Isn't it good, Freddy?... Freddy... Freddy...

SFX: MAGICAL HARP

WIFE: Freddy...Freddy ...Breakfast time.

FREDDY: Wha...Who?

WIFE: Here's a nice bowl of cereal.

FREDDY: NO! I feel like ...like a... MILKSHAKE.

SFX: MAGICAL HARP UNDER

FAIRY: A great way to shake up your mornings: Carnation Instant Breakfast.

(LOCAL ANNCR TAG)

TITLE
DREAM FAIRY
ART DIRECTOR
BARBARA GELB
WRITER
THOMAS POLDRE
CREATIVE DIR.
ROBERT HAWTON
AGENCY
MacLAREN: LINTAS INC.
CLIENT
CARNATION INSTANT BREAKFAST
PRODUCTION COMP
THE AIR COMPANY
PRODUCTION PRODUCER
RICK SHURMAN
AGENCY PRODUCER
DONNA HUFFMAN

LIZ: (To dog) Walkies ...walkies... (dog barks)

CHARLES: Uh... mummy?

LIZ: What is it, Charles?

CHARLES: I'm going to be King one of these days, right?

LIZ: Don't bug me Charles, you're first in line... and...

CHARLES: But, Mumsy, Mumsy, Mumsy, I have an idea.

LIZ: I thought it was a little brighter in here.

CHARLES: Let me go and be King of Canada 'til...

LIZ: Canada! That's where they had the Diet Pepsi Taste Drive.

CHARLES: Well, yeah but...Mumsy...

LIZ: And it's back this year.

CHARLES: Well yeah, ok, because last year more than half the Diet Coke drinkers who received Diet Pepsi Taste Packs said they preferred the taste of Diet Pepsi.

LIZ: This Taste Drive, that's why you want to be King of Canada isn't it Charles?

CHARLES: Well...

LIZ: Charles...?

CHARLES: Okay so I want to be King of Canada so I can get a Diet Pepsi Taste Pack. What's wrong with that?

LIZ: Nothing dear, oh here's your brother Andrew.

ANDREW: Just thought I'd mention Diet Pepsi with Nutrasweet is suitable for carbohydrate and calorie reduced diets. So there, Charles.

ANDREW: Gotta go, nature calls.

LIZ: Thank you dear.

CHARLES: Hey, sprog. I'm first in line for the throne, ok?

ANNCR: Diet Pepsi. Get with the taste.

TITLE
KING FOR A DAY
WRITER
BRENT PULFORD
CREATIVE DIR.
GRAY ABRAHAM
AGENCY
J. WALTER THOMPSON ADVERTISING
CLIENT
PEPSI-COLA CANADA

PRODUCTION COMP
REDWOOD STUDIOS
PRODUCTION PRODUCER
ANDRE JACQUEMIN
AGENCY PRODUCER
ANDY WILLIAMSON
MUSIC/SOUND
ANDRE JACQUEMIN

ANNCR: Even back in grade school, the members of the Automobile Journalists Association were not easily impressed.

TEACHER: And that's Einstein's breakthrough theory of relativity. Any comments? Yes Billy?

BILLY: (RASPBERRY)

ANNCR: And years later, when it came to picking the best cars of the year, not much had changed.

SFX: (RASPBERRY)

ANNCR: Until one day they saw the new 1989 Nissan Maxima.

SFX: WHISTLES

ANNCR: They were so impressed they named it "Best New Sedan of the Year". Choose the car the critics did. Visit you Nissan dealer. And bring your relatives.

Nissan. Built for the Human Race.™

ANNCR: Even in 1969, the members of the Automobile Journalists Association were not easily impressed.

FILTERED TV: "This is one small step for man, one giant leap for mankind"

SFX: (RASPBERRY)

ANNCR: And years later, when it came to picking the best cars of the year, not much had changed.

SFX: (RASPBERRY)

ANNCR: Until one day they saw the new 1989 Nissan 240SX.

SFX: WHISTLES

ANNCR: They were so impressed they named the 240SX "Best New Sports Coupe of the Year". So why not choose the car the critics did. Just moonwalk over to your Nissan dealer.

Nissan. Built for the Human Race.™

ANNCR: Once upon a time, there were 60 different babies who had one thing in common. They hated everything. Like baby food.

SFX: RASPBERRY

ANNCR: Brothers and sisters.

SFX: SPITOOEY

ANNCR: And kindergarten.

SFX: SNORE

ANNCR: And when they grow up, they became the Automobile Journalists Association of Canada. And they hated everything.

SFX: RASPBERRY

Until the day they saw the luxurious new Nissan Maxima and the sporty 240SX.

SFX: WOLF CALLS, WHISTLES

ANNCR: And voted them Best New "Sedan" and "Sports Coupe" of 1989. So why not choose the cars the critics did. Just visit your Nissan dealer.

SFX: RASPBERRY THAT TURNS INTO ENGINE

Nissan. Built for the Human Race.™

TITLE
MAXIMA
240 SX
WRITER
TERRY O'REILLY
CREATIVE DIR.
RICHARD HADDEN/
GEOFFREY B. ROCHE
AGENCY
CHIAT DAY ADVERTISING
CLIENT
NISSAN
PRODUCTION COMP
THE AIR COMPANY
PRODUCTION PRODUCER
RICK SHURMAN
AGENCY PRODUCER
AUDREY TELFER

SFX: Sounds inside airplane.

VOICE: Look this way! Seatbelts off!

ANNCR VO: In the Army, any soldier who's ever jumped out of a plane knows a certain feeling.

VOICE: Stand up, hook up!

ANNCR VO: We can tell you the feeling comes during an 800-foot low level jump.

VOICE: Check static line, check equipment!

ANNCR VO: We can talk about the sensation...

VOICE: Winds fine!

ANNCR VO: How the chill travels through your skin, and up your spine, and that everybody has their own name for it.

VOICE: Stand by!

ANNCR VO: Like the 'Big Chill' and 'Catching the Wave', but you'll only know the real feeling by doing it.

VOICE: Go!

SFX: OUTSIDE THE PLANE/ WIND

ANNCR VO: Find out what it feels like being a member of the Canadian Armed Forces... to experience challenges met and courage realized. Join men and women in action. We're in the Yellow Pages under recruiting.

BASE: The Canadian Armed Forces. Choose a career. Live the adventure.

SFX: SOUNDS ON SHIP

1ST VOICE: Burke! Martino! On deck.

2ND VOICE: Check your regulators.

1ST VOICE: Up to the side.

ANNCR VO: In the Navy, any sailor who's ever made a night dive knows there's a certain feeling.

1ST VOICE: Let's all remember! No lights until fifteen feet.

ANNCR VO: We can tell you the feeling comes forty feet down surrounded by blackness with only one light.

1ST VOICE: Ready.

ANNCR VO: We can tell you the sensation. The pressure of water against your mask. The stillness.

1ST VOICE: Okay let's get into it. Burke! Over!

ANNCR VO: And that everybody has their own name for it. Like Spacewalk...The Isolation Tank. But you'll only know the real feeling...

2ND VOICE: You're up next Martino!

SFX: SPLASH/ SOUND OF REGULATOR UP TO END.

ANNCR VO: By doing it. Find out what it feels like being a member of the Canadian Armed Forces...to experience challenges met...and courage realized. Join men and women in action. We're in the Yellow Pages under recruiting.

BASE: The Canadian Armed Forces. Choose a career. Live the adventure.

TITLE
**BIG CHILL
SPACEWALK**
ART DIRECTOR
BILL NEWBERY
WRITER
BOB CORMACK
AGENCY
**McLAUCHLAN, MOHR,
MASSEY**
CLIENT
**DEPARTMENT OF
NATIONAL DEFENCE**
PRODUCTION COMP
**HARRIS/COLE
PRODUCTIONS**

A

GOLD

AUDIO

Air Canada's Executive Class. Convenient, comfortable, almost completely effortless. Some say it's the way business travel was meant to be.

TITLE
FLYING OFFICE
ART DIRECTOR
YVES SIMARD
WRITER
**CHERYL REAY/
LOUIS GAUTHIER/
JEAN DUVAL**
CREATIVE DIR.
YVES SIMARD
AGENCY
**COSSETTE
COMMUNICATION-
MARKETING (MONTREAL)**
CLIENT
**AIR CANADA
'EXECUTIVE CLASS'**
PRODUCTION COMP
**RAWI SHERMAN
FILMS INC.**
DIRECTOR
OUSAMA RAWI
CAMERA MAN
OUSAMA RAWI
PRODUCTION PRODUCER
KATE DALE
AGENCY PRODUCER
NICOLE TARDIFF
FILM EDITOR
JIM MUNRO
MUSIC/SOUND
ERIC HARRY

  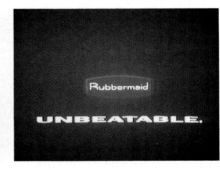

A

SILVER

VIDEO

The spot opens revealing a two level stage covered in Rubbermaid products.

These products are arranged like percussion instruments.

Four drummers stand behind the various product arrays.

They begin to drum on the product's lids, sides and bottoms.

They play for approx. 26 seconds as the camera swoops in and among them—capturing the excitement.

AUDIO

SFX: Plus the sound of four drummers playing on Rubbermaid products.

As the last beat is heard we cut to a dark screen where we read:

LOGO: RUBBERMAID

SUPER:
UNBEATABLE

TITLE
UNBEATABLE
ART DIRECTOR
**HOWARD ALSTAD/
DUNCAN BRUCE**
WRITER
**MARTA CUTLER/
PHILIPPE CARNEAU**
CREATIVE DIR.
ALLAN KAZMER
AGENCY
**DDB NEEDHAM
WORLDWIDE
ADVERTISING INC.**
CLIENT
**RUBBERMAID
CANADA INC.**
PRODUCTION COMP
**THE DIRECTORS FILM
CO. LTD.**
DIRECTOR
MARCO BRAMBILLA
CAMERA MAN
NICK ALLEN-WOOLFE
PRODUCTION PRODUCER
CANDACE CONACHER
AGENCY PRODUCER
BETTE MINOTT
FILM EDITOR
BOB KENNEDY
MUSIC/SOUND
**ROSNICK
PRODUCTIONS INC.**

SILVER

TITLE
SIDE-STEP
ART DIRECTOR
MARTIN SHEWCHUK
WRITER
MARTIN SHEWCHUK
CREATIVE DIR.
TONY HOUGHTON
PHOTOGRAPHER
MICHAEL RAFELSON
AGENCY
**LEO BURNETT
COMPANY LTD.**
CLIENT
**THOMSON CONSUMER
ELECTRONICS**
PRODUCTION COMP
VIDEOGENIC CORP.
DIRECTOR
DAVE GREENHAM
CAMERA MAN
JEFF HADDOW
PRODUCTION PRODUCER
DAVE GREENHAM
AGENCY PRODUCER
BRENDA SURMINSKI
FILM EDITOR
DAVE GREENHAM
TALENT
LYNN ROSENBLOOD

VIDEO	AUDIO
1. Open on super. (3.74)	LYN: Like I think they call this one "side step"
2. Beauty shot of lavender radio. GE LOGO (2.09)	well like there's not just one...OK...
3. Beauty shot of purple radio. GE LOGO (1.67)	...like really there's two
4. Beauty shot of both radios. GE LOGO (6.28)	So...like...I thing they call both of these "Side Step"...like one is purple and one is lavender...which is so cool 'cause...like...for sure a lot of stuff would go with it...
5. CU of nail polish. (1.66)	...like your nail polish
6. CU of lipstick. (1.31)	...or your lipstick
7. Beauty shot of lavender radio. GE LOGO (3.08)	...and like that is so important...OK...
8. CU magazines. (2.11)	'cause like I read a lot of ...like of those fashion magazines...
9. CU headphones. (2.56)	and they say...like...it's so important to match your audio equipment...
10. Beauty shot of purple radio. (2.07) GE LOGO.	...with like...your make-up and stuff...
11. End on GE LOGO and super. (2.97)	...no really...it's true...

Total time: 29.54 approx.

SILVER

TITLE
COMMUTER STATION
ART DIRECTOR
YVES SIMARD
WRITER
**CHERYL REAY/
LOUIS GAUTHIER/
JEAN DUVAL**
CREATIVE DIR.
YVES SIMARD
AGENCY
**COSSETTE
COMMUNICATION-
MARKETING (MONTREAL)**
CLIENT
**AIR CANADA
'EXECUTIVE CLASS'**
PRODUCTION COMP
**RAWI SHERMAN
FILMS INC.**
DIRECTOR
OUSAMA RAWI
CAMERA MAN
OUSAMA RAWI
PRODUCTION PRODUCER
KATE DALE
AGENCY PRODUCER
NICOLE TARDIFF
FILM EDITOR
JIM MUNRO
MUSIC/SOUND
ERIC HARRY

AUDIO

Rapidair. So convenient, business travelers hardly give it any thought at all.

S I L V E R

TITLE
LAVA LAMP
ART DIRECTOR
DOUG BRAMAH
WRITER
BASIL MINA
CREATIVE DIR.
BILL DURNAN
AGENCY
MacLAREN: LINTAS INC.
CLIENT
AGREE SHAMPOO
PRODUCTION COMP
DIRECTORS FILM HOUSE
DIRECTOR
ROB QUARTLY
PRODUCTION PRODUCER
MARY ANN TEVLIN
AGENCY PRODUCER
SANDY STERNE
FILM EDITOR
DAVID BUDOR - BANANAZZ
MUSIC/SOUND
TED ROSNICK

VIDEO	AUDIO
1. Open on two girls in situ, one holding the pack.	FVI: This is Agree Shampoo.
2. She points to the other pack.	That's Agree Conditioner. Use it and you get no oil, no silicone, no gunk in your hair. So what *do* you get? You get this really neat, hand-held lava lamp.
3. Cut to other girl, holding pack.	
4. Cut to packs. Super "Don't you Agree?"	MVO: New oil & silicone-free Agree beats build-up for clean, beautiful hair.

TITLE
THE BRASS RING
ART DIRECTOR
HOWARD ALSTAD
WRITER
PHILIPPE GARNEAU
CREATIVE DIR.
ALLAN KAZMER
AGENCY
DDB NEEDHAM WORLDWIDE ADVERTISING INC.
CLIENT
DIGITAL EQUIPMENT OF CANADA
PRODUCTION COMP
THE DIRECTORS FILM CO. LTD.
DIRECTOR
MARCO BRAMBILLA
CAMERA MAN
STANLEY MESTEL
PRODUCTION PRODUCER
CANDACE CONACHER
AGENCY PRODUCER
BETTE MINOTT
FILM EDITOR
BOB KENNEDY
MUSIC/SOUND
TED ROSNICK

VIDEO

Open on a magnificent hall. An older man stands proudly in front of a throne. The throne faces a huge floor area on which rests a Persian carpet. On the middle of the carpet is a plinth supporting a radiant brass ring. Three groups of people flank the carpet on different sides. Each group consists of three individuals. One member from each group stands while the others remain seated behind. Suddenly the leader Creon speaks:

Creon surges forward indicating with his pointing arm.

AUDIO

CREON (THE LEADER) O.C.: This is no mere exercise. I am here to designate one of you as my chief advisor... One whose initiative and creativity will help us seize the future.

Your challenge... Get me the brass ring. But, there is a caveat, you must remove it without setting foot on the carpet.

Cut to the first group. Consulting briefly among themselves we see a man rise from the group. With a satisfied smile his colleagues make way for him as he approaches the carpet.

The first man assumes that his arm length will suffice. He approaches the carpet and bends over to reach. He has come within inches but cannot reach the ring.

Cut to the next group. This group chooses to link arms to extend their reach. CU of two hands securing a grip. Pulling back we find them bracing at the carpet edge. The lead candidate leans forward, straining to reach. A profile shot of the ring shows his hand barely a half inch away. One of the grips slips and he falters, setting foot on the carpet.

ANNCR: (V.O.) Finding the right computer company to help your business isn't easy.

ANNCR: (V.O.) You need a company that's flexible and responsive. Not just big. You need the right hardware and software. But connectivity must be assured.

Cut to our last candidate calmly sharing counsel with his colleagues. A nod of ascent runs through the group as the main candidate confidently approaches the carpet. The candidate looks Creon in the eye, then appears to bow. Cut to Creon standing up, his face beaming with delight.

Cut to our candidate. He is calmly rolling up the carpet towards the pedestal.

Arriving at the pedestal, our candidate grasps the brass ring.

SUPER: DIGITAL
You'll like our thinking.

ANNCR: V.O. Most of all you need a computer company that can provide the simple, creative solutions your business demands.

ANNCR: (V.O.) Who has all of this?

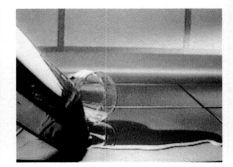

TITLE
EGG
ART DIRECTOR
JEFF LAYTON
WRITER
BORIS DAMAST
CREATIVE DIR.
BORIS DAMAST
AGENCY
**BAKER LOVICK
ADVERTISING**
CLIENT
BLACK & DECKER
ADVERTISER'S SUPERVISOR
BARRY BOUSFIELD
PRODUCTION COMP
**THE DIRECTORS FILM
COMPANY**
DIRECTOR
GILLEAN PROCTOR
CAMERA MAN
CHRIS TAMARO
PRODUCTION PRODUCER
KAREN SILVER
AGENCY PRODUCER
**KEN MacDOUGALL/
GORD STANWAY**
FILM EDITOR
MICK GRIFFIN
MUSIC/SOUND
**ROSNICK
PRODUCTIONS INC.**
ACCOUNT SUPERVISOR
MARK VIVIAN

VIDEO	AUDIO
Open on egg falling through the air in slow motion and crashes to the floor. Spillbuster sucks up egg. A foot enters frame and shatters the shell. Spillbuster eats shell.	ANNCR: The nice thing about Black & Decker's new cordless Spillbuster is you can feed it almost anything.
Cut to glass lying on its side with spilled liquid beside it. Spillbuster enters and consumes the liquid.	ANNCR: And a little drink to wash it down.
SUPER: Black & Decker Logo. The people who brought you Dustbuster.	ANNCR: The cordless Spillbuster from Black & Decker.

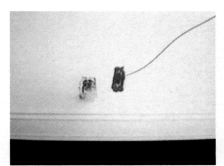

TITLE
CORD
ART DIRECTOR
JEFF LAYTON
WRITER
BORIS DAMAST
CREATIVE DIR.
BORIS DAMAST
AGENCY
**BAKER LOVICK
ADVERTISING**
CLIENT
BLACK & DECKER
ACCOUNT SUPERVISOR
MARK VIVIAN
PRODUCTION COMP
**THE DIRECTORS FILM
COMPANY**
DIRECTOR
GILLEAN PROCTOR
CAMERA MAN
CHRIS TAMARO
PRODUCTION PRODUCER
KAREN SILVER
AGENCY PRODUCER
**KEN MACDOUGALL/
GORD STANWAY**
FILM EDITOR
MICK GRIFFIN
MUSIC/SOUND
**ROSNICK
PRODUCTIONS INC.**
ADVERTISER'S SUPERVISOR
BARRY BOUSFIELD

VIDEO	AUDIO
Open on a carpeted room. A cord is seen lying on the floor plugged into a wall socket. We see the cord tighten as it is pulled constantly.	Music.
Enter the Dustbuster Upright. It easily glides across the frame.	ANNCR: Presenting the cordless Dustbuster Upright Powerbrush... from Black & Decker.
Back to the cord as it gets yanked out of the wall—taking some of the wall with it.	
The Dustbuster Upright gets wheeled back in to clean up the mess—and is conveniently snapped in place on the wall.	ANNCR: It simply picks up where the others leave off.
SUPER: Black & Decker Logo. The people who brought you Dustbuster.	ANNCR: The cordless Dustbuster Upright Powerbrush from Black & Decker.

TITLE
LUNCH BREAK
ART DIRECTOR
DOMENIC SALLESE
WRITER
**MIKE O'REILLY/
TOM GOUDIE**
CREATIVE DIR.
RICK DAVIS
AGENCY
YOUNG & RUBICAM LTD.
CLIENT
SCOTT'S FOOD SERVICE
PRODUCTION COMP
**PARTNERS FILM
COMPANY**
DIRECTOR
BRONWEN HUGHES
CAMERA MAN
GUY FURNER
PRODUCTION PRODUCER
SHERRI SAITO
AGENCY PRODUCER
CYNTHIA WHITE
MUSIC/SOUND
**DAVID BEARE -
THE AIR COMPANY**

VIDEO	AUDIO		
Distant shot of prison with SUPER: "Kentucky Fried Chicken presents The Lunch Break".		Close up of can.	SFX: Dramatic music. Heavy breathing.
Guard patrolling roof.	SFX: Night time atmosphere.	Search lights frantic in yard.	
Guard with search light.		Distant shot of prison with searchlights.	
Light on cell window.	SFX: Dramatic music starts.	SUPER: The drinks are free.	ANNCR: (V.O.) From September 12th until October 9th, the drinks are free with any small chicken package during lunch at Kentucky Fried Chicken.
Close up on cell window.	VOICE ON P.A.: Red alert! The drinks are free. The drinks are free.	SUPER: September 12 to October 9.	
	SFX: Sirens start.	SUPER: "Kentucky Fried Chicken and Colonel's Face".	
Far shot of search lights on cell wall.	SFX: General panic with sirens throughout.	Pop can pops up into scene, then leaves.	
Silhouette of guards with dogs.	SFX: Dogs barking.		
Glimpse of can in search-light.			

TITLE
HALLELUJAH
ART DIRECTOR
AVRIL RAVENSCROFT
WRITER
**BRUCE McCALLUM/
HEATHER CHAMBERS**
AGENCY
PALMER BONNER BCP
CLIENT
**SCHOLL PLOUGH
CANADA INC.**
PRODUCTION COMP
**DEREK VANLINT
& ASSOCIATES**
DIRECTOR
DEREK VANLINT
CAMERA MAN
DEREK VANLINT
PRODUCTION PRODUCER
CHRIS MONEY
AGENCY PRODUCER
CAROL VILA-YOUNG
FILM EDITOR
BOB KENNEDY
MUSIC/SOUND
MCS

VIDEO	AUDIO
Open on an early morning. Setting some-where in cottage country.	SFX: Peaceful morning sounds like you would hear at the cottage… water gently slapping up against the shoreline, the distant sound of little birds, loons calling to each other.
MS of two loons floating along the water.	
WS of soft, rippling water across the lake.	
Dissolve to small, quaint cottage on an attrac-tively landscaped lot.	As we approach the cottage you can hear the murmur of a conversa-tion inside, the sizzling of breakfast being made.
MS of tiny outhouse to the side of the cottage, little dog waiting outside the door.	SINGERS: Hallelujah! Hallelujah. Hallelujah. Hallelujah.
Beauty shot of Correctol package dissolves on final scene.	
SUPER: Use as directed for occasional constipa-tion…	

TITLE
BODY PAINT
ART DIRECTOR
PAUL HAINS
CREATIVE DIR.
PAUL HAINS
AGENCY
PALMER BONNER BCP
CLIENT
CARLING O'KEEFE BREWERIES
PRODUCTION COMP
PARTNERS' FILM CO.
DIRECTOR
JIM SONZERO
CAMERA MAN
JEFF PRIESS
PRODUCTION PRODUCER
PETER GRECH
AGENCY PRODUCER
KAY BROWN
FILM EDITOR
MICK GRIFFEN
MUSIC/SOUND
CONNIE VANBEEK

VIDEO

This commercial consists of B&W footage (all in close-up) of a male and a female who have been body painted with the "Black Label stripe graphics".

Shots would include: neck, bicept, shoulder, back, leg, abdomen, eye.

Inter cut with these are close-ups of Go-Go dancers and the new bottle with painted label.

End shot of paint brush on label. Reveals the colour red.

AUDIO

SFX & music throughout.

SUPER: The Legend is Black.

LABEL: Black Label Beer.

TITLE
PASSION
CREATIVE DIR.
DAN PEPPLER
AGENCY
DONER SCHUR PEPPLER
CLIENT
HONDA CANADA INC.
PRODUCTION COMP
MISTRAL FILMS
DIRECTOR
JOHN LLOYD
CAMERA MAN
MICHAEL BUCKLEY
PRODUCTION PRODUCER
ANDREA HUBERT
AGENCY PRODUCER
JO-ANN PURSER
FILM EDITOR
RAY COLE
MUSIC/SOUND
DAVID FLEURY MUSIC

VIDEO

Open on black & white shot of helicopter flying over cityscape.

Dissolve to attractive 24–28 year old girl in designer jeans and white T-shirt leaning against her new Civic Hatchback Si.

Dissolve to CU of girl's face. Series of dissolves of girl walking towards camera and then away and off to side of camera.

Wide shot of girl by car. Dissolve off leaving car on its own—frame changes to colour.

AUDIO

MUSIC: Heavy rock.

V.O.: Presenting the new Honda Civic Hatchback Si . . . or, how to turn your ex boyfriend into nothing more than a dot in the mirror.

TITLE
PLAYING WITH FIRE
ART DIRECTOR
JOHN SPEAKMAN
WRITER
TERRY BELL
CREATIVE DIR.
GARY PROUK
AGENCY
SCALI, McCABE, SLOVES
CLIENT
LABATT'S
PRODUCTION COMP
THE PARTNERS' FILM COMPANY
DIRECTOR
PETER MOSS
CAMERA MAN
PETER MOSS
PRODUCTION PRODUCER
JOANNE WOOD/ KELVIN FOSBERRY
AGENCY PRODUCER
SYLVIA MAGUIRE
FILM EDITOR
RICHARD UNRUH
MUSIC/SOUND
STRESS INC/ MARK STAFFORD

VIDEO   **AUDIO**

Open on shot of blazing sun.
SUPER: Playing with fire.
Cut to medium shot within the living room of a cottage. The camera makes its way towards the sliding glass doors which lead to a deck. We see through the door. Bodies of men and women in bathing suits sprawled out on the deck. There is a slightly ominous feel to the shooting like a Helmut Newton picture. As we pass through the doors, we hear a radio and outdoor ambience. There are bottles of Blue on small tables beside the people.

SFX: Wind...small transistor radio from which we hear the DJ talk about the incredible heat wave. Playing on the radio behind DJ is Arthur Brown's "Fire".

As the camera passes over a small alarm clock it goes off. A hand fumbles with it and shuts it off. In unison, everybody turns over to tan the side of them not exposed to the sun.

SUPER: It's the way we play.

ANNCR: If you're going to turn up the heat, Why not play...for real.

ANNCR: Labatt's Blue. It's the way we play.

TITLE
OVERTAKE
ART DIRECTOR
HOWARD ALSTAD
WRITER
PHILLIPE GARNEAU
CREATIVE DIR.
ALAN KAZMER
AGENCY
DDB NEEDHAM WORLDWIDE ADVERTISING INC.
CLIENT
AUDI DIVISION, VOLKSWAGEN CANADA INC.
PRODUCER
BETTE MINOT
PRODUCTION COMP
THE PARTNERS' FILM COMPANY
FILM EDITOR
BRANT LAMBERMONT
MUSIC/SOUND
TED ROSNICK

VIDEO   **AUDIO**

Quick cuts of racing footage with intercuts of beauty shot footage.

Cut to black.
SUPER: Why settle for moving with the times.

Quick cuts car footage.

Cut to black.
SUPER: When you can overtake them.

Cut to race finish.

Cut to black. Audi Logo.
SUPER: Advancing the art of engineering.

Music and effects.

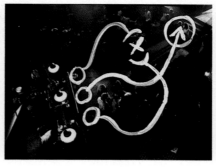

TITLE
JOHN MADDEN
ART DIRECTOR
JOHN SPEAKMAN
WRITER
**TERRY BELL/
GARY PROUK**
CREATIVE DIR.
GARY PROUK
AGENCY
**SCALI, McCABE,
SLOVES (CANADA) LTD.**
CLIENT
**LABATT BREWING
CO. LTD.**
TALENT
**KEVIN O'KEEFE/
NANCY SABOVICH**
PRODUCTION COMP
**PAINTED HORSE
PRODUCTIONS**
DIRECTOR
PAUL CADE
CAMERA MAN
STANLEY MESTEL
PRODUCTION PRODUCER
MARILYN KASTELIC
AGENCY PRODUCER
SYLVIA MAGUIRE
FILM EDITOR
**RICHARD UNRUH/
BRANT LAMBERMONT**
MUSIC/SOUND
**MARK STAFFORD -
STRESS INC.**

VIDEO

This commercial represents a parody of the John Madden type announcer.

Open on an overhead shot within a crowded bar. The shot resembles an overhead shot of a football field.

Cut to tight shot as woman enters bar.

Cut to shot of four men at bar leaning into frame like offensive front four.

AUDIO

SFX: Of football game. We hear the crowd roar, the sounds of blocks and tackles.

ANNCR 1: Here's MacGuire coming onto the field . . .

ANNCR 2: And, this could be the last play of the season for these guys, Bubba . . .

ANNCR 1: . . . that's the truth, pardner . . .

Cut to two guys at bar with bottles of Blue in their hands. They put bottles of Blue down and move from bar.

Cut to shot of third man at bar as he makes his way towards woman.

Cut to one of the first two men at bar as he intercepts third man.

Cut to hero as he arrives at woman who entered bar.

ANNCR 2: Third down and long and here's the snap. Looks like play action and what a block by Crawford he just threw on Martin. Crushed 'em. MacGuire's in the clear and Bukowski made the big play! and what a play! Let's look at it again!

We now return to overhead shot and rewind tape. We see the entire sequence of events covered in a couple of seconds.

Now using the overhead camera, we re-run the sequence as the announcer describes the play and uses a grease pencil to circle the key players.

Cut to tight shot as our hero arrives at woman.

Woman shrugs non-committally.

SUPER: It's the way we play.

ANNCR 1: They trapped Bell going the wrong way, levelled Martin, cleared a lane here and Bukowski and MacGuire hooked up to make it to the one.

ANNCR 2: Yeah first and goal, and what should be an easy six.

HERO: Buy you a Blue?

WOMAN: Let's talk about it.

ANNCR 2: Well Bubba?

ANNCR 1: Heck of a play pardner.

TITLE
NOT IN SERVICE
ART DIRECTOR
RANDY DIPLOCK
WRITER
RANDY DIPLOCK
CREATIVE DIR.
GARY PROUK
AGENCY
**SCALI, McCABE,
SLOVES (CANADA) LTD.**
CLIENT
**CANADIAN CHILDRENS
FOUNDATION**
TALENT
SARA MCLAREN
PRODUCTION COMP
**THE PARTNERS FILM
CO. LTD.**
DIRECTOR
GREG SHEPPARD
CAMERA MAN
STANLEY MESTEL
PRODUCTION PRODUCER
CHARLENE KIDDER
AGENCY PRODUCER
SYLVIA MAGUIRE
FILM EDITOR
**MICHAEL LAMBERMONT/
BOB MANN**
MUSIC/SOUND
**RICK SHURMAN -
THE AIR COMPANY**

VIDEO

Open on black.

Flash cut to MS of telephone booth. It's raining and a 12-year-old girl is inside.

Cut to black.

Flash cut to CU girl picking up receiver.

Cut to black.

Flash cut to ECU of girl pressing numbers.

Cut to black.

Flash cut to ECU of girl playing nervously with phone cord.

Cut to black.

Flash cut to more numbers being pushed.

AUDIO

SFX: Rain/cars under pictures.

V.O.: In Canada, like other countries, child abuse exists.

The abuse can range from verbal to sexual.

In fact, 1 in 8 Canadian kids are victims.

And like other countries, we have a child helpline.

But there is a difference.

Cut to black.

Flash cut to CU girl's hand on phone near numbers but not pushing buttons.

Cut to black.

Flash cut to girl pushing last button.

Cut to black.

Fade on Super: Help connect the Kids Help Phone.
Flash cut to CU girl hanging up phone.
Fade on Super: Call 449-8888 or give at any Bank of Montreal.

Cut to black.

Bell recording: I'm sorry, the number you have dialed is not in service . . . I'm sorry, the number you have dialed is not in service.

VIDEO	AUDIO				
VIGNETTE #1 Open in barbershop. Girl dumps clothes/books/ sporting goods into lap of young man getting hair cut. Cut to close up of girl shaking head. Cut to wide shot...girl exiting barbershop... young man runs after her. VIGNETTE #2 Cut to medium close up of young man with hose in hand washing car. Cut to medium close up of girl driving car out of car wash.	GROUP SINGERS: (Rolling Stones song "You Can't Always Get What You Want") You can't always get what you want... You can't always get what you want...	Cut to young man standing with hose watching as car drives away. VIGNETTE #3 Cut to girl picking up laundry hamper in laundromat. Cut to extreme close up of young man getting up, off counter, where he has been sitting. Cut to girl walking out of laundromat, turning, she smiles at young man. Cut to young man leaning against bank of dryers.	You can't always get what you want... And if you try sometime...	VIGNETTE #4 Cut to girl looking back in rear view mirror. Cut to young man on hill watching as car drives away. Cut to medium close up of pair of jeans. Pop on Super: Levi Logo.	GROUP SINGERS CONTINUE You get what you need. VOICE OVER: Some loves come and go. VOICE OVER: Others last forever.

TITLE
SOME LOVES
ART DIRECTOR
BRIAN HARROD
WRITER
IAN MIRLIN
CREATIVE DIR.
BRIAN HARROD/ IAN MIRLIN
AGENCY
HARROD & MIRLIN
CLIENT
LEVI STRAUSS
PRODUCTION COMP
THE DIRECTORS FILM COMPANY
DIRECTOR
JEREMIAH CHECHIK
CAMERA MAN
OARILSZ WOLISKI
PRODUCTION PRODUCER
MARYANN TEVLIN
AGENCY PRODUCER
ANGELA CARROLL
FILM EDITOR
RON VESTER (BLUEFIELDS)
MUSIC/SOUND
ROSNICK PRODUCTIONS

VIDEO	AUDIO		
We open looking across a lake, somewhere in Northern Ontario. It is night. A beautiful, blue-silvery moon begins to rise over the trees. Beside the lake is a deserted road. A Volkswagen is parked on the shoulder. It appears to be empty. Camera zooms in slowly for a closer look. Cut to a close shot of the Volkswagen's rear lights. They are dark. Cut to a side view of the car. It still appears empty. Suddenly a woman pops up in the car, followed by a man. She fixes her hair and adjusts her blouse. He smooths his shirt.	MUSIC: "Blue Moon". It is an older, bluesier version, simply orchestrated with singers. V.O.: If the unexpected happens to your Volkswagen, we now provide the new Guaranteed Mobility Service. Should you need help, just find a phone and call us, any time of day or night, for problems like: a failed battery, or a blown fuse, even if your Volkswagen breaks down.	Cut to close-up of front headlights flaring. Cut to wide shot of lake and blue moon. The car drives off screen. The Volkswagen Logo dissolves into the moon. SUPER: Guaranteed Mobility Service. Ask your dealer for details.	SFX: Car starts. ANNCR: Of course that only happens once in a... SINGERS: "Blue Moon ...da da da da dum de dum..." (fades underneath).

TITLE
BLUE MOON
ART DIRECTOR
DUNCAN BRUCE
WRITER
MARTA CUTLER
CREATIVE DIR.
ALLAN KAZMER
AGENCY
DDB NEEDHAM WORLDWIDE ADVERTISING LTD.
CLIENT
VOLKSWAGEN CANADA INC.
PRODUCTION COMP
DEREK VAN LINT AND ASSOCIATES
DIRECTOR
STEVE THURSBY
CAMERA MAN
STEVE GORDON
PRODUCTION PRODUCER
KAREN KING
AGENCY PRODUCER
BETTE MINOTT
FILM EDITOR
BOB KENNEDY
MUSIC/SOUND
DAVID FLEURY MUSIC
ANIMATION
ANNE SMELTZER

TITLE
STAMP COLLECTING
ART DIRECTOR
DAVID SNIDER
WRITER
MAURA MacNEILL
CREATIVE DIR.
PETER LANYON
AGENCY
COSSETTE
CLIENT
CANADA POST CORPORATION
PRODUCTION COMP
ANIMATION HOUSE
DIRECTOR
BOB FORTIER
PRODUCTION PRODUCER
CHRISTINE DAVIS
AGENCY PRODUCER
CATHY WILLOWS
FILM EDITOR
ALAN MESTEL
MUSIC/SOUND
RICK SHURMAN
ANIMATOR
STEVE EVANGELOTOS

VIDEO

AUDIO

Mounted Policeman gallops into frame. Horse rears and gallops off.

Killer whale explodes from bottom of frame.

Figure skater glides into frame, pirouettes and glides off.

Dog trots into frame, wags his tail and wanders away.

Astronaut stamp appears at bottom of frame and blasts out the top.

Train stamp chugs across the frame and disappears in tunnel.

SFX: Horse hoofs galloping and whinny.

SFX: Seagulls. Water breaking.

SFX: Appropriate music.

SFX: Dog pants and barks as he wags his tail.

SFX: Count down and blast off.

SFX: Steam engine and whistle.

Ducks fly into frame in rough formation. One duck departs and lands at the bottom of the frame.

Fade to Super: Canada Post Corporation.

SFX: Ducks quacking, flap of wings.

V.O. Stamp Collecting. A real life adventure.

TITLE
OREO DOME
ART DIRECTOR
JOE CAMILLERI
WRITER
JOE CAMILLERI/ KURT HAGAN
CREATIVE DIR.
STU EATON
AGENCY
FOSTER/McCANN-ERICKSON ADVERTISING
CLIENT
CHRISTIE BROWN & CO.
PRODUCTION COMP
STUDIO 422
DIRECTOR
WAYNE TRICKET
AGENCY PRODUCER
COLLEEN FLOYD
MUSIC/SOUND
ERIC HARRY MUSIC

VIDEO

AUDIO

Open on Oreo cookie with 2/3 of top missing, exposing the white icing inside.

Camera moves around as 3 parts of the cookie top move around and into position to complete the top.

SUPER: Oreo Dome.

MUSIC: Marching band version of 'Mr. Christie' theme.

SFX: Mechanical sounds of roof closing, crack of baseball and bat, cheer of crowd.

TITLE
TALENT NIGHT
ART DIRECTOR
DAVID ADAMS
WRITER
SANDY LEMM
CREATIVE DIR.
BILL DURNAN
AGENCY
MacLAREN: LINTAS INC.
CLIENT
MOLSON GOLDEN
PRODUCTION COMP
McWATERS
DIRECTOR
PETER THOMSON
CAMERA MAN
GEORGE WILLIS
PRODUCTION PRODUCER
MARG WHITE
AGENCY PRODUCER
SANDY COLE
FILM EDITOR
ANDY ATTALIA
MUSIC/SOUND
ACROBAT

VIDEO | **AUDIO**

Master shot of 7 people at the table. Each has a beer. Banner behind them on the wall. The guys amazed at what they're seeing.

SFX: General ambience.

Last two words of "Hound Dog" being sung a capella.

Intercut to amazed facial looks.

Folks start to applaud.

SFX: Crowd applause.

ELVIS: "Thank you, ladies and gentlemen... That used to wow 'em in Las Vegas... I'll be back in an hour... thank you..."

Cut to Wayne shaking his head.

WAYNE: It couldn't be...

Cut to Louise.

LOUISE: Well... they say he's alive...

Cut to Dennis.

DENNIS: Sure sounds like him...

Through frame walks a black man in complete Elvis-style wardrobe. Wayne makes a comment to the man.

WAYNE: Lookin' good!

"Elvis" replies to Wayne.

ELVIS: Thank you, son.

All the folks at the table stare at each other in silence, then on cue make a single-word comment.

EVERYONE: Naw.

Product shot. An empty bottle of Golden with a filled glass beside it.

ANNCR V.O.: Smooth Molson Golden. And the life at Riley's.

TITLE
CONFETTI
ART DIRECTOR
MARTIN SHEWCHUK
WRITER
MARTIN SHEWCHUK
CREATIVE DIR.
TONY HOUGHTON
PHOTOGRAPHER
MICHAEL RAFELSON
AGENCY
LEO BURNETT CO. LTD.
CLIENT
THOMSON CONSUMER ELECTRONICS
PRODUCTION COMP
VIDEOGENIC CORPORATION
DIRECTOR
DAVE GREENHAM
CAMERA MAN
JEFF HADDOW
PRODUCTION PRODUCER
DAVE GREENHAM
AGENCY PRODUCER
BRENDA SURMINSKI
FILM EDITOR
DAVE GREENHAM
TALENT
LYNN ROSENBLOOD

VIDEO | **AUDIO**

1. Open on Super. (3.19)

LYN: Confetti... like I'm gonna talk about Confetti but not like real confetti... I'm sure.

2. Beauty shot of radio. GE LOGO. (5.29)

...like this tape deck is called the "Confetti"

3. CU shot of coloured pins. (3.50)

...because like you get these little coloured pins... which look kinda like confetti...

4. CU of speaker. (4.16)

...and you use them to do like... designs... like right on the speakers...

5. CU of speaker with pins in it. (4.80)

...like you could put your initials or like your boy-friend's initials... like right on it... OK...

6. Beauty shot of radio. GE LOGO. (4.60)

...and like even if you break up... you like... don't have to throw the whole thing away...

7. CU of coloured pins. (1.71)

...you like... just take the pins out.

8. End on GE LOGO and Super. (2.53)

I'm sure... which is like really cool don't you think... I do.

Total Time: 29.78 approx.

TITLE
LONDON
ART DIRECTOR
DAVE KELSO
WRITER
BILL LOWER
CREATIVE DIR.
**DAVE KELSO/
BILL LOWER**
AGENCY
**J. WALTER THOMPSON
ADVERTISING**
CLIENT
WARDAIR CANADA LTD.
PRODUCTION PRODUCER
DAN KRECH
AGENCY PRODUCER
PAT WHITE
FILM EDITOR
DAN KRECH
MUSIC/SOUND
DAVID FLEURY

VIDEO	AUDIO
See board.	Looking for regular scheduled flights to London that are far from regular? Then fly one of the world's best airlines. Wardair Canada. Because business class or economy, it's in a class all its own.

TITLE
AMSTERDAM
ART DIRECTOR
DAVE KELSO
WRITER
BILL LOWER
CREATIVE DIR.
**DAVE KELSO/
BILL LOWER**
AGENCY
**J. WALTER THOMPSON
ADVERTISING**
CLIENT
WARDAIR CANADA LTD.
PRODUCTION PRODUCER
DAN KRECH
AGENCY PRODUCER
PAT WHITE
FILM EDITOR
DAN KRECH
MUSIC/SOUND
DAVID FLEURY

VIDEO	AUDIO
See board.	One of the world's best airlines now flies regularly scheduled flights to Amsterdam. Wardair Canada.

TITLE
PARIS

ART DIREECTOR
DAVE KELSO

WRITER
BILL LOWER

CREATIVE DIR.
DAVE KELSO/
BILL LOWER

AGENCY
J. WALTER THOMPSON
ADVERTISING

CLIENT
WARDAIR CANADA LTD.

PRODUCTION PRODUCER
DAN KRECH

AGENCY PRODUCER
PAT WHITE

FILM EDITOR
DAN KRECH

MUSIC/SOUND
DAVID FLEURY

VIDEO	**AUDIO**
See board.	One of the world's best airlines now flies regularly scheduled flights to Paris. Wardair Canada.

A

SILVER

TITLE
**P. JAMMER &
NITE JAMMER
CONFETTI
SIDE-STEP**
ART DIRECTOR
MARTIN SHEWCHUK
WRITER
MARTIN SHEWCHUK
CREATIVE DIR.
TONY HOUGHTON
PHOTOGRAPHER
MICHAEL RAFELSON
AGENCY
LEO BURNETT CO. LTD.
CLIENT
**THOMSON CONSUMER
ELECTRONICS**
PRODUCTION COMP
**VIDEOGENIC
CORPORATION**
DIRECTOR
DAVE GREENHAM
CAMERA MAN
JEFF HADDOW
PRODUCTION PRODUCER
DAVE GREENHAM
AGENCY PRODUCER
BRENDA SURMINSKI
FILM EDITOR
DAVE GREENHAM
TALENT
LYNN ROSENBLOOD

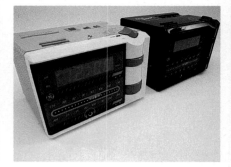

VIDEO | **AUDIO**

1. Open on Super. (3.00)

LYN: OK...now these two are like so cool okay.

2. Beauty shot of p'jammer. GE LOGO. (2.09)

...because they are like an alarm clock and a radio...

3. Beauty shot of nite jammer. GE LOGO. (2.00)

...or like a radio and an alarm clock...

4. Beauty shot of p'jammer. GE LOGO. (3.18)

...or like vice-versa.

5. Beauty shot of nite jammer. GE LOGO. (2.50)

...okay so like if someone says, hey, that's an alarm clock...

6. Beauty shot of p'jammer. GE LOGO. (2.23)

...or if someone else says...like...hey, that's a radio...you can say

7. Beauty shot p'jammer & nite jammer. GE LOGO. (4.70)

...like..."Stop you're both right." It's an alarm clock and a radio...or it's a radio and an alarm clock.

8. CU headphones. (4.93)

...and like they also come with these neat headphones that...like ...fit right in your ears and like you can roll them up and keep them...

9. Beauty shot p'jammer & nite jammer. GE LOGO. (2.20)

right in...like...the side of the radio...or the alarm clock...or whatever.

10. End on GE LOGO and Super. (2.91)

Like...let's not get into this again...

Total time: 29.74 approx.

VIDEO | **AUDIO**

1. Open on super. (3.74)

LYN: Like I think they call this one "side step"

2. Beauty shot of lavender radio. GE LOGO (2.09)

well like there's not just one...OK...

3. Beauty shot of purple radio. GE LOGO (1.67)

...like really there's two

4. Beauty shot of both radios. GE LOGO (6.28)

So...like...I thing they call both of these "Side Step"...like one is purple and one is lavender...which is so cool 'cause...like...for sure a lot of stuff would go with it...

5. CU of nail polish. (1.66)

...like your nail polish

6. CU of lipstick. (1.31)

...or your lipstick

7. Beauty shot of lavender radio. GE LOGO (3.08)

...and like that is so important...OK...

8. CU magazines. (2.11)

'cause like I read a lot of ...like of those fashion magazines...

9. CU headphones. (2.56)

and they say...like...it's so important to match your audio equipment...

10. Beauty shot of purple radio. (2.07) GE LOGO

...with like...your make-up and stuff...

11. End on GE LOGO and super. (2.97)

...no really...it's true...

Total time: 29.54 approx.

A

SILVER

TITLE
LONDON
AMSTERDAM
PARIS
ART DIRECTOR
DAVE KELSO
EDITOR
BILL LOWER
CREATIVE DIR.
DAVE KELSO/
BILL LOWER
AGENCY
J. WALTER THOMPSON
ADVERTISING
CLIENT
WARDAIR CANADA LTD.
PRODUCTION PRODUCER
DAN KRECH
AGENCY PRODUCER
PAT WHITE
FILM EDITOR
DAN KRECH
MUSIC/SOUND
DAVID FLEURY

VIDEO	**AUDIO**
See board.	Looking for regular scheduled flights to London that are far from regular? Then fly one of the world's best airlines. Wardair Canada. Because business class or economy, it's in a class all its own.

VIDEO	**AUDIO**
See board.	One of the world's best airlines now flies regularly scheduled flights to Paris. Wardair Canada.

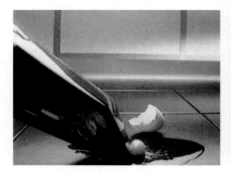

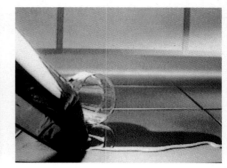

TITLE
EGG
CORD
ONE STEP
ART DIRECTOR
JEFF LAYTON
EDITOR
BORIS DAMAST
CREATIVE DIR.
BORIS DAMAST
AGENCY
BAKER LOVICK
ADVERTISING
CLIENT
BLACK & DECKER
ADVERTISER'S SUPERVISOR
BARRY BOUSFIELD
PRODUCTION COMP
THE DIRECTORS FILM
COMPANY
DIRECTOR
GILLEAN PROCTOR
CAMERA MAN
CHRIS TAMARO
PRODUCTION PRODUCER
KAREN SILVER
AGENCY PRODUCER
KEN MacDOUGALL/
GORD STANWAY
FILM EDITOR
MICK GRIFFIN
MUSIC/SOUND
ROSNICK
PRODUCTIONS INC.
ACCOUNT SUPERVISOR
MARK VIVIAN

VIDEO

Open on egg falling through the air in slow motion and crashes to the floor. Spillbuster sucks up egg. A foot enters frame and shatters the shell. Spillbuster eats shell.

Cut to glass lying on its side with spilled liquid beside it. Spillbuster enters and consumes the liquid.

SUPER: Black & Decker Logo. The people who brought you Dustbuster.

AUDIO

ANNCR: The nice thing about Black & Decker's new cordless Spillbuster is you can feed it almost anything.

ANNCR: And a little drink to wash it down.

ANNCR: The cordless Spillbuster from Black & Decker.

VIDEO

Open on CU of power-brush being attached to unit.

CU of step covered with confetti as powerbrush crosses frame cleaning up mess.

Cut to wide shot of long, wide staircase and butler near top cleaning with powerbrush.

SUPER: Black & Decker. The people who brought you Dustbuster.

AUDIO

ANNCR V.O.: The outstanding feature

Let's show you what we mean...

...one step at a time.

The cordless DustBuster PowerBrush from Black and Decker.

AUDIO

Air Canada's Executive Class. Convenient, comfortable, almost completely effortless. Some say it's the way business travel was meant to be.

TITLE
FLYING OFFICE
FLYING SKYSCRAPER
COMMUTER STATION
ART DIRECTOR
YVES SIMARD
WRITER
CHERYL REAY/
LOUIS GAUTHIER/
JEAN DUVAL
CREATIVE DIR.
YVES SIMARD
AGENCY
COSSETTE
COMMUNICATION-
MARKETING (MONTREAL)
CLIENT
AIR CANADA
'EXECUTIVE CLASS'
PRODUCTION COMP
RAWI SHERMAN
FILMS INC.
DIRECTOR
OUSAMA RAWI
CAMERA MAN
OUSAMA RAWI
PRODUCTION PRODUCER
KATE DALE
AGENCY PRODUCER
NICOLE TARDIFF
FILM EDITOR
JIM MUNRO
MUSIC/SOUND
ERIC HARRY

 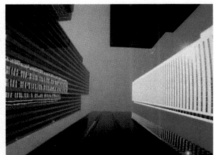 

AUDIO

Around the world, everyday, thousands of business people count on Air Canada to get them to work and to get them home again.

TITLE
LOSING MY HAIR
OREO FOURTH
SEND ME A POSTCARD
ART DIRECTOR
BARRY CHEMEL
WRITER
KURT HAGAN
CREATIVE DIR.
STU EATON
AGENCY
**FOSTER McCANN-
ERICKSON ADVERTISING**
CLIENT
CHRISTIE BROWN & CO.
PRODUCTION COMP
**McWATERS &
ASSOCIATES**
DIRECTOR
PAUL CADE
CAMERA MAN
STEVE RAMSAY
AGENCY PRODUCER
JAN CRAIG
FILM EDITOR
ANDY ATTELAI
MUSIC/SOUND
DR. MUSIC

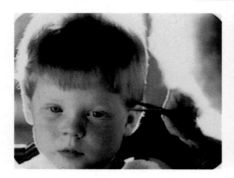

Mr. Christie, you make good cookies.

VIDEO	AUDIO				
	AS RECORDED	MS grandmother and toddler reaching into glass to pull Oreo out.	Birthday greetings, bottle of wine	MS grandmother and boy on bench as boy takes bite of Oreo.	need me, will you still
	MUSIC: The Beatles' "When I'm 64" exact lyrics from song:	CU small boy as he sneezes.	If I'd been out	MS grandfather and toddler as toddler feeds Oreo to grandfather.	feed me, When I'm sixty-four.
CU small boy having his bangs cut.	SINGER: When I get older	MS grandmother and boy sitting on a park bench as boy looks through binoculars.	till quarter to three	CU small boy eating Oreo.	
MS grandmother and boy, grandmother wipes his face with towel.	Losing my hair	CU Oreo bag.	Would you lock	MS grandmother and small boy on park bench, she leans over to kss boy on the head.	
MS toddler reaching into Oreo bag.	Many years from	CU boy opening an Oreo cookie.	the door		
Over the shoulder shot of grandfather laughing with grandmother.	now	MS grandmother and boy on park bench, grandmother reaches for Oreo.		SUPER: Mr. Christie, you make good cookies.	
MS grandfather and toddler sharing a glass of milk and an Oreo.	Will you still be sending me a	CU boy smiling with arm outstretched, camera pans over his arm to Oreo in his hand.	will you still		
ECU glass of milk as toddler's hand drops Oreo into the glass.	Valentine				

Mr. Christie, you make good cookies.

VIDEO	AUDIO				
	MUSIC: The Beatles' "When I'm sixty-four" exact lyrics from song.	Boy speaking into tin can telephone.	Give me your answer	2 kids sitting on bench with Oreo bag, eating Oreos.	When I'm sixty-four.
Kid writing with a crayon.	SINGER: Send me a post card	Grandma with other tin can telephone laughing.		SUPER: Mr. Christie you make good cookies.	
CU of cat.		2 boys laughing with grandpa as one boy reaches into Oreo bag.	fill in a form		
Kid licking stamp.	Drop me a line				
Kid pounding stamp down on letter with fist.	stating point of view	2 kids painting on an easel.			
Girl with grandpa, both raising airs in the air.	Indicate precisely	3 kids, grandma and grandpa holding hands in a circle and falling down.	Mine forever more		
Boy and girl, boy waving his arms.	what you mean to say				
Grandpa and boy looking at birds in cage.	Yours sincerely	WS boy and grandma talking to each other across the yard via a tin can telephone.	Will you still need me		
2 boys sitting down on bench. Grandpa opening Oreo bag as one boy falls backwards off bench.	wasting away	Girl gives Oreo to dog.	Will you still feed me		

TITLE
ROAD WARRIOR
ART DIRECTOR
MICHAEL CROSS
WRITER
ALLEN SCHOPP
CREATIVE DIR.
ALLEN SCHOPP
AGENCY
KERT ADVERTISING
CLIENT
**TORONTO CITY CYCLING
COMMITTEE**
PRODUCTION COMP
**NELVANA -
BEAR SPOTS**
DIRECTOR
CLIVE SMITH
PRODUCTION PRODUCER
NORM STANGL
AGENCY PRODUCER
SANDRA SPEARS
FILM EDITOR
RICK SAFRUK
MUSIC/SOUND
**THE EINSTEIN
BROTHERS**
ANIMATION
**FERENC ROFUSZ/
GREG HILL**

VIDEO

AUDIO

Fade in on CU of male cyclist. He is dressed in casual street clothes. He veers at camera.

Camera pulls back to reveal cyclist on a city street. We see two story buildings in the background. He weaves through traffic towards oncoming traffic and turns left onto a one way street causing chaos among the motorists.

Cyclist begins to transform into a locomotive as he approaches the green light at the intersection. As the light changes from amber to red, he becomes an express train, charging through the intersection causing further mayhem.

Cyclist transforms into a bowling ball rolling down a sidewalk. Pedestrians are being knocked down as they leap out of the way.

SFX: Street sounds

SFX: Honking and brakes screeching

SFX: Bowling ball rolling down alley

SFX: Bowling pins being hit

The ball transforms back into the cyclist as we segue into night. He is hard to distinguish. He is dressed in black and throws a cape over his face as he approaches camera.

A car zooms past in the foreground and cyclist is revealed. He weaves towards the camera as a headlight shines on him and wipes out the screen.

Segue back into daylight. As cyclist approaches camera he reacts to the off screen cavalry call.

Cut to group of cyclists coming over a ridge towards the camera. They are dressed in proper cycling attire and have a look of determination on their faces.

SFX: Calgary bugle charge and stampeding horses

ANNCR V.O.: Don't be a road warrior.

Cut to reaction shot of the cyclist looking humble and scared. The cavalry approaches the cyclist and totally engulf him as they pass.

A whirlwind is created, and as it dies down the cyclist is left standing in the middle of the street without his bicycle.

Camera views back of cyclist as he watches the group ride on.

Dissolve out and Super: Cycle safely. Our reputation is riding on you. The Toronto City Cycling Committee

ANNCR: Cycle safely. Our reputation is riding on you.

TITLE
MEN'S/WOMEN'S POINT OF VIEW
ART DIRECTOR
JIM GAULEY
WRITER
SUSAN ROBERTSON/ JOHN McINTYRE
CREATIVE DIR.
JOHN McINTYRE
AGENCY
CAMP ASSOCIATES ADVERTISING
CLIENT
ONTARIO WOMEN'S DIRECTORATE
DIRECTOR
LARRY MOORE
CAMERA MAN
DAVID HERRINGTON
PRODUCTION PRODUCER
CANDACE CONACHER
AGENCY PRODUCER
BOB KIRK
FILM EDITOR
NORM O'DELL
MUSIC/SOUND
JOHN WELSMAN

VIDEO — **AUDIO**

TITLE: It happens every day SCENE: Door being kicked in with heel of shoe.

"It's the one thing I learned to do, get mad and hit."

TITLE: It maims SCENE: Boiling water on stove.

"She doesn't know what's coming, she doesn't know what's going to happen next."

TITLE: It scars SCENE: Hands on telephone.

"I'd yell at her, threaten her, cut her off from her friends."

TITLE: It always gets worse SCENE: Knife being pulled from drawer.

"It got worse. Instead of maybe hitting her in the arms, I'd grab her by the neck and push her into the wall."

TITLE: There's no excuse SCENE: Woman recoiling from slap.

"I thought I had the right because she's my wife."

TITLE: It's a crime SCENE: Police officer securing back door.

"In the police station they explained to me that I was being charged with assault. It was a criminal offense."

TITLE: Seek help SCENE: Park, two men walking on path toward camera.

"I love my wife and kids more than anything in the world, I lost them…because of my violence."

TITLE: Wife Assault Stop the violence. If you are a man who needs help, write Family Violence Queen's Park Toronto Logo Ontario Women's Directorate.

"At least 1 in 10 women is assaulted by her partner. The violence must be stopped."

VIDEO — **AUDIO**

TITLE: Wife Assault SCENE: Interior door, woman's hands resisting, man's hands forcing open.

"He'd get himself into this rage and then he'd punch…"

TITLE: It happens every day SCENE: Hands rinsing bloodied facecloth.

"I had to cry quietly so the neighbours wouldn't hear."

TITLE: It maims SCENE: Tumble down stairwell.

"They had to bring me into surgery to sew me up…"

TITLE: It scars SCENE: Man's hand interrupting woman phoning.

"So you are humiliated, isolated from your family, isolated from your friends."

TITLE: It's hard to escape SCENE: Low angle, living room in some disarray. Figure of man walking away.

"I felt like a prisoner, I thought I had nothing, no place to go."

TITLE: It always gets worse SCENE: Silhouette of man approaching.

"He wouldn't stop until I'd be literally out cold."

TITLE: It's a crime SCENE: Residential street, policeman locking culprit in police car.

"My husband was charged with assault. That's the law."

TITLE: You're not alone SCENE: Group of women and child in living room.

"I found out there were people I could talk to. I'm feeling a lot better about myself."

TITLE: Call the Wife Assault Help Line Ontario's Women's Directorate.

"One in ten women is assaulted by her partner. If you are a woman who needs help, call the Wife Assault Help Line, listed in your phone book."

IF YOU'RE THE BEST, DEMAND THE BEST.

**Demand perfection.
Print it on a Heidelberg.**

DIRECTIONS 2 was printed in Canada on a Heidelberg Speedmaster.

THIS AIN'T NO PARTY

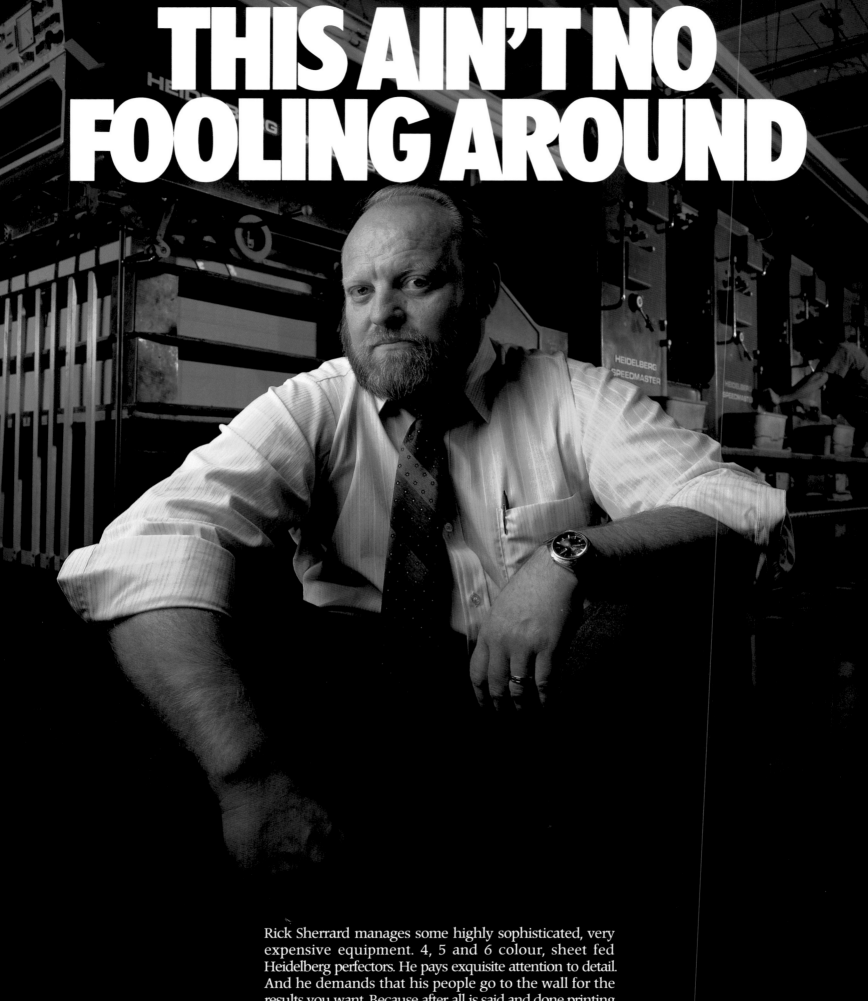

THIS AIN'T NO FOOLING AROUND

Rick Sherrard manages some highly sophisticated, very expensive equipment. 4, 5 and 6 colour, sheet fed Heidelberg perfectors. He pays exquisite attention to detail. And he demands that his people go to the wall for the results you want. Because after all is said and done printing comes down to the quality of the people. And their commitment to their craft. So if you buy print, buy MIL. Because you couldn't pay other printers to do what we do. And we're not kidding.

M&L

Matthews Ingham and Lake Inc. 1366 Don Mills Road, Don Mills, Ontario, Canada M3B 2X2 (416) 445-8800

THE QUEEN OF TEARS

Virtually locked in a small, darkened screening room in Yorkton, Sask. for five days to watch 50 hours or so of films, French-Canadian actress Marie Tifo is edgy—much edgier than the other jury members at the Short Film & Video Festival. There are a few times she's ready to tear out her curly, dirty-blond hair. "I don't like being in a room all day," she moans. "I must have a little sunshine—yes?"

She is also much more demonstrative emotionally than the other jurists, breaking into tears at the end of Michel Brault's film on wife abuse, L'Emprise. "I'm such a mess," Tifo exclaims, wiping her eyes and attempting to laugh through her tears, then promptly bursting into them again.

Cry again she does during a few other films, but there's one in particular, Lori Spring's Inside/Out, the story of a young

◆

Pratiquement emprisonnée pendant cinq jours dans l'obscurité d'une petite salle de projection de Yorkton, en Saskatchewan, pour regarder des films pendant une cinquantaine d'heures, l'actrice canadienne française Marie Tifo est énervée, beaucoup plus que les autres jurés du festival du court métrage et de la vidéo. On la sent prête, plusieurs fois, à s'arracher à poignées ses cheveux blond cendré bouclés. "Je n'aime pas rester enfermée toute la journée, gémit-elle, il me faut un peu de soleil, n'est-ce pas?"

Elle est aussi beaucoup plus démonstrative que les autres: elle éclate en sanglots à la fin du film de Michel Brault sur les femmes battues, L'Emprise. "Je suis dans un état épouvantable", fait-elle en s'essuyant les yeux et en essayant de rire à travers ses larmes, avant de se remettre à pleurer.

BY • PAR
LAWRENCE O'TOOLE

PHOTOS
CHRISTIAN BELPAIRE

Marie Tifo is

Quebec's

Meryl Streep

Marie Tifo

est la

Meryl Streep

du Québec

LA LARME A L'OEIL

FEBRUARY • FÉVRIER 1989   31

TITLE
THE QUEEN OF TEARS
ART DIRECTOR
EVELYN STOYNOFF
EDITOR
KAREN HANLEY
DESIGNER
**AUDREY GOTO/
EVELYN STOYNOFF**
PHOTOGRAPHER
CHRISTIAN BELPAIRE
PUBLICATION
ENROUTE MAGAZINE
CLIENT
AIR CANADA
PUBLISHER
AIRMEDIA
PHOTO DIRECTOR
LISA BURROUGHS

Through a clever little box attached to viewers' TVs, marketers are electronically tracking the impact of advertising on consumer buying habits

TUBE TESTS

Every Thursday night about 6 p.m., Norma Pruitt has a date at the local supermarket in Toronto. That's when she meets her husband, Vance, after work to do their grocery shopping. When the Pruitts return home, they put away their groceries, have dinner and watch TV. Using a special keypad, Norma then fills out an "electronic questionnaire" that appears on the screen. She inputs information about her grocery pur-

BY • PAR WILI LIBERMAN
ILLUSTRATION
BALVIS RUBESS

Grâce à une boîte attachée au petit écran, les responsables marketing dépistent électroniquement l'impact de la publicité télévisée sur la consommation

TÉLÉ TESTS

Tous les jeudis soirs vers 18 h, Norma Pruitt a rendez-vous au supermarché du quartier à Toronto. Elle rencontre son mari, Vance, après le travail pour acheter avec lui leurs produits d'épicerie. Quand les Pruitt rentrent chez eux, ils rangent provisions, dînent et regardent la télé. Se servant d'un bloc numérique spécial, Norma remplit un "questionnaire électronique" qui s'affiche à l'écran. Elle introduit des données sur les

75

TITLE
TUBE TESTS
ART DIRECTOR
EVELYN STOYNOFF
EDITOR
KAREN HANLEY
DESIGNER
**AUDREY GOTO/
EVELYN STOYNOFF**
ILLUSTRATOR
BALVIS RUBESS
PUBLICATION
ENROUTE MAGAZINE
CLIENT
AIR CANADA
PUBLISHER
AIRMEDIA

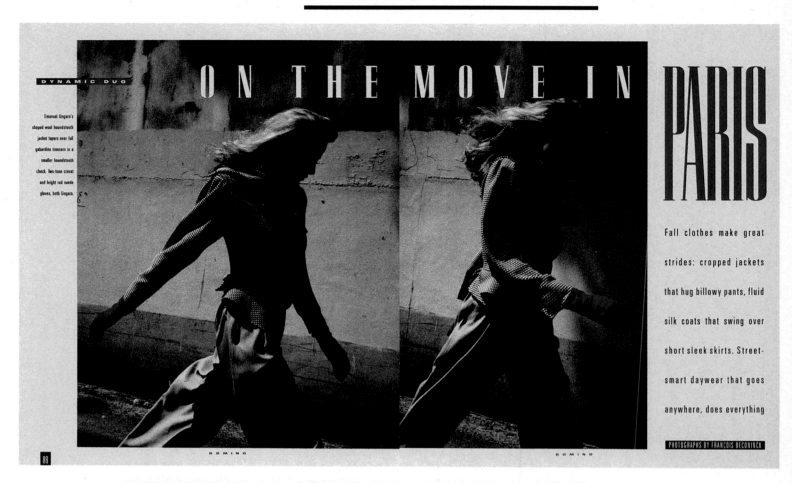

TITLE
ON THE MOVE IN PARIS
ART DIRECTOR
KAREN SIMPSON
DESIGNER
KAREN SIMPSON
PHOTOGRAPHER
FRANCOIS DECONINCK
PUBLICATION
DOMINO MAGAZINE
PUBLISHER
THE GLOBE AND MAIL

TITLE
LIP READING
ART DIRECTOR
**GEORGES HAROUTIUN/
BONITA COLLINS**
EDITOR
SALLY ARMSTRONG
DESIGNER
VALERIE RIOUX
PHOTOGRAPHER
MICHEL PILON
DESIGN FIRM
MAG GRAPHICS
PUBLICATION
HOMEMAKERS
PUBLISHER
TELEMEDIA PROCOM

The Russians call him difficult,
the Parisians say he's wild.
The whole world wonders if
the Kirov is big enough for....

MR. RAZZMATAZZ

● Ruzimatov: A tartar, on stage and off ●

WITH HIS LONG, DARK HAIR HANGING IN TANGLED CURLS over a downcast face, Faruk Ruzimatov appears sullen, exhausted – a sinewy waif lost in the mirrored rehearsal hall of Leningrad's hallowed Kirov Theatre. Only his costume – black tights and scarlet top slashed in a V to his navel – gives him away as a dancer. But then Ruzimatov takes to the air. He leaps like a bolt of lightning and lands like a butterfly, his laconic expression transformed by a blazing passion. Treading air, eyes burning and teeth flashing, the waif is spectacular.

When he lands he turns inward again, his exhaustion palpable. He dons a tatty white bathrobe and slips quietly away. But long after he is gone, the empty room still crackles with the energy of an electric storm.

In the sober world of the Kirov ballet, stars officially don't exist. "We purposely don't advertise our dancers. Advertising is artificial," says artistic director Oleg Vinogradov. And after losing first Rudolf Nureyev and then Mikhail Baryshnikov to the West, the Kirov has been understandably careful about exposing its latest male-lead sensation to the outside world. Still – in the few appearances he has made in the West, the young 5-foot-9 dancer has been hailed as an emerging giant of international ballet.

That much became abundantly clear during the Kirov's seven-week season in Paris last winter. "Ruzimatov was the rave of Paris," reports Victor Melnikoff, the Montreal impresario who just presented the Soviet dancer in a charity gala at Place des Arts on September 1. And when he and his partner, Altynai Assylmuratova, performed as guests with Baryshnikov's American Ballet Theatre in New York last spring, Ruzimatov astonished the most jaded dance audience in the world. In one of the more understated notices, *The New York Times* described the performance of the Soviet pair in the ABT's *La Bayadère* as "passionate and superb." Before he left town New York had adopted Ruzimator as one of its own, even to the point of giving him a new (continued on page 122)

DOMINO

THE BELZBERG INHERITANCE

Sam Belzberg (left) still casts a long shadow over First City Financial. But the next generation has come of age, bringing a new vision to this western dynasty's continental reach

BY LARRY BLACK

Only 60 years old and in excellent health, Sam Belzberg, the acknowledged patriarch of First City Financial Corp. Ltd., is not about to retire any time soon. But a second generation of Belzbergs is taking charge of much of the $4.9-billion business empire Sam and his brothers, Hy and Bill, founded 27 years ago. Sam's son, Marc, 34, and Hy's son Brent, 38, are inheriting responsibility for First City's key divisions: Brent of the $3.4-billion Toronto-based trust company, and Marc of the family's hugely profitable New York merchant bank. But with the power, the cousins have also inherited the Belzberg reputation—one of the most controversial in North American business.

In the last decade, "Belzberg" has become one synonym for hostile corporate raiding. On business pages across North America, the Belzbergs have been described as quick-flip artists and as greenmailers and chastised for questionable practices such as

32 CANADIAN BUSINESS MARCH 1989

MARCH 1989 CANADIAN BUSINESS 33

TITLE
MR. RAZZMATAZZ
ART DIRECTOR
KAREN SIMPSON
DESIGNER
KAREN SIMPSON
PUBLICATION
DOMINO MAGAZINE
PUBLISHER
THE GLOBE AND MAIL

TITLE
THE BELZBERG INHERITANCE
ART DIRECTOR
JIM IRELAND
EDITOR
WAYNE GOODING
DESIGNER
JIM IRELAND
PUBLICATION
CANADIAN BUSINESS MAGAZINE
PUBLISHER
CB MEDIA

TITLE
FIASCO AL FRESCO
ART DIRECTOR
KAREN SIMPSON
DESIGNER
KAREN SIMPSON
PHOTOGRAPHER
DANIEL MINASSIAN
PUBLICATION
DOMINO MAGAZINE
PUBLISHER
THE GLOBE AND MAIL

TITLE
TIME FRAMES
ART DIRECTOR
JAMES IRELAND
EDITOR
JOCELYN LAURENCE
DESIGNER
JAMES IRELAND
PHOTOGRAPHER
GEORGE WHITESIDE
PUBLICATION
CANADIAN ART
PUBLISHER
KEY PUBLISHERS CO. LTD.

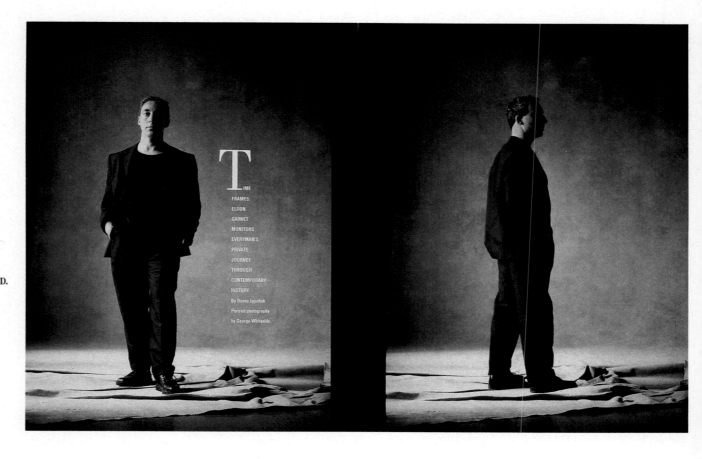

THE RESTLESS
THE YOUNG AND

To Hani Rashid and Lise Anne Couture, the earthquake that struck Los Angeles on December 3, 1988, was no fluke. The two young architects saw it as a sign that their gods were pleased. As finalists in an international competition to design a new monument for downtown L.A., the answer to New York's Statue of Liberty, Couture and Rashid had come to Tinseltown with an audacious proposal for a bizarre antimonument they called Steel Cloud. Unlike anything that had ever been lifted off a drafting table, it was meant to make the earth move. And it worked: The tremor that greeted their arrival was minor compared with the cultural aftershocks that followed the jury's announcement of their victory. Unknown and unheralded, Canada's Hani Rashid and Lise Anne Couture had truly arrived. And in their not entirely humble opinion, modern architecture had entered a new epoch.

At 29 and 30 respectively, Couture and Rashid are typical of architects their age in that none of their designs has ever been built. But there is nothing typical about the confidence with which they now tread the world stage. Dressed in baggy corduroys and a green T-shirt on a grey Sunday morning in the couple's small and spartan Manhattan studio, Rashid eulogizes his project – "clouds that rain culture" – with the high-flying conceits of a visionary. Couture, formal in a grey suit and almost demure in her manner, seems more practical. But the way her hazel eyes brighten with every one of her partner's rhetorical flourishes proves that there is no disagreement between these two. They believe in destiny – especially their own. "Audacity, drive, tenacity – whatever it takes, we do it," says Rashid, black eyes glowing. "Our teachers engrained into us that there are those who lead and those who follow. It sounds pompous, but we intend to lead."

L.A. HATES THEM, JURIES LOVE THEM: LISE ANNE COUTURE AND HANI RASHID DESIGN TO PROVOKE AND PLAN TO WIN

Situated directly on top of the Hollywood Freeway, Steel Cloud would be a 1,600-foot-long tangle of girders and boxes comprising parks, cinemas, museums, multistory fish tanks and laser light shows. It looks like the Orwellian nightmare of *Blade Runner* interpreted by a Soviet Constructivist; like "a bad accident on the southbound 101," according to one of many disgruntled Angelenos. In fact, the public reaction to Steel Cloud has been overwhelmingly negative. "If people said it was wonderful, we would be concerned," says Rashid. "It would mean that our (continued on page 105)

BY JOHN BARBER

KILLSHOT

In an excerpt from his forthcoming novel, America's foremost crime writer finds the dark underbelly of Toronto the Good

he Blackbird told himself he was drinking too much because he lived in this hotel and The Silver Dollar was close by, right downstairs. Try to walk out the door past it. Try to come along Spadina Avenue, see that goddamn Silver Dollar sign, hundreds of lightbulbs in your face, and not be drawn in there. Have a few drinks before coming up to this room with a ceiling that looked like a road map, all the cracks in it. Or it was the people in The Silver Dollar talking about the Blue Jays all the time that made him drink too much. He didn't give a shit about the Blue Jays. He believed it was time to get away from here, leave Toronto and the Waverley Hotel for good and he wouldn't drink so much and be sick in the morning. Follow one of those cracks in the ceiling.

The phone rang. He listened to several rings before picking up the receiver, wanting it to be a sign. He liked signs. The Blackbird said, "Yes?" and a voice he recognized asked would he like to go to Detroit. See a man at a hotel Friday morning. It would take him maybe two minutes.

In the moment the voice on the phone said, "Detroi-it" the Blackbird thought of his grandmother, who lived near there, and began to see himself and his brothers with her when they were young boys and thought, This could be a sign. The voice on the phone said, "What do you say, Chief?"

"How much?"

"Out of town, I'll go 15."

The Blackbird lay in his bed staring at the ceiling, at the cracks making highways and rivers. The stains were lakes, big ones.

"I can't hear you, Chief."

"I'm thinking you're low."

"All right, gimme a number."

"I like 20,000."

"You're drunk. I'll call you back."

"I'm thinking this guy staying at a hotel, he's from here, no?"

"What difference is it where he's from?"

"You mean what difference is it to me. I think it's somebody you don't want to look in the face."

The voice on the phone said, "Hey Chief? F—you. I'll get somebody else."

This guy was a punk, he had to talk like that. It was OK. The Blackbird knew what this guy and his people thought of him. Half-breed tough guy one time from Montreal, maybe a little crazy, they gave him dirty jobs to. If you took the jobs, you took the way they spoke to you. You spoke back if you could get away with it, if they needed you. It wasn't social, it was business.

He said, "You don't have no somebody else. You call me when your people won't do

fiction by ► **ELMORE LEONARD** ◄

TITLE
THE YOUNG AND THE RESTLESS
ART DIRECTOR
KAREN SIMPSON
DESIGNER
KAREN SIMPSON
PHOTOGRAPHER
E.J. CAMP
PUBLICATION
DOMINO MAGAZINE
PUBLISHER
THE GLOBE AND MAIL

TITLE
KILL SHOT
ART DIRECTOR
LINDSAY BEAUDRY
WRITER
ELMORE LEONARD
DESIGNER
FERNANDA PISANI
ILLUSTRATOR
CHRISTINE BUNN
PUBLICATION
TORONTO MAGAZINE
PUBLISHER
THE GLOBE AND MAIL

TITLE
TWISTS AND TURNS
ART DIRECTOR
BARBARA SOLOWAN
EDITOR
SHEILA HIRTLE
DESIGNER
BARBARA SOLOWAN
PHOTOGRAPHER
JOHN BENTHAM
PUBLICATION
HOMES
CLIENT
TORONTO LIFE MAGAZINE
PUBLISHER
KEY PUBLISHERS CO. LTD.

TITLE
THE DEVIL AND THIERRY MUGLER
ART DIRECTOR
GAYLE GRIN
EDITOR
DONNA NEBENZAHL
DESIGNER
GAYLE GRIN
ILLUSTRATOR
JEFF HENNING
PUBLICATION
FASHION AND BEAUTY MAGAZINE
PUBLISHER
THE GAZETTE, MONTREAL
FASHION EDITOR
IONA MONAHAN

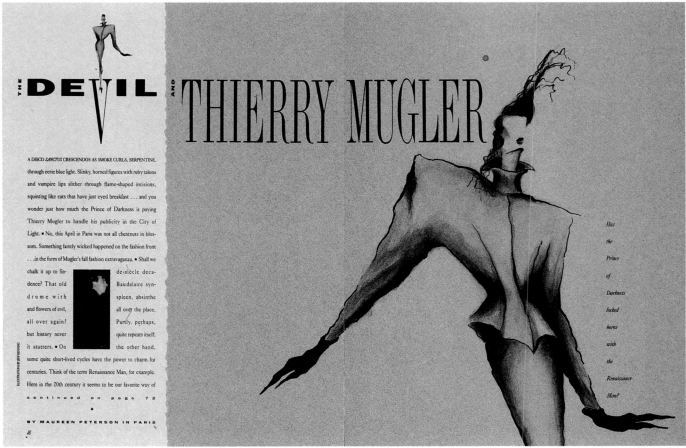

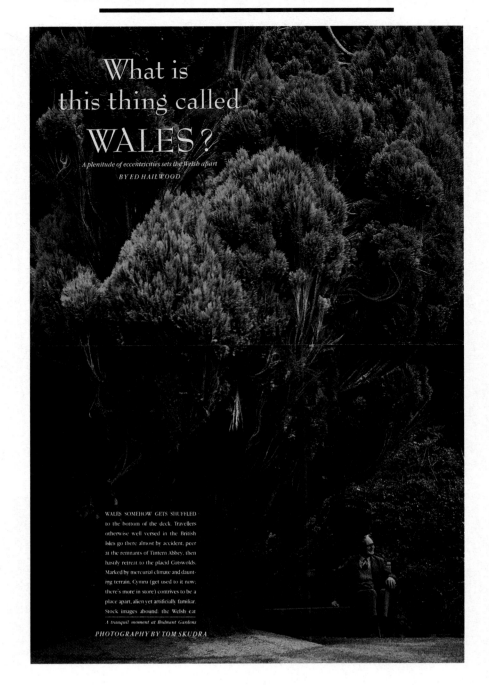

What is this thing called WALES?

A plenitude of eccentricities sets the Welsh apart
BY ED HAILWOOD

WALES SOMEHOW GETS SHUFFLED to the bottom of the deck. Travellers otherwise well versed in the British Isles go there almost by accident, peer at the remnants of Tintern Abbey, then hastily retreat to the placid Cotswolds. Marked by mercurial climate and daunting terrain, Cymru (get used to it now; there's more in store) contrives to be a place apart, alien yet artificially familiar. Stock images abound: the Welsh eat
A tranquil moment at Bodnant Gardens

PHOTOGRAPHY BY TOM SKUDRA

TITLE
WHAT IS THIS THING CALLED WALES?
ART DIRECTOR
NADIA MARYNIAK
EDITOR
JACK McIVER
DESIGNER
NADIA MARYNIAK
PHOTOGRAPHER
TOM SKUDRA
PUBLICATION
DESTINATIONS
PUBLISHER
THE GLOBE AND MAIL

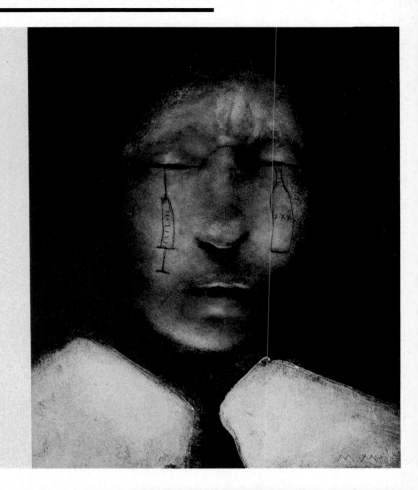

Dealing with the demons

The office addict no longer faces an endless private hell. Enlightened employers and progressive clinics will reach out to begin the healing.

By Alan Morantz
Illustrations by Matt Mahurin

Paul Court* never had a problem with drugs until he reached his late twenties. In his early working life he traveled the world with rock-and-roll bands, working at staging and lighting jobs. He left that about seven years ago to start a software company in Toronto. It was then, at the age of 29, that he began making more than $300,000 a year and surrounding himself with new things and new ideas. "It was nothing to show off my $70,000 Porsche and $400,000 home," he recalls, ruefully. "I always had to buy $1,500 hand-made suits. I went to Hawaii five times one year, once renting a helicopter to fly all over the islands. I had to stay in the best hotels, even if it cost me $350 a night. I was making like there was no tomorrow."

He was hanging out with a fast-running crowd. And he was introduced to cocaine. As his dependency grew and the supply of coke became plentiful, he began looking forward to parties where he knew it would be available. This diversion was costing him at least $4,000 a month, sometimes $6,000.

A few years later, the American computer company for which he distributed software wanted to break a 20-year agreement with him. And that set in motion his denouement. "I spent three years in court and $120,000 in legal fees fighting them, and I had to close the business," he recalls. "I finally won close to $500,000, but I ended up putting it all up my nose. It was not until I lost my wife and the confidence to start over in business that I realized I had a problem, although I spent months denying it. During this time I had several jobs in the computer field, but they ended up being washed out because I couldn't function."

* The names of the two addicts in this story, Paul Court and Robert Smith, are pseudonyms.

48 VISTA

ALL THE RIGHT MOVES

This summer, bold detail will set you apart from the crowd

COORDINATION · ANNIE NIKOLAJEVICH
PHOTOS · SHIN SUGINO

IMPULSIONS

Coupes classiques, couleurs relaxes et finition raffinée, le bon ton de cet été . . .

PROGRESSIVELY NEUTRAL

A cream suit and patterned shirt show off a cream and green, polka-dot tie with matching pocket hanky, all by Byblos. McGregor socks, Zodiac olive shoes

PROGRESSIVEMENT NEUTRE

Un complet crème et une chemise imprimée font ressortir une cravate a pois vert et crème et la pochette assortie, le tout de Byblos. Chaussettes de McGregor et chaussures vert olive de Zodiac

WHERE TO BUY: SEE PAGE 40
AUTRES DÉTAILS EN PAGE 40

TITLE
DEALING WITH THE DEMONS
ART DIRECTOR
ROD DELLA VEDOVA
EDITOR
ROD McQUEEN
DESIGNER
KELLY de REGT
CREATIVE DIR.
ROD DELLA VEDOVA
ILLUSTRATOR
MATT MAHURIN
PUBLICATION
VISTA MAGAZINE
PUBLISHER
VISTA PUBLICATIONS

TITLE
ALL THE RIGHT MOVES
ART DIRECTOR
EVELYN STOYNOFF
EDITOR
KAREN HANLEY
DESIGNER
AUDREY GOTO/ EVELYN STOYNOFF
PUBLICATION
ENROUTE MAGAZINE
CLIENT
AIR CANADA
PUBLISHER
AIRMEDIA
PHOTO DIRECTOR
LISA BURROUGHS

COLOR

IT'S STRONG. IT'S SCULPTURAL. IT'S ALMOST SURREAL. IN A
SEASON OF NEUTRALS, DRAMATIC EYES, A FOCUSED MOUTH,
HAIR THAT SHIMMERS WITH GOLDEN SHINE CREATE THEIR
OWN INDIVIDUAL STATEMENTS. THE PALETTE IS SIMPLE BUT
ITS MESSAGE IS NO LESS DEFINITE: VIOLET ON THE EYELIDS
PLAYS OFF A TAWNY BEIGE MOUTH. GOLD
SHADOW POINTS UP RUBY RED. TITIAN HAIR IS
THE STAR FRAME FOR A WATERCOLORED FACE.
SUBTLETY OR ALL-OUT GLAMOUR,
THE SECRET IS TECHNIQUE. PRECISION
WORKS SMALL MIRACLES.
BALANCE IS THE KEY.

SHADOW PLAY

A PAINT BOX OF VIBRANT SHADES FROM YVES SAINT LAURENT'S CALYPSO COLLECTION (LEFT). ROUGE INTENSE NO. 6 LIPSTICK FILLS OUT A
LUSCIOUS MOUTH. WHITE AND GOLD EYESHADOW FROM THE NO. 85 AND 87 EYESHADOW POWDER DUOS SCULPT A FINELY ARCHED EYE. (ABOVE) FROM
CHRISTIAN DIOR'S SIMPLICITE COLLECTION, SULTRY TONES TO GLIDE ON WITH EASE. FROST AND VIOLET EYESHADOW MAKE EYES THE FOIL
FOR THE PALEST OF LIPS, HERE BRUSHED WITH ELEGANCE. DIOR'S NEWEST SHADE FOR SUMMER, SAHARA BEIGE POUDRE PLUS FINE POLISHES THE
LOOK. HAIR THESE EIGHT PAGES BY RAY CIVELLO. MAKEUP BY ALAN MILROY, BOTH OF CIVELLO.

FUCHSIA FUSION

(LEFT) FROM SHISEIDO'S MOISTURE MIST EYE SYSTEM NO. 37. A SWATH OF PURPLE, PURE AND SIMPLE. HAIR IS GLOSSY, GLEAMING WITH SILKY
RICH VITAMIN-PACKED ZACHI SHAMPOO AND MOISTURE RINSE CONDITIONER. (ABOVE) HEARTBREAKER LIPS IN A HOTHOUSE COLOR.
CRIMSON PINK MOISTURE MIST. BY SHISEIDO. BEAUTY NOTE: STRONG SHADOW SHADES MAKE THE BOLDEST STATEMENT WHEN THEY ARE WORN
ALONE. TO SET LIPSTICK, BLOT AND WHISK LIPS WITH A TOUCH OF LOOSE POWDER.

SILVER

TITLE
COLOR
ART DIRECTOR
BRAD MacIVER
EDITOR
TIM BLANKS
DESIGNER
BRAD MacIVER
PHOTOGRAPHER
CHRIS NICHOLLS
PUBLICATION
TORONTO LIFE FASHION
PUBLISHER
**KEY PUBLISHERS
CO. LTD.**

Stephen Jones, 31, made and sold his designs one by one after graduating from his millinery course in London. His first full collection, in 1984, was inspired by a trip to Montreal. This fall's line, lightly referred to as "Room Service," features pink satin linings and boudoir luxury; here, the "Cloud 9" swan feather hat.

DOMINO

76

With her first line of prewashed silks, in 1980, Katharine Hamnett, now 40, became a British star. Her political T-shirts made headlines in 1984 (she wore one saying "58% DON'T WANT PERSHING" to meet Margaret Thatcher). Her collection features romantic looks such as this velvet veiled hat and matching velvet cape.

DOMINO

77

Born in Istanbul 34 years ago, Rifat Ozbek (who does a mean Diana Vreeland impression) says he learned design by studying architecture. His first collection, in 1984, followed an African theme; now he favors minimalist pieces. Here, long metallic beads shine on a black jersey bodysuit and wrap skirt, with long leather gloves.

DOMINO

80

Betty Jackson, 39, introduced her first collection under her own label in 1981, and two years later was named England's Woman Designer of the Year. An eclectic sense of texture and color is her trademark, as in this maroon striped waistcoat and red striped tie teamed with an oversized striped jacket and printed shirt.

DOMINO

81

SAVAGE PENCILS

Artists who'll drop-kick your sensibility through the goal posts of good taste BY GARY MICHAEL DAULT

Art today is so exhaustively pluralist, so triumphantly and, at the same time, so wearyingly elastic in its inclusions, that one can scarcely posit the existence any longer of a truly distaff art, a soft underbelly of expression cradled beneath the body of art's high-cultural concerns. There is work, however, that is just that. Nobody knows for certain what to call it and so it gets referred to, mostly, as comic art.

Which is not a very useful term. It does not usually refer, for example, to the popular art of the syndicated comic strips or to the graphic sophistication of the drawing-room-comedy cartoons that enliven the pages of magazines like *The New Yorker*. Rather, the term tends to be reserved for the sort of drawing (little of this sensibility gets manifested as painting) that finds its way into the grotty, fly-by-night anthologies called graphzines (fanzines for drawing junkies). These raw, often rude, inevitably Rabelaisian publications are born out of a heady sense of freedom and licence, punched up onanistically onto the screens of backstreet monitors and laser-printed into the grateful hands of an audience — mostly other comix artists — who see marginalization as independence, tastelessness as creative tension, vulgarity as a rolling-back of the super-ego and a hot tool for blasting and bombardiering the insufficiently conscious mind into fresh new attitudes to truth.

The art of Montreal's Henriette Valium (Patrick Henley) is like an irridescent sock in the jaw. Brilliantly and energetically drawn, written in an English that is Beckettian, a French that is an outrageously silly patois ("Il a changé toutes mes Roches de Kriptonite Rouge en petits blocs de Hash Bruns!!" complains the artist's sleazoid Superman), and a woozily bilingual hybrid that is neither, Valium's cartoons squarely confront the miserable excesses of the world with the uproarious power of outrage.

Toronto artist/illustrator Sean Leaning's cartoon strips in Peter Dako's graphzine *Casual Casual* inevitably star a plucky but shakily rendered, Chaplinesque Everyman named Mr. D. (probably Leaning's reading of Dako himself) placed in predicaments that are poignant and grotesque in equal measure. Here, in his slicker, upscale illustrative style, is a Leaning one-shot morality play: a man cuckolded by TV, his partner having been literally sucked in by what she has seen.

Contrary to popular belief, the men and women who draw for the graphzines and who read and collect them are not invariably and unalterably psychopaths and lunatics. Among the artists represented on these pages is a medical illustrator and sculptor (Dave Geary); two all-purpose illustrators (Sean Leaning and Henriette Valium, a.k.a. Patrick Henley); an editor (of the influential Toronto graphzine *Casual Casual*), desktop publisher and musician (Peter Dako); and two prolific painters (Julie Voyce and Carel Moiseiwitsch). All of them have work to do during the daytime that is culturally validated and intellectually respectable. There is a cherry moon of satire-fuelled madness, however, that rises into their studio windows when day is done, transforming them into guerrilla graphists, art-outlaws hightailing it up into the hills of competitionless enjoyment from which they make their ragged raids on the imperialist programs of the art establishment. These are the artists your instructors warned you about, artists whose wicked triumph it is to fire-bomb whatever you knew about Good Taste and erect on its ashes edifices of irreverence, bunkers of radical unself-consciousness.

The term comic art doesn't help anything. Indeed, it muddies the graphic waters. These artists are and are not funny. They are often too angry to be funny (Carel Moiseiwitsch's feverishly epic story "Fatal Fellatio," too intense to reproduce here, begins as black humor,

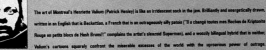

Carel Moiseiwitsch, citizen of a more enlightened planet than ours, but currently based in Vancouver, employs her razor-slashed style in a feminist war against both oppressive systems of patriarchal command and generalized (usually male-generated) manifestations of earth-wide lunacy like The Bomb. Moiseiwitsch plants graphic detonators in unlikely places — such as the Vancouver Art Gallery, which, next August, will host her exhibition *Siren*, a deconstruction of the *femme fatale*.

The comic drawings of Saskatoon artist/sculptor/illustrator Dave Geary often take the shape of ambiguously positioned graphic constructions that perform simultaneously as a satire of and loving homage to his favorite moments in the history of modernist art. Geary has enough admiration for Malevitch and the Russian avant-garde, for example, to pervert Suprematist houses into futurist airplanes and to gather Suprematist artifacts into this radiantly optimistic, happy-families tableau.

A
SILVER

OPPISITE PAGE

TITLE
LONDON'S NEXT WAVE
ART DIRECTOR
KAREN SIMPSON
DESIGNER
KAREN SIMPSON
PHOTOGRAPHER
JURGEN TELLER
PUBLICATION
DOMINO MAGAZINE
PUBLISHER
THE GLOBE AND MAIL
HAND LETTERING
MARY MARGARET O'HARA

A
SILVER

TITLE
SAVAGE PENCILS
ART DIRECTOR
JAMES IRELAND
WRITER
GARY MICHAEL DAULT
DESIGNER
JAMES IRELAND
PUBLICATION
CANADIAN ART
PUBLISHER
KEY PUBLISHERS CO. LTD.

A
S I L V E R

TITLE
THE DIRT WORKERS
ART DIRECTOR
TERESA FERNANDES
EDITOR
MARQ de VILLIERS
DESIGNER
TERESA FERNANDES
PHOTOGRAPHER
TOM SKUDRA
PUBLICATION
TORONTO LIFE
MAGAZINE
PUBLISHER
KEY PUBLISHERS
CO. LTD.

They come each year to plant and tend and harvest the produce for our tables, then go back home, a little richer, a little more travelled. But however long they come, they are forever outsiders

THE DIRT WORKERS

BY LINDALEE TRACEY, WITH PHOTOGRAPHY BY TOM SKUDRA

Katerina Banman and her daughter, Net, tumble barefoot down the stairs into the dark, sticky-hot kitchen. It's 4:45 a.m., a mid-July morning in 1988. They are silent except for two or three words whispered in German. The light from the open refrigerator outlines Katerina's puffy face and hunched shoulders. Her tiredness is like a second skin, rubbed raw under her long, sombre cotton dress.

"My mother says she is sorry for this bad place," Net mumbles from behind her broom.

"*Si, ja,*" Mrs. Banman echoes, offering a shrug as apology.

Inside the unpainted clapboard house, bare boards cover up holes in the walls, and the rooms are scarred with peeling wallpaper. There are no backs to the kitchen chairs, no dressers, no shelves. Clothing is piled in heaps on the floor or hung from nails in the wall. The curtains are tacked to the window frames.

Katerina, her husband, Pieter, and their four children are Mexican Mennonites who have been coming to Canada to work every summer for eight years now. The house is provided free by their employer, Bert De Brouwer, a farmer

By eleven we've picked clean whatever cucumbers there are, filling 122 baskets. "I like more pay by the hour than by how many pickles," Pieter sighs

In a good year, the Banmans can earn $20,000 for seven months of stoop work, money that goes back into their farm in Mexico. Practice doesn't make the labor easier. "It always hurts," says fifteen-year-old Net

in Kent County, 290 kilometres west of Toronto. It's the Banmans' second year working for De Brouwer in his cucumber, bean and tomato fields. He will employ about thirty-four workers this season, ten of them from offshore. A quiet, shy man with rosy Dutch cheeks, De Brouwer says he couldn't do without the foreigners: "They say you gotta grow yer own labor, but I only got two kids. And only one of them's interested in farm work."

In the last twenty years, the farm population of Ontario has decreased by forty-five per cent. Farmers are depending less on their families and more on paid labor. But the small wages don't attract as many students or the large Québécois families that once did the planting, hoeing and picking. The ones who do come often leave midseason for better-paying work. In 1987, of the 1,664 Canadians contracted to work in Kent County, twenty-four per cent quit.

Every year, Ontario produces $500 million worth of fruits and vegetables, and we spend almost fifty per cent of our food budgets on these items, consuming an average of 500 pounds per person per year. Farmers desperately need stoop workers to get the crops to our tables, and increasingly they're turning to offshore laborers—in 1983, Ontario farmers hired 4,500 seasonal workers; by 1988, the number was up to 8,000. The workers come from Jamaica, Mexico, Trinidad and Tobago, Barbados and dot islands in the Caribbean, with Jamaica supplying almost half of the total.

Begun in 1966, the federally incorporated Foreign Seasonal Agricultural Workers Program allows workers into Canada for up to eight months, although the average contract is fifteen weeks. The participating farmers must cover airfare and supply housing. Some of the laborers are asked for by name; they come each year to the same farm and are almost part of the family. When they go back home they are a little richer, a little more travelled, returning

VALERIE SCOTT
OF CORP:
"EVER SINCE I
WAS FIVE
I DREAMED OF
GETTING INTO
THE SEX
INDUSTRY"

HOOKERS

Street Fight

In the war between the

homeowners and the hookers,

is the real issue propriety

or property values?

L AST DECEMBER 10, A DRAMA WAS enacted on an elegant residential street in Cabbagetown. Wearing white sweatshirts emblazoned with a red circle and oblique line slashed across the graphic image of a hooker bending to solicit a john in a car, a handful of neighbors took to the pavements. Except for their sweatshirts and the missionary gleam in their eyes, they looked like any group of upwardly mobile Torontonians you might see in a movie lineup on a Saturday night. Armed with cameras and coming on like a preppy lynch mob, they confronted a chunky, confused-looking prostitute.

"Go away. Go do what you do on someone else's street," one man snarled in disgust. The prostitute stood her ground. With a whaddaya-wanna-make-of-it tone she replied, "I'm a hooker and I work Ontario Street."

"You're suffering. You're abused by pimps," came a sermon, but its recipient remained unmoved. Then, in hysterical tones, another voice shouted: "We're sick of you. You've lowered our property values. You have no idea what you're doing to the people who have spent hun-

dreds of thousands of dollars to live on this street."

"I live here," the exasperated woman sputtered, although when grilled as to where, she could only hurl invective. Finally, she spewed venomously: "Buddy, I've lived in this area for twenty-six years. What made this your fucking area?"

There are a few ironies bound up in the downtown hooker wars, and the Ontario Street standoff throws them into high relief. What we have here is a clash in which the real issues have been obscured. They've been obscured because the adversaries aren't acknowledging what those issues are. What the Cabbagetown residents will admit about street soliciting is that it is a nuisance. What they won't say is that it offends their moral sensibilities and threatens their property values. This is not the first time outraged citizens have agitated to make prostitutes go away, but it is the first time that there may be nowhere else in town for them to go. What's going on, then, is a turf war. The street, a pricey chunk of real estate, is up for grabs. But

BY WENDY DENNIS

Photography by Nigel Dickson.

NOVEMBER 1988 TORONTO LIFE 85

something else is also up for grabs, something that in the mêlée hardly anybody seems to be noticing. At stake is the future of a city. A city that, in altering its priorities and pimping its sense of community to the highest bidder, is in grave danger of losing its innocence.

There was a time when downtowners viewed prostitution as part of the donnée of urban life. If you chose to live downtown, you chose also to tolerate, maybe even cherish, as part of the texture of everyday experience, the hootchy-cootchy vitality. If streetwalkers belonged to that sometimes seamy world, so be it.

Since the early 1970s, a confluence of forces has conspired to radically disrupt this harmony. With the push to revitalize the downtown core, Cabbagetown's flops and rooming houses gradually vanished, transformed by the white-painters and, later, the sandblasters, who kept tenants to make the mortgage. As real estate prices spiralled, however, a more affluent group, many of them suburban refugees, moved in, grandly upgrading properties and squeezing out those tenants who once had called the neighborhood their own. Property values leaped to the point where some houses on prime streets were turning over for close to half a million dollars. Not only had the houses been transformed; so too, in some cases, had the sensibilities of their owners. With a significant investment to protect, some residents no longer viewed hookers as part of the local color.

Parallel to those developments were others. In 1977, in the wake of citizen outrage at the murder of shoeshine boy Emanuel Jaques, and increasingly eager to attract more tourist dollars, civic officials padlocked body-rub parlors and cleaned up Yonge Street. Displaced from Yonge, some of the hookers began to move eastward to Church Street, although certain corners, like Jarvis and Gloucester, Isabella and Huntley, had been active hooker turf long before. When Church Street began to sprout smart cafés in the early eighties, the hookers migrated eastward again, off familiar territory and onto neighboring streets where they began do-

ing deals under the noses of residents.

Barry Smith is a lawyer with a let's-skip-the-pleasantries manner who, along with his wife, Judy, bought a house on Cabbagetown's Ontario Street during the real estate boom of 1981. Smith was born and raised in Toronto, but had spent the previous ten years living on a twenty-five-acre property in the bucolic environs of Stouffville. Their two daughters having grown, the Smiths decided to return to the

FRONTLINERS

LIKE LAURIE EDMISTON

(ABOVE) SYMPATHIZE WITH

SANDRA JACKSON AND BARRY

SMITH, WHO ARE TROUBLED

BY HOOKERS IN THEIR

NEIGHBORHOOD; BUT THE

SOCIAL WORKERS SAY A LEGAL

CRACKDOWN WOULD ONLY

WORK AGAINST KIDS TRYING

TO BEAT THE STREET

city. It was the charm of the downtown core, with its movie houses, theatres and lively multicultural enclaves, that seduced them back. Other than what Smith describes as a "few drunks" in the neighborhood, Ontario Street seemed the ideal place to locate.

In 1984, a year prior to the passage of Bill C-49, the country's current antisoliciting law, Barry Smith wrote the first of many letters to his alderman. It said that "prostitutes and other undesirable characters" had "begun" to appear in his neighborhood. In fact, Barry Smith's neighborhood had for decades been in the part of town known as Track 1 (an area bordered by Church, Parliament, Isabella and Dundas streets), which was a stroll for the city's hookers and a nesting ground for many of its hoodlums and vagrants. Nevertheless, Smith was not alone in complaining that these unsavory elements were beginning to clash with the scenery. Soon Smith and several hundred other like-minded citizens met with the police, who saw Bill C-49 as a law with more enforcement clout than the legislation it was replacing. So Smith and his cohorts pestered politicians to support it, and in December 1985, Bill C-49 was passed. What Smith soon realized was that despite what he saw as "this lovely piece of legislation," the problem seemed to be getting worse.

So, to prod the powers-that-be once again, in the summer of 1987 the South of Carlton Community Association, headed by Smith, made a conscious decision to attract press, gambling that the media would lick their chops over a gamy story. Soon *Globe*, *Star* and *Sun* residents learned that Cabbagetown residents were being greeted, after a hard day's work, by hookers and johns thrashing about on their patios. Tales emerged of streets clogged with the bumper-to-bumper traffic of cruising johns and suburban gawkers, and of residents who practically had to don hip boots to get through the debris of dildos, syringes and used condoms piling up on their properties. An October 25, 1987, *Sunday Star* piece, alliteratively headlined "Hookers haunt homes along The Track," described a scenario in which residents had become prisoners in their own

SANDRA JACKSON AND BARRY SMITH

homes, children could no longer play outside and pimps roamed the streets with baseball bats. The situation seemed so alarming and grim it was as if, without anybody else having noticed, Cabbagetown had become the Bronx, and only Charles Bronson could set things right.

By November, the South of Carlton Community Association had swung into Phase 2 of its crusade to win the media's sympathy and the mayor's attention. The group began what Barry Smith prefers

now to refer to as neighborhood "street walks." He is somewhat touchy on this subject since some observers, including certain members of the press, have described these as vigilante tactics. In any event, wearing their sweatshirts, a small group of residents would cruise Ontario and Seaton streets three or four nights weekly and, according to Smith, "politely ask the girls to move"; over three months, he says there was only the December 10 confrontation. If they were standing on a

street corner, "the girls" would then tell the residents that they were no longer on the residents' turf. Barry Smith's tone turns incredulous at the notion that the hookers would think they had the right to share the public domain of a street corner.

On a cold Saturday afternoon at the end of that month, about 200 residents sweatshirted up again, blocked traffic at the corner of Ontario and Carlton streets, milled about eating hot dogs that were being cooked on the terrace of Melanie's res-

88 TORONTO LIFE · NOVEMBER 1988

NOVEMBER 1988 TORONTO LIFE 87

TITLE
DRUGS IN THE CITY
ART DIRECTOR
TERESA FERNANDES
EDITOR
MARQ de VILLIERS
DESIGNER
TERESA FERNANDES
ILLUSTRATOR
GENE GREIF/
KATHY BOAKE
PUBLICATION
TORONTO LIFE
PUBLISHER
KEY PUBLISHERS
CO. LTD.

The car was full of smoke. Something subterranean rippled through his heavy body and his eyes closed. For a minute and a half by the dashboard clock, he looked like a small black child, unlined, untouched, sleeping.

Ry Cooder was on the radio. "Borderline," I thought. I never noticed before how beautiful that song is. Over his bulky shoulder I could see the low breeze-block shape of Saint Philip's school. I went to that school when I was a kid. This is my hometown. I have a black crack dealer leaning in my passenger window and the car is full of crack smoke. I feel wonderful. I have fireflies in my blood. Things change.

I grew up on Calvington Drive in Downsview, about a mile from where we are now. In 1952, my father paid $11,000 for a brick bungalow on a 100-foot lot. Behind our house there was a farmer's field. It smelled of horses and cut grass. Beyond this farm, the land rolled north and west and east, trees and fallow fields, red barns and silos and rusting tractors. In the winter it was so cold the trees would crack, a sound like a bone breaking you'd hear in the night. Snow fell all winter long, drifting into dunes where the wind blew. The silences were as deep as sleep. I had pictures of fighter planes Scotch-taped to the slanted ceiling over my bed. Corsairs and Spitfires from the war that was just over. My sister slept across the hall. She was three that first winter, a Reynold's baby with red cheeks in a pink snowsuit so stiff she couldn't get up if she fell over. I'd carry her up the snowbanks as tall as my father and slide her down again on her pink snowsuit. A cold white sun burned in a high blue sky. She'd laugh and the shiny cloth would hiss on the frozen snow.

He let his breath out in a long reptilian sigh and his face grew leathery again. Ry Cooder was singing in Spanish.

"The best," he said again.

"How much for that?" I asked, nodding at the bowl.

"You try this for free. Man, I don't stiff you. You try this one time only, you won't be asking me, How much for that."

That was true.

"Well, you think about it, man. I got business to do."

He reached in and shook my hand and said, "Nice car, man," and gave me a huge grin.

"Rented," I said.

"Yeah," he said, pulling back and walking away toward the arcade. "I know."

Metro is putting another ninety-seven bodies into the drug squads this year. The RCMP's Toronto O Division had eighty-eight people working on drug enforcement and they just put a street crew out last year, a first for them. Why? Because they *had to.*

The drug trade in Toronto is a perfect paradigm of the Greed Years. Crack seizures are up from six hits in 1986 to hundreds in 1988. In 1986, the Metro squads seized 273 grams of heroin; last year they picked up 2,381 grams. This year it looks as if they'll top that by early fall. Cocaine busts are also up, from 867 in 1986 to 2,267 in 1988. The amount of hash seized last year was up more than 100 per cent over 1987. Last September it became illegal to bring *High Times* into Canada because so many people were writing away to Superior Growers Supply in East Lansing, Michigan, for metal halide grow lamps and hydroponic culture tanks. Homegrown sinsemilla now labs out to thirty per cent active tetrahydrocannabinol, a hell of a lot stronger than anything you or your buddies might have smoked in your daddy's Buick back in '71. Drug dealing in Toronto is a Growth Industry.

Illustrations by Gene Greif

Heroin has its fans. About seventy per cent of the heroin sold in Canada comes in by air from the Golden Triangle countries of Laos, Thailand and Burma. Southwest Asia, called the Golden Crescent, ships us the rest. The Golden Crescent countries are Pakistan, Afghanistan and Iran. Pakistan poppy growers planted almost twenty per cent more poppies in 1988 than in any year before. In Afghanistan, the poppy fields are controlled by the mujahideen. They produced around 750 tonnes of opium last year, most of which is processed into heroin. And in Toronto, a high percentage of the dealers are Iranian.

Along the Danforth and in Parkdale, you can buy a deck of number four heroin, which is about twenty to twenty-five per cent pure, for anywhere from seventy to seventy-five dollars, given the supply. Depending on the source country, a kilo of number four pure heroin goes for $100,000 to $200,000 in Canada. Twenty-eight grams of that will sell for $10,000. One gram runs from $500 to $700 if it's uncut. Some of the money paid for it goes back to Iran and Libya and Afghanistan to pay for car bombs and surface-to-air missiles.

Chemicals are very popular. Run mainly by the Lobos, the Satan's Choice and the Queensmen, from processing labs in the rural areas north of the city, the trade operates out of topless bars and blind pigs all over Toronto. Angel dust, acid, speed, MDA, psilocybin mushrooms, homegrown or imported, they're all over town. There isn't a high school kid in the city who couldn't get any one of these drugs within twenty-four hours.

But the White Queen of the trade is cocaine. Toronto is in love with this drug. Coke is everywhere now. You can't do a three-sixty in any downtown bar without bumping someone's spoon arm and getting a snarl and a curse. In the bars and clubs around Yorkville and Yonge and Eglinton and Queen Street West, guys get used to their dates walking away tired and coming back from the bathroom with a slight case of postnasal drip and a whole new attitude. The powder-room express.

The White Queen of the drug trade is cocaine. Toronto is in love with this drug. You can't do a three-sixty in any downtown bar without bumping someone's spoon arm and getting a snarl and a curse

Competition. Free enterprise. Market rules. A level playing field. That's all the dealers ever ask for. Iranians. Italians. Colombians. The Tongs. Motorcycle gangs. Vietnamese syndicates. Hong Kong businessmen. Presbyterians with striped ties and clean shaves and great forehand smashes. Teenagers living on The Kingsway offer twenty-four-hour home delivery. High school cafeterias sound like the Swiss bourse. In Toronto, *anyone* can play the game.

Most of the coke in Toronto comes from syndicates operating out of Medellín and Cali in Colombia. Most of the coca paste they need comes from Peru. Here again, as in Afghanistan and Iran, there's a strong connection between revolutionary armies and the drug trade. In Peru, the Sendero Luminoso guerrillas are providing armed escorts for coca-paste caravans on their way to the processing labs. And some of that money pays for AK-47s and plastique and rocket-propelled grenades so men with ethical astigmatisms and hearts cut out of basalt can blow babies to God in the name of Freedom.

The trade is relatively polite. You don't have to go to some Third World hellhole where the language is hard and the water foul and the hygiene medieval. You can carry on business with gentlemen on their car phones, with beepers and laptop computers and a price list for bribes and protection all the way from Rio to Dorval.

Freight handlers and airport security guards are buying Corvettes and inground pools. There are day-jobbers working late nights and all they have to do is drive an '87 Subaru to the Woodbine Centre and leave it outside the west entrance at three o'clock in the afternoon, get out and walk away. A week later they pick up $3,000 in cash. Other guys with excess mortgage money are asked to put out $30,000 in cash on a Monday and collect $40,000 on the following Saturday night.

Market rules. Supply and demand. Five years ago a kilo of pure Medellín coke went for $60,000. Now, the price of a kilo of coke sitting in a burgundy leather briefcase on a rosewood tabletop in an airport-strip hotel suite is down to $25,000. And it's pure. Ninety-nine per cent. As pure as modern technology and Central American ingenuity can make it.

Bazuco has some aficionados. It's coca paste you smoke. It's the Number One drug for South American boys and girls. But crack. . .crack is special. Smoked, it slams through the lung walls and burns like gasoline on water, all slithery blue fire in the blood. Crack is so potent that some people with the right receptors get addicted in one go. Cocaine can stop your heart in thirteen seconds. Suck up a line on any Saturday night and there's one chance in a hundred you'll spend the rest

GETTING WIRED

A nice suburban girl turned night-shift stripper slips into the freebase abyss. By Ken Campbell

She's a stripper—a truly bizarre concept, or so she's felt in those moments of Alien Perspective. She goes by the name Cherrye. It isn't her real name, of course; few people know her real name, even fewer use it. It's getting to the point where you wonder if she remembers it herself.

It may be hard to believe, but she's basically a nice girl. The product of a typical, two-parent suburban hearth, she had a standard education, in a standard school, in a standard community; yet for whatever complex web of motivations, she's opted for stripping.

The money's good, and she's been at it for over two years. But where her bankbook once read in the thousands and she lived alone in a spotless one-bedroom at Yonge and Eglinton, now it doesn't look as if she's going to meet this month's rent. She was thinking of moving anyway.

She's on the night shift, a "house girl," booked at the same midtown bar three out of four weeks. The night shift kicks in at 6:30—but it's 7:45, and Cherrye's nowhere to be found. This will be the third night in a row. The other girls mutter and shake their heads—a strange brew of disgust and jealousy. *They* know where she's at. The word gets around about things like this. Cherrye's at the coke den she's mentioned, the one over on Harbord Street, navigating through a fog of freebase smoke.

The DJ hasn't even bothered to write in her name on the schedule this time. The girls have filled him in on what's what. And in retrospect, he should have seen it coming. About four weeks ago, Cherrye asked him to hold $150 of her day's take. She was going out to a base-party and didn't want the temptation of spending it. It was just past midnight when she called: she was just getting a cab, she'd be right down, have the money ready.

It's 10:55, and business is picking up. The shows are back-to-back; customers are whooping it up. It's Friday night and there isn't a spare chair in the house. And it's *hot,* a humid, sticky July night. Then again, the heat in here isn't just a product of the climate. So many bodies, so tightly packed, in so small a space. . .and then liberally doused with that holy trinity: Sex, Booze and Loud Music. . . . Not to mention the snorting of some fine, white powder in darker corners of cars, doorways, booths and washroom stalls.

Coke is just suddenly everywhere. Ten years ago, pot was the ubiquitous drug. Maybe hash. Sometimes acid. But coke? Until sometime around 1986, when a phenomenon that had hit American cities years earlier came to Toronto. *Why* it happened is tough to say. Maybe Noriega and the boys find it easier to make deals with the right side of the ballot: Reagan, Bush, Mulroney. Today, every strip club has at least one connection, and the booze cans have degenerated into little more than cash-bar coke dens. The club where Cherrye works doesn't differ from other clubs. The trade flourishes, particularly with the girls. More and more customers are discovering the advantages of dealing in a strip club: not only does it provide an excuse to meet the girls, but you can make a dollar or two while you're at it. No one makes *good* money at it—to do that, you can't be constantly sampling the merchandise. But they make enough, because these "coke weasels" sell low-grade crap.

The reason they can get away with it is because it's a seller's market. If a guy buys a few grams ($100 each), he can cut them into at least six "quarters" (forty dollars each). Befriend the right girl, she drums up business among her co-workers, and he can dump maybe two grams of this garbage in a night. That's $280 to play with, which is what he does. It lets him pay for his evening, buy a few rounds, look like a great guy. . .which is the point, isn't it? Coke is still a glamour drug. Mr. Businessman uses it to impress the girls. He likes to have them flock to his table. And he likes to bring along a few office buddies to see how popular he is.

The girls like having a number of these sources—that way, one is usually around at all times. Yet you still have to wonder at the unabashed stupidity that some of them display. They elect to stay after work to round up some extra cash, freelancing for five-dollar bills. But, to get themselves in the mood, they buy a quarter, or two, or five. They spend all the money they just made and have to start again, by which time they're in need of more in-the-mooding.

Of course, Cherrye has graduated from these neophyte worries. Which happens to be Cherrye's problem. It also happens to be the reason she makes a cameo appearance at 11:05. There's no way she's going to get paid for her shift—if she's even still working here at all. But working isn't her concern. It seems she's been given the boot from Harbord. She ran out of money two days ago and found she could cocksuck her way to supply. Oral sex is where it's at. Cold, quick and kinky. Coke promotes kink, if it promotes sex at all. It worked quite a while, but the host tired of her blow-for-blow payment schedule.

In the change room, under lights brighter than she's seen for days, Cherrye isn't looking too good: red eyes, hoarse voice (fifty hours of smoking and yapping), hollow stare, sickly pallor and that telltale acne breakout on her lower face. Cherrye's been basing her brains out. Plus, she looks to have dropped another pound or two. If she doesn't stop losing weight, she won't be able to work *anywhere.*

After a cursory sniff about, and finding that all the stuff is Out There, with the customers, she determines to make a go at rustling up some cash. Two hours till close. Sounds good, yet once in her underwear and on the floor, it loses appeal. Five bucks here, five bucks there—it takes too bloody *long*! And she just does not have the patience to sit and listen to some jerk babble about himself! And what the hell will she end up with, anyway? Fifty? A hundred at best? What is *that* going to buy? It would take that just to get back to where she was. This whole scene, right here, is Mickey Mouse. She lets her opinion be known. The girls listen to her ramble and curse, and a few wonder at the change in her personality. But no one says anything. They avoid her and kind of hope she goes away.

Illustration by Kathy Boake

Then again, Cherrye's attitude may be a defence, a personal defence mechanism against that increasing and sickening suspicion that the other girls know exactly where she's been, exactly whom she's been with, exactly what she's been doing. And maybe she recalls her own disgust with a dancer called Marina, who was rumored to be using her mouth for coke: how Marina swore about Cocaine Anonymous, about being all cleaned up, all changed, never touch it again; how she would disappear again, resurfacing three days later, five pounds lighter, ten years older. Cherrye had wondered how anyone could let their integrity slide so.

The more she thinks about that sort of thing, the more she wants that flying feeling back. Somebody, out in that sea of male, has to be holding. Sure, she has no money, but that is no problem. Maybe it is terrible to be so premeditated about it, but what the hell's the difference, anyway? Is there a *real* difference between profiting from dancing naked on a stage or on a little table box and sucking some guy off? Of course not. Moral acquittal. Case dismissed.

OK, she's been at it nearly three nights, but what the hell. It's Friday night! One more night of fun, *then* she'll get caught up on some sleep, *then* she'll have a good meal, *then* she'll get her bookings straightened around, *then* it'll be back to normal, solid lifestyle. On Monday.

But she has to deal with tonight. And then she sees the answer: Derrick. Derrick is here. Derrick always has something. And pretty good, too, he gets it from his lawyer pals. Derrick *is* Mr. Businessman. He likes to buy the round, and occasionally distributes small bags of white powder. All for nothing but a little bit of attention. Most of the other girls aren't too thrilled when Cherrye moves in on the already overloaded table. And they are even less thrilled, fifteen or so minutes of private Cherrye-Derrick whispering later, when Derrick announces he'll be heading out. He goes out to his car. Cherrye hurries to get her gear.

Yet a date with destiny is a date with destiny—you don't go willingly, it *drags* you. Or grabs you painfully by the arm when walking by, which is precisely what happens to Cherrye. Destiny has taken the guise of that rotund, shaggy biker Cherrye has been dodging. He has been sitting in the corner, near the back of the room. She hadn't noticed him come in.

She owes him $360 from two weeks ago. It seems he wants his money. With a guilty nod, she tries to calm him. She tells him that he's right, tells him she is sorry, tells him how she's been sick these last days, tells him that she's been having problems with her boyfriend, her landlord, says she has *some* of his money right now, it's back in the change room, in her locker. He can have that right now, and she'll make the rest doing tables this very night. Chill out. She'll be right back.

Cherrye goes into the change room, gathers up all her equipment and splits via the back door. Derrick is waiting in the car.

There is a party about to begin! Screw the biker. She'll deal with him next week. There's nothing to worry about, everything will be fine. Right now, she's got to find a test tube, some baking soda and some ice. . . .

TRYCLOPS

PHOTOGRAPHY BY FLORIA SIGISMONDI

NORTHERN LIGHTS

SHINING MOMENTS IN LAMP DESIGN

These cunningly crafted, apparently flying objects discharging their rays at all eight corners of the room are the substantive result of a conjuring trio of industrial designers based in Toronto. Jack Smith and Stephen Boake, of Designwerke, and Miles Keller, formerly of Designwerke and now of Kerr Keller, have together and individually produced the four extraterrestrial light sources pictured herein: Tryclops, Trycycle, Sail and Galaxy.

TRYCLOPS, by Designwerke, consists of three (or if desired, four) 50W halogen lamps mounted on spheres. They, quite free of cords and other tangle-able sources of current, rest loosely on two conducting rails supported by six-foot slivers of wired glass mounted on twin triangular floor bases (right), which house the necessary transformer and serve as storage places for temporarily unwanted lamps. Freed of ridged connections, the direction of each beam is limited only by the rails on which the sphere rests. This lamp is not yet CSA approved; it is still under development.

Homes   March 1989   **31**

NORTHERN LIGHTS

GALAXY

32   Homes   March 1989

Homes   March 1989   **33**

TITLE
NORTHERN LIGHTS
ART DIRECTOR
BARBARA SOLOWAN
EDITOR
SHEILA HIRTLE
DESIGNER
BARBARA SOLOWAN
PHOTOGRAPHER
FLORIA SIGISMONDI
PUBLICATION
HOMES
CLIENT
TORONTO LIFE
PUBLISHER
**KEY PUBLISHERS
CO. LTD.**

PORTFOLIO

ANITA KUNZ

HER ILLUSTRATIONS GIVE WORDS NEW MEANINGS

BY PETER GIFFEN

ANITA KUNZ

IS SHE BEING DISINGENUOUS? COY? YOU TELL ONE OF CANADA'S MOST SUCCESSFUL ILLUSTRATORS, ANITA KUNZ, THAT A PAINTING IN HER PORTFOLIO IS GOOD, AND SHE, LOOKING AT YOU WIDE-EYED, ASKS, "DO YOU REALLY THINK SO?" YOU WONDER IF SHE IS REALLY SERIOUS. AFTER ALL, HER WORK HAS APPEARED IN A WHO'S WHO OF CANADIAN AND INTERNATIONAL MAGAZINES. AND SHE IS

a former gold medal winner at the National Magazine Awards.

But no, Kunz is not fishing for compliments. The 32-year-old Toronto illustrator is genuinely modest. Talking about her work, she says, only half jokingly, "I agonize over every job. I know it's my last and my career is finished. When it's done, I don't know if I like it or hate it. I'm just glad to put it in a Federal Express bag and send it off." This wins you over. You are both part of the league of chronic self-doubters. Of course, there is one important difference: Her worries are unfounded.

If this weren't enough to impress you, then there is her

artistic integrity. When Kunz graduated from the Ontario College of Art 11 years ago, she immediately started doing freelance illustrations for McCann-Erickson, working on a high-profile Del Monte campaign. But she decided to give this up to devote herself to editorial assignments. Where many illustrators do editorial in the hope of one day getting at the big bucks of advertising, Kunz opted

right, illustration for the **Art Directors Club of Toronto** 1985 awards show. Designer **Ann Ames** *opposite page, top:* for an article in **New Scientist** magazine about how religion and science explain the same miracles. Art director **Chris Jones**

for creative freedom. And though she stands near the top of her field, commanding from $300 to $3,000 for an illustration, she still must do the occasional ad work to help pay the bills.

It is this integrity of artistic vision that makes her illustrations so compelling, so resonant. They are not mere pretty decorations. They have depth, and they flow out of her convictions. "I try to tackle themes that have to do with social and political issues," she says. "Though lately I've been less interested in political ones, because everything that goes on in the world, all the wars, have to do with man's nature rather

left, illustration for an article in the **London Sunday Times Magazine** about losing weight. AD **Gilvrie Misstear** *overleaf,* two paintings for a story about lying in the **Washington Post Magazine.** AD **Michael Walsh**

than isolated political events. I suppose my role is to look at things in an oblique way, find [visual] parallels, and somehow tap into what keeps man repeating his mistakes. I am unhappy doing things that exist only on one level."

Still, there is no shortage of socially and politically committed artists around. What sets her apart, besides her native talent, is her relationship to the written word. Kunz is the quintessential illustrator, elucidating printed matter by painted example. For an assignment, she will carefully read the article or book, cutting through to the core of the author's intentions, and then create her illustrations according to these insights. As Teresa Fernandes, art director for *Toronto Life* magazine, notes, "She is able to read a manuscript and capture its essence."

However, this insistence on understanding sometimes makes illustration a laborious process. When painting the cover for Thomas Pynchon's complicated novel, *Gravity's Rainbow,* in 1984, she had to ponder the book's meaning for two weeks before even attempting a drawing.

As an illustrator, Kunz rarely resorts to literal renderings of text. She prefers an "oblique" approach, looking at the story from a different angle than the author, so that her painting adds another dimension to its meaning. For a rather dry *Rolling Stone* article about the Epstein-Barr virus, Kunz did a wrenching picture of a woman pierced through by coiled snakes to show the pain of a virus sufferer, which gave the piece much needed emotional impact.

Even without a story's inspiration, Kunz refuses to paint pretty pictures. A poster she did for the Canadian Opera Company's 1986/87 season does not take the obvious route, portraying a scene or a figure from a production. Instead, it encapsulates the COC's whole season in one image: that of a singer with seven arms, each representing one of the year's operas. For example, a limb wearing a bloodstained blouse with tartan border stands for Donizetti's *Lucia di Lammermoor,* and another, sporting a jester's costume and mask, for Verdi's *Rigoletto.*

Occasionally Kunz will even use her illustrations to help compensate for a particularly one-sided story. She recalls, "I did a cover for *Quest* magazine of Pierre Trudeau, just as he was leaving office. The article was written by George Woodcock, who is something of an anarchist. It was really scathing. Rather than do a gruesome portrait of him that would have paralleled the article, I just did a very normal portrait, that I guess sort of ennobled him, but which acted as a counterbalance."

As a child growing up in Kitchener/Waterloo, Ontario, Kunz was first introduced to the concept that art should have substance as well as flash by her uncle Robert Kunz, an illustrator in educational publishing. His motto, "art for education," and work taught her that illustration should never be done for its own sake, but must have a higher purpose. This was later reinforced when Kunz became a student at OCA and fell under the tutelage of New York illustrator Doug Johnson. At this time, her eyes were also opened to "the possibilities of what illustration has to offer" by *Weekend*

top, poster for the **Canadian Opera Company.** Design **Taylor & Browning** *right,* book cover for **Random House.** AD **Keith Sheridan** *far right,* magazine cover for **The Boston Globe Magazine.** AD **Lucy Bartholomay**

MICHEL TOURNIER
THE FOUR WISE MEN

top, illustration for **Regardie's** magazine. AD **Fred Woodward** *left,* for the **British Grand Prix Tennis Tournament.** Design **Hutton-Staniford Design Group** *far left,* cover for **Rolling Stone.** AD **Fred Woodward** *overleaf,* illustration for a **Rolling Stone** article about the Epstein-Barr virus. AD **Fred Woodward**

magazine, a Canadian newspaper supplement then art directed by Robert Priest and Derek Ungless, who commissioned pieces from topflight artists around the world. "I'd be looking through the magazine," says Kunz, "and there would be something by [British illustrator] Sue Coe, and I'd say, 'Oooo yuk! That's the ugliest thing I've ever seen.' Then I'd see it was an article about rape and it clicked: 'It's got to be ugly.'"

British illustrators, with their conceptual style, so impressed Kunz that in 1982 she went to England to pursue her career. But unemployment was high there and she managed to get only three assignments during her six-month stay (though she was told that this was quite a feat for a colonial newcomer). Disappointed, Kunz returned to Toronto and started sending slides of her work to prominent magazine art directors all over North America.

The ADs took notice and Kunz's career took off. Her illustrations have since appeared in such prominent foreign publications as *Esquire, New York Times Magazine, Playboy, Time,*

Newsweek, Atlantic, Sports Illustrated and *New Scientist;* and at home in *Saturday Night, Toronto Life* and *Report on Business.* Even so, she sometimes has trouble getting due recognition. Last year, more than a half-dozen New York reps wouldn't accept her as a client because her illustrations were "too editorial." "It was humiliating," says Kunz, "One woman told me, 'If you put more business suits on [your figures], then I'll see what I can do.' I *hate* drawing business suits, computers, anything with a graph."

Despite her aversion for this type of art, Kunz runs her own business very efficiently. She shares a studio in downtown Toronto with commercial photographer Brian Smale, who spends most of his time working in the States. Though far removed from the bulk of her clients, she keeps in regular contact with various art directors via phone and fax machine. When she gets an assignment and has read the manuscript, she generally forgoes rough sketches and starts drawing right away on illustration board. A copy of this is faxed to the art director. Once it is approved, she begins painting in a series of watercolor glazes, each layer sprayed with fixative. The finished painting is then shipped by courier to the client. From beginning to end, a project can be done without her leaving the studio.

PORTFOLIO

YURI DOJC

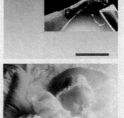

OPPISITE PAGE

TITLE
ANITA KUNZ PORTFOLIO
ART DIRECTOR
**GEORGES HAROUTIUN/
BONITA COLLINS**
EDITOR
PETER GIFFEN
ILLUSTRATOR
ANITA KUNZ
DESIGN FIRM
MAG GRAPHICS
PUBLICATION
**APPLIED ARTS
QUARTERLY**
PUBLISHER
APPLIED ARTS INC.

SEXY, FUNNY AND PAINTERLY, YURI DOJC'S PHOTOGRAPHS DEMONSTRATE A UNIQUE PERSPECTIVE
BY PETER GIFFEN

THE FIRST SENTENCE OF HIS SINGLE-PAGE AUTOBIOGRAPHY READS: "AS AN ADOLESCENT YURI DOJC WAS IN TRAINING TO BE ALBANIA'S FIRST COSMONAUT UNTIL HE DISCOVERED THAT THE PROPOSED PROPULSION SYSTEM OF THE ANXNILO 1 WAS SOLID TNT, AT WHICH TIME HE DECIDED THAT ABSENCE WAS THE BETTER PART OF VALOR." BESIDES THE CORRECT SPELLING OF DOJC'S name, the document is entirely a work of fiction. Still, it does tell you something important about the Toronto-based photographer: that he is one funny guy.

Dojc is the kind who sends his receptionist a strip-a-gram for her birthday. When he recalls the occasion, laugh lines crinkle in the corners of his eyes. This is not a nice way of saying he is aging and has crow's feet. Even though he has a handsome face looks years younger. No, they are genuine laugh lines that appear as a huge grin spreads across his face.

It is the same grin that he gives you at the end of a tour of his well-appointed downtown studio, where he works with his wife Eva, an assistant and the receptionist. He stands at the back of the building by his pride and joy, the bins of kitsch collected during his travels. Displaying in turn plastic models of the Statue of Liberty, an egg, an ice-cream cone, a two-headed monster and a dinosaur, he confides with an Eastern European accent that is not Albanian, "I have more toys than my two kids." Not only does he have them, he uses them. Two plastic marlin, for

opposite page: PERSONAL WORK SHOT AT TORONTO'S CHERRY BEACH.

right, top to bottom: PRINT AD ART DIRECTED BY **SANDRA DAMIANI** OF **ERIK TRINTER** ADVERTISING FOR **SPORTING LIFE.**

ANNUAL REPORT DESIGNED BY **BRIAN TSANG** OF **THE SPENCER FRANCEY GROUP** FOR **T.G. BRIGHT & CO.**

PRINT AD ART DIRECTED BY **PATTI DISCLASCIO** OF **LEO BURNETT** FOR **PROCTER & GAMBLE.**

TRAFFIC·STOPPERS

YURI DOJC

SPORTING LIFE

example, appear in a shoot he did for a swimming and fitness article in *Toronto Life* magazine. Or there is the picture of a miniature tyrannosaur about to chomp on the derrière of a model, which became a successful poster image.

As one might suspect, there is more to Yuri Dojc than his familiar with his work know that he is a man passionately devoted to his photographic art. Over the past 15 years, he has established a reputation for himself as a first-rate shooter with a perspective uniquely his own. "When I flip through a magazine and see a picture, I don't even need to look at the credits, I know it's Yuri's, even though it is like nothing he has done before," says Lindsay Beaudry, art director for *Toronto* magazine. The range of his work is extensive, from the humorous shots to serious advertising photos to moody and evocative personal work.

What connects it all is a fine-art sensibility. As Dela Kilian, AD at Toronto's Design Force, notes, "He has an innate sense for positioning

Her mother and grandmother wore it before her. Now Luvs will protect it for her own grandchildren.

$3ºº OFF

Luvs

74 APPLIED ARTS QUARTERLY

APPLIED ARTS QUARTERLY *75*

TITLE
YURI DOJC PORTFOLIO
ART DIRECTOR
**GEORGES HAROUTIUN/
BONITA COLLINS**
EDITOR
PETER GIFFEN
PHOTOGRAPHER
YURI DOJC
DESIGN FIRM
MAG GRAPHICS
PUBLICATION
**APPLIED ARTS
QUARTERLY**
PUBLISHER
APPLIED ARTS INC.

colors together that enhance one another and gets a great vibrancy. He also has a fabulous sense of composition, for positioning and space. He doesn't crowd his pictures."

In part, Dojc owes this strongly developed aesthetic sense to his upbringing in Czechoslovakia. His father was dean of a college and his mother was an art "fanatic," who duly infected her son. "All the books I read as a kid," he recalls, "were biographies of such artists as Picasso, Cézanne, Modigliani and Gauguin. Reading about them gave me ideals, a different lifestyle and energy. I always wanted to escape a bourgeois way of life." Today his own home contains an extensive library, and Dojc still reads compulsively, about photography, art and religion, especially Zen Buddhism. He has developed such an unrelenting enthusiasm for his chosen profession that he once ran after Richard Avedon in New York City to ask for an autograph.

Dojc's coming to Canada can be considered part of an extended vacation. In the summer of 1968, while he was holidaying in England as a young university psychology student, the Soviets invaded his country. He decided then to see more of the world, rather than return home. After a year in the British Isles, he stood one day in Trafalgar Square, trying to determine where to go next. Confronted by trade commissions from Australia, New Zealand and Canada, he opted to go to Canada, for no other reason than it brought him closer to relatives in New York.

Since then, his life has been marked by a number of such spur-of-the-moment decisions that have radically altered its course. By the winter of 1970, he had become disillusioned with Canada's harsh climate and the menial jobs he had to do in order to eke out a living. He announced his intention to move to Spain to his then-girlfriend, Eva, during a car ride. "I was so surprised," she recalls, "that I put on the brakes and we swung around 360 degrees into a ditch. He turned to me and said, 'I didn't think you cared.'" This unusual display of affection convinced Dojc to stay on, and by May of that year the two were married. For the last three years, Eva has worked with Yuri, acting as a producer, administrator, negotiator and "the buffer zone leading up to and at the shoot."

In 1971, at the suggestion of a friend, he decided to take a photography course at Toronto's Ryerson Polytechnical Institute, though he had neither camera nor money to buy one. His father in Czechoslovakia had to send him an East German Exakta. Dojc's knowledge of photography was rudimentary, to say the least. It took him three months to figure out that he needed a light meter. But he learned, and his training accelerated when he became the photo editor of Ryerson's weekly newspaper, *The Eyeopener.* "It made a hell of a difference to my future life," says Dojc. "You had your own assistant, your little studio and you had incredible responsibilities. Every week you had to come up with an issue. While the other kids were in the pub drinking, I was in the darkroom."

Leaving school in 1973, he started lugging his portfolio to every ad agency and magazine in town. Work came slowly and the first years were lean. Gradually his client base grew as word got around that he he produced work that was off-beat and, in many cases, sexy. A 1978 magazine ad campaign that he shot for Toronto clothing retailer Harry Rosen shows a young woman in various states of partial dress lying on the white-tiled floor of a washroom. She is surrounded by a group of fashionably attired men striking bizarre poses. One man, for example, is holding a cabbage in front of his head. The ads provoked an outcry from women's groups, who claimed some sort of rape fantasy was being enacted. The clothing stores were picketed and a couple of bomb threats made. According to Reid Bell, president of Reid Bell Associates, the agency responsible for the campaign, "All hell broke loose. But with all the media play, we got $200,000 or $300,000 worth of free advertising."

Dojc is bothered by the straitlaced reactions some of his racier work elicits: "It is bit sexually uptight here. There is confusion between

opposite page and above, PERSONAL WORK

15 seconds of Club Med...

could you imagine a week?

above, top to bottom: ART DIRECTOR **LIAM McDONNELL,** AGENCY **NATHAN FRASER,** CLIENT **CLUB MED.**

ART DIRECTOR **STEPHEN THURSBY,** AGENCY **DDB NEEDHAM,** CLIENT **VOLKSWAGEN CANADA.**

below, AGENCY **G&G ADVERTISING,** CLIENT **SUSAN SHOE.**

next page: SPREAD FROM *AU COURANT* MAGAZINE ART DIRECTED BY **DELA KILIAN** OF **DESIGN FORCE** FOR **HAZELTON LANES.**

76 APPLIED ARTS QUARTERLY

APPLIED ARTS QUARTERLY *77*

FALL FASHION

Big Shooters

BY SHIRLEY GREGORY & MYRON ZABOL

DESIGNER INSPIRATION FOR THE FALL 1989 BUSINESS SUIT FLOWED FROM TWO DISTINCT ERAS IN MALE FASHION. IN PRE-WORLD WAR ONE ITALY, PROMINENT MILANESE BANKERS POPULARIZED AN ELEGANT, DOUBLE-BREASTED STYLE OF SUIT, CUT TO FLATTER BROAD SHOULDERS AND LEAN HIPS. IT WAS WITH THIS PROFILE IN MIND THAT NEW YORK MENSWEAR DESIGNERS OF THE MID-'50S REBELLED AGAINST THE EXAGGERATED, BIG BAND ERA ZOOT SUIT, WITH ITS OVERSIZED SHOULDERS AND PEG PANTS, CREATING SUITS THAT WERE LOOSER AND BOXIER. THESE TWO INFLUENCES — THE 1910 *PANINARO* (TRANSLATION: CAFE WASTREL), AND THE 1955 JAZZ DEVOTEE—MERGE IN THIS FALL'S COLLECTION OF DESIGNER SUITS. AT RIGHT, HUGO BOSS'S DOUBLE-BREASTED CASH-MERE BLAZER SETS OFF A PAISLEY VEST, PAT-TERNED TIE, STRIPED SHIRT AND DOUBLE-PLEATED TROUSERS. A BOSS DOUBLE-BREASTED, CINNAMON-COLORED COAT AND PURPLE CASH-MERE SCARF COMPLETE THE TRENDY, MULTI-COL-ORED AND MULTI-TEX-TURED NEW FALL LOOK.

FROM GEORGIO ARMANI'S MANI COLLECTION COMES THIS ELEGANT, DOUBLE-BREASTED SUIT. THE WIDE LAPELS, LONGER JACKET AND SLIM LINE GIVE THIS TRADITIONAL SUIT A MODERN PRESENTATION. ALDEN OF NEW ENGLAND SHOES, COURTESY HARRY ROSEN. FOR HER, A TWO-PIECE KNIT SUIT BY PORTS INTERNATIONAL WITH HIS MANI COAT OVER HER SHOULDERS. HER JEWELRY BY ANNE KLEIN; SHOES COURTESY HOLT RENFREW.

THE FORTIES

THE MOBILIZED ECONOMY

The Second World War brought incredible heartache and sacrifice, yet the threat of fascism galvanized the nation and shaped the entire decade. Wartime production, controlled from Ottawa by the guiding hand of Munitions and Supply Minister C.D. Howe, zoomed to untold heights, and a host of industries, from aviation companies and forest-products makers to mines and shipbuilders, benefited mightily. Once unimaginable technological leaps became routine as the world careened painfully into the atomic age. And ordinary people? They either enlisted or rolled up their sleeves. And they went to banks like the one below and put their money on our way of life.

OPPISITE PAGE

TITLE
BIG SHOOTERS
ART DIRECTOR
ROD DELLA VEDOVA
WRITER
SHIRLEY GREGORY
DESIGNER
**KELLY de REGT/
CHRIS HOY**
CREATIVE DIR.
ROD DELLA VEDOVA
PHOTOGRAPHER
MYRON ZABOL
PUBLICATION
VISTA
PUBLISHER
VISTA PUBLICATIONS

THE FORTIES

WAR MEASURES ACTS

PHIL GARRATT AND HIS TEAM AT DE HAVILLAND CANADA LTD. COULDN'T BUILD MOSQUITO BOMBERS FAST ENOUGH TO SUIT MUNITIONS AND SUPPLY MINISTER C.D. HOWE. SO HOWE FOUND PEOPLE WHO COULD

Garratt (left) with a brooding Air Marshal L.S. Breadner at the unveiling of the first Canadian Mosquito in 1942. de Havilland Canada's general manager was an affable bear of a man, more suited to the cottage industry pace of Depression-era aviation than the punishing demands of wartime

The atmosphere was in marked contrast to the warm day outside as eight men filed into the de Havilland Canada Ltd. boardroom at Downsview, Ont., in May, 1943. The directors' meeting had been called by Ralph Bell, the federally appointed director-general of aircraft production, to discuss de Havilland Canada's production problems with the Mosquito bomber program. Bell, a stocky, cherubic-faced shipping executive from Halifax who had been dragooned into wartime service as a "dollar-a-year" man by Munitions and Supply Minister C.D. Howe, coldly recited the contents of cables about the Mosquito, which had gone back and forth from de Havilland Canada to Ottawa. All of them pointed to one damning fact: the program, which had begun in September, 1941, should already have yielded more than 200 finished aircraft. Now, with the spring of 1943 almost over, the company had turned out precisely 26 planes. The performance was especially disappointing in view of the fact that the company was the Canadian subsidiary of Britain's de Havilland Aircraft Co., the firm that had given birth to the Mosquito in the first place. More important, the Canadian government, as Bell pointed out, was committed to building 400 of the wooden bombers for the British Aviation Ministry by the end of August.

Such was the unforgiving nature of wartime corporate culture. After Sept. 10, 1939, when Canada joined Britain and France in declaring war on Germany, Ottawa gradually mobilized the nation's resources to produce the arms and supplies that would lead to victory. Then, in April, 1940, as Hitler's armies smashed through Denmark and Norway, Howe took on the munitions and supply portfolio and raced to create the industrial equivalent of a Nazi panzer division. Federal emergency powers became absolute as Howe and his assistants threw up new companies and commandeered others in order to meet a bewildering array of production goals. Arms-making of any type became a cutthroat, viciously political business in which the naive or the slow of foot risked being trampled.

As he sat listening to Bell, de Havilland Canada Managing Director Phil Garratt could hear footfalls. The private company had been founded as a wholly owned subsidiary by the legendary aviator and designer Sir Geoffrey de Havilland in 1928 as a foreign outpost to assemble his popular light planes. A succession of British and Canadian managers had been granted the autonomy to build the firm, and they gradually did, increasing employment at Downsview from 30 in 1935 to 195 at the outset of the Second World War. After that, however, a barrage of war programs transformed de Havilland Canada from a successful but modest aircraft builder into a large and successful military contractor.

Until the Mosquito program came along, that is. By early spring, 1943, Bell's executive assistant, Fred Smye, had been sent to Downsview to find out why plans and production were diverging. He soon drafted a report that told of overlapping managerial fiefdoms, petty disagreements over plant methods and near chaos when it came to getting timely delivery of parts, or parts that were usable at all, from a host of subcontractors.

It was clear that de Havilland Canada's problems were due to more than growing pains. Bell had already asked the board to respond to Smye's report, and Garratt, with the backing of some of his fellow directors, had bluntly said that any problems were internal and would be solved by his managers.

Mosquitos like the one in this A.J. Casson painting were fast enough that they were rarely caught by Nazi searchlights. Even if they were hit, the wooden planes were durable enough that they usually remained airborne

TITLE
THE MOBILIZED ECONOMY
ART DIRECTOR
DONNA BRAGGINS
EDITOR
THE EDITORS OF CANADIAN BUSINESS
DESIGNER
DONNA BRAGGINS
CREATIVE DIR.
JIM IRELAND
PUBLICATION
CANADIAN BUSINESS
PUBLISHER
CB MEDIA

TITLE
EXTREMES OF FORTUNE
ART DIRECTOR
DONNA BRAGGINS
EDITOR
**THE EDITORS OF
CANADIAN BUSINESS**
DESIGNER
DONNA BRAGGINS
CREATIVE DIR.
JIM IRELAND
PUBLICATION
CANADIAN BUSINESS
PUBLISHER
CB MEDIA

POWER IS **DIVERSITY** *Harold Steele*

P OWER IS MASTERY IN MORE THAN ONE TRADE, THE ABILITY TO COMMAND PROFITS AND INFLUENCE IN A VARIETY OF INDUSTRIES.

Harry Steele knows better. Better than skeptics who have doubted that he could spin gold from straw, better than adversaries who have resisted his brawny charms. Usually he's been right, even if his outspokenness has seen him vilified as Atlantic Canada's ugly capitalist.

Steele, the head of Newfoundland Capital Corp. Ltd., has spent a lifetime butting heads with convention. He cashed in a long and distinguished career in the navy in disgust over the unification of the Armed Forces. He then accepted a vice-president's post at Eastern Provincial Airways only to abruptly quit a year or so later, bitterly complaining that EPA was badly managed. Scarcely a year later, he was back with a vengeance, snapping up control of the airline and imposing his profitable vision on it.

Twenty-four years served in the Canadian military taught Newfoundland's Harry Steele a thing or two about the importance of diversification: always keep some force in reserve and never commit everything to one strategy

Steele doesn't go out of his way to make friends. A long and bitter strike at EPA in the early 1980s was a dark chapter in labor relations history. (Steele was censured by the Canadian Labour Relations Board for unfair labor practices.) And he willfully incurred the wrath of a fellow son of the Rock, Premier Brian Peckford, when he relocated EPA's headquarters from Gander, Nfld., to Dartmouth, NS, depriving Newfoundland of one of its largest employers.

Yet, as a tycoon who captures the imagination both of local peers and the man on the street, Steele has won hero status for not only managing the impossible task of turning EPA around but unloading it for a handsome $20 million onto a buyer from central Canada (the then Canadian Pacific Air Lines Ltd.). And since that 1984 sale, he has set an electric pace that makes even the Jodreys, Sobeys and Irvings appear lethargic by comparison.

In the past few years, Steele has turned his attention to trucking, shipping, hotels and auto sales. And following the model of his good friend Conrad Black, Steele is rapidly assembling a sprawling network of media properties. His *Halifax Daily News* is challenging the longtime newspaper supremacy of the Dennis family in Nova Scotia's capital, and his *Sunday Express* has broken the mighty Thomson monopoly in St. John's, Nfld. He has also gobbled up weeklies, radio stations and magazines in three Atlantic provinces and in Ontario, and is eager to pull more media properties into his stable.

The Bay Street analysts who study Newfoundland Capital, Steele's holding company, still aren't ready to believe that reliable profits can flow from such an odd assortment of activities. But Steele, the millionaire serviceman who made money even with his early investment in the bankrupt Albatross Motel in Gander, has made a career of—and a sizable fortune from—proving the skeptics wrong. And by bending his workers to his will: As he once told the the Dartmouth Chamber of Commerce: "You'll have more seasickness with your crew in their hammocks smelling bilge than on deck where the wind is free."

PORTRAIT BY JOE FLEMING

POWER IS **INDUSTRY LEADERSHIP** *Robert Stollery*

P OWER IS BEING AMONG THE BIGGEST AND BEST AT WHAT YOU DO. IT IS THE ABILITY TO SET THE PACE FOR AN ENTIRE INDUSTRY.

Robert Stollery is little known outside the construction trade and a small circle of well-heeled corporate clients. But his work is easy to spot: it is an imposing part of the skylines of major cities across North America. Stollery has built the tallest office tower in Minneapolis; Citicorp's western regional headquarters in Los Angeles; municipal landmarks such as the West Edmonton Mall; and structures of every description in Canada's Far North, where Stollery's PCL Construction Ltd. is the only contractor with a permanent presence.

A project is only as good as its foundation. Bob Stollery built PCL Construction on his own experience as a tradesman. Now PCL has climbed into North America's top five and he's constructed an empire of bricks and mortar

Stollery's philosophy is simple. PCL bids on everything, from $50 jobs to assignments that run into the hundreds of millions of dollars, and then moves heaven and earth to bring its projects in on time and on budget. It's a simple formula that has seen the $1.3-billion (sales) PCL emerge as one of the top five general contractors on the continent.

Not too many years ago, the Edmonton-based PCL was known as a builder of modest homes, garages and schoolhouses in the Prairies and in the North. Stollery has been faithful to that heritage. Soon after joining PCL in 1949 as a field engineer, he was trekking about the Northwest Territories in snowshoes helping plan the pioneer community of Inuvik. Yet while his commitment to the North is unshaken, it is Stollery who has placed the name of the firm that Ernie Poole founded in 1906 on a much bigger map.

A fierce nationalist, Stollery takes pride in being among the first Canadian contractors to wrest energy megaproject work away from the foreign contractors who once froze Canadian firms out of the business. And his success at casting off PCL's image as an exclusively western Canadian concern is evident from the green-and-gold PCL colors that grace the hoardings of the two most important office complexes now underway in Toronto, BCE Place and the 68-story Scotia Plaza. These will house the head offices of Wood Gundy Inc. and the Bank of Nova Scotia, respectively.

From Stollery's perspective, the key to maintaining his power in the hotly competitive construction industry has been to share it. Almost from the moment he bought PCL from the founder's sons in 1977, Stollery began selling off stock to his managers: some 470 employees now collectively own more than half the company. The busiest word in his vocabulary is respect—respect not only for the managers, supervisors and foremen, who because of their shareholdings are inclined to think of themselves as self-employed entrepreneurs, but for all 3,000 workers in the PCL ranks. For Stollery, a bricklayer and plasterer in his university days, a compelling rationale lies behind this respect: "There's never a moment in the day when I don't realize that PCL's growth and profits are being generated out there in the field, not here in our office."

PORTRAIT BY DENNIS NOBLE

TITLE
POWER LIST
ART DIRECTOR
JIM IRELAND
EDITOR
JOANN WEBB
DESIGNER
**DONNA BRAGGINS/
DAVID WOODSIDE**
PUBLICATION
CANADIAN BUSINESS
PUBLISHER
CB MEDIA

BLACK & WHITE

And Donatella all over.
At home with Italy's top fashion mogul

SHE NEVER RELAXES HER SENSE OF STYLE

SLEEPING BEAUTY

A fter one glimpse of Donatella Girombelli's dramatically appointed Ancona home, it is no surprise to learn that she rules Italy's most powerful fashion empire. The *padrona di casa* is clearly a woman who knows her own mind. All of the public space – foyer, living room, dining room and hall – in her small but elegant two-story residence is an uncompromising study in black and white. Black leather chairs rest on highly polished black marble floors; billowing white taffeta curtains blow in the ceiling-high windows. White classical sculptures alternate with contemporary Italian art works. And when Girombelli herself arrives, announced by the clicking of high heels, to greet an early-morning guest, she is also dressed from head to toe in black, from her Genny suit – she owns the line – to her black stockings and gleaming black leather pumps. A necklace of large pearls and matching earrings provide a dash of white. Black, white and ivory are the only colors Girombelli wears: As she explains, they satisfy not only the esthetic challenges posed by her long red hair and pale complexion, but also her "mania for organization."

PHOTOGRAPHS BY TOM LEIGHTON

With a schedule like hers, it's easy to see why Girombelli prefers to keep things simple. At 45, she heads Genny Holding Company, a burgeoning fashion house that encompasses eight lines, including Genny, Byblos and Christian Lacroix. Soaring sales and skyrocketing international popularity – last year's profits topped $220 million, with more than 1,800,000 items exported to 30 different countries – have made the company a force in the made-in-Italy phenomenon currently sweeping the world. Sitting on her gold mine, Girombelli is safely ensconced as one of a handful of superpowers in today's thriving Italian fashion industry.

But the company is about more than profits. Since its inception 27 years ago, Genny has been a fertile training ground for young talent: Both Gianni Versace and Claude Montana got their start here. And since Girombelli took the helm nine years ago (after the death of her husband, Arnaldo, who founded the company), it has also served as an expression of her taste, producing clothes as sleek, stylish and well-made as the upscale urban professionals who wear them – as the boss herself. "There is enormous res-

SET FOR PRIVATE AFFAIRS

CLASSIC PIECES...

IN CONTEMPORARY SETTINGS

pect for Girombelli," says Rietta Messina, spokeswoman for the Milan-based Association of Italian Clothing Manufacturers. "She knows how to come up with a fresh, high-style product at low prices."

At home Girombelli relaxes her schedule but not her sense of style. Two years ago she moved to Ancona, a smiling city of 110,000 on the Adriatic coast, to begin renovations on a two-floor apartment she had bought a dozen years earlier. Part of a converted 18th-century Nembrini-Gonzaga palace (once the residence of a local archbishop), the apartment sits in the heart of the town's exclusive old quarter, where dark, narrow, cobble-stoned streets alternate with sunlit Renaissance squares. Spurning interior decorators, Girombelli designed the apartment in her own image.

A carefully orchestrated mix of geometric marble ornaments in shades of ochre, white and black atop mahogany Empire pieces gives the house a subdued, almost austere tone. The round white dining-room table, a massive marble slab set on a base of carved leonine legs, signals another of Girombelli's strong preferences: She always entertains on the small scale, hosting infrequent dinners for a few close friends from outside the fashion business; she adamantly insists that her private and public life remain separate. Shunning the glittering parties in Milan, she prefers quiet weekends in her

white seaside villa 15 minutes to the south, or homey evenings in town chatting with her 18-year-old son, Leonardo, in his separate flat upstairs. She has never remarried, and has no known love interests.

But Girombelli's sumptuous sleeping quarters reveal a hidden, warmer side. Here, wood-panelled closets conceal a collection of antique silk and lace nightdresses – white, of course. And a lace-covered antique *bateau-lit* becomes a dining table each morning as she breakfasts on toast and lemon tea under the eyes of a voluptuous 19th-century nude.

"I am not an early riser," she admits, lazily pulling back a taffeta curtain to reveal the stunning view: the 15th-century Piazza del Plebiscito, dominated by the Renaissance Palace of Government, a statue of Pope Clement XII and, up a ramp of stairs, the Church of San Domenico. "I try not to let my work take over my life completely." Most workdays start at 10 a.m. or later, when her chauffeur, Antonio, drives her across town to oversee production at the Genny factory. But at least twice a week, the tempo is more hectic. Those mornings Girombelli boards an 8:20 a.m. plane for day trips to Milan, where she meets with buyers and organizes runway shows and the twice-yearly collections. "I get all the excitement I need on those trips," she says when asked why she doesn't live in Milan, Italy's fashion capital. "Besides, Ancona is a very healthy atmosphere, say they have switched to part-time work to avoid shifts that play havoc with their home lives. "There are so many better options for young women today than going into nursing," says Carol Helmstadter, the fifty-six-year-old president of the Wellesley nurses' union local. Her colleague, Sheila Croft, a thirty-year veteran of the profession and a Wellesley graduate, agrees. "I forbade my two daughters to even think of nursing as a career," she tells reporters. "People come up to me and ask me, 'Are you still nursing?' Can you imagine people asking that of a lawyer or an accountant?"

One nurse says, "I wouldn't want to be a patient anywhere right now. That's an honest statement"

It is surprising how candid and forthright these nurses are, but for many of them the time for grumbling over the lunchroom table has passed. After months of trying to work within the system, they have realized that going public is the only way to get action. They are not a group of inexperienced rookies or publicity-seeking militants. They are highly skilled and dedicated nurses. Take Carol Helmstadter, for instance—tall, poised, married to a university professor, mother of three adult daughters—she is a nursing graduate of Columbia University, class of '56, and a critical-care nurse in the neurosurgical unit at Wellesley. "It's not easy for us," she says, "but if we don't speak out for ourselves, no one is going to help us."

Incidents such as the one described by Molnar only serve to remind them how much is at stake. While no crisis took place on Wellesley's ICU that day, Molnar knows it could happen all over again: at the time, approximately 100 out of 500 nursing positions at the hospital were vacant, and this continues to be the case now. There are similar shortages at other hospitals in the city. "I wouldn't want to be a patient anywhere right now. And that's an honest statement," she says.

Early warnings about the crisis were ignored

Toronto's nursing shortage has been almost three years in the making, and it has taken as long to acknowledge and document it. In 1983 and 1984 the vacancy rate for the 16,000 nursing positions in Metro's hospitals was a fraction of one per cent. By March 1988 it had risen to 7.1 per cent. Some hospitals are much harder hit than others. Many of the suburban institutions are relatively well staffed, while in downtown Toronto, with its high concentration of teaching hospitals with specialized units, the vacancy rate can be much higher than the Metro average. Most affected are the high-stress areas: critical care, long-term care and psychiatric care.

By last summer, as the shortage worsened, 1,300 hospital beds had been closed—twelve per cent more than in 1987. While summer bed closures are customary, usually most of them reopen by fall. But last September, half of them didn't, and some institutions were literally begging for nursing applicants. Oversize ads appeared regularly on the first page of *The Globe and Mail* medical classified section. One day it would be Wellesley pleading: "We're so eager to talk to you about your career, we want you to call collect!" The next day it would be St. Michael's: "Handle with care, that's what we'll do with your nursing career."

Then in October, Albert Horlock, an Orangeville man, lay in a helicopter with a bleeding aneurysm while Toronto General Hospital and Sunnybrook Medical Centre argued for twenty minutes about which one had sufficient staff to admit him. Dr. Murray Girotti, TGH's director of trauma, stated at the time that the lack of nurses would mean cases like Horlock's would happen over and over again.

And they did. During the first week of December, Gary McDougall, who had sustained multiple compound fractures when hit by a car, waited seven hours for admission to one of the teaching hospitals equipped with the necessary cardiac facilities to operate on him. A few days before Christmas, Charles Coleman died following heart bypass surgery at St. Michael's. His operation had been postponed eleven times.

Partly as a result of intensive media coverage, the province ordered an investigation into each of the incidents amid charges at Queen's Park from the opposition that the shortage of nurses, lack of beds and waiting lists for surgery could no longer be tolerated. But Girotti, a member of a provincial task force on critical care and a chair of its subcommittee on manpower requirements, doesn't see the situation improving: "There may not be patients refused, but there will be delays. For places like Toronto we are seeing clearly that the shortage of nurses is one of the bottlenecks in accessibility."

As early as the fall of 1986, *The Toronto Star* and

OPPISITE PAGE

TITLE
BLACK AND WHITE
ART DIRECTOR
KAREN SIMPSON
DESIGNER
KAREN SIMPSON
PHOTOGRAPHER
TOM LEIGHTON
PUBLICATION
DOMINO
PUBLISHER
THE GLOBE AND MAIL

The Globe and Mail had reported that unhappy nurses were fleeing their profession. Yet at the time, such accounts were often dismissed as anecdotal and exaggerated. Figures from the College of Nurses of Ontario indicated that there was a small but steady growth of registrants, from 98,633 in 1982 to 105,729 in 1987, and Minister of Health Elinor Caplan assured the public that nursing schools were full.

People ask, 'Are you still nursing?' Can you imagine people asking that of an accountant or lawyer?

But there were warnings that all was not well. In November 1986 the ministry's advisory committee on nursing manpower undertook a special staffing survey. Its report, published in April 1987, said: "While there is an adequate overall supply of RNs and RNAs. . .employers in the Toronto area are having difficulties in filling permanent positions for RNs, particularly in critical-care units. Small increases in vacancy rates for RNs in a number of regions suggest that the province may be moving into a shortage situation."

Equally frightening was the evidence from the U.S., often a harbinger of trends in Canada, that American nursing schools were experiencing a marked decrease in enrolment. Although a similar drop had not occurred here, the difficulties Toronto hospitals were having with staffing, as well as recent strikes in two provinces, were making it harder and harder to ignore what the nurses were saying.

And Toronto nurses were intent on being heard. On November 10, 1987, the executive of Local 94 of the Ontario Nurses' Association, representing some 500 union nurses at the Wellesley Hospital, wrote directly to Elinor Caplan: "At our hospital we are desperately short-staffed. Staff nurses, particularly in the intensive care units, are working 16 to 24 hours in a row, which is unsafe for patients and destructive to nurses' morale and health. The operating room, the recovery room and the critical-care areas are especially short staffed. At one point our operating room was short 19 nurses out of 48."

Carol Helmstadter, at the time vice-president of membership for the Wellesley local, says the letter, which was signed by 200 nurses, was written out of sheer desperation. "We were in our local meeting and a number of nurses from the operating room joined us," she recalls. "They said things were just impossible. Several of the operating rooms had been closed down and we were using the emergency nursing team to do surgery in the middle of the night because they had so many patients waiting."

Helmstadter, who returned to nursing seven years ago after a twenty-year absence to raise a family, says that she and her fellow nurses agonized about going public with their complaints. "I'm not an activist by nature," she says quietly, "but I was appalled by the conditions under which nurses work now."

To its letter to Caplan, Local 94 received a terse reply suggesting that the nurses make known their quality-of-work issues through their collective agreement process. Despite repeated attempts, the local couldn't obtain a meeting with the minister. Caplan said later, "It would be inappropriate for me to meet or intervene in what is a local issue between the nursing union and hospital management." She pointed to the fact that Ontario nurses had recently negotiated a three-year collective agreement and that they are among the most highly paid nurses in the country.

Many Toronto nurses are not buying this argument. They say that it is the government, through the Ministry of Health, that funds the Ontario Hospital Association, which in turn negotiates with the 49,000-member Ontario Nurses' Association, and that they are not happy with the compensation provisions of the collective agreement. These stipulate that regular hospital RNs earn between $15.85 and $18.55 an hour; intensive care nurses, who have additional training and work with critically ill patients, make only forty cents an hour more. There's also little provision for experience. Elaine Rumleskie, for example, started nursing in 1986 at the bottom of the salary scale: $29,000. By last fall, she was making about $33,000. Ten years from now she estimates she would have been earning only $39,000, and under the present compressed salary scale that's where she'd have remained for the rest of her career. She says that, as far as she is concerned, such compensation doesn't reflect her education, her capabilities or how hard she worked.

But salaries are just one reason why nurses are leaving the profession. Margaret Molnar and Rumleskie were members of the Wellesley local's executive at the time of the letter to Caplan. Both are highly skilled critical-care nurses, the kind most sought-after by the hospitals. The decisions they made last year are indicative of why Toronto has a nursing shortage. In the spring of 1988, Molnar decided to switch from full-time work to part-time. She wanted to take a course once a week, but her full-time rotation schedule required that she alternate regularly between day and night work. "It looked to me as if I would miss half my lectures," she says. As a part-time employee she would have more control in scheduling her workdays and she would also receive up to fourteen per cent of her salary in lieu of benefits—benefits for which she was already eligible through her husband's employer.

Hospitals have begun to literally beg for nurses

Last fall, Elaine Rumleskie left nursing altogether to study political science, with plans to go into law. Her reasons are closely tied to her sense of self-esteem as a nurse. "I originally transferred to ICU because you're supposed to know a lot more to work there," she says. "I thought I'd get more respect, but the nurses who had been there for thirty years were rarely called upon to act as consultants in any patient decisions." The defections from the profession are not lost on the nursing leadership. "The problem is with society's attitude to women's work," says Glenna Cole Slattery, the chief executive officer of the Ontario Nurses' Association, whose own daughter gave up nursing for a job in the insurance industry. "The loss of women like Isabella is sad," says Cole Slattery, whose happiest hours were spent as a bedside nurse. "My daughter loved the work but hated the system."

She charges that nurses have very little say in their own industry. "Nursing is ninety-eight-per-cent female, and yet there are fewer than two per cent women on the hospital boards as trustees. I would further submit to you that none of them are nurses." Almost as if to compensate for the lack of nursing clout in the hospital hierarchy, Cole Slattery takes great pride in ONA's brand-new $10-million Toronto headquarters, which contains her office. "Bought and paid for," she says briskly. "Thrifty women, these nurses." Grey-haired and small in stature, photos of her grandchildren arranged around her desk, Cole Slattery may appear to be the prototypical nurse. But she represents a new voice in nursing—that of unionism and feminism. "As soon as the caregiver starts to care for herself, she stops being liked," she says. "Why make nurses feel guilty? They're not guilty; they're angry. Is the public waiting for a nurse to make a fatal mistake from fatigue and burnout? Does the health care system have to fall to its knees before we see some changes?"

Pointing out that nurses have been subsidizing the health care system with their time and talents since the days of Florence Nightingale, she says, "There's no nursing shortage. There's a shortage of nurses who are willing to work under the conditions that are in hospitals today, for the money that they're paid."

In March 1988, the nurses' union published a position paper, *An Industry in Crisis: Ontario Nurses Speak Out on the Nursing Shortage*, based on the findings of a study done for the union by Goldfarb Consultants. The report warned that "one in seven working nurses, one in six in Toronto, say that they will probably not keep working as nurses. As many as one in four will leave their present job for a different type of facility."

Although the Goldfarb report made clear the nurses were fed up with the way they were being treated, a wait-and-see attitude prevailed among those in a position to act on the findings. One reason for this inaction was that during 1988 just about every other organization in the province with any jurisdiction in the nursing field had a manpower task force examining the shortage, including the Ontario Ministry of Health, the Registered Nurses' Association of Ontario (RNAO) and the Hospital Council of/*Continued on page 64*

TITLE
FLORENCE DOESN'T WORK HERE ANYMORE
ART DIRECTOR
TERESA FERNANDES/ JANICE GOLDBERG
EDITOR
MARQ de VILLIERS
DESIGNER
JANICE GOLDBERG
ILLUSTRATOR
LANE SMITH
PUBLICATION
TORONTO LIFE
PUBLISHER
KEY PUBLISHERS CO. LTD.

永尚太

VEILED MYSTERY
MODEST, BUT SUGGESTIVE OF
THE BODY BENEATH

Yohji Yamamoto wool
V-necked blouse and cropped
pants, left, and
sleeveless dress with slit
back and layered,
colored underskirts, right.

孤近太

A BOXY JACKET
A SOFTLY SWALLOWTAILED BLOUSE
DRAMATIC EXITS

Comme des Garçons single-
breasted jacket with transparent
sleeves over a tank top
and gathered bloomers, left.
Issey Miyake pleated
blouse with back V and three-
quarter sleeves, right.

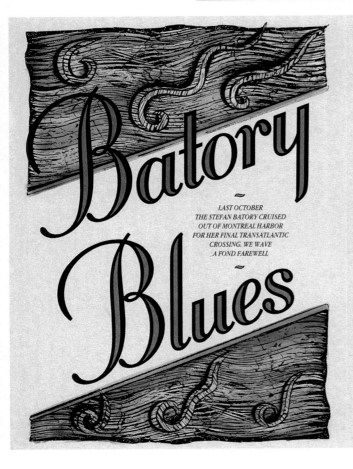

By AUDREY THOMAS · Illustrations by FRANK VIVA

I'm an emotional person and somehow I wanted more than this: fireboats spouting plumes of water, crowds waving white hankies, a band on the quay, dignitaries shaking hands with the captain before hurrying down the gangway; maybe an ambassador or, at the very least, Joe Clark. It is October 7, 1987, 4:42 p.m. (I know because I ask a young man with a digital watch) and the Polish ocean liner the *Stefan Batory* is moving slowly away from Montreal's Iberville Passenger Terminal, Pier 5, to begin voyage number 140, her last regular crossing of the North Atlantic. Nine days from now she is scheduled to sail up the Thames to Tilbury Landing Stage, disgorge passengers for Britain, then on later that day to Rotterdam and by October 20 dock in Poland. Except for a lengthy cruise down the east coast of South America from November 7 to January 4 and a West Indies/Cuba cruise from January 17 to March 22, she is finished, about to be retired, victim not only of old age and the high cost of fuel but also of the generally accepted belief that time is money and that being so, who could possibly afford to take a ship that is so slow and on which you are most unlikely to meet "useful" contacts.

The ship's resident band has been on deck for some time, playing assorted un-Polish tunes such as "Alexander's Ragtime Band," "It's a Long, Long Way to Tipperary" and "Bill Bailey, Won't You Please Come Home." Rumor has it that someone or perhaps more than someone has defected. However, baggage is still being loaded – huge crates marked Gdynia, Gdynia, Gdynia. Poles going home are obviously making good use of the generous baggage allowance. The crates are big enough to hold major appliances or even pianos. But suddenly it's all done, the hatches covered, the gangway pulled away and the band switches to the Polish national anthem (whose opening bars sound like a song I knew as a kid, "Down by the Station"). The small crowd that has waited – relatives, people from the North American agent's office of the shipping company, a dark-haired man with a briefcase – begins to wave. Someone has put up a large red-and-white banner: Batory Good Ambassador for Poland/Farewell with Fond Memories. There are a few streamers attached to the boat and I have brought some with me; I give some to my friend Ellen, who is travelling with me, and to the man with the digital watch. A Polish woman rushes up. "Please, where do you get those?" I tell her I brought them and pull off some more rounds for her and her friend. "No, no," she protests, but I say, "Yes, yes," and we laugh and exchange kisses. "Luftschlangen," the package says – they are made in Germany. "Schwer entflammbar," flameproof. The woman is about 60. I quickly turn the package so the German writing doesn't show. Ellen, the two women, myself, the man with the digital watch, lean over the rail, throw our rainbow colored streamers. Goodbye, goodbye. The dark-haired man with the briefcase follows us down to the end of the pier. "Jack! Jack!" a woman yells, "get another ship!" He gives the thumbs-up sign, but it's hard to believe him.

This is not only the last regular transatlantic crossing of the *Stefan Batory* but the last time, perhaps, that any passenger liner will sail in or out of Montreal. Thousands of people have crossed on the *Stefan Batory*; she indeed has been "Good Ambassador for Poland," both the original *Batory* and this one, bought from the Dutch in 1968, over 40 years of service altogether. As an ex-American who left that beautiful, benighted, Commie-hating country a long time ago (by ship, I might add) and emigrated from England to Montreal with an English husband and 4½-month-old daughter (again by ship, the old *Empress of France*), it has always delighted me that ships from the Eastern bloc were free to dock in Canada. And it occurs to me now that just as a matter of diplomacy, Canada might do well to help Jack find another ship.

"What we have here," I say to Ellen as we leave the rail and go down to have our first drink of Bison Brand vodka, "is not just a ship but a symbol." Our friend Mick Henry sees us and comes over to join us. He is grinning from ear to ear. He's off to Berlin for the winter. "Oh, isn't it wonderful," he says. He has been on this ship before, as have I. Ellen has never been on any ship. By nightfall I can see that she is taking to shipboard life like – like what? "Like a duck to water!" she suggests. October 6 was the full moon, the Hunter's Moon; from where we stand on deck, it bobs in the sky as though being bounced gently by the languid hand of God. Couples are strolling, groups already forming; music is floating up to us whenever a door is opened: "Moon River," "I Could Have Danced All Night." Already some couples are doing the quickstep or fox trot in the Grand Lounge. The same songs I heard on my last two voyages – golden oldies. The moon a golden oldie too, up there in the October sky. In some ways travelling on the *Stefan Batory* is like the reverse of what happened to Mia Farrow in *The Purple Rose of Cairo*: we enter the movie's world, a movie of the 1950s.

The CBC is on board with a camera crew – they will get off tomorrow with the pilot. Our tablemates, Fran and Tom, have asked them if they want a "human interest" story. They met on the *Stefan Batory*, on a westward crossing, in the 1970s. She had been divorced a long time when she met him and he was a widower, 17 years older. Fran is one of those people everyone talks to, and during the voyage she will provide us with all kinds of information (such as the presence of a poodle in Cabin X, strictly forbidden, who is given plates of food by a steward after money has changed hands beneath a dinner napkin). I tell them I saw the CBC interviewing a woman who was wearing a homemade sweater with a little passenger liner knitted into it. I couldn't get close enough to see if it was the *Stefan Batory* sailing on that dark blue woollen ocean. I'm nearsighted and was afraid the woman would think I was trying to nuzzle her breast. Fran says we are all going to be on *The Journal*, so when the television crew pans the dining room, we wave like mad and make faces, hoping the dear ones at home might see us. There is a Polish television crew as well and they remain for the whole voyage. Media types look like media types any-

OPPISITE PAGE

TITLE
SUN SIGNS

ART DIRECTOR
KAREN SIMPSON

DESIGNER
KAREN SIMPSON

PHOTOGRAPHER
WALTER CHIN

PUBLICATION
DOMINO

PUBLISHER
THE GLOBE AND MAIL

TITLE
BATORY BLUES

ART DIRECTOR
NADIA MARYNIAK

EDITOR
JACK McIVER

DESIGNER
NADIA MARYNIAK

ILLUSTRATOR
FRANK VIVA

PUBLICATION
DESTINATIONS

PUBLISHER
THE GLOBE AND MAIL

where, not just the way they dress (casually chic) but the way their eyes move around a space. Always looking for a good story. (Always hanging around the bar.) Around 2:50 a.m. on Saturday we pass through the Strait of Belle Isle and enter the North Atlantic. Now we are truly on an ocean voyage and our menus will say, at the bottom, "Saturday, October 10, Atlantic Ocean." There is a particular thrill associated with this, for we are now in the waters that many sailors consider the most dangerous of the world.

The brochure advertising the *Stefan Batory*'s Farewell Cruise program describes the ship as a "charming, graceful old lady, abounding in woodwork and brass." Peter Kohler, a tall, thin young man who is vaguely 1920s in dress and manner (cloth cap, tweed jacket, rather superior) and a fanatic about passenger liners (he was on the last sailing of the *France* and can be seen on deck wearing his *France* T-shirt under his jacket surrounded by clumps of people asking him questions), gives two excellent lectures. He

says that the ship represents a "lost era of craftsmanship." It is neither ultramodern nor frumpy, rather like what I imagine a good English club would be. Beautiful wood panelling, comfortable chairs, covered in leather or wool, arranged for conversation or solitude. Well-stocked bars, although a wealthy woman has brought her own cocktail onions for vodka Gibsons, with drinks at dangerously low prices. You don't sign for the drinks, however, you pay in Polish scrip or U.S. dollars. And, as in a good club, once

you are in there is no further class distinction. The *Stefan Batory* is a determinedly one-class ship. This is not strictly a socialist innovation, for the Holland America Line ship the *Maasdam*, which later became the *Stefan Batory*, was also a one-class ship except for 59 superior cabins on the Boat Deck. Many of my college friends travelled on the *Maasdam* and her sister ship, the *Ryndam*, in the 1950s, and one of the things they loved was having the run of the ship. Even that tiny first class was done away with after the Poles re-

Getting Away SAY GOODBYE TO THE SAFE AND SEDATE AS CLOTHES BARE ALL FOR SPRING. BRIGHT, FANCIFUL LEATHERS TAKE YOU BY THE HAND IN STYLE

Whimsical leather bag with steamboat appliqué and smoke-cloud closure, Hermes. Colorful beaded clutch in an African motif, Renaud Pellegrino.

Left page, top to bottom; pink leather stacked cones, Ipso Factor. Evening bag with giant satin flower, Joceiyne Imbert for Jean Louis Imbert. Fuchsia triangle bag, Jean Marlaix for La Bagagerie. Right page, top to bottom; gold leather pouch, Philippe Model. Accordion bag, Ipso Factor. Buttoned leather dice on a long string, Patrick Kelly.

Polka-dot door-opener (below left). Lacroix's eye-boggling version of the Kelly, clasped in rhinestones for swanning in the spotlight, $1,395. (Right) the wing tip like never before by Emma Hope, $295. Both at Creeds. Acid green chiffon scarf, $98. From Little Lanes at Hazelton Lanes. Genny's red satin wisp of a dancing shoe (below right) keeps company with Prada's no-nonsense handbag as briefcase. Slipper, $275. At Genny. Bag, $650. At Holt Renfrew.

FIRST additions

*When fashion goes classic, the trimmings take centre stage.
This season even the chicest chemise basks in the reflected glory
of the real attention-getters, accessories that make their own look-at-me
statements. Some of them are brash. Some of them are circumspect.
But they all aim to take glorious advantage of every situation.*

PHOTOGRAPHED BY SHUN SASABUCHI

OPPISITE PAGE

TITLE
CARRIED AWAY
ART DIRECTOR
**KAREN SIMPSON/
MARTHA WEAVER**
DESIGNER
MARTHA WEAVER
PHOTOGRAPHER
MITCHELL FEINBERG
PUBLICATION
DOMINO
PUBLISHER
THE GLOBE AND MAIL

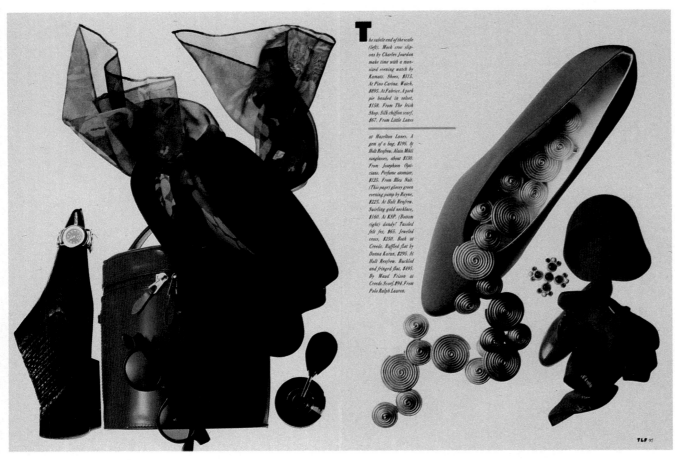

The subtle end of the scale (left). Mock croc slip-ons by Charles Jourdan make time with a man-sized evening watch by Kamatz. Shoes, $115. At Pino Carina. Watch, $895. At Fabrice. A pork pie banded in velvet, $158. From The Irish Shop. Silk chiffon scarf, $67. From Little Lanes at Hazelton Lanes. A gem of a bag, $195. At Holt Renfrew. Alain Mikli sunglasses, about $130. From Josephson Opticians. Perfume atomizer, $125. From Bleu Nuit. (This page) glossy green evening pump by Rayne, $225. At Holt Renfrew. Swirling gold necklace, $160. At KSP. (Bottom right) dandy! Tasseled felt fez, $65. Jeweled cross, $250. Both at Creeds. Ruffled flat by Donna Karan, $295. At Holt Renfrew. Buckled and fringed flat, $495. By Maud Frizon at Creeds. Scarf, $94. From Polo Ralph Lauren.

TITLE
FIRST ADDITIONS
ART DIRECTOR
BRAD MacIVER
EDITOR
TIM BLANKS
DESIGNER
ALEX GOSSE
PHOTOGRAPHER
SHUN SASABUCHI
PUBLICATION
TORONTO LIFE FASHION
PUBLISHER
**KEY PUBLISHERS
CO. LTD.**

Il Pleut

(Ômbrēla). Also umbrellia,

umbrilla, umbrello

umbrillo, umbrellow, umbrella

From umbra, Shade

Left. Eliza Doolittle meets Yhoji Yamamoto in a black wool parasol. Above. Black exploding tassels printed on white nylon, by Chantal Thomas.

DOMINO

Above, tiny pompoms and sheer chiffon on bamboo frame, by Jean-Paul Gaultier. Right. Georges Grespar's peaked parasole trimmed in ruched chiffon.

DOMINO

Is your heart at rest,

Now you have got a

Shadow, an umbrella?

~ fletcher 1624 ~

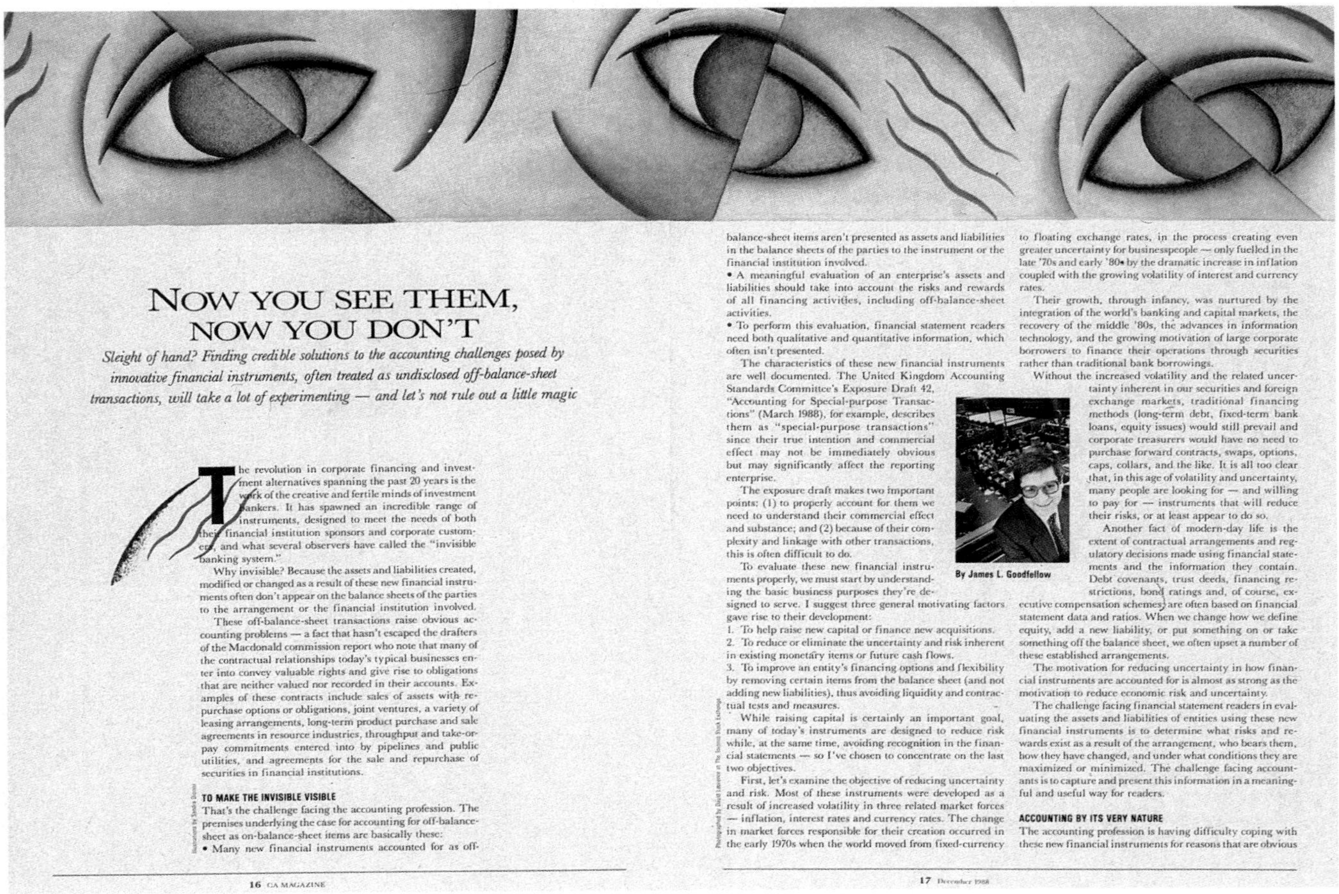

NOW YOU SEE THEM, NOW YOU DON'T

Sleight of hand? Finding credible solutions to the accounting challenges posed by innovative financial instruments, often treated as undisclosed off-balance-sheet transactions, will take a lot of experimenting — and let's not rule out a little magic

The revolution in corporate financing and investment alternatives spanning the past 20 years is the work of the creative and fertile minds of investment bankers. It has spawned an incredible range of instruments, designed to meet the needs of both their financial institution sponsors and corporate customers, and what several observers have called the "invisible banking system."

Why invisible? Because the assets and liabilities created, modified or changed as a result of these new financial instruments often don't appear on the balance sheets of the parties to the arrangement or the financial institution involved.

These off-balance-sheet transactions raise obvious accounting problems — a fact that hasn't escaped the drafters of the Macdonald commission report who note that many of the contractual relationships today's typical businesses enter into convey valuable rights and give rise to obligations that are neither valued nor recorded in their accounts. Examples of these contracts include sales of assets with repurchase options or obligations, joint ventures, a variety of leasing arrangements, long-term product purchase and sale agreements in resource industries, throughput and take-or-pay commitments entered into by pipelines and public utilities, and agreements for the sale and repurchase of securities in financial institutions.

TO MAKE THE INVISIBLE VISIBLE

That's the challenge facing the accounting profession. The premises underlying the case for accounting for off-balance-sheet as on-balance-sheet items are basically these:

- Many new financial instruments accounted for as off-balance-sheet items aren't presented as assets and liabilities in the balance sheets of the parties to the instrument or the financial institution involved.
- A meaningful evaluation of an enterprise's assets and liabilities should take into account the risks and rewards of all financing activities, including off-balance-sheet activities.
- To perform this evaluation, financial statement readers need both qualitative and quantitative information, which often isn't presented.

The characteristics of these new financial instruments are well documented. The United Kingdom Accounting Standards Committee's Exposure Draft 42, "Accounting for Special-purpose Transactions" (March 1988), for example, describes them as "special-purpose transactions" since their true intention and commercial effect may not be immediately obvious but may significantly affect the reporting enterprise.

The exposure draft makes two important points: (1) to properly account for them we need to understand their commercial effect and substance; and (2) because of their complexity and linkage with other transactions, this is often difficult to do.

By James L. Goodfellow

To evaluate these new financial instruments properly, we must start by understanding the basic business purposes they're designed to serve. I suggest three general motivating factors gave rise to their development:

1. To help raise new capital or finance new acquisitions.
2. To reduce or eliminate the uncertainty and risk inherent in existing monetary items or future cash flows.
3. To improve an entity's financing options and flexibility by removing certain items from the balance sheet (and not adding new liabilities), thus avoiding liquidity and contractual tests and measures.

While raising capital is certainly an important goal, many of today's instruments are designed to reduce risk while, at the same time, avoiding recognition in the financial statements — so I've chosen to concentrate on the last two objectives.

First, let's examine the objective of reducing uncertainty and risk. Most of these instruments were developed as a result of increased volatility in three related market forces — inflation, interest rates and currency rates. The change in market forces responsible for their creation occurred in the early 1970s when the world moved from fixed-currency to floating exchange rates, in the process creating even greater uncertainty for businesspeople — only fuelled in the late '70s and early '80s by the dramatic increase in inflation coupled with the growing volatility of interest and currency rates.

Their growth, through infancy, was nurtured by the integration of the world's banking and capital markets, the recovery of the middle '80s, the advances in information technology, and the growing motivation of large corporate borrowers to finance their operations through securities rather than traditional bank borrowings.

Without the increased volatility and the related uncertainty inherent in our securities and foreign exchange markets, traditional financing methods (long-term debt, fixed-term bank loans, equity issues) would still prevail and corporate treasurers would have no need to purchase forward contracts, swaps, options, caps, collars, and the like. It is all too clear that, in this age of volatility and uncertainty, many people are looking for — and willing to pay for — instruments that will reduce their risks, or at least appear to do so.

Another fact of modern-day life is the extent of contractual arrangements and regulatory decisions made using financial statements and the information they contain. Debt covenants, trust deeds, financing restrictions, bond ratings and, of course, executive compensation schemes are often based on financial statement data and ratios. When we change how we define equity, add a new liability, or put something on or take something off the balance sheet, we often upset a number of these established arrangements.

The motivation for reducing uncertainty in how financial instruments are accounted for is almost as strong as the motivation to reduce economic risk and uncertainty.

The challenge facing financial statement readers in evaluating the assets and liabilities of entities using these new financial instruments is to determine what risks and rewards exist as a result of the arrangement, who bears them, how they have changed, and under what conditions they are maximized or minimized. The challenge facing accountants is to capture and present this information in a meaningful and useful way for readers.

ACCOUNTING BY ITS VERY NATURE

The accounting profession is having difficulty coping with these new financial instruments for reasons that are obvious

16 CA MAGAZINE — 17 December 1988

OPPISITE PAGE

TITLE
IL PLEUT
ART DIRECTOR
KAREN SIMPSON
DESIGNER
KAREN SIMPSON
PHOTOGRAPHER
SATOSHI SAIKUSA
PUBLICATION
DOMINO
PUBLISHER
THE GLOBE AND MAIL
HAND LETTERING
DONALD ROBERTSON

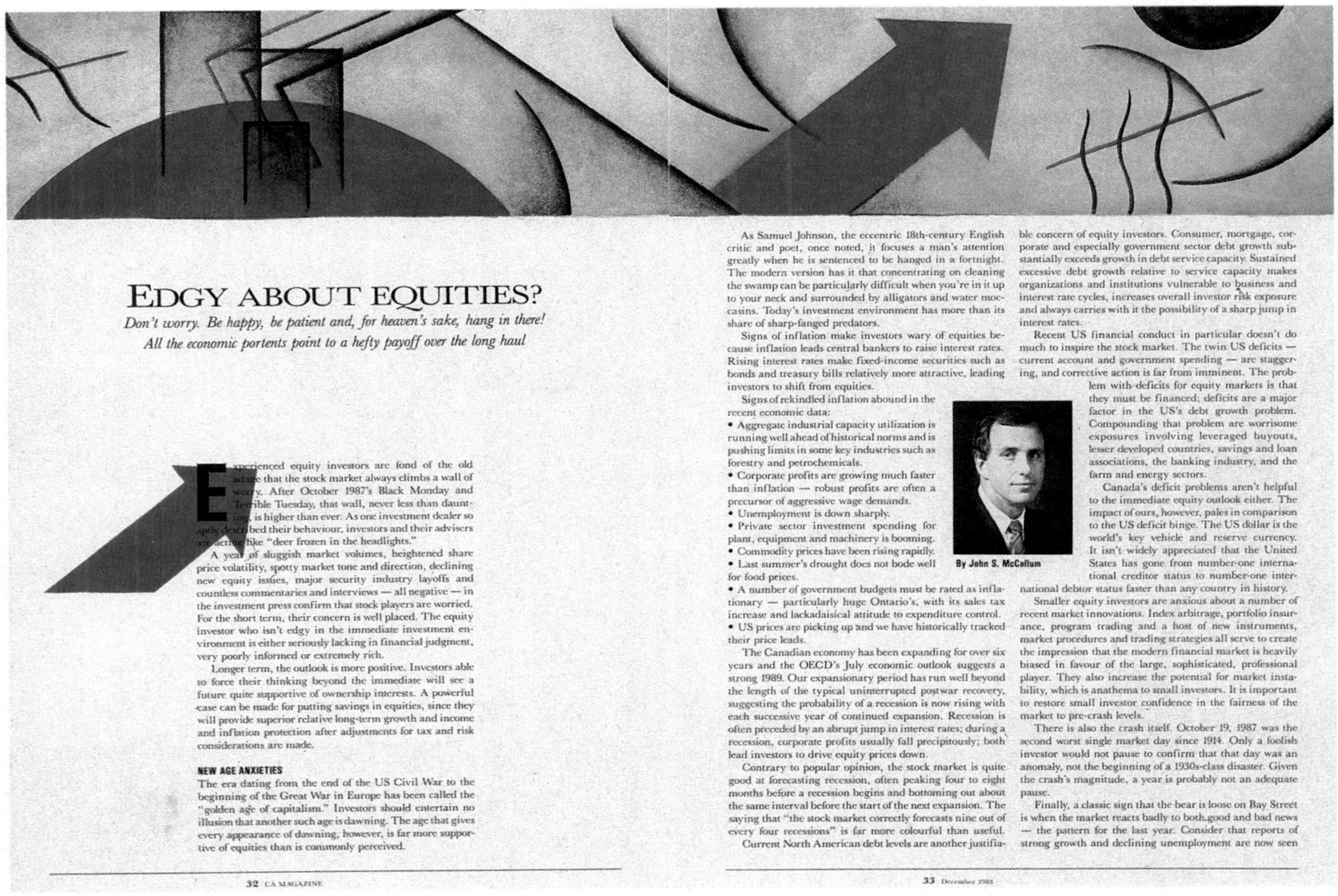

EDGY ABOUT EQUITIES?

Don't worry. Be happy, be patient and, for heaven's sake, hang in there! All the economic portents point to a hefty payoff over the long haul

Experienced equity investors are fond of the old adage that the stock market always climbs a wall of worry. After October 1987's Black Monday and Terrible Tuesday, that wall, never less than daunting, is higher than ever. As one investment dealer so aptly described their behaviour, investors and their advisers are acting like "deer frozen in the headlights."

A year of sluggish market volumes, heightened share price volatility, spotty market tone and direction, declining new equity issues, major security industry layoffs and countless commentaries and interviews — all negative — in the investment press confirm that stock players are worried. For the short term, their concern is well placed. The equity investor who isn't edgy in the immediate investment environment is either seriously lacking in financial judgment, very poorly informed or extremely rich.

Longer term, the outlook is more positive. Investors able to force their thinking beyond the immediate will see a future quite supportive of ownership interests. A powerful case can be made for putting savings in equities, since they will provide superior relative long-term growth and income and inflation protection after adjustments for tax and risk considerations are made.

NEW AGE ANXIETIES

The era dating from the end of the US Civil War to the beginning of the Great War in Europe has been called the "golden age of capitalism." Investors should entertain no illusion that another such age is dawning. The age that gives every appearance of dawning, however, is far more supportive of equities than is commonly perceived.

As Samuel Johnson, the eccentric 18th-century English critic and poet, once noted, it focuses a man's attention greatly when he is sentenced to be hanged in a fortnight. The modern version has it that concentrating on cleaning the swamp can be particularly difficult when you're in it up to your neck and surrounded by alligators and water moccasins. Today's investment environment has more than its share of sharp-fanged predators.

Signs of inflation make investors wary of equities because inflation leads central bankers to raise interest rates. Rising interest rates make fixed-income securities such as bonds and treasury bills relatively more attractive, leading investors to shift from equities.

Signs of rekindled inflation abound in the recent economic data:

- Aggregate industrial capacity utilization is running well ahead of historical norms and is pushing limits in some key industries such as forestry and petrochemicals.
- Corporate profits are growing much faster than inflation — robust profits are often a precursor of aggressive wage demands.
- Unemployment is down sharply.
- Private sector investment spending for plant, equipment and machinery is booming.
- Commodity prices have been rising rapidly.
- Last summer's drought does not bode well for food prices.
- A number of government budgets must be rated as inflationary — particularly huge Ontario's, with its sales tax increase and lackadaisical attitude to expenditure control.
- US prices are picking up and we have historically tracked their price leads.

By John S. McCallum

The Canadian economy has been expanding for over six years and the OECD's July economic outlook suggests a strong 1989. Our expansionary period has run well beyond the length of the typical uninterrupted postwar recovery, suggesting the probability of a recession is now rising with each successive year of continued expansion. Recession is often preceded by an abrupt jump in interest rates; during a recession, corporate profits usually fall precipitously; both lead investors to drive equity prices down.

Contrary to popular opinion, the stock market is quite good at forecasting recession, often peaking four to eight months before a recession begins and bottoming out about the same interval before the start of the next expansion. The saying that "the stock market correctly forecasts nine out of every four recessions" is far more colourful than useful.

Current North American debt levels are another justifiable concern of equity investors. Consumer, mortgage, corporate and especially government sector debt growth substantially exceeds growth in debt service capacity. Sustained excessive debt growth relative to service capacity makes organizations and institutions vulnerable to business and interest rate cycles, increases overall investor risk exposure and always carries with it the possibility of a sharp jump in interest rates.

Recent US financial conduct in particular doesn't do much to inspire the stock market. The twin US deficits — current account and government spending — are staggering, and corrective action is far from imminent. The problem with deficits for equity markets is that they must be financed; deficits are a major factor in the US's debt growth problem. Compounding that problem are worrisome exposures involving leveraged buyouts, lesser developed countries, savings and loan associations, the banking industry, and the farm and energy sectors.

Canada's deficit problems aren't helpful to the immediate equity outlook either. The impact of ours, however, pales in comparison to the US deficit binge. The US dollar is the world's key vehicle and reserve currency. It isn't widely appreciated that the United States has gone from number-one international creditor status to number-one international debtor status faster than any country in history.

Smaller equity investors are anxious about a number of recent market innovations. Index arbitrage, portfolio insurance, program trading and a host of new instruments, market procedures and trading strategies all serve to create the impression that the modern financial market is heavily biased in favour of the large, sophisticated, professional player. They also increase the potential for market instability, which is anathema to small investors. It is important to restore small investor confidence in the fairness of the market to pre-crash levels.

There is also the crash itself. October 19, 1987 was the second worst single market day since 1914. Only a foolish investor would not pause to confirm that that day was an anomaly, not the beginning of a 1930s-class disaster. Given the crash's magnitude, a year is probably not an adequate pause.

Finally, a classic sign that the bear is loose on Bay Street is when the market reacts badly to both good and bad news — the pattern for the last year. Consider that reports of strong growth and declining unemployment are now seen

32 CA MAGAZINE — 33 December 1988

TITLE
SERIES ON FINANCIAL INSTRUMENTS
ART DIRECTOR
JUDY MARGOLIS
DESIGNER
CHRISTINE STOCKBAUER
ILLUSTRATOR
SANDRA DIONISI
TYPOGRAPHER
JOHN SHARDALOW
PUBLICATION
CA MAGAZINE
PUBLISHER
CA MAGAZINE

TITLE
THE DEFINITIVE EYE
ART DIRECTOR
JIM IRELAND
EDITOR
JOCELYN LAURENCE
DESIGNER
JIM IRELAND
PHOTOGRAPHER
ARNAUD MAGGS
PUBLICATION
CANADIAN ART
PUBLISHER
**KEY PUBLISHERS
CO. LTD.**

A Canadian Art portfolio
By Arnaud Maggs

The Definitive Eye

The five Canadian artists who appear on the following pages represent some of the best this country has to offer. Renée Van Halm, John Clark, Allyson Clay, Guido Molinari and Bernie Miller are all producing work that is individually diverse but uniformly intelligent and engaging. What makes this portfolio particularly special is the participation of photographer Arnaud Maggs. Himself an artist, this is in fact Maggs' first commercial shoot in almost a decade.

RENÉE VAN HALM
I've always worked within architectural contexts using a variety of images. This Jack Bush painting is part of a larger installation called *Recreation*. The piece was a direct response to my interest in contextualizing paintings. I wanted to talk about the relationship between paintings and other kinds of consumer objects—how we accommodate them and the extent to which the display of these objects adds a lot to their meaning and preservation.

JOHN CLARK
I work with images that often come from the imagination and all the things the imagination can unlock, which include possible narratives, memory and dreams. Since I moved to Alberta, I've been using clearer, stronger colors because the light here is particularly beautiful and clear. When I lived in Nova Scotia, the light was very grey and I did grey paintings. I don't have the sense of a closed studio. I'm directly influenced by my environment and I welcome that.

STAN WATTS
TRUCK DRIVER, CANADIAN CARTAGE

Watts has hauled everything from steel to groceries on every major highway that feeds into Toronto, as well as on all major downtown streets, for fifteen years. He currently drives a 10,000-pound, eighteen-wheel tractor trailer—one of the biggest rigs on the road (it can haul as much as 60,000 pounds). Traffic volume and congestion, illegally parked cars (Watts has had to go from door-to-door in search of drivers to remove their vehicles so he can make a delivery) and narrow intersections, roads and alleys (Watts has backed his rig into alleys that are so narrow he can't wedge a finger between the side mirror and the wall) make truck driving in Toronto, he says, "so frustrating you could scream sometimes." As well, inadequate docking facilities mean that drivers often have to wait in line for hours to make deliveries—which ties up traffic and ultimately adds costs to merchandise.

Apart from the city's physical restrictions (roads were designed before eighteen-wheelers were even conceived of), Watts, like many others, cites driver discourtesy as a major headache. Watts says drivers often fail to let trucks into traffic—both downtown and on freeways—or cut them off, forcing them to gear down through fifteen to twenty gears (depending on how fast they were going). "It

takes ages to build up your speed again," he says, "which slows down traffic."

A TRUCK DRIVER'S SOLUTIONS
◊ Ban parking on all major downtown business streets from 7 to 9 a.m.;
◊ Restrict parking on all major downtown business streets to one side only;
◊ To decrease traffic congestion and increase the number of people using car pools, restrict one lane on the Gardiner Expressway, the Don Valley Parkway and highways 401 and 427 to cars with three or more passengers between 7 and 9 a.m. and 4 and 6 p.m.;
◊ Increase the number of traffic police so rules and regulations can be better enforced;
◊ Extend downtown shipping and receiving hours from 4 to 8 p.m. to avoid competing with rush-hour traffic;
◊ To crack down on freeway speeding and dangerous lane changes, give Department of Transportation drivers authority to use radar and issue speeding tickets;
◊ Build no-exit express lanes (a skyway?) for Highway 401 from Dixie Road to Markham Road (where traffic clogs up during rush hour).

- - - - - - -

CHRIS WATSON
VAN DRIVER, PUROLATOR

A ten-year veteran of downtown driving, Watson says, "Toronto's not growing bigger, it's getting taller," and the resulting increase in traffic has left parking for commercial vehicles—especially couriers—high and dry. Watson says there's simply no space left on the streets. Thus couriers are forced to park illegally, or to park blocks away from their destinations. In the early morning, between 7 and 9:30 a.m., the tow-away zones make their lives even more difficult.

A COURIER'S SOLUTIONS
◊ Between 6 and 7 a.m. restrict the downtown core to commercial traffic only so that couriers and trucks can get

a head start on deliveries (and exit before rush hour begins);
◊ Implement one or two commercial-vehicle-only unloading zones for each major block within the downtown core;
◊ To encourage more people to leave their cars at home and make greater use of car pools, insurance companies should offer lower rates to car-pool passengers and drivers;
◊ Ensure all downtown buildings have street numbers clearly posted. Traffic is often backed up by drivers—both commercial and commuter—who slow down while searching for their specific destinations.

- - - - - - -

EARL FRIMETH
TAXI DRIVER, DIAMOND TAXI

Frimeth has driven a cab throughout downtown for more than thirty years. He says there are too few roads and a lack of enforcement of existing traffic laws. Frimeth looks back wistfully to the days of Metro chairman Fred Gardiner, who ignored road-building naysayers (he called them "panty-waists") and went ahead and constructed some of Toronto's major throughways, including the Don Valley Parkway and what became the Gardiner Expressway. He blames members of Metro council for our traffic woes, saying they are too concerned with getting reelected (thus caving in to local pressures) and not concerned enough with building roads that will benefit all citizens of the greater Toronto area.

A CAB DRIVER'S SOLUTIONS
◊ Increase the number of Green Hornets so current no-stopping and no-parking laws can be better enforced;

◊ Remove all restrictions to entering neighborhood roads during certain hours: "People shouldn't have the right to block off their streets";
◊ Build the Spadina Expressway: "It'll take traffic out of residential areas";
◊ No parking at all on major business streets (including Kingston Road and the Danforth) during rush hours;
◊ To encourage more people to go downtown by GO Transit, outlying stations should provide free parking (in expanded lots) and, as an added incentive, GO commuters should ride free on Fridays (governments would provide a subsidy);
◊ Build the cross-town subway line across Sheppard Avenue;
◊ Give double-parked cars higher fines than cars parked illegally at curbs;
◊ Large truck shipments downtown should be at night.

- - - - - - -

ANDY McCABE
DRIVER-ATTENDANT, METRO AMBULANCE

Andy McCabe has been driving his ambulance in the downtown core for seven years, a period during which he's noticed a "phenomenal increase in vehicular and pedestrian traffic." While congestion (which can double the time it takes to reach an accident victim) and poorly maintained roads (which can be extremely dangerous for spinal-injury patients) rate high on his list of major traffic problems, lack of driver courtesy and ignorance of the rules of driving are number one. Increasingly, McCabe notes, cars fail to pull over to the side of the road and stop, as required by law, to make way for ambulances on emergency runs. Instead, they either pull over and keep moving, come to a complete stop right in the middle of the road or, worse, attempt to race the ambulance.

AN AMBULANCE DRIVER'S SOLUTIONS
◊ Maintain public awareness campaigns, such as last year's "Seconds can save" campaign, to educate the driving public about the laws of conduct pertaining to emergency vehicles;
◊ Make Bay and Yonge one-way. Variations on this idea include making these streets one-way between 3 and 9 p.m. on weekdays or making them one-way all day on weekdays only;
◊ Make more streets in the downtown area one-way; for

example, east-west arteries such as Dundas and Queen, and north-south roads such as Jarvis and Church;
◊ Prohibit parking—and permit stopping for commercial vehicles only—on major business streets all day on weekdays;
◊ Prohibit trucks from driving in the downtown core between 9 a.m. and 5 p.m. on weekdays but permit them to make deliveries at night. With insufficient docking and parking facilities and narrow roads and intersections, trucks are a major source of slowdowns during peak traffic hours;
◊ Ticket bicycle couriers who disobey the traffic rules. (McCabe has seen a number of injured bike couriers due to dash-and-dart riding techniques.);
◊ Police should sustain the recent crackdown on drivers who deliberately block intersections;
◊ Give emergency-vehicle drivers authority to write down and report to police the licence numbers of drivers who blatantly impede their progress. Drivers should then be given a warning by police along with printed reminders of proper procedure. Further infractions should result in legal action;
◊ Encourage drivers to use bicycles during warm months by introducing bike-only lanes (for example, Church or Jarvis, or Richmond, Adelaide or Front streets).

- - - - - - -

TITLE
ROADS SCHOLARS
ART DIRECTOR
**TERESA FERNANDES/
MARTHA WEAVER**
EDITOR
MARQ de VILLIERS
DESIGNER
MARTHA WEAVER
PHOTOGRAPHER
RUSSELL MONK
PUBLICATION
TORONTO LIFE
PUBLISHER
**KEY PUBLISHERS
CO. LTD.**

TITLE
THE FIXER
ART DIRECTOR
BRUCE RAMSAY
EDITOR
NORMAN SNIDER
DESIGNER
KASPAR deLINE
ILLUSTRATOR
SETH
PUBLICATION
SATURDAY NIGHT
PUBLISHER
HOLLINGER PUBLICATIONS INC.

competition within them was brutal. A young outsider interested in the interlocking careers of law and politics had more chance of being noticed among the Tories, who were seldom overburdened with young talent. Neither at St. Francis Xavier nor at law school at Laval did Mulroney distinguish himself as a brilliant academic mind. Rather, he impressed those around him with his ability to get things done in campus politics and ingratiate himself with those of his peers and superiors who counted in terms of climbing the greasy pole. He made himself invaluable, for instance, to John Diefenbaker. Trusting the student politician as an English-speaker, Diefenbaker relied on Mulroney to give him primer lessons on Quebec, territory as foreign to the prime minister as the moons of Mars. Similarly, when Mulroney moved on to law school at Laval, he befriended a group of the young anglo Quebec gentry, which included Michael Meighen, grandson of a Tory prime minister and now a Toronto lawyer, and Peter White, now Mulroney's principal secretary. There was no better incarnation of English Quebec's respectably alienated than these young Tories. As a group, they were obsessed with the eternal domination of Quebec politics by the Liberals, and like Mulroney they were hungry for the comforts and privileges that went with political power.

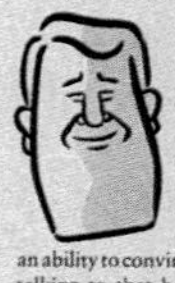

The anglo gentry of Montreal were considerably less stuffy than their Toronto equivalents, and they were also interested in having a good time. Mulroney had Irish charm and conviviality in abundance, as well as an ability to convince whoever it was he was talking to that he believed in everything they did. According to friends from this time, Mulroney's whole conversation was predicated, whether he was talking about fishing or politics, on exaggeration that they fondly understood to be exaggeration. (It was an innate proclivity that translated quickly into career advantage. Mulroney made with ease the small transition from exaggeration to public-relations pitch. Observers less charitable than his friends would come to characterize this glib hyperbole as a lack of probity.) In those early years, Mulroney also imbibed the first law of Tory politics, an unequivocal partisanship that enjoined "*on tire toujours sur les Rouges*" – you always slam the Grits.

The Laval group made their way from Quebec City to the business, legal, and political world of Montreal in the mid-1960s, and Brian Mulroney went with them. One of their francophone allies, Bernard Roy, helped Mulroney get his first job at the establishment law firm of Howard, Cate, Ogilvy. While Mulroney did not particularly stand out in terms of ability, he did possess certain natural advantages. First of all, there was his Irish background. The Irish are historic mediators between the French and English in Quebec, sharing a religion with one and a language with the other: there has always been much intermarriage between the French and Irish communities. In the politics of Quebec, Meighen or White, pure anglos, could win a seat only on the West Island of Montreal, whereas Mulroney's political possibilities were broader. Then there was his class background: Mulroney could move easily and amiably between workers and management. This was the key to his success in settling the disputes on the Montreal waterfront in the mid-1960s.

The skills involved in such mediations were essentially those of impersonation. With his Baie Comeau background, Mulroney could call upon all the tavern manners necessary to convince union leaders after a night of drinking that he was essentially on their side and that they should shave a couple of cents an hour off their wage demands. Dealing with management, he further developed the gentleman's façade learned at St. Francis Xavier and Laval. (Only romantics from the middle class dress and behave like factory workers. Ambitious boys from the working class learn quickly the flat necessity of a genteel front to clothe the primitive appetites that drive the worlds of business and politics.) There was scarce doubt, however, where Brian Mulroney's allegiance ultimately lay: the route to money and high position was in acting for management, never the unions.

Of the Laval group, Mulroney was clearly the poorest and hungriest. The demands of high office in the late twentieth century are such that whoever wants it has to be driven by furies. Mulroney's father died just after Brian had gone on to Montreal. A friend from that time remembers the funeral at the family's modest apartment. Mulroney's father's pension was not going to go far, and he was faced with supporting his mother, younger brother, and youngest sister. In those days, young lawyers didn't make much, and Mulroney's contemporaries were impressed with their friend's nerve when he told his law firm that unless his salary was raised he was going back to Baie Comeau. (Mulroney's firm valued him highly enough to grant him an increase, which enabled him to move his family to Montreal.) The friend recalls Mulroney's first suit, a matter of desperate concern because he could never get it to fit properly. In this context, the fifty pairs of Gucci loafers discovered in his Sussex Drive closet are thoroughly comprehensible.

If there was a single key to Brian Mulroney's character, it was a hunger for success defined in the most unvarnished terms: big job, big house, a looker for a wife. Although he could mediate between business and labour, his loyalty was to the dominant power in any situation. Nor was Mulroney the sort to take a quixotic gamble. Staying firmly in the back rooms of Quebec Tory politics, he realized that a run at a seat in Parliament under either Stanfield or Clark was a loser's game. He couldn't afford to lose, even once. He had not come all the way from Baie Comeau to place his bets on anything less than a sure thing.

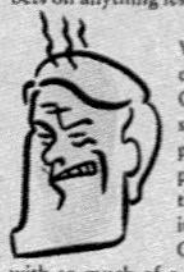

When Mulroney decided to run for the Conservative leadership in 1976, his implicit promise to the party was so novel that they could not accept it: he was a bilingual Catholic from Quebec with so much of a winner's gloss that he offended their alienated instincts. In 1976, Mulroney looked to his party to have too much of the style of a Liberal. It took almost a decade of Joe Clark's blunderings to convince the Tories of the practical value of Mulroney's attractions. His success in the corporate boardrooms and political back rooms of Montreal was based on qualities more visceral than cerebral. He understood the art of the deal, he understood the art of pragmatic friendship known as networking, he understood the art of quid pro quo. When the American-owned Iron Ore Company of Canada hired Mulroney to become their local president, they knew they were getting a glossily packaged member of Canada's branch-plant class. He could finesse their labour problems in Schefferville and polish the company's image. After his experience on the Cliche Commission, he was well versed in the skills of self-presentation on television. It was also Mulroney's pride that he could get on with anybody. In the province of Quebec he was supremely well-connected. If the Iron Ore Company wanted to talk to the provincial Liberals, well, he could set up lunch with Robert Bourassa.

The Tory values of loyalty and self-interest could be mutually contradictory at times: it took the genteel virtue of hypocrisy to reconcile them. In 1982, Mulroney publicly shook hands with Joe Clark at the Ritz

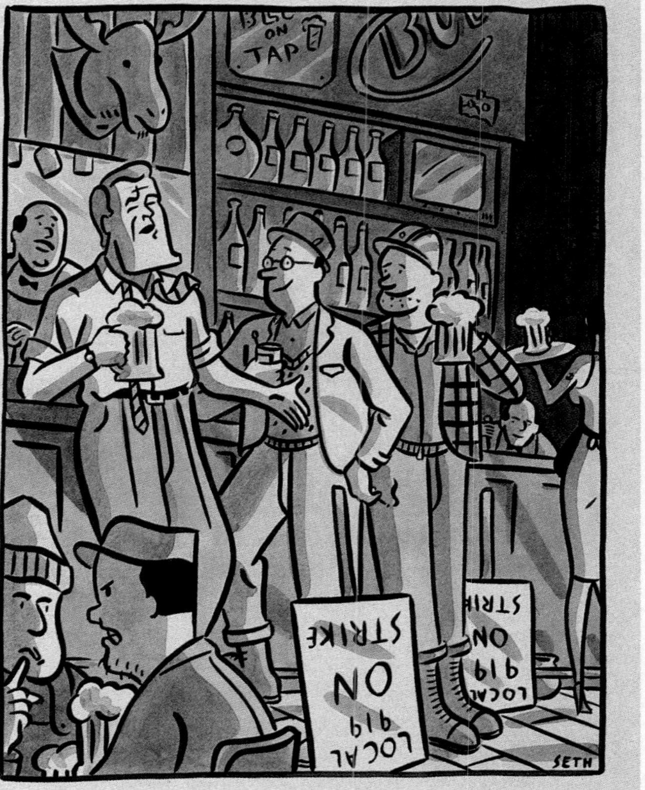

With his folksy Baie Comeau background, Mulroney could convince union leaders that he was really on their side

Carlton Hotel in Montreal while preparing the leadership campaign that would ultimately unseat Clark. Though he recruited Claude Wagner for the election of 1972, in 1976, when they were both candidates for the Tory leadership, the Mulroney camp leaked through Peter White information about Wagner's trust fund that ultimately eliminated Wagner from the race. Then there was the other major lesson of the greasy pole: suck up, kick down. At Howard, Cate, Ogilvy, Mulroney was known for his extreme deference to the senior partners and their wives and daughters. On the campaign stump, Mulroney raged defiance at picketing strikers and unionists. Neither was an act of personal preference, just pious obeisance to the social hierarchy as a practical ladder to success.

While the corporate arts of impersonation and slick self-presentation served Mulroney well behind the scenes, they seldom endeared him to the public once he moved into the arena of parliamentary politics. What was amiable and likable in a boardroom was unctuous and phoney on television. It was felt that Mulroney gave up too much to his social self. The oft-made comparisons between Brian Mulroney and Ronald Reagan were ultimately false. The difference was seemingly between a proficient television performer and a lesser one. Yet Reagan used all his considerable theatrical skills to propound a message he clearly believed. Where Reagan had the advantage of a simple creed – the American way – to propound, Mulroney gave little evidence of having wrestled with all the devilishly elusive and complicated Canadian dilemmas of identity. He never mastered the accent of sincerity that is shaped, after all, by an inner loyalty to the truth of one's experience. Mulroney never gave evidence of much propensity to inner reflection. The actor's virtues of impersonation that served him well in labour mediation and corporate public relations left him with the actor's vices: attenuation of self, an immense vanity, and a desire to flatter and please the audience. The more sincere he tried to be, the phonier he seemed. Just as Reagan was always well liked, no matter how outrageous the scandals that plagued his government, Mulroney would never be trusted, no matter what his government achieved. The electorate still looked to its leaders to provide an example in character. The noble self is boldly defined, its purposes clearly conceived and openly avowed. In odd ways both Thatcher and Reagan could each lay claim to a noble self. But it often seemed that Brian Mulroney had achieved success at the cost of his integrity. In the election of 1984, though, it scarcely mattered. John Turner was much worse in every conceivable way. Universal rejection of the Liberals and Turner's blunders combined to relegate latent mistrust of Mulroney to the background. Nonetheless, the genetic defects of the Conservative animal were simmering in embryo waiting to hatch once it gained power.

After Turner's leadership victory at the Liberal convention in the spring of 1984, Mulroney and his party had difficulty recruiting the type of candidate they wanted in Quebec. Instead of high-quality men and women from the universities and the more prestigious corporations, the Tories, with a few exceptions such as Marcel Masse, could attract only low-level opportunists. (Paradoxically, the probusiness fever of the early 1980s worked against the Tory recruitment programme. A bilingual woman administrator, say, from the University of Sherbrooke with a Harvard MBA would be too engrossed in building up her own little company to take a chance on running for Parliament.) Consequently, many of the candidates that they did recruit were attracted to politics by its spoils and rapidly proved embarrassing to Mulroney in office. What's more, the Quebec caucus was largely rural. Not only were they regionalists but their concerns were intensely parochial. They focused more on local issues – whether Hyundai would build a branch plant in their riding, who would sell the land, who would get the jobs there – than they did on national concerns. Quebec Tories cared little about federal nation building. As long as Quebec's interests were looked after, they were quite satisfied. The rest of the country left them indifferent at best, and actively hostile at worst.

MULRONEY WAS MOST LOYAL TO CRONIES HE'D MET ON HIS WAY UP. HIS VERY BEST PALS GOT PLUM JOBS

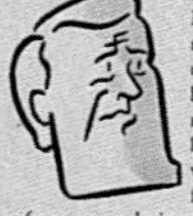

As prime minister, Mulroney sought to reconcile the various elements of his party; his programme was never one of strongly held vision and conviction. Instead he fashioned a patchwork of accommodation. As Allan Gregg has observed, the real split in the party was not left and right but pro- and anti-Dief. In contesting the Tory leadership, Mulroney had first wooed the Diefenbaker cowboys such as Robert Coates, since they were the portion of the party most alienated from Joe Clark. The Diefenbaker cowboys most certainly had a strong vision of the country, one that had remained unchanged since the mid-1950s. Reactionary to the core, they believed in capital punishment and strong censorship; they were anti-abortion and against bilingualism and the metric system. Mulroney knew that the country rejected their atavistic and mean-spirited values but felt compelled to mollify the cowboys by opening up their concerns for debate. So the electorate watched the spectacle of Mulroney dissenting from a motion to reinstate capital punishment, which members of his own party had introduced.

The Diefenbaker cowboys proved embarrassing in another way. The scandal involving Coates and a B-girl in Lahr, West Germany, was less an example of yahoo lust run amok than the rebound of Coates's mistrust and dislike of the permanent civil service. After twenty-seven years on the back benches, Coates was determined in a particularly high-handed way to show the military bureaucracy at the department of national defence just how little he needed them. Almost immediately after taking office he alienated his senior civil servants. The subsequent scandal in Lahr must be seen, at least in part, as the successful effort of disgruntled bureaucrats like Duncan Edmonds who, seeking to rid the department of an inadequate chief, spoke of the incident to Dan Turner of the *Ottawa Citizen*.

Still, Mulroney's most powerfully interpreted cliché was "Ya dance with who brung ya." He was most loyal to those cronies and pals whom he had met on his climb to power. Mulroney in office was like a local mayor who had lured a large concern into town: his best buddies and cronies would get the plum jobs; those citizens humble enough not to have antagonized the mayor over the years would be allowed to

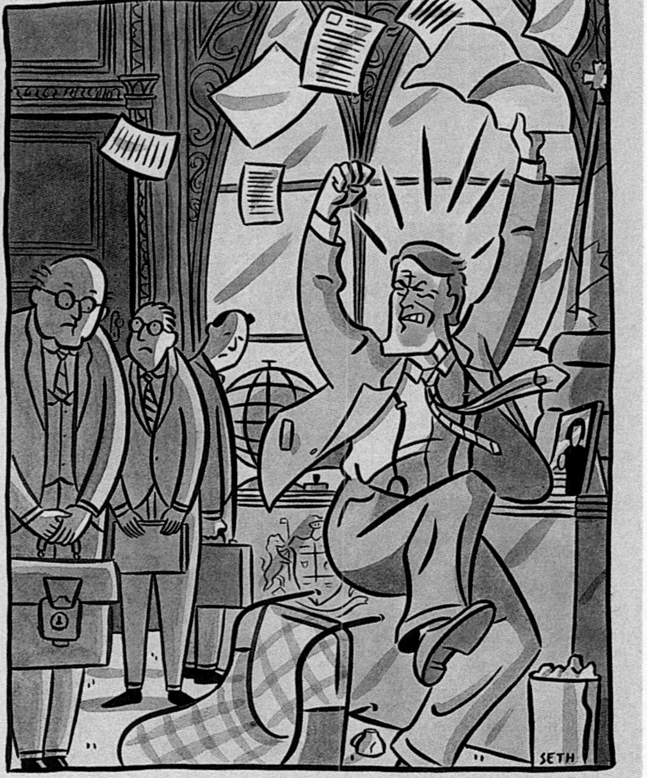

Behind closed doors, the P.M.'s small-town instincts let loose major tantrums and small-minded recriminations

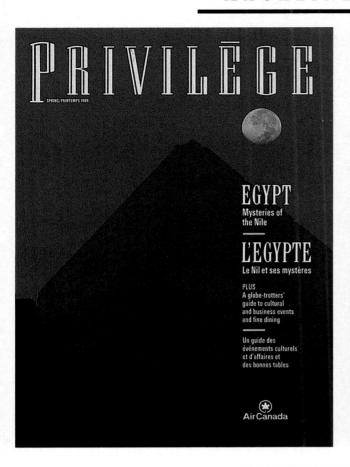

TITLE
EGYPT
ART DIRECTOR
B.T. GILLEN
EDITOR
KAREN HANLEY
PHOTOGRAPHER
**RON WATTS/
FIRST LIGHT**
PUBLICATION
PRIVILEGE
PUBLISHER
AIRMEDIA
PHOTO DIRECTOR
LISA BURROUGHS

TITLE
THE EDGE
ART DIRECTOR
NADIA MARYNIAK
EDITOR
JACK McIVER
DESIGNER
NADIA MARYNIAK
PHOTOGRAPHER
KAREN LEVY
PUBLICATION
DESTINATIONS
PUBLISHER
THE GLOBE AND MAIL

TITLE
SEPTEMBER 1988
ART DIRECTOR
KAREN SIMPSON
DESIGNER
KAREN SIMPSON
PHOTOGRAPHER
JOSE PICAYO
PUBLICATION
DOMINO
PUBLISHER
THE GLOBE AND MAIL

TITLE
BEGINNER'S CLUCK
ART DIRECTOR
ULRIKE BENDER
ILLUSTRATOR
THEO DIMSON
PUBLICATION
HARROWSMITH
PUBLISHER
**TELEMEDIA
PUBLISHING INC.**

TITLE
KILLING TIME
ART DIRECTOR
CARMEN DUNJKO
EDITOR
JOHN FRASER
DESIGNER
KASPAR deLINE
PHOTOGRAPHER
BURROUGH'S PICTURES
PUBLICATION
SATURDAY NIGHT
PUBLISHER
**HOLLINGER
PUBLICATIONS INC.**

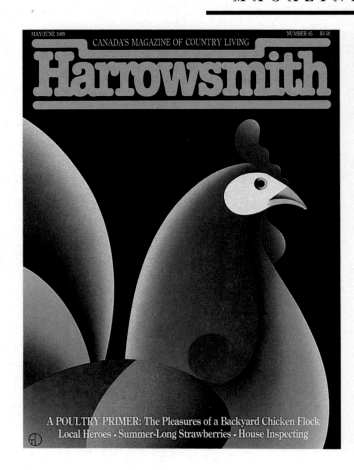

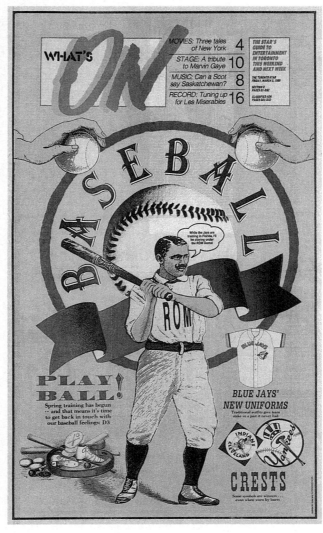

SILVER

TITLE
SALSA IN THE CITY
EDITOR
PAT McCORMICK
DESIGNER
KAM WAI YU
PUBLICATION
WHAT'S ON
PUBLISHER
**THE TORONTO STAR
NEWSPAPER**

TITLE
BASEBALL
EDITOR
PAT McCORMICK
DESIGNER
KAM WAI YU
PUBLICATION
WHAT'S ON
PUBLISHER
**THE TORONTO STAR
NEWSPAPER**

TITLE
BIG IS BACK
ART DIRECTOR
THERESE SHECHTER
EDITOR
SARAH MURDOCH
DESIGNER
THERESE SHECHTER
PUBLICATION
**THE FINANCIAL TIMES
OF CANADA**
PUBLISHER
**JOHN MacFARLANE/
THE FINANCIAL TIMES
OF CANADA**

TITLE
POLICE PAYOFF
ART DIRECTOR
REVA POMER
EDITOR
TED MUMFORD
CREATIVE DIR.
IRENE GRAINGER
PUBLICATION
NOW
PUBLISHER
**NOW
COMMUNICATIONS INC.**
PRODUCTION MANAGER
JOHN COX

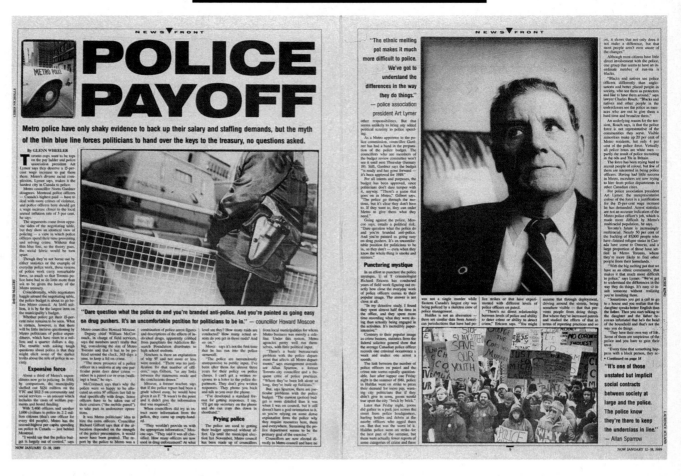

TITLE
LEAPIN' LIZARDS
EDITOR
PAT McCORMICK
DESIGNER
KAM WAI YU
PUBLICATION
WHAT'S ON
PUBLISHER
**THE TORONTO STAR
NEWSPAPER**

TITLE
MARCEL MARCEAU
EDITOR
PAT McCORMICK
DESIGNER
KAM WAI YU
PUBLICATION
WHAT'S ON
PUBLISHER
**THE TORONTO STAR
NEWSPAPER**

Only because the land had forsaken them did Maria Quievac see her son disappearing. The drought had so caked him with dust that she hurried outside to wipe his face and hands. ❧ *"José!"* she called out, brushing past her husband as if he didn't exist. ❧ Alfredo stood by as she took the large blue cloth to the boy's face. Alfredo could barely swallow from the dryness of his throat. He watched her caresses, her mouth pursed with motherly concern. Alfredo recalled their marriage night, when the heat was filled with moisture and with promise. ❧ Now, the earth lifted around them to whirl away like smoke. Most of their cornstalks were dead. Those still alive were brittle, the ears small and hard. They had been eating black and crumbly tortillas for days. Even the beans, soaked for a day longer than usual, ended up chewy and flavorless. And no amount of prayer seemed enough to save them from this misfortune. ❧ So it was with strange relief that Alfredo heard his wife scream. For a moment he thought that the boy was gone, burned out of his mother's heart by the blistering and unforgiving heat, no longer hunted by this harsh life. ❧ But Maria held out José's arm for her husband while she clamped the cloth to her mouth to quell what had taken shape in her throat. A small area above the boy's left elbow had disappeared. There was

The harsh Guatemalan sun kills crops and dreams, but it also brings truths to light— in fantastic and hideous ways.

UNDER A BLINDING SUN

By Omar S. Castañeda

Illustration by
Jamie Bennett

SILVER

TITLE
UNDER A BLINDING SUN
ART DIRECTOR
JENNIFER NAPIER
WRITER
OMAR S. CASTENEDA
DESIGNER
JENNIFER NAPIER
ILLUSTRATOR
**JAMIE BENNETT/
REACTOR**
PUBLICATION
**SPECIAL REPORT
SUMMER /89**
PUBLISHER
**WHITTLE
COMMUNICATIONS**

nothing there, no blood or flesh or pain, just an empty space that revealed the ground below, gray and lifeless.

Maria dared not speak for fear some unknown thing might leap from her mouth. Her eyes went as wild and full of bewilderment as a baby's.

Alfredo leaned down and put his arm around her. He tried lifting her to her feet, but the weight of horror crushed his wife down.

"It is nothing," he said. "It will be all right. Won't it?"

José, still a gangly and awkward boy, nodded slowly. He twirled his finger in the space of his arm, then held the hole to his eye like a periscope.

Alfredo led Maria into the hut, where he placed his trembling wife into the hammock. He sat with her until she closed her eyes and slept. The boy went away.

From the kitchen, Alfredo's mother glared.

"That wife," she said.

Alfredo stepped back. "Don't wake her. It is difficult for her."

"And no wonder! The way she carries on about a son! Is she blind?"

Alfredo rubbed his eyes with both hands.

"Leave her," Consuela said. "She is so wife for my son. Does she make love like a wife should?"

"I will not have this!"

"Dios! She stays awake all night, not for you, but because she fears the dark will steal her son. All these years!"

"Please go," Alfredo said.

He looked down into Maria's face, gentle in the 'day, undisturbed as she lay dreaming while others walked about. No, he knew it was not the dark orbits of planets but the brilliant sun, but mid revealing, that stole life away.

Alfredo gathered two candles, one red, the other white; a piece of copal-resin; several cigars; and a small bottle of rum. He looped the long tassel of his belt around the items, then tied them all into a ball that hung at his waist. He would go visit the idol Maximón, now that his prayers in church had produced nothing. He had given the priest his chance, but it seemed beyond those blessed saints to save them. And sorrow is a heartworm gnawing at vulnerable flesh.

At the guardian's hut he paid one quetzal for the privilege of seeing Maximón. The guardian brought Alfredo in, then extinguished the lights except for a solitary candle. He brought the wood idol out from the back shadows to stand illumined by that one flickering light. Alfredo could feel hope flutter inside his heart.

Maximón wore two felt hats, tens of scarves around his neck, and uncountable layers of clothes. The brilliant colors seemed to glow under the candle. The guardian placed a short cigar into the hole of Maximón's mouth to finish the preparation.

Alfredo prayed for rain to kill the drought. He prayed for just

ZOMBIES

The zombies that lurch through our fiction, comic books, and movies are based on Haitian folklore. In the 1920s, American journalist W.B. Seabrook introduced the legend to the U.S. and proposed a scientific explanation for it after visiting plantations in Haiti. Seabrook brought back reports of deathlike laborers whose eyes were "staring, unfocused, unseeing" and whose faces were "not only expressionless, but incapable of expression." Described to him as genuine zombies—walking corpses—they first struck him as garden-variety idiots. He later hypothesized that they were live people of ordinary intelligence, first drugged to induce a temporary deathlike coma, then stolen from their caskets and given another drug to keep them subservient.

Alfredo would go visit the idol Maximón, now that his prayers in church had produced nothing.

enough corn so that he and his wife and mother could eat, for food so that his family might make it through this terrible time and live long enough to honor the *cofradía*—the brotherhood—the patron saints, and all the deities of the Tzutuhil people.

"Do this for me," he pleaded, "and unclasp the fear pinned inside Maria. Lift the veil from her eyes."

The guardian walked with Alfredo to the street. "We are all saddened for you," he said.

Alfredo found Maria busily piling swatches of cloth in the middle of the room. José sat inundated, like Maximón, by shirts, pants, Alfredo's old hats, and Maria's scarves, sandals strung around his neck like a necklace. She had splashed jewelry onto him to shine like disks of water.

"Look!" Maria cried.

She lifted up the veil of clothes. José's knees had evaporated, and his right shoulder was gone. Under the hats, the scalp had vanished. Maria's lips moved with her anguish.

"He's leaving us," she whimpered.

Alfredo's mother spoke. "She wants to cover him with clothes, as if the weight alone will make him live?"

"What do you know of how I feel?"

Alfredo stepped between the women.

"You have your son!" Maria cried.

Consuela touched Alfredo's firm arm.

Maria stared up at Alfredo, pleading with her eyes for Alfredo to save their son, but he turned from her and looked deeply into the boy's face. José's eyes were those of a sailor, distantly yearning, not for the betraying land of their small fields but for the horizon and the sea swells like rolling papaya.

"Does it hurt?" Alfredo asked.

"Oh, yes," Maria said. "Yes!"

And beside his mother's crying, the boy's jaw and neck slowly dissolved to become more mottled air.

She opened her mouth, wet with sadness, and prayed loudly to whatever gods cared to hear: "Deign to come. Deign to catch the dust of earth, deign to clean what has been endangered, O Five Destinies. Deign to come, our uncles, our priests, Seven Serpent, Urgent Flower, Deign to come and see what there is to salvage. Scour this black longing."

Her prayer came again, louder and louder as if to shut out the unhappy world and her despair.

Consuela hissed in the shadows.

"Be kind," Alfredo said.

That night he fell asleep hearing his wife's prayers. He too had prayed, but quietly, in bed, pleading for Maximón to save them.

And in the morning he found his wife still awake, squeezing blood from wounds in her breasts. She tried coating the areas she saw vanishing from her son, hoping to paint with her blood the absent limbs.

"Pray for your son," she yelled, "not for rain! Our son, Alfredo. Pray for our son!"

Only her boy's distant eyes, faint and illusory, remained above the vanishing torso. Below, only wisps of shoulder, ghosts of flesh in that nebulous son.

"How can you be so unloving? How can you stand and watch your son disappear from our lives? How?"

"You are my wife," he said, and left.

She screamed out her hate of him. Consuela watched from the doorway.

All around them, the drought ran like a rabid dog. Homes lost their children, their elders. The sky was forever a maelstrom of dirt and brittle plants; above, the sun burned the life from birdsong and downed the gluttonous vultures. Men refused to smile at one another even when humor, how-

ever maniacal, was all that could save them from total desperation; and to smile would allow the heat to steal the moisture of their mouths. Children looked thirstily at mothers, crying over dying family. It was a year of the green calendar, of destruction.

Alfredo went again to Maximón, but the line to pray extended

"Just clarity for Maria," Alfredo said. "I will die so you may clear the moon from her eyes."

down to the empty riverbed. Back in his field, Alfredo opened the veins of his prized turkey and pleaded with the sun. He pierced his tongue with the point of a knife and dripped the blood into the soil.

"Just clarity for Maria," he said. "I will die so you may clear the moon from her eyes. Just clarity," he said.

Behind him, Maria came running with a bundle of clothes. She cursed him, holding out the cloth that cradled now only the eyes of her son. Like a cat peering from a stack of wood, the boy's eyes

A

SILVER

TITLE
THE FIXER
ART DIRECTOR
BRUCE RAMSAY
EDITOR
NORMAN SNIDER
DESIGNER
KASPAR deLINE
ILLUSTRATOR
SETH
PUBLICATION
SATURDAY NIGHT
PUBLISHER
**HOLLINGER
PUBLICATIONS INC.**

A

SILVER

TITLE
CITYLIFE SERIES
ART DIRECTOR
TERESA FERNANDES
EDITOR
MARQ de VILLIERS
DESIGNER
LINA McPHEE
ILLUSTRATOR
BARRY BLITT
PUBLICATION
TORONTO LIFE
PUBLISHER
**KEY PUBLISHERS
CO. LTD.**

The most salient fact about Brian Mulroney is that he is the first prime minister born into the Canadian working class. His career, as well as being a testimony to social mobility in this country, is a story of one individual's eager assimilation of the values of the branch-plant class. It is also the story of a socially disadvantaged though passionately ambitious young man on the rise prepared to stroke and appease whatever powers could hasten his advance. For Mulroney, growing up in an isolated town on the north shore of the St. Lawrence in Quebec, any consideration of whether it should have been Canadians or Americans who owned the town's paper mill would have been a luxury. The critical difference between respectability and welfare lay in whether or not the mill employed you.

At St. Francis Xavier University in Nova Scotia in the 1950s, the campus Conservative club offered more opportunity of advancement than did an association with the Liberals. Campus Liberal clubs were universally recognized as the incubators of future cabinet ministers, senior bureaucrats, and lawyers with clout. Thus, the

Despite Mulroney's huge desire to please, the more sincere he tries to be, the phonier he sounds

Brian Mulroney has a natural talent for appeasing the powerful and cutting a deal. What he doesn't have is a coherent vision of Canada

by NORMAN SNIDER

Saturday Night/NOVEMBER 1988 **35**

Carlton Hotel in Montreal while preparing the leadership campaign that would ultimately unseat Clark. Though he recruited Claude Wagner for the election of 1972, in 1976, when they were both candidates for the Tory leadership, the Mulroney camp leaked through Peter White information about Wagner's trust fund that ultimately eliminated Wagner from the race. Then there was the other major lesson of the greasy pole: suck up, kick down. At Howard, Cate, Ogilvy, Mulroney was known for his extreme deference to the senior partners and their wives and daughters. On the campaign slump, Mulroney raged defiance at picketing strikers and unionists. Neither was an act of personal preference, just pious obeisance to the social hierarchy as a practical ladder to success.

While the corporate arts of impersonation and slick self-presentation served Mulroney well behind the scenes, they seldom endeared him to the public once he moved into the arena of parliamentary politics. What was amiable and likable in a boardroom was unctuous and phoney on television. It was felt that Mulroney gave up too much to his social self. The oft-made comparisons between Brian Mulroney and Ronald Reagan were ultimately false. The difference was seemingly between a proficient television performer and a lesser one. Yet Reagan used all his considerable the-

Reagan was always well liked, no matter how outrageous the scandals that plagued his government, Mulroney would never be trusted, no matter what his government achieved. The electorate still looked to its leaders to provide an example in character. The noble self is boldly defined, its purposes clearly conceived and openly avowed. In odd ways both Thatcher and Reagan could each lay claim to a noble self. But it often seemed that Brian Mulroney had achieved success at the cost of his integrity. In the election of 1984, though, it scarcely mattered. John Turner was much worse in every conceivable way. Universal rejection of the Liberals and Turner's blunders combined to relegate latent mistrust of Mulroney to the background. Nonetheless, the genetic defects of the Conservative animal were simmering in embryo waiting to hatch once it gained power.

After Turner's leadership victory at the Liberal convention in the spring of 1984, Mulroney and his party had difficulty recruiting the type of candidate they wanted in Quebec. Instead of high-quality men and women from the universities and the more prestigious corporations, the Tories, with a few exceptions such as Marcel Masse, could attract only low-level opportunists. (Paradoxically, the probusiness fever of the early 1980s worked against the Tory recruitment programme. A bilingual woman

looked after, they were quite satisfied. The rest of the country left them indifferent at best, and actively hostile at worst.

As prime minister, Mulroney sought to reconcile the various elements of his party; his programme was never one of strongly held vision and conviction. Instead he fashioned a patchwork of accommodation. As Allan Gregg has observed, the real split in the party was not left and right but pro- and anti-Dief. In contesting the Tory leadership, Mulroney had first wooed the Diefenbaker cowboys such as Robert Coates, since they were the portion of the party most alienated from Joe Clark. The Diefenbaker cowboys most certainly had a strong vision of the country, one that had remained unchanged since the mid-1950s. Reactionary to the core, they believed in capital punishment and strong censorship; they were anti-abortion and against bilingualism and the metric system. Mulroney knew that the country rejected their atavistic and mean-spirited values but felt compelled to mollify the cowboys by opening up their concerns for debate. So the electorate watched the spectacle of Mulroney dissenting from a motion to reinstate capital punishment, which members of his own party had introduced.

The Diefenbaker cowboys proved embarrassing in another way. The scandal involving Coates and a B-girl in Lahr, West Germany, was less an example of yahoo lust run amok than the rebound of Coates's mistrust and dislike of the permanent civil service. After twenty-seven years on the back benches, Coates was determined in a particularly high-handed way to show the military bureaucracy at the department of national defence just how little he needed them. Almost immediately after taking office he alienated his senior civil servants. The subsequent scandal in Lahr must be seen, at least in part, as the successful effort of disgruntled bureaucrats like Duncan Edmonds who, seeking to rid the department of an inadequate chief, spoke of the incident to Dan Turner of the *Ottawa Citizen*.

Still, Mulroney's most powerfully interpreted cliché was "Ya dance with who brung ya." He was most loyal to those cronies and pals whom he had met on his climb to power. Mulroney in office was like a local mayor who had lured a large concern into town: his best buddies and cronies would get the plum jobs; those citizens humble enough not to have antagonized the mayor over the years would be allowed to

MULRONEY WAS MOST LOYAL TO CRONIES HE'D MET ON HIS WAY UP. HIS VERY BEST PALS GOT PLUM JOBS

atrical skills to propound a message he clearly believed. Where Reagan had the advantage of a simple creed – the American way – to propound, Mulroney gave little evidence of having wrestled with all the devilishly elusive and complicated Canadian dilemmas of identity. He never mastered the accent of sincerity that is shaped, after all, by an inner loyalty to the truth of one's experience. Mulroney never gave evidence of much propensity to inner reflection. The actor's virtues of impersonation that served him well in labour mediation and corporate public relations left him with the actor's vices: attenuation of self, an immense vanity, and a desire to flatter and please the audience. The more sincere he tried to be, the phonier he seemed. Just as

administrator, say, from the University of Sherbrooke with a Harvard MBA would be too engrossed in building up her own little company to take a chance on running for Parliament.) Consequently, many of the candidates that they did recruit were attracted to politics by its spoils and rapidly proved embarrassing to Mulroney in office. What's more, the Quebec caucus was largely rural. Not only were they regionalists but their concerns were intensely parochial. They focused more on local issues – whether Hyundai would build a branch plant in their riding, who would sell the land, who would get the jobs there – than they did on national concerns. Quebec Tories cared little about federal nation building. As long as Quebec's interests were

38 Saturday Night/NOVEMBER 1988

Behind closed doors, the P.M.'s small-town instincts let loose major tantrums and small-minded recriminations

Saturday Night/NOVEMBER 1988 **39**

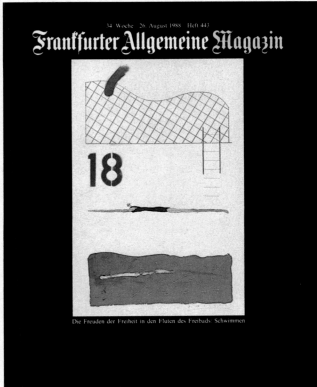

A

SILVER

TITLE
**PHILIP MORRIS'S
BIG BITE**
ART DIRECTOR
JANET FROEHLICH
WRITER
L.J. DAVIS
ILLUSTRATOR
ANITA KUNZ
PUBLICATION
**THE NEW YORK TIMES
MAGAZINE**
PUBLISHER
THE NEW YORK TIMES

A

SILVER

TITLE
SCHWIMMEN
ART DIRECTOR
**HANS-GEORG
POSPISCHIL**
WRITER
INGRID HEINRICH-JOST
DESIGNER
**BERNADETTE
GOTTHARDT**
ILLUSTRATOR
**JEFF JACKSON/
REACTOR**
PUBLICATION
**FRANKFURTER
ALLEMEINE**
PUBLISHER
**FRANKFURTER
ALLEMEINE
ZEITUNG GMBH**

A
SILVER

TITLE
TALKIN 'BOUT AN EVOLUTION
ART DIRECTOR
FRED WOODWARD
EDITOR
JANN WENNER
ILLUSTRATOR
ANITA KUNZ
PUBLICATION
ROLLING STONE MAGAZINE
PUBLISHER
STRAIGHT ARROW PUBLISHERS INC.

TITLE
STUNG
ART DIRECTOR
FRED WOODWARD
EDITOR
JANN WENNER
ILLUSTRATOR
ANITA KUNZ
PUBLICATION
ROLLING STONE
PUBLISHER
STRAIGHT ARROW PUBLISHERS INC.

TITLE
MINOR PROBLEMS
ART DIRECTOR
PETER deGANNES
ILLUSTRATOR
MALCOLM MacPHAIL
PUBLICATION
OTTAWA MAGAZINE
PUBLISHER
OTTAWA MAGAZINE INC.

THE HISTORY OF ROCK & ROLL

Talkin' Bout an Evolution
BY ANITA KUNZ

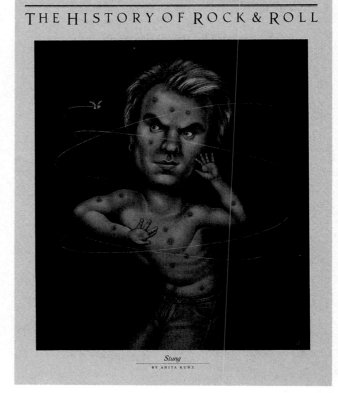

THE HISTORY OF ROCK & ROLL

Stung
BY ANITA KUNZ

MINOR
PROBLEMS

Why it's so difficult for bad kids from lower-income families to turn good

THE ELDEST SON

IT WAS INEVITABLE. JUST ABOUT THE WORST thing that could have happened to him finally did. One quiet Ottawa night, when most people were watching TV or helping their kids with homework, a young man walked into a convenience store, grabbed about $500, and on the way out was shot in the chest. The ugly red hole perilously close to his heart took him within an inch of his existence.

The reasons he was shot are cloudy. No violence was committed during the robbery, but a crowbar was brandished at the owner. There was a question of whether he was giving himself up, or trying to flee.

There's a good chance the police who came on the scene that night knew his name. Even at 18 years of age, Joseph Jude (all the names of the family in this article are, of course, fictional) had crossed the line many times, so maybe only a gun could bring him back over it. Some may have thought it wasn't the worst thing that could have

happened to him, that maybe in some cruel way it was the best.

That terrible notion even crossed his mother's mind. A painful thought for any mother to have about her son. But after years of watching him go in and out of the Youth Services Bureau (YSB), the Children's Aid Society (CAS), group homes, the courts, training schools, halfway houses and jail; after agonizing for so many years over his trespasses, and searching until she was blind with grief for some sign of improvement and hope, the thought wasn't entirely unexpected.

FLY IN DINER

Transform your backyard into a popular eatery with this guide to bird feeding techniques

BY PETER WHELAN

January. Early morning. Bed. I huddle deeper under the blankets and shrink from the cold, grey day. I am diving back toward sleep when the thought hits: I wonder who came for breakfast? Moments later I peer into the snowy backyard. Yes, there are guests. They hop about and gossip as they eat. One sings. They are red and blue and yellow, tiny black eyes gleaming with vitality. They touch my cold yard with life. Suddenly the day is less hostile. I enter it, smiling.

The cost of reconstituting this morning grouch is a handful of grain and a smidgeon of work. Some say they feed birds in the winter to help the birds. I do it to help my sanity. For whatever reasons, birding in its many forms is the fastest growing hobby in North America and the second largest, after gardening. Recent studies showed 51 million people in the United States watch birds and $500-million (U.S.) was spent there on bird food in a winter. It is helpful but not necessary to know the birds first. Many a bird feeder is simply someone with a yard and a zest for life.

York Region offers a host of winter birds for those who reach out and offer food. A new star is the house finch, a transplant from the Far West that is spreading through the area. The red-splashed male warbles richly all winter, one of the few warm singers in cold weather. Few new feeders lack long for several or a dozen. Watch a bustling black-capped chickadee and try not to smile; such a cheery elf is hard to resist. I say a chickadee a day keeps the shrink away. Feel twice repaid for the food as woodpeckers and nuthatches not only perch fearlessly a few metres away, but eat harmful insects from your trees at no extra charge. American

HARVEY CHAN

TITLE
FLY IN DINER
ART DIRECTOR
KELLY MICHELE de REGT
EDITOR
LORIE SCULTHORP
DESIGNER
DAN KISHCHUK
ILLUSTRATOR
HARVEY CHAN
PUBLICATION
YORK MAGAZINE
PUBLISHER
FOCUS MAGAZINES INC.

PRIVATE EYES

The investigation business in Canada is booming, thanks to lawyers who have a growing need for private eyes and ears

By Robert Coates

ANTHONY KUNKEL STARES through his windshield at the cold suburban dawn. He's been parked in this west Toronto subdivision since an hour before sunrise, using a private investigator's two cardinal talents — watching and waiting. Suddenly, the waiting pays off. A figure emerges from a two-storey brick house halfway down the block and Kunkel coils into action.

He grabs a still camera and reels off three quick shots with the auto-winder. In one smooth motion the camera is replaced by the video camera that Kunkel has been cradling in his lap for the past two hours. Unsuspecting, the man down the street climbs into his car as Kunkel lets the camera roll. The investigator's adrenaline has shot from zero to 60 in less than 10 seconds; the 25-year-old private eye lives for these moments of activity that offset the long hours of waiting. Aiming the video camera at the man in the driveway, Kunkel starts to sing: "You oughtta be in pictures..."

The object of Kunkel's serenade is the focus of an insurance claim arising from a personal injury lawsuit. But the insurance company and its legal counsel want more information on the man's condition before settling the suit. So an investigation agency has been called in, and today the job has landed in Kunkel's lap. How disabled is the claimant? Is he working? If so, where? Kunkel is about to find out — the car down the street is rolling out of the driveway.

"We'll take him by the nose," Kunkel says, pulling away from the curb and leading the subject's late-model Ford to the first corner. He then takes a turn, lets the Ford go past, and is soon following at a comfortable distance, two cars behind. As he winds through the suburban streets, Kunkel prays that the subject doesn't run any yellow lights.

While driving, he tells of a colleague who ran into trouble following a particularly feisty subject. "The guy was nuts," Kunkel says. "He'd been harassing a public official and they wanted to find out who he was. But he burned the investigator and then chased him all over Mississauga. Thank God the cops showed up."

As the driver of the Ford leads him farther from Toronto, Kunkel reminisces about other cases. "I followed a psychic once," he muses. "He said he was psychic. He couldn't have been too psychic."

Then there was the time he watched someone for seven days, renting a different coloured van every morning. The subject didn't suspect a thing. "Some people just seem to be able to smell you," Kunkel says. "Others, you can smack 'em across the face with the camera and they don't catch on."

Kunkel is one of the growing legion of private investigators across the country who dig up the dirt on an individual or a company for a price. Along with insurance companies and private businesses, law firms are becoming regular users of investigation agencies, turning to private eyes for a wide variety of services.

Investigators regularly interview witnesses for lawyers involved in litigation; trace missing heirs in estate cases; gather street-level information on trademark and copyright infringements; and compile corporate profiles for lawyers involved in mergers and acquisitions. They've even been known to track down lawyers' clients who've skipped out on their legal bills.

Most modern investigators are eager to dispel the hard-boiled gumshoe image that has evolved around private sleuths since the heyday of Sam Spade. They want to be known as professionals providing a professional service. "There's no magic to investigation," says Doug Misiak of the Toronto office of Sahlen International Inc., "just legwork, phone calls, knocking on doors. It takes good common sense, a little bit of luck and a lot of perseverance."

Private investigators are licensed and regulated by most provincial governments. They have no more powers or liberties than the average person — no guns, no running red lights, no trespassing in the line of duty. "It would be a lot easier to do illegal stuff, but we have to maintain our credibility," says Kunkel. A resourceful investigator should be able to get the information and still stay on the right side of the law, he says.

But, let us cut to the chase, as they say. The driver of the blue Ford is leaving the crowded anonymity of the highway for a deserted country road and Kunkel is cursing. The Ford pulls up to an empty intersection and Kunkel slides in directly behind, still cursing, willing himself invisible.

"Don't look back... don't look back," he pleads, while the light takes forever to change. Finally the subject turns a corner, still blissfully ignorant, and Kunkel stretches out the gap between the cars for some breathing room. "If I was as dumb as you I'd commit myself," he chides his target. Kunkel makes no bones about his view of the "bad guys". "I used to think about being a cop until a good friend who was a police officer was shot and killed," he reflects. "This is just

SANDRA DIONISI

TITLE
PRIVATE EYES
ART DIRECTOR
BRUCE WRIGHTE
ILLUSTRATOR
SANDRA DIONISI
DESIGN FIRM
INK
PUBLICATION
CANADIAN LAWYER
PUBLISHER
CANADA LAW BOOK

TITLE
THE SQUEEZED GENERATION
ART DIRECTOR
LINDSAY BEAUDRY
EDITOR
JOHN FITZGERALD
DESIGNER
FERNANDA PISANI
ILLUSTRATOR
STEVE REDMAN
PUBLICATION
TORONTO
PUBLISHER
THE GLOBE AND MAIL

BY JOHN FITZGERALD

THE SQUEEZED GENERATION

When baby boomers find they have both their kids and their parents to care for, obligation can become a vise

The fury of the attack was what surprised her. Helen was standing in the kitchen of her north Toronto home one morning talking on the telephone. Her children were out, her husband was at work and her 80-year-old mother – who with age had developed bouts of paranoia – suddenly became angry that not enough attention was being paid. "She grabbed a can with an open lid from the top of the bin and came at me," Helen recalls. "My own mother!"

For several long minutes, the two women were locked in a macabre slow-moving dance across the kitchen floor, the mother clinging fiercely to Helen's dress with one hand and wielding the can with the glistening serrated edge with the other. "I can't tell you what those moments were like," Helen says with sadness and disbelief. "When I finally calmed my mother down and wrestled the thing away from her, she apologized. 'I must be a sinner,' she said. She knew what she'd done. And that hurt me more than anything else. Sometimes," Helen goes on, "I could just scream. I've got the business to run. I've got a teenaged son having problems in school who needs me. And I've got my mother, whom I love a great deal, living with us. It just gets to be too much sometimes. I find myself taking a drink or two every night now just to get through it."

The woman's real name isn't Helen – "I don't want to sound like an ungrateful daughter, airing the family laundry and all," she says as she begs for the privacy of a pseudonym (given to all but the officials in this story). But her story could be told by anyone shouldering responsibility for a needy elderly relative as well as a job, a household, a young family and the everyday *Sturm und Drang* of getting by. Sociologists describe the Helens of society as "The Squeezed Generation," the mortgaged, middle-aged people sandwiched between the competing demands of their own lives, their children and their elderly parents. For now, personal accounts like theirs are footnotes in the sprawling chapters of family life. But they are also distant early-warning signals of a problem that looms ahead.

Many of the people caring for elderly parents are resentful and frustrated by the lack of options, says an expert. "They see their lives going by. Fast"

It's a problem of colliding numbers. Already the squeeze is starting to close in on baby boomers. Parents in that bulge of the population are beginning to see their own young families move inexorably into their most expensive years – the teenaged years of clothes, cars and university tuition – just as medical science is mastering the mechanics of prolonging life for the elderly. By 2001, according to the Ontario government's white paper on health and social service strategies for the province's seniors, the number of people between the ages of 65 and 74 will increase by approximately 38 per cent; in the over-85 group, those who will undoubtedly require the most extensive services, it's 110 per cent. Coincidentally, governments grappling with the upward spiral of social service costs – education and, particularly, health care – are starting to pass on an even greater share of those responsibilities to families. Sooner or later, the squeeze will be everybody's problem. And when its vise constricts the boomers, the problem of coping will become one of the most pressing social issues of the 1990s.

If the experience of today's squeezed generation is any indication, boomers are going to find it a tough challenge. "Many of the people we've seen are doing what they're doing out of a sense of love and/or duty," says Sunnybrook Medical Centre's Jassy Tracey, who is coordinating a study on the needs of those families who care for elderly parents suffering from

Illustration by Steve Redman

dementia. "But many of these people are also resentful, frustrated and angry by the absence of options. They're doing their part but they know of very few adequate support systems to help them. It's already too late for some of these people. They see their lives going by. Fast."

That sense of confinement, of aloneness, is compounded, in a case like Helen's, by competing loyalties to parents and children. Part owner of a homemaker service, she has a 16-year-old son, a 19-year-old daughter and her own, somewhat erratic, mother living at home with her and her husband. "It's tough on the family," says Helen, struggling to put a face on the emotional turbulence at home. "The kids naturally want to play the stereo and bring their friends in. And the phones are ringing and I'm running around trying to do the household chores and the shopping. Mother gets very anxious and nervous with all the activity. She screams at the kids, telling them not to bring their friends home or that they're running me to the ground. She attacks them in defence of me. They try to be reasonable, but I know they resent her behavior."

The pressures on Janet drove her to gain 25 pounds and seek psychotherapy

Janet works in a Toronto design firm. Now 50, she and her husband have two children in university living at home. Close by is Janet's 77-year-old mother, a widow for the past

THE SQUEEZED GENERATION

19 years, whom she visits twice a week and speaks to every day. The pressures on Janet recently drove her to gain 25 pounds and seek extensive psychotherapy. "My mother has never let go of any of us," she says. "She interferes. When she heard my daughter was planning a trip to Europe, she was on the phone in two seconds, asking me how I could allow my daughter to go, with all the violence over there, and what kind of a mother was I? She's after me all the time. Get me this. Do that. The kids need a lot of time and support as well, especially financially. I have to ration the time. There's probably disappointment on mother's part that I'm not the daughter she expected. Part of me wants to be, hence the guilt."

"I feel pulled in so many different ways." This time the speaker is Doris, a 49-year-old counsellor with a social agency. She steeples her fingers together as if in supplication, and recites her own heavy litany: four grown children, three grandchildren, a 77-year-old father and a 92-year-old mother-in-law in nursing homes and a mother living nearby who argues that for years she was a parent and now, at 74, it's her turn to be taken care of. "Last year," says Doris, "I had a daughter at home, my father went into a medical crisis and we had my son's wedding. I can't tell you how much I was running around. The stress was incredible. My kids want part of me. My mother and father and mother-in-law need me. I think, What about me? No matter how hard I try I end up feeling there are needs somewhere I'm not meeting. My own daughter gave me a sweater recently as a joke. It said, 'Avenge yourself: Live long enough to be a burden to your children.'"

Old age doesn't have to mean a downhill slide into alienation and helplessness, of course. Many seniors not only look after themselves but provide crucial financial, logistical and emotional support for their children and grandchildren. Eventually though, age, illness or a meagre income forces them to call on the younger ones for help in return. Already, families provide the bulk of care to the elderly: an estimated 75 per cent of the health care needs of Canada's 2.9 million people over 65. In part, that's because of the high cost of putting one's parents into an institution. Families of the 45,000 elderly Ontarians in nursing homes and homes for the aged pay between $700 a month for a bed in a government-subsidized home and as much as $3,000 a month for a top-of-the-line private rest home. And already such facilities are packed. According to the Metro Community Services department, in October, 1986, the average length of time people waited between application and admission to a seniors' home was 104 days; by the end of 1988 it had risen to more than 250 days.

Every passing day makes the question of what to do with dependent elderly people more acute. "If we just continue on the way we've been going," says Mavis Wilson, Ontario's minister for senior citizens' affairs, "the provincial health budget in the future is going to be astronomical. The challenge for all of us is to come up with some innovative ways to deal with all the numbers." Wilson, 39, wants to deal with the impending crisis by encouraging people to stay *out* of institutions. "Most of the elderly want to remain as independent as they can for as long as they can," she says. "Families should be responsible for families and communities responsible for each other. The government should be there to assist the community in that job but not take it over." In many cases, that means those who do take it over will be younger members of the family with other responsibilities – the squeezed.

Of course, that's the way it's always been in other times and other cultures. But those cultures – the Chinese and Japanese, for example – exact a price of social rigidity and narrow horizons. In this society, the desire to help may be there, but the rules are muddled.

"My own daughter gave me a sweater recently as a joke," recalls Doris. "It said, 'Avenge yourself: Live long enough to be a burden to your children'"

"No matter what you do, it's a lose-lose situation," sighs Mark, an electronics company executive and, at 38, himself a father with a young family. He and his wife, Kim, a junior partner with a fledgling marketing firm, bought a larger house so they could take in Kim's parents. Her mother was a victim of Parkinson's disease. "Their families on both sides had been wiped out in the Holocaust," Mark recalls. "How could we not feel we had to do everything after what had happened to them? They were fine people. My father-in-law had a heart condition and we knew the burden was too much for him looking after a wife with Parkinson's. He literally had to carry her on his back from room to room.

"We felt desperate for him," he continues. "Morally, we had to take them in. But we had no freedom anymore. We had to stay with her, dress her, take her to the bathroom, do everything for her. It seems that if you don't do anything, you feel guilty, and what you do do has a price."

The young couple modified their house for the new occupants, putting in railings, an intercom, even a separate kitchen and bathroom. "It cost plenty to make the adjustments and of course we weren't reimbursed. There's no government money for this. We kept wondering what we'd do if something happened to my father-in-law. He was a great help with his wife and very self-reliant. What we'd feared happened, and he died three years ago. And for 15 months, until she was able to get a bed in a nursing home, my mother-in-law was here. It's hard on everyone living with a person who's sick. There was my mother-in-law's coughing fits and the accidents and the spitting up. It was like having a young child in the house again, only we were watching her deteriorate. At some point, you end up thinking this can only be happening to you."

How Mark and Kim faced their problem seems singularly heroic – and probably atypical. Boomers are the most coddled generation in history, and the one that has experimented most with family values. How many others like them would be willing to make similar sacrifices? Says University of Toronto gerontologist Blossom Wigdor, "Baby boomers are very individualistic, very competitive. They're not by nature team players. They love their parents, but they also want to get on with their own lives. They find it difficult for someone to invade their space."

"I'd send money if it was needed," says Ken, a 39-year-old trust company vice-president. "I visit every few months – but I let my sister handle the day-to-day things." Ken's widowed mother, 78, is now in a nurs-

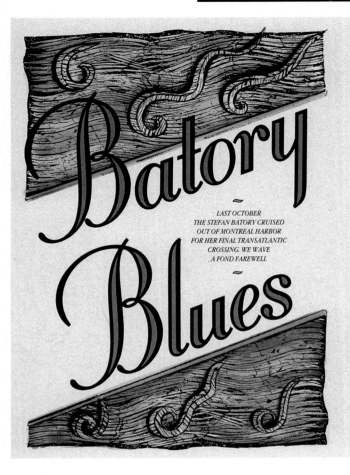

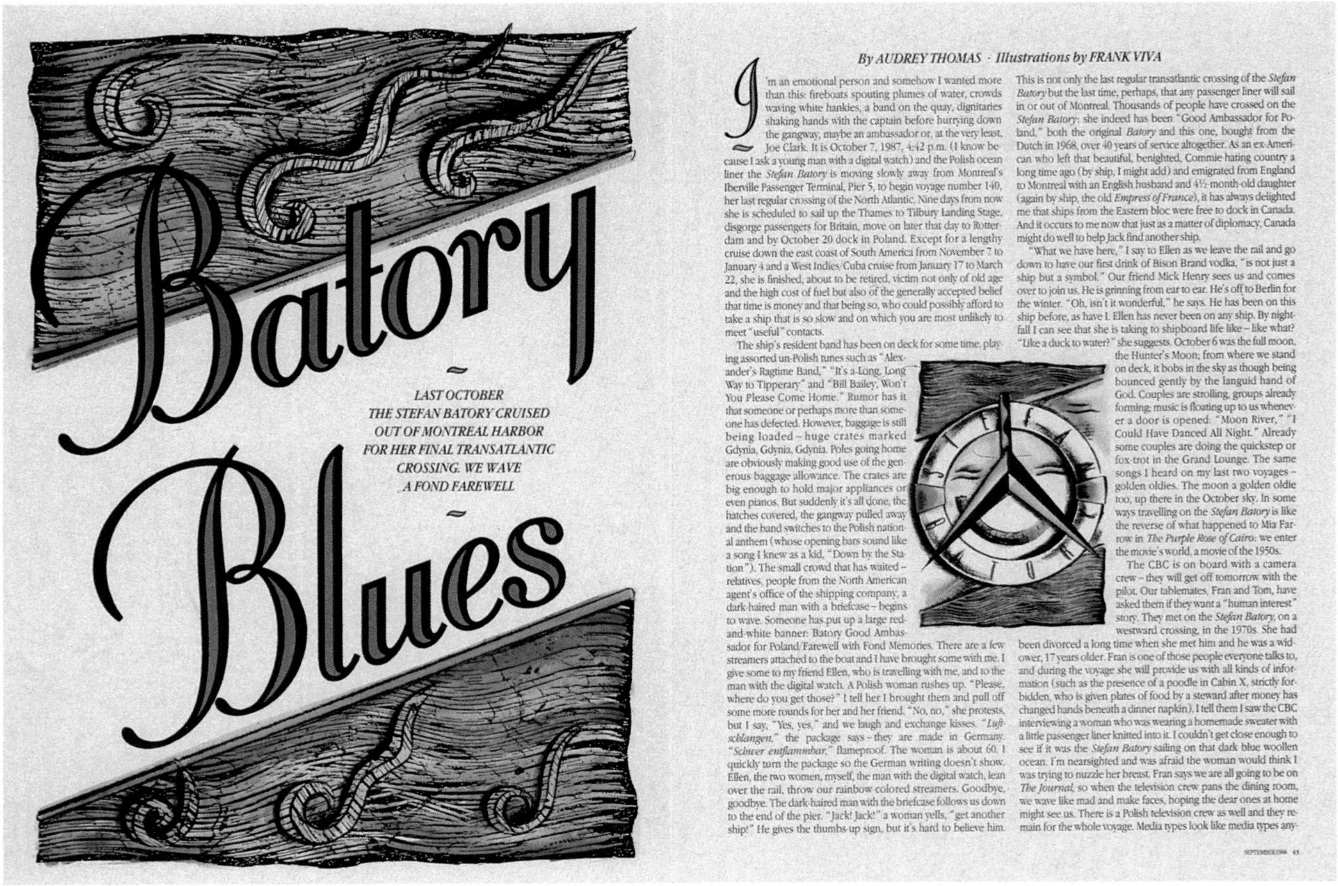

Batory Blues

LAST OCTOBER
THE STEFAN BATORY CRUISED
OUT OF MONTREAL HARBOR
FOR HER FINAL TRANSATLANTIC
CROSSING. WE WAVE
A FOND FAREWELL

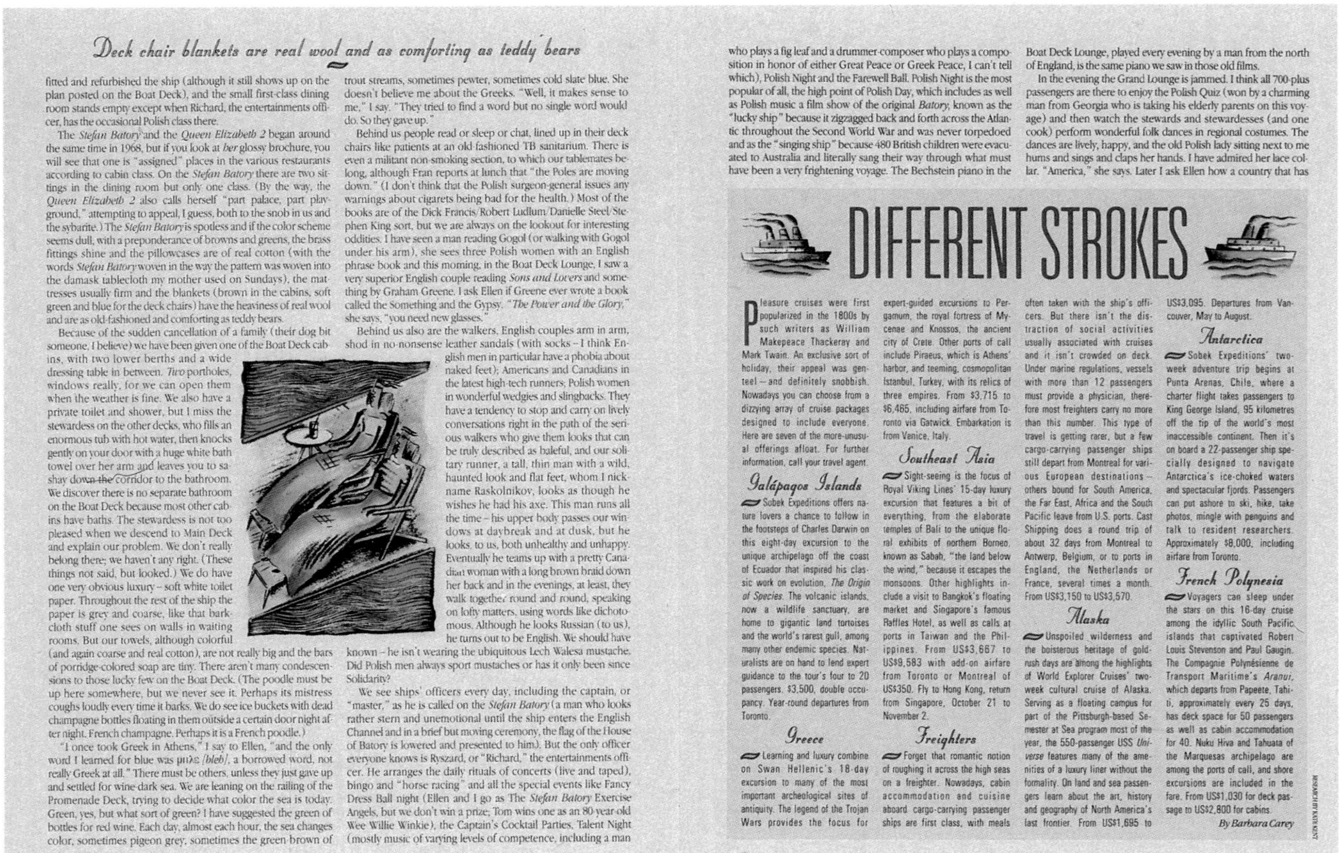

By AUDREY THOMAS · Illustrations by FRANK VIVA

I'm an emotional person and somehow I wanted more than this: fireboats spouting plumes of water, crowds waving white hankies, a band on the quay, dignitaries shaking hands with the captain before hurrying down the gangway, maybe an ambassador or, at the very least, Joe Clark. It is October 7, 1987, 4:42 p.m. (I know because I ask a young man with a digital watch) and the Polish ocean liner the *Stefan Batory* is moving slowly away from Montreal's Iberville Passenger Terminal, Pier 5, to begin voyage number 140, her last regular crossing of the North Atlantic. Nine days from now she is scheduled to sail up the Thames to Tilbury Landing Stage, disgorge passengers for Britain, move on later that day to Rotterdam and by October 20 dock in Poland. Except for a lengthy cruise down the east coast of South America from November 7 to January 4 and a West Indies/Cuba cruise from January 17 to March 22, she is finished, about to be retired, victim not only of old age and the high cost of fuel but also of the generally accepted belief that time is money and that being so, who could possibly afford to take a ship that is so slow and on which you are most unlikely to meet "useful" contacts.

The ship's resident band has been on deck for some time, playing assorted un-Polish tunes such as "Alexander's Ragtime Band," "It's a Long, Long Way to Tipperary" and "Bill Bailey, Won't You Please Come Home." Rumor has it that someone or perhaps more than someone has defected. However, baggage is still being loaded – huge crates marked Gdynia, Gdynia, Gdynia. Poles going home are obviously making good use of the generous baggage allowance. The crates are big enough to hold major appliances or even pianos. But suddenly it's all done, the hatches covered, the gangway pulled away and the band switches to the Polish national anthem (whose opening bars sound like a song I knew as a kid, "Down by the Station"). The small crowd that has waited – relatives, people from the North American agent's office of the shipping company, a dark-haired man with a briefcase – begins to wave. Someone has put up a large red-and-white banner: Batory Good Ambassador for Poland/Farewell with Fond Memories. There are a few streamers attached to the boat and I have brought some with me. I give some to my friend Ellen, who is travelling with me, and to the man with the digital watch. A Polish woman rushes up, "Please, where do you get those?" I tell her I brought them and pull off some more rounds for her and her friend. "No, no," she protests, but I say, "Yes, yes," and we hug and exchange kisses. "*Luftschlangen*," the package says – they are made in Germany. "*Schwer entflammbar*," flameproof. The woman is about 60. I quickly turn the package so the German writing doesn't show. Ellen, the two women, myself, the man with the digital watch, lean over the rail, throw our rainbow-colored streamers. Goodbye, goodbye. The dark-haired man with the briefcase follows us down to the end of the pier. "Jack! Jack!" a woman yells, "get another ship!" He gives the thumbs-up sign, but it's hard to believe him.

This is not only the last regular transatlantic crossing of the *Stefan Batory* but the last time, perhaps, that any passenger liner will sail in or out of Montreal. Thousands of people have crossed on the *Stefan Batory*; she indeed has been "Good Ambassador for Poland," both the original *Batory* and this one, bought from the Dutch in 1968, over 40 years of service altogether. As an ex-American who left that beautiful, benighted, Commie-hating country a long time ago (by ship, I might add) and emigrated from England to Montreal with an English husband and 4½-month-old daughter (again by ship, the old *Empress of France*), it has always delighted me that ships from the Eastern bloc were free to dock in Canada. And it occurs to me now that just as a matter of diplomacy, Canada might do well to help Jack find another ship.

"What we have here," I say to Ellen as we leave the rail and go down to have our first drink of Bison Brand vodka, "is not just a ship but a symbol." Our friend Mick Henry sees us and comes over to join us. He is grinning from ear to ear. He's off to Berlin for the winter. "Oh, isn't it wonderful," he says. He has been on this ship before, as have I. Ellen has never been on any ship. By nightfall I can see that she is taking to shipboard life like – like what? "Like a duck to water?" she suggests. October 6 was the full moon, the Hunter's Moon; from where we stand on deck, it bobs in the sky as though being bounced gently by the languid hand of God. Couples are strolling, groups already forming, music is floating up to us whenever a door is opened: "Moon River," "I Could Have Danced All Night." Already some couples are doing the quickstep or fox trot in the Grand Lounge. The same songs I heard on my last two voyages – golden oldies. The moon a golden oldie too, up there in the October sky. In some ways travelling on the *Stefan Batory* is like the reverse of what happened to Mia Farrow in *The Purple Rose of Cairo*: we enter the movie's world, a movie of the 1950s.

The CBC is on board with a camera crew – they will get off tomorrow with the pilot. Our tablemates, Fran and Tom, have asked them if they want a "human interest" story. They met on the *Stefan Batory*, on a westward crossing, in the 1970s. She had been divorced a long time when she met him and he was a widower, 17 years older. Fran is one of those people everyone talks to, and during the voyage she will provide us with all kinds of information (such as the presence of a poodle in Cabin X, strictly forbidden, who is given plates of food by a steward after money has changed hands beneath a dinner napkin). I tell them I saw the CBC interviewing a woman who was wearing a homemade sweater with a little passenger liner knitted into it. I couldn't get close enough to see if it was the *Stefan Batory* sailing on that dark blue woollen ocean. I'm nearsighted and was afraid the woman would think I was trying to nuzzle her breast. Fran says we are all going to be on *The Journal*, so when the television crew pans the dining room, we wave like mad and make faces, hoping the dear ones at home might see us. There is a Polish television crew as well and they remain for the whole voyage. Media types look like media types any-

Deck chair blankets are real wool and as comforting as teddy bears

fitted and refurbished the ship (although it still shows up on the plan posted on the Boat Deck), and the small first-class dining room stands empty except when Richard, the entertainments officer, has the occasional Polish class there.

The *Stefan Batory* and the *Queen Elizabeth 2* began around the same time in 1968, but if you look at *her* glossy brochure, you will see that one is "assigned" places in the various restaurants according to class. On the *Stefan Batory* there are two sittings in the dining room but only one class. (By the way, the *Queen Elizabeth 2* also calls herself "part palace, part playground," attempting to appeal, I guess, both to the snob in us and the sybarite.) The *Stefan Batory* is spotless and if the color scheme seems dull, with a preponderance of browns and greens, the brass fittings shine and the pillowcases are of real cotton (with the words *Stefan Batory* woven in the way the pattern was woven into the damask tablecloth my mother used on Sundays), the mattresses usually firm and the blankets (brown in the cabins, soft green and blue for the deck chairs) have the heaviness of real wool and are as old-fashioned and comforting as teddy bears.

Because of the sudden cancellation of a family (their dog bit someone, I believe) we have been given one of the Boat Deck cabins, with two lower berths and a wide dressing table in between. *Two* portholes, windows really, for we can open them when the weather is fine. We also have a private toilet and shower, but I miss the stewardess on the other decks, who fills an enormous tub with hot water, then knocks gently on your door with a huge white bath towel over her arm and leaves you to sashay down *the* corridor to the bathroom. We discover there is no separate bathroom on the Boat Deck because most other cabins have baths. The stewardess is not too pleased when we descend to Main Deck and explain our problem. We don't really belong there; we haven't any right. (These things not said, but looked.) We do have one very obvious luxury – soft white toilet paper. Throughout the rest of the ship the paper is grey and coarse, like that barkcloth stuff one sees on walls in waiting rooms. But our towels, although colorful (and again coarse and real cotton), are not really big and the bars of porridge-colored soap are tiny. There aren't many condescensions to those lucky few on the Boat Deck. (The poodle must be up here somewhere, but we never see it. Perhaps its mistress coughs loudly every time it barks. We do see ice buckets with dead champagne bottles floating in them outside a certain door night after night, French champagne. Perhaps it is a French poodle.)

"I once took Greek in Athens," I say to Ellen, "and the only word I learned for blue was *ρπόξ* /*bleh*/, a borrowed word, not really Greek at all." There must be others, unless they just gave up and settled for wine dark sea. We are leaning on the railing of the Promenade Deck, trying to decide what color the sea is today: Green, yes, but what sort of green? I have suggested the green of bottles for red wine. Each day, almost each hour, the sea changes color, sometimes pigeon grey, sometimes the green brown of

trout streams, sometimes pewter, sometimes cold slate blue. She doesn't believe me about the Greeks. "Well, it makes sense to me," I say. "They tried to find a word but no single word would do. So they gave up."

Behind us people read or sleep or chat, lined up in their deck chairs like patients at an old fashioned TB sanitarium. There is even a militant non-smoking section, to which our tablemates belong, although Fran reports at lunch that "the Poles are moving down." (I don't think that the Polish surgeon-general raises any warnings about cigarets being bad for the health.) Most of the books are of the Dick Francis/Robert Ludlum/Danielle Steel/Stephen King sort, but we are always on the lookout for interesting oddities. I have seen a man reading Gogol (or walking with Gogol under his arm), she sees three Polish women with an English phrase book and this morning, in the Boat Deck Lounge, I saw a very superior English couple reading *Sons and Lovers* and something by Graham Greene. I ask Ellen if Greene ever wrote a book called the Something and the Gypsy, "*The Power and the Glory*," she says, "you need new glasses."

Behind us also are the walkers, English couples arm in arm, shod in no-nonsense leather sandals (with socks – I think English men in particular have a phobia about naked feet); Americans and Canadians in the latest high-tech runners, Polish women in wonderful wedgies and slingbacks. They have a tendency to stop and carry on lively conversations right in the path of the serious walkers who give them looks that can be truly described as baleful, and our solitary runner, a tall, thin man with a wild, haunted look and flat feet, whom I nickname Raskolnikov, looks as though he wishes he had his axe. This man runs all the time – his upper body passes our windows at daybreak and at dusk, but he looks, to us, both unhealthy and unhappy. Eventually he teams up with a pretty Canadian woman with a long brown braid down her back and in the evenings, at least, they walk together, round and round, speaking on lofty matters, using words like dichotomous. Although he looks Russian (to us), he turns out to be English. We should have known – he isn't wearing the ubiquitous Lech Walesa mustache. Did Polish men always sport mustaches or has it only been since Solidarity?

We see ships' officers every day, including the captain, or "master," as he is called on the *Stefan Batory* (a man who looks rather stern and unemotional until the ship enters the English Channel and in a brief but moving ceremony, the flag of the House of Batory is lowered and presented to him). But the only officer everyone knows is Ryszard, or "Richard," the entertainments officer. He arranges the daily rituals of concerts (live and taped), bingo and "horse racing" and all the special events like Fancy Dress Ball night (Ellen and I go as The *Stefan Batory* Exercise Angels, but we don't win a prize; Tom wins one as an 80-year-old Wee Willie Winkie), the Captain's Cocktail Parties, Talent Night (mostly music of varying levels of competence, including a man

who plays a fig leaf and a drummer-composer who plays a composition in honor of either Great Peace or Greek Peace, I can't tell which), Polish Night and the Farewell Ball. Polish Night is the most popular of all, the high point of Polish Day, which includes as well as Polish music a film show of the original *Batory*, known as the "lucky ship" because it zigzagged back and forth across the Atlantic throughout the Second World War and was never torpedoed and as the "singing ship" because 480 British children were evacuated to Australia and literally sang their way through what must have been a very frightening voyage. The Bechstein piano in the Boat Deck Lounge, played every evening by a man from the north of England, is the same piano we saw in those old films.

In the evening the Grand Lounge is jammed. I think all 700-plus passengers are there to enjoy the Polish Quiz (won by a charming man from Georgia who is taking his elderly parents on this voyage) and then watch the stewards and stewardesses (and one cook) perform wonderful folk dances in regional costumes. The dances are lively, happy, and the old Polish lady sitting next to me hums and sings and claps her hands. I have admired her lace collar. "America," she says. Later I ask Ellen how a country that has

DIFFERENT STROKES

Pleasure cruises were first popularized in the 1800s by such writers as William Makepeace Thackeray and Mark Twain. An exclusive sort of holiday, their appeal was genteel – and definitely snobbish. Nowadays you can choose from a dizzying array of cruise packages designed to include everyone. Here are seven of the more unusual offerings afloat. For further information, call your travel agent.

Galápagos Islands

Sobek Expeditions offers nature lovers a chance to follow in the footsteps of Charles Darwin on this eight-day excursion to the unique archipelago off the coast of Ecuador that inspired his classic work on evolution, *The Origin of Species*. The volcanic islands, now a wildlife sanctuary, are home to gigantic land tortoises and the world's rarest gull, among many other endemic species. Naturalists are on hand to lend expert guidance to the tour's four to 20 passengers. $3,500, double occupancy. Year-round departures from Toronto.

Greece

Learning and luxury combine on Swan Hellenic's 18-day excursion to some of the most important archeological sites of antiquity. The legend of the Trojan Wars provides the focus for expert-guided excursions to Pergamum, the royal fortress of Mycenae and Knossos, the ancient city of Crete. Other ports of call include Piraeus, which is Athens' harbor, and teeming, cosmopolitan Istanbul, Turkey, with its relics of three empires. From $3,715 to $6,465, including airfare from Toronto via Gatwick. Embarkation is from Venice, Italy.

Southeast Asia

Sight-seeing is the focus of Royal Viking Lines' 15-day luxury excursion that features a bit of everything, from the elaborate temples of Bali to the unique floral exhibits of northern Borneo, known as Sabah, "the land below the wind," because it escapes the monsoons. Other highlights include a visit to Bangkok's floating market and Singapore's famous Raffles Hotel, as well as calls at ports in Taiwan and the Philippines. From US$3,667 to US$9,593 with add-on airfare from Toronto or Montreal of US$350. Fly to Hong Kong, return from Singapore, October 21 to November 2.

Alaska

Unspoiled wilderness and the boisterous heritage of gold-rush days are among the highlights of World Explorer Cruises' two-week cultural cruise of Alaska. Serving as a floating campus for part of the Pittsburgh-based Semester at Sea program most of the year, the 550-passenger USS *Universe* features many of the amenities of a luxury liner without the formality. On land and sea passengers learn about the art, history and geography of North America's last frontier. From US$1,695 to

Freighters

Forget that romantic notion of roughing it across the high seas on a freighter. Nowadays, cabin accommodation and cuisine aboard cargo-carrying passenger ships are first class, with meals often taken with the ship's officers. But there isn't the distraction of social activities usually associated with cruises and it isn't crowded on deck. Under marine regulations, vessels with more than 12 passengers must provide a physician, therefore most freighters carry no more than this number. This type of travel is getting rare, but a few cargo-carrying passenger ships still depart from Montreal for various European destinations – others bound for South America, the Far East, Africa and the South Pacific leave from U.S. ports. Cast Shipping does a round trip of about 32 days from Montreal to Antwerp, Belgium, or to ports in England, the Netherlands or France, several times a month. From US$3,150 to US$3,570.

US$3,095. Departures from Vancouver, May to August.

Antarctica

Sobek Expeditions' two-week adventure trip begins at Punta Arenas, Chile, where a charter flight takes passengers to King George Island, 95 kilometres off the tip of the world's most inaccessible continent. Then it's on board a 27-passenger ship specially designed to navigate Antarctica's ice-choked waters and spectacular fjords. Passengers can put ashore to ski, hike, take photos, mingle with penguins and talk to resident researchers. Approximately $8,000, including airfare from Toronto.

French Polynesia

Voyagers can sleep under the stars on this 16-day cruise among the idyllic South Pacific islands that captivated Robert Louis Stevenson and Paul Gauguin. The Compagnie Polynésienne de Transport Maritime's *Aranui*, which departs from Papeete, Tahiti, approximately every 25 days, has deck space for 50 passengers as well as cabin accommodation for 40. Nuku Hiva and Tahuata of the Marquesas archipelago are among the ports of call, and shore excursions are included in the fare. From US$1,030 for deck passage to US$2,800 for cabins.

By Barbara Carey

TITLE
BATORY BLUES
ART DIRECTOR
NADIA MARYNIAK
EDITOR
JACK McIVER
DESIGNER
NADIA MARYNIAK
ILLUSTRATOR
FRANK VIVA
PUBLICATION
DESTINATIONS
PUBLISHER
THE GLOBE AND MAIL

TITLE
FOOL'S GOLD
ART DIRECTOR
CARMEN DUNJKO
EDITOR
MORDECAI RICHLER
ILLUSTRATOR
STEVE BRODNER
PUBLICATION
SATURDAY NIGHT
PUBLISHER
**HOLLINGER
PUBLICATIONS INC.**

TITLE
MIND OVER BATTER
ART DIRECTOR
**TERESA FERNANDES/
JANICE GOLDBERG**
EDITOR
MARQ de VILLIERS
DESIGNER
JANICE GOLDBERG
ILLUSTRATOR
PETER de SEVE
PUBLICATION
TORONTO LIFE
PUBLISHER
**KEY PUBLISHERS
CO. LTD.**

FICTION

Milk Bread Beer Ice

"During those twenty-four hours they released into the mild air of the marriage counsellor's office millions of words: their longest conversation"

What's the difference between a gully and a gulch?" Barbara Cormin asks her husband, Peter Cormin, as they speed south on the interstate. These are the first words to pass between them in over an hour, this laconic, idle, unhopefully offered, trivia-contoured question.

Peter Cormin, driving a cautious sixty miles an hour through a drizzle of rain, makes no reply, and Barbara, from long experience, expects none. Her question concerning the difference between gullies and gulches floats out of her mouth like a smoker's lazy exhalation and is instantly subsumed by the hum of the engine. Two minutes pass. Five minutes. Barbara's thoughts skip to different geological features, the curious wind-lashed forms she sees through the car window, and those others whose names she vaguely remembers from a compulsory geology course taken years earlier — arroyos, cirques, terminal moraines. She has no idea now what these exotic relics might look like, but imagines them to be so brutal and arresting as to be instantly recognizable should they materialize on the landscape. Please let them materialize, she prays to the grooved door of the glove compartment. Let something, *anything*, materialize.

This is their fifth day on the road. Four motels, interchangeable, with tawny, fire-retardant carpeting, are all that have intervened. This morning, Day Five, they drive through a strong brown and yellow landscape, ferociously eroded, and it cheers Barbara a little to gaze out at this scene of novelty after 1,700 miles of green hills and

BY CAROL SHIELDS

TITLE
MILK BREAD BEER ICE
ART DIRECTOR
CARMEN DUNJKO
EDITOR
CAROL SHIELDS
ILLUSTRATOR
JOHN CRAIG
PUBLICATION
SATURDAY NIGHT
PUBLISHER
HOLLINGER PUBLICATIONS INC.

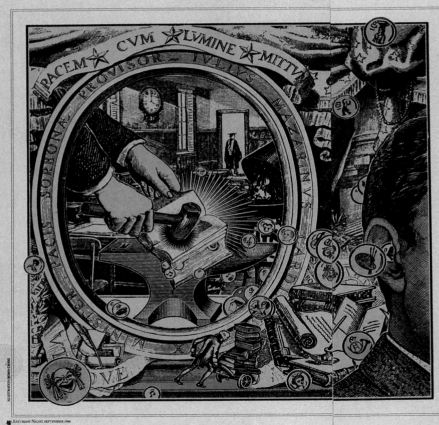

LEARNING ON THE LOW ROAD

People who are wholly ignorant of art, philosophy, literature, music, and history seem to do very well at university today

A university teacher in the humanities is like a blacksmith working in the basement of a nuclear-power station. He does the same old job with the same old tools, but above his head he hears the hum of machinery and the marching feet of the technocrats.

The same job, the same tools. The requirements for teaching subjects like Greek and English are unchanging. True, there are overhead projectors and assorted other audiovisual aids available. But these are of little use in humane subjects, and people who enjoy them are often entertainers rather than teachers. A well-lit classroom with a lectern and desks, a blackboard with chalk and eraser, and, of course, books in the library are the ingredients of a course in philosophy, and not even all of those are essential. A professor goes behind the lectern and talks to students, who may or may not take notes. So it was in the medieval university; so it is now.

From this it might be thought that the instructor in Greek or philosophy places modest demands on the university budget. And indeed, they are modest. But go into any big university in Canada and observe the classrooms where such a person must teach. Chances are the lighting will be poor, the desks rickety and covered with gum and graffiti, the walls in need of paint, the lectern dam-

by Patrick O'Flaherty

TITLE
LEARNING ON THE LOW ROAD
ART DIRECTOR
BRUCE RAMSAY
EDITOR
PATRICK O'FLAHERTY
DESIGNER
KASPAR deLINE
ILLUSTRATOR
JOHN CRAIG
PUBLICATION
SATURDAY NIGHT
PUBLISHER
HOLLINGER PUBLICATIONS INC.

TITLE
**SEXUAL ETIQUETTE
FOR THE '90s**
ART DIRECTOR
**TERESA FERNANDES/
MARTHA WEAVER**
WRITER
MARTHA WEAVER
EDITOR
MARQ de VILLIERS
ILLUSTRATOR
BARRY BLITT
PUBLICATION
TORONTO LIFE
PUBLISHER
**KEY PUBLISHERS
CO. LTD.**

TITLE
HOME TRUTHS
ART DIRECTOR
**TERESA FERNANDES/
MARTHA WEAVER**
EDITOR
MARQ de VILLIERS
DESIGNER
MARTHA WEAVER
ILLUSTRATOR
ANITA KUNZ
PUBLICATION
TORONTO LIFE
PUBLISHER
**KEY PUBLISHERS
CO. LTD.**

TITLE
**FLORENCE DOESN'T
WORK HERE ANYMORE**
ART DIRECTOR
**TERESA FERNANDES/
JANICE GOLDBERG**
EDITOR
MARQ de VILLIERS
DESIGNER
JANICE GOLDBERG
ILLUSTRATOR
LANE SMITH
PUBLICATION
TORONTO LIFE
PUBLISHER
**KEY PUBLISF
CO. LTD.**

Florence Doesn't Work Here Any More

BY ANNA PRODANOU

Why Toronto's nurses are fed up, burned out—and no longer willing to be silent nightingales

I was in intensive care with a patient who was developing ventricular arrhythmia, a heartbeat irregularity that can lead to cardiac arrest and requires that the patient receive a continuous infusion. As I was attending to this patient, a doctor called me next door to suction the lungs of a second patient who, if not treated immediately, would be put on a ventilator to help him breathe and, once hooked up, might never come off the unit again. Meanwhile, in the third room was a patient who was scheduled for peritoneal dialysis, or exchange of waste products, every fifteen minutes on the dot. When this patient's nurse left on a much-needed break, she was not replaced, and I was asked to cover for her. During this same thirty-minute period, I was also asked by another nurse, who had to step away to get supplies, to keep an eye on a patient in Room 4. All I knew about this last patient was that she was on life supports and that she was restless."

The speaker is Margaret Molnar, twenty-six, a critical-care nurse in the medical and surgical intensive care unit (ICU) of Wellesley Hospital. Her voice is anxious but controlled—it's not every day that she speaks about her work to a roomful of reporters.

Molnar is one of several critical-care nurses, most of them members of the executive of Local 94 of the Ontario Nurses' Association, who along with NDP Leader Bob Rae have called this press conference on a bright September morning in the media room of a building adjacent to Wellesley. One by one they speak of their own experiences: the shifts that keep them away from their families on weekends and holidays, the low pay, poor opportunities for further training, stress, the lack of recognition from administration and the public and, above all, the shortage of help by the bedside.

One of the nurses, twenty-five-year-old Elaine Rumleskie, announces she is about to leave the profession altogether. Margaret Molnar and several others

ILLUSTRATIONS BY LANE SMITH

---

say they have switched to part-time work to avoid shifts that play havoc with their home lives. "There are so many better options for young women today than going into nursing," says Carol Helmstadter, the fifty-six-year-old president of the Wellesley nurses' union local. Her colleague, Sheila Croft, a thirty-year veteran of the profession and a Wellesley graduate, agrees. "I forbade my two daughters to even think of nursing as a career," she tells reporters. "People come up to me and ask me, 'Are you still nursing?' Can you imagine people asking that of a lawyer or an accountant?"

It is surprising how candid and forthright these nurses are, but for many of them the time for grumbling over the lunchroom table has passed. After months of trying to work within the system, they have realized that going public is the only way to get action. They are not a group of inexperienced rookies or publicity-seeking militants. They are highly skilled and dedicated nurses. Take Carol Helmstadter, for instance—tall, poised, married to a university professor, mother of three adult daughters—she is a nursing graduate of Columbia University, class of '56, and a critical-care nurse in the neurosurgical unit at Wellesley. "It's not easy for us," she says, "but if we don't speak out for ourselves, no one is going to help us."

Incidents such as the one described by Molnar only serve to remind them how much is at stake. While no crisis took place on Wellesley's ICU that day, Molnar knows it could happen all over again: at the time, approximately 100

Early warnings about the crisis were ignored

out of 500 nursing positions at the hospital were vacant, and this continues to be the case now. There are similar shortages at other hospitals in the city. "I wouldn't want to be a patient anywhere right now. And that's an honest statement," she says.

Toronto's nursing shortage has been almost three years in the making, and it has taken as long to acknowledge and document it. In 1983 and 1984 the vacancy rate for the 16,000 nursing positions in Metro's hospitals was a fraction of one per cent. By March 1988 it had risen to 7.1 per cent. Some hospitals are much harder hit than others. Many of the suburban institutions are relatively well staffed, while in downtown Toronto, with its high concentration of teaching hospitals with specialized units, the vacancy rate can be much higher than the Metro average. Most affected are the high-stress

areas: critical care, long-term care and psychiatric care.

By last summer, as the shortage worsened, 1,300 hospital beds had been closed—twelve per cent more than in 1987. While summer bed closures are customary, usually most of them reopen by fall. But last September, half of them didn't, and some institutions were literally begging for nursing applicants. Oversize ads appeared regularly on the first page of *The Globe and Mail* medical classified section. One day it would be Wellesley pleading: "We're so eager to talk to you about your career, we want you to call collect!" The next day it would be St. Michael's: "Handle with care, that's what we'll do with your nursing career."

Then in October, Albert Horlock, an Orangeville man, lay in a helicopter with a bleeding aneurysm while Toronto General Hospital and Sunnybrook Medical Centre argued for twenty minutes about which one had sufficient staff to admit him. Dr. Murray Girotti, TGH's director of trauma, stated at the time that the lack of nurses would mean cases like Horlock's would happen over and over again.

And they did. During the first week of December, Gary McDougall, who had sustained multiple compound fractures when hit by a car, waited seven hours for admission to one of the teaching hospitals equipped with the necessary cardiac facilities to operate on him. A few days before Christmas, Charles Coleman died following heart bypass surgery at St. Michael's. His operation had been postponed eleven times.

Partly as a result of intensive media coverage, the province ordered an investigation into each of the incidents amid charges at Queen's Park from the opposition that the shortage of nurses, lack of beds and waiting lists for surgery could no longer be tolerated. But Girotti, a member of a provincial task force on critical care and a chair of its subcommittee on manpower requirements, doesn't see the situation improving: "There may not be patients refused, but there will be delays. For places like Toronto we are seeing clearly that the shortage of nurses is one of the bottlenecks in accessibility."

As early as the fall of 1986, *The Toronto Star* and

One nurse says, "I wouldn't want to be a patient anywhere right now. That's an honest statement"

Gunrunners, Fundraisers and Keepers of the Orange Faith

BY HOWARD GOLDENTHAL

How this city's loyalist, law-abiding (with one arms-smuggling exception) Irish community is troubled by the troubles in Northern Ireland

IN BELFAST, WHERE MURDER-gangs and political parties are often indistinguishable, there is no such thing as a walk-in constituency office. You press the buzzer and after a few moments the door to the Progressive Unionist Party headquarters, barely visible through the spiderweb of steel netting, pops open. A face-level camera jutts from the wall near the front of the empty corridor. In Belfast, you are always under surveillance.

Paranoia and fear permeate this city. So much death, so much hate. Twenty years of guerrilla warfare—the IRA trying to blast Ulster into the Irish republic, and the loyalists carrying out their own terrorist campaigns to stay British—has institutionalized assassinations, kneecappings and bombings. Toronto seems much more than just an ocean away.

You are led into a barren back room by three young, tough-looking men. On one wall is a picture of Edward Carson, a hero to the Ulster loyalists and the founder of the original Ulster Volunteer Force (UVF) in the early part of this century. After a few moments of tense table-tapping, the door opens and a tall, rotund man enters. His name is Ken Hagan, a one-time resident of Toronto and now the political researcher for the reconstituted Progressive Unionist Party, an organization that, like its paramilitary wing, the UVF, sees itself as the guardian of Protestantism and the throne in the six counties that constitute Ulster.

ILLUSTRATIONS BY MARSHALL ARISMAN

Hagan returned to Belfast from his relatively quiet life in Toronto in 1969, the year political murder became a way of life in Northern Ireland. He scoffs at the suggestion that the outbreak of violence and his arrival in Ulster may be connected. "You think I went back to organize the defence of Belfast?" he asks sarcastically.

In May 1987, over a year before our conversation, Liverpool police charged Hagan with smuggling weapons to the UVF, between 1980 and 1986, via Liverpool (through men named Albert Watt, a Torontonian then living by the Mersey; and Trevor Cubbins, who ran a Liverpool trucking company) and Toronto (through Howard Anthony Wright, a member of the Canadian militia; and William Charles Taylor, an Etobicoke electrician). "They were trying to make out that I was the linkman with Belfast," says Hagan, "linking up Liverpool and Canada, because I lived in Canada, you know, and stuff like that."

prohibited weapons and committing him to stand trial).

"I don't know if this fellow Taylor is a first- or second-removed generation from Northern Ireland," says Hagan, who had no further legal troubles from Liverpool authorities due to the fact they couldn't come up with any evidence to establish his guilt. (However, he is now banned from entering the mainland under the British Prevention of Terrorism Act.) "I haven't a clue, never met the chap, but probably he thought in his own way he was going to do something to eradicate the IRA."

The smuggling began in 1980, when a number of sealed packages addressed to people who had died were sent from Canada to Scotland, where they would be smuggled on to Ulster. Three of the packages were intercepted by Scottish customs agents in Glasgow in 1981—one contained a submachine-gun, while the other two contained handguns—but over the years many more got through, a fact that

Paranoia and fear permeate Belfast. So much death, so much hate. Twenty years of guerrilla warfare has institutionalized assassinations, kneecappings and bombings. Toronto seems much more than just an ocean away. Yet for members of our city's Irish community, the troubles over there affect the lives of friends and family

Meanwhile, in a separate, though related, action last September in Canada, Howard Anthony Wright was standing trial in Toronto's district court on University Avenue. The tall Anthony Perkins look-alike was facing charges of conspiring (with ten unindicted co-conspirators, among them Watt, Cubbins and Taylor) to smuggle weapons from Toronto to Belfast during that same six-year period.

For nearly two weeks, witness after witness took the stand, each adding details about the illegal enterprise. The alleged mastermind behind the operation was William Charles Taylor, originally from Belfast, who in Britain faces a charge of "conspiring to introduce firearms that are likely to cause harm to others" (part of Britain's antiterrorist legislation) and is now fighting an extradition order for his role in the gunrunning (two months ago, the Canadian government added to his troubles, charging him with possession of

didn't become clear until five years later.

On Christmas Day in 1986, the RCMP raided William Charles Taylor's Etobicoke home. Inside, among other items, was a UVF weapons list, and one of the items fit the description of a firearm that the Royal Ulster Constabulary had found in a loyalist house in Belfast five years earlier. Also found at the Taylor address was a hollowed-out Chrysler engine block, which was about to be used to smuggle weapons through Liverpool. The inner wall of the engine had been lined with lead to prevent X-ray machines from detecting the deadly cargo.

When the first Toronto packages of guns were being sent overseas in 1980, the UVF, according to the London-based anti-Nazi journal *Searchlight*, was also scrounging around Europe and the U.S. looking for other sources of firepower. The search took them to a seedy café in Antwerp, Belgium, run by the violent

TITLE
**THE INCIDENTAL
TOURIST**
ART DIRECTOR
JIM IRELAND
EDITOR
WAYNE GOODING
DESIGNER
DONNA BRAGGINS
ILLUSTRATOR
STEVE ATTOE
PUBLICATION
CANADIAN BUSINESS
PUBLISHER
CB MEDIA

SPECIAL REPORT

THE INCIDENTAL TOURIST

WHEN THE BUSINESS TRAVELER HITS
TOWN ON A TWO-DAY BLITZ, TIME IS PRECIOUS.
HERE'S HOW TO MAKE THE MOST OF IT

BY ROSS FISHER

For the business person, travel in the late 1980s is more survival than arrival. Getting in and out of airports is a lot tougher than it was a decade ago, and few travelers would now agree with the old slogan, "Getting there is half the fun."

Nevertheless, the knowing traveler can do quite well by following this guide to six business capitals. Included you'll find such arcane traveler's lore as the best airlines for hurried schedules and advice on navigating the downtown core. But can you get more out of a two-day trip than jet lag and, maybe, a solid deal? It *is* possible to enjoy a strange city without joining the herds of idle tourists. You can penetrate the silver vaults in London, or find peace by the Pacific in Vancouver. No matter how unfamiliar the city, there's an attraction for every taste.

This is the age of megacities. From London to Toronto, from Vancouver to Montreal, a business traveler increasingly gets the feeling he or she is part of some huge man-hive. It would take the best part of a day to cross London; a morning

before you've gone from downtown Toronto, conducted a business meeting 20 kilometres north in Markham, and returned to your hotel.

How pleasant then to stay in a well-managed, personalized property where you are a guest and not a checkout number. All the hotels listed here have what the American travel writer Andrew Harper calls the Q factor—the intangible summary impression that separates the merely good from the truly special. Special weight has been given to friendliness, attentiveness and efficiency. Most of the hotels offer concierge service or the attention of the owner-manager. If you need a hard-to-get ticket for the city's best play or a table at an exclusive restaurant, a concierge can perform wonders. All of the hotels are centrally located, and, as the guide on pages 76 and 78 indicates, they are ready to host the most demanding guest.

With a well-equipped home base, you'll be surprised how easy it is to stop and smell the flowers without losing time along the way.

SPECIAL REPORT

MONTREAL
DEALING AT A LEISURELY PACE
IN CANADA'S DISTINCT SOCIETY

GETTING IN Air Canada is the dominator in this city with more flights and better terminal facilities than any other carrier.
WHERE TO STAY The Ritz-Carlton offers glamour without flashy ostentation. A major renovation is adding new world know-how to old-world style. Rooms include marble bathrooms and terry-cloth robes, three telephones (including one in the bathroom), and a safe that can hold an attaché case. There's a complimentary overnight shoeshine service and in-house movies on closed circuit.

Madame Marie-Louise Villeneuve's Château Versailles justly ranks as one of North America's greatest small hotels. This 70-room jewel is tough to get into, but once in, you're never likely to stay elsewhere. The rooms are beautifully furnished, many with chandeliers and fireplaces. The rates are a bargain, and the Villeneuve family is renowned for its helpfulness.
GETTING AROUND A compact downtown means you can walk almost everywhere. For longer distances the subway is fast, efficient and cheap.
DINING OUT In summer, the Ritz Garden (at the Ritz-Carlton), with its charming duck pond. Mick Jagger was almost tossed out of here because he came sans jacket. Lunch: $40 for two. All year round, a Montreal tradition is supper in the Maritime Bar at the Ritz-Carlton. Dinner: $80 for two. A top lunch spot in the financial district is Chez Delmo, spe-

cializing in fresh seafood. You can eat oysters at the mahogany bar or wait for a table. Lunch: $30 for two (211-15 Notre Dame St. W.; 514/849-4061). Le Paris is a favorite of Montrealers; the food is exactly what you'd find in a Paris bistro. Dinner: $40 to $55 for two (1812 St. Catherine St.; 514/937-4898). Les Halles is popular with the young business crowd and PR types. Chic, fun and relatively expensive. Dinner: $120 for two (1450 Crescent St.; 514/844-2328).
DIVERSIONS The 200-acre Botanical Gardens, Sherbrooke Street E. at Pie IX Boulevard contain one of the world's largest collection of plants under glass and the largest dwarf tree (bonsai) exhibit outside Asia. You can walk through a tropical rainforest, a desert, and enjoy the world's largest orchid display. And no visitor should miss Place Jacques Cartier in Old Montreal. A colorful slice of city life with its flower vendors, street musicians, boutiques and outdoor restaurants.

John Angus, a director of the high-tech firm Eco Corp., advises a trip to St. Denis Street below Sherbrooke Street. "By day or night, it's an enjoyable experience. You feel like you are in another country. Drop in and sit at the bar of a bistro or have dinner alone or with company. You'll understand what Quebecers mean when they say 'Quebec is a distinct society.' "

OTTAWA
CAPITAL AMUSEMENTS FOR
THE SEASONED MUSEUM MAVEN

GETTING IN For frequency, choose Air Canada. If you are flying from the west, try Canadian Airlines International, and

you can't ignore the super cabin service of Wardair. In short, Ottawa-bound travelers are spoiled.
WHERE TO STAY About as establishment as you can get is the luxurious Four Seasons, where luxury treatment is de rigueur. Frequent visitors get additional pampering: 50-time visitors are entitled to their own monogrammed dressing gowns. Regulars also get fruit, flowers and special attention.

Cartier Place is a luxury all-suites business hotel that offers residential atmosphere. Suites are available with fridge, dishwasher, stove, dishes, linen and cutlery. In-house laundry rooms for guests.
GETTING AROUND Deserved or otherwise, Ottawa residents recommend that strangers to the city ask cab drivers how far it is to their destination. Some newcomers have found themselves on a tour of the outskirts when they were, in fact, only three blocks from their destination.
DINING OUT Ottawa insiders declare the best value and best food is served at the Ritz. The eclectic menu ranges from fettucine with clams to veal with three mustards. Popular and crowded. Dinner: $30 for two (274 Elgin St.; 613/235-7027). Another travelers' favorite is Le Jardin. Seafood and rack of lamb are the specialties, served in the ambience of a private house. Dinner: $70 for two (127 York St.; 613/238-1828).
DIVERSIONS In winter, visitors can bring their skates for a spin on the ice-bound Rideau Canal. In summer, take a walk through Bytown, Ottawa's colorful old market area. Call your MP in advance and arrange for him to take you to lunch or breakfast at the parliamentary restaurant. Ottawa is also blessed with an extraordinary variety of museums, including the new National Gallery of Canada.

Jalynn Bennett is vice-president of corporate development at Manufacturers Life Insurance Co. in Toronto. London, Paris, Washington and Ottawa are frequent stops in a busy career that combines politics and business, but she has a special fondness for Ottawa. "I like to visit the Parliamentary Library, one of the most spectacular public spaces anywhere. I also visit the numismatic museum in the Bank of Canada. It's a fascinating history of our country in paper and coinage."

TITLE
THOSE WHOOP-DE-DO YEARS
ART DIRECTOR
TERESA FERNANDES
EDITOR
MARQ de VILLIERS
DESIGNER
TERESA FERNANDES
ILLUSTRATOR
ROSS MacDONALD
PUBLICATION
TORONTO LIFE
PUBLISHER
KEY PUBLISHERS CO. LTD.

TITLE
HOST TO THE WORLD
ART DIRECTOR
JIM SARFATI
WRITER
ELEANOR BERMAN
DESIGNER
JIM SARFATI
ILLUSTRATOR
ROSS MACDONALD/ REACTOR
PUBLICATION
FREQUENT FLYER
PUBLISHER
OFFICIAL AIRLINE GUIDE

TITLE
PERSIAN GULFS
ART DIRECTOR
**TERESA FERNANDES/
MARTHA WEAVER**
EDITOR
MARQ de VILLIERS
DESIGNER
MARTHA WEAVER
ILLUSTRATOR
NORMAND COUSINEAU
PUBLICATION
TORONTO LIFE
PUBLISHER
**KEY PUBLISHERS
CO. LTD.**

IS THE CITY THAT WORKS STILL WORKING?

NEWCOMERS

Persian Gulfs

*The Iranian arrival and
what their problems are, how
the city fails them, and what
this says about Toronto*

BEHIND THE PREPOSTEROUSLY postmodernist Miracle Foodmart complex that anchors the southeast corner of Sheppard and Yonge lies a leafy, quiet neighborhood of bungalows and two-storey homes, late-model compacts and scaled-down station wagons, mature trees and no sidewalks. Old Suburbs; a bit tattered around the edges, by contemporary North York standards, but still charming. Drive north on Bales Avenue until you're smack against the back end of Miracle Foodmart and you come to a cluster of eight identical two-storey brownstones. A woman wearing a chador, the traditional Iranian veil that leaves only the face exposed, sits beside several toddlers playing on the grass. She looks up, then lowers her eyes quickly; she is separated from Khomeini's Iran by a matter of days. Inside unit 47, an apartment door is open. There is no furniture in sight; eight men and women and a couple of children sit on a carpet on the bare floor. They are the future of Toronto, although you might have difficulty convincing the neighbors of this fact.

The Bales Avenue Newcomer Project provides tempo-

rary accommodation to a constantly fluctuating stream of refugees, and acts as a link between Employment and Immigration Canada, a vast bureaucracy, and its neediest clients. Of the 152,098 immigrants that came to Canada legally last year, more than half ended up in Ontario and nearly two-thirds of those settled in Metropolitan Toronto. These include refugees fleeing political, racial or religious persecution in their countries of origin.

Walk into the offices of any frontline service dealing with refugees, like the Bales Avenue Project, and what you'll see is representative of the world's trouble spots at that moment in time. A decade ago it was Central Americans, Pakistanis and southern Asians, especially the boat people. Over the past few years it has been Afghans, Tamils from Sri Lanka, Chileans, and Iranians escaping the war with Iraq and Khomeini's harshly uncompromising vision of Islam.

Nooshin Shafai, a community worker, is standing in the doorway of her basement office at Bales. She is a compact, outgoing woman with kind eyes who is engaged in an in-

BY DAVID HAYES

*Names of people denoted by an asterisk have been changed at their request.

Illustrations by Normand Cousineau

INSIDE UNIT 47 AT THE BALES AVENUE NEWCOMER
PROJECT, A DOOR IS OPEN. THERE IS NO FURNITURE IN SIGHT; A GROUP OF IRANIAN MEN,
WOMEN AND CHILDREN—THE FUTURE OF TORONTO—SIT ON A CARPET ON THE FLOOR

IS THE CITY THAT WORKS STILL WORKING?

tense conversation in Farsi, the principal language of Iran, with a young couple: a dark, timid woman in her early 20s and her tall, serious-looking husband. "They lived in Turkey for two years after getting out of Iran," Shafai explains to me later. "They're educated. He was an engineer and she was a university student. There was some kind of trouble with the Khomeini regime and they were in danger. These people tend to have low

WALK INTO ANY OF THE
FRONTLINE SERVICES
DEALING WITH REFUGEES,
LIKE THE BALES AVENUE
NEWCOMER PROJECT, AND
WHAT YOU WILL SEE IS
REPRESENTATIVE OF THE
WORLD'S TROUBLE SPOTS

expectations because they've been living in places like Turkey or Pakistan. They've applied to come to Canada, have been accepted, and have received visas. They are legal landed immigrants when they arrive. But for many, it can take as long as two years, which is difficult to accept when you've just escaped from a repressive country and you're trying to reach a safe haven. There are always smugglers who say to them, 'Give me $15,000 and I'll send you this week.' They may be legitimate refugees, but they decide to come to Canada illegally and claim refugee status when they arrive so they can start their new lives sooner. But many find that it's not so easy."

Nooshin Shafai is the daughter of a university professor in Tehran. Her husband, Habib, was a deputy minister in the Ministry of Industry and Mines during the reign of the Shah, Mohammad Reza Pahlavi. After the revolution, when Khomeini came to power in 1979, the civil service was purged and Habib Shafai was "retired." He was also placed on a blacklist, which meant, among other things, he could not obtain a passport. Life had changed in other ways. The war with Iraq was growing increasingly bloody, and the Shafai's elder son, who was 17, would soon be drafted into the military, a chilling thought when one considers that Iran—with a population three times that of

Iraq—considered its thousands of young soldiers an easily expendable resource. So the Shafais made what was for them a radical decision: a smuggler was paid to take Habib and his son over the mountains into Turkey while Nooshin, who was free to travel, flew to Switzerland with their remaining children, an 18-year-old daughter and 10-year-old son. Getting themselves into Canada was relatively simple: they were sponsored by Habib's

brother, an academic at the University of Manitoba who had been settled in Canada since the 1960s.

Nooshin Shafai applied for an interpreter's job at Pearson Airport but ended up working as a Farsi-speaking counsellor for a community organization. For several years that job meant trips to the airport, usually after midnight when the day's flights had ended, to act as an interpreter for Iranian refugees and help them find lodging at hostels. Sometimes she put them up in her own home. As more arrived, it became apparent that Iranians were in a weird kind of limbo. Although their numbers weren't large—of 25,000 in Canada, about 13,000 live in Ontario, with most in Toronto—there was no community focus nor recognized spokespersons because there really was no community, a condition the Shafais hope to change. Iranians in Toronto today are an ethnic community in the earliest stage of formation, and how they are adjusting to Toronto—and Toronto to them—tells us about our city, and ourselves.

Words like immigrant and refugee are highly charged and frequently misunderstood. The terms bear a relationship to each other exactly like that of brandy and cognac: all refugees are immigrants, although not all immigrants are refugees. There are

---

IS THE CITY THAT WORKS STILL WORKING?

IT BECAME APPARENT THAT IRANIANS WERE
IN A WEIRD KIND OF LIMBO. THOUGH THEIR NUMBERS WEREN'T LARGE, THERE WAS NO COMMU-
NITY FOCUS NOR RECOGNIZED SPOKESPERSONS BECAUSE THERE REALLY WAS NO COMMUNITY

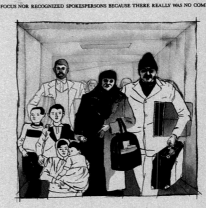

three classes of immigrant. Independent applicants are awarded points according to age, education, job training and experience, demand for specific occupations, proficiency in either official language and something called "personal suitability," which takes into account "adaptability, motivation, initiative, resourcefulness and other similar qualities." Immigrants are also sponsored by family members living in Canada, subject to a number of criteria that include the sponsor's ability to financially support a relative for up to ten years. Finally, there are refugees. Immigration Canada recognizes the definition of refugee adopted by the United Nations: "any person who, by reasons of race, religion, nationality, membership in a particular social group, or political opinion. . .is unable, or, by reason of such fear, is unwilling to avail himself of the protection of that country."

By Canadian law, anyone able to take refuge in a country of first asylum before coming to Canada must do so. Iranian refugees, for example, who escape to Turkey or India are expected to apply for entry into Canada from those countries. Only after being approved by Canadian visa officers will they be allowed to enter as landed immigrants. In practice, however, as many as 3,000 arrive illegally each month. They claim refugee status at airports and border crossings and are permitted to stay until

their claims have been processed. They cannot work but do receive welfare. The review process is so backlogged that there are 60,000 refugee claimants—of which Iranians are the second most numerous behind Sri Lankans—waiting for their cases to be settled or an amnesty to be declared, which Canada last did two years ago. (New government legislation that will crack down on refugee claimants will be in place in early 1989.) While some refugee claimants are no doubt economic migrants hoping to circumnavigate lengthy application procedures, media reports referring to "very wealthy" refugee claimants who are "impeccably dressed" and "clutching briefcases" are misleading. Being well-off doesn't mean you are immune from persecution; sometimes it increases the risk. Legitimate refugees flee their homeland by whatever means they can, and the very fact that they are refugees usually precludes orderly—and time-consuming—bureaucratic procedures.

A small number of Iranians have lived in Toronto for years. Many were university students who remained after their studies were completed and became physicians, academics and businesspeople. The first real wave of immigration began in the late seventies with an exodus of Iranians who feared reprisals because of ties to the Shah's government. They were what immigration

---

Dealing with the demons

*The office addict no longer faces an endless private hell.
Enlightened employers and
progressive clinics will reach out to begin the healing.*

By Alan Morantz
Illustrations by Matt Mahurin

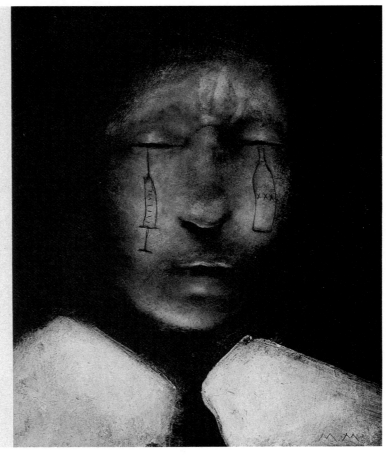

P aul Court* never had a problem with drugs until he reached his late twenties. In his early working life he traveled the world with rock-and-roll bands, working at staging and lighting jobs. He left that about seven years ago to start a software company in Toronto. It was then, at the age of 29, that he began making more than $300,000 a year and surrounding himself with new things and new ideas. "It was nothing to show off my $70,000 Porsche and $400,000 home," he recalls, ruefully. "I always had to buy $1,500 hand-made suits. I went to Hawaii five times one year, once renting a helicopter to fly all over the islands. I had to stay in the best hotels, even if it cost me $350 a night. I was making like there was no tomorrow."

He was hanging out with a fast-running crowd. And he was introduced to cocaine. As his dependency grew and the supply of coke became plentiful, he began looking forward to parties where he knew it would be available. This diversion was costing him at least $4,000 a month, sometimes $6,000.

A few years later, the American computer company for which he distributed software wanted to break a 20-year agreement with him. And that set in motion his denouement. "I spent three years in court and $120,000 in legal fees fighting them, and I had to close the business," he recalls. "I finally won close to $500,000, but I ended up putting it all up my nose. It was not until I lost my wife and the confidence to start over in business that I realized I had a problem, although I spent months denying it. During this time I had several jobs in the computer field, but they ended up being washed out because I couldn't function."

* The names of the two addicts in this story, Paul Court and Robert Smith, are pseudonyms.

48 VISTA

Willard
& Kate

*"He felt her
contentment as she
listened to him,
a contentment she had
never had a chance
to enjoy before
his retirement"*

WILLARD COWLEY LIVED WITH HIS WIFE in a stone house set back from the street in a grove of trees. A sun parlor overlooked the garden, the windows opening onto a flowering apple tree in the spring. Willard was a well-known scholar, tall and angular, self-confident and bold. Waving his long, powerful arms, he talked earnestly and with great openness to his students, but then, because he was 65, he retired. In his retirement, he took long walks. At home, he sat at the supper table talking to his wife about the affairs of the day. She had soft grey eyes and a wistful smile and the way she listened now, sitting at the table, made him want to talk to her. She seemed to draw him out, asking questions. After a time, he didn't notice that he didn't miss the classroom, or the audience of old, scholarly friends. They were dying off anyway. She was his audience, and soon he was talking to her as intimately as he would talk to himself. He felt her contentment as she listened to him, a contentment she had *never* had a chance to enjoy before his retirement.

Her eyesight was failing and so he began to read the newspapers to her. They would get into bed early, and in bed he would read to her as she lay quietly curled beside him, sometimes questioning him. Letting his reading glasses slip down to the tip of his nose, he would link his hands behind his head and answer her questions till her heavy breathing told him she had fallen asleep.

He had always liked to read the newspapers slowly and deliberately and any story about archeology, about the lost past, interested him. Only a few months before he retired, he had written an/*Continued on page 150*

FICTION BY BARRY CALLAGHAN

TITLE
DEALING WITH DEMONS
ART DIRECTOR
ROD DELLA VEDOVA
EDITOR
ROD McQUEEN
DESIGNER
KELLY de REGT
CREATIVE DIR.
ROD DELLA VEDOVA
ILLUSTRATOR
MATT MAHURIN
PUBLICATION
VISTA
PUBLISHER
VISTA PUBLICATIONS

TITLE
WILLARD & KATE
ART DIRECTOR
**TERESA FERNANDES/
MARTHA WEAVER**
EDITOR
MARQ de VILLIERS
DESIGNER
MARTHA WEAVER
ILLUSTRATOR
BRAD HOLLAND
PUBLICATION
TORONTO LIFE
PUBLISHER
**KEY PUBLISHERS
CO. LTD.**

TITLE
WHAT A DAY!
ART DIRECTOR
BEDA ACHERMAN
EDITOR
ALAN FORMAN
ILLUSTRATOR
**MAURICE VELLEKOOP/
REACTOR**
PUBLICATION
MANNER VOGUE
PUBLISHER
**CONDE NAST
VERLAG GMBH**

OPPISITE PAGE

TITLE
**HISTORY & TRADITIONS
OF JAZZ**
ART DIRECTOR
JONATHAN TUTTLE
DESIGNER
JONATHAN TUTTLE
ILLUSTRATOR
**MAURICE VELLEKOOP/
REACTOR**
PUBLICATION
PURSUITS - SUMMER /89
PUBLISHER
**WHITTLE
COMMUNICATIONS**

THE LAST FARMER
An American Memoir

BY HOWARD KOHN

HOWARD KOHN, a contributing editor of this magazine, first wrote about his father's farm for ROLLING STONE in 1977 (RS 244). This is an excerpt from 'The Last Farmer: An American Memoir,' by Howard Kohn, published in September by Summit Books. Copyright © 1988 by Howard Kohn.

HALFWAY UP the Lake Huron coast of Michigan is the Saginaw Valley, and near the northern extreme of the valley, in a German community, is the farm that Heinrich Kohn homesteaded and passed on to his son, Johann Kohn, who passed it on to his son, Fredrick Kohn, who is my father. The farm did not pass on to me.

When I was eighteen, my time on the farm came to an end, that slow, unforgettable time of cow milking and haying and woodcutting, chore upon chore in raw weather – an unchanging time, a time that seemed a sentence of indeterminate length from which escape at times was doubtful. I left in August of 1965, moving on to California, New York, Florida, Washington, D.C., and elsewhere. I felt, when I left, that I had been granted a new life: the traveling life of a writer.

Sixteen years later, I happened to be back at the farm on a stopover between assignments. Diana, my second wife, was with me. A light rain fell before dawn on the third day of our visit, but when it stopped, I expected my father to have us out in the navy beans, sickling the last of the summer weeds. This was a weekday, a workday, and I certainly did not expect him to say, as he did, "Go ahead, go enjoy yourselves."

We found a boat livery and planked a canoe in the river and were miles out of reach when, back on the farm, my father fell off the roof of the house.

He landed on his lower back, half on the sidewalk, half on the lawn. In that moment, after almost seventy years of the farming life without one night in a hospital, having been brought down suddenly to earth, flattened on his back, the wind knocked out of him, sweat drying on his skin, an elbow opened to the bone, three vertebrae cracked, gazed at by grandchildren fearing the worst, my father, against all common sense, picked himself up and went about his day as if nothing had happened.

Had he died that morning, I cannot say how the past few years would have turned out. He and I, and whatever lay between us, would have been fixed at that point – he in his place in old America, with his Germanic standards in his 120-acre farm, and I in no particular place at all.

But he did not die. He forced himself erect and walked into the house. He let my mother wash and wrap his elbow. Then, as planned, he got into his pickup to give a ride to my brother Roy's wife, Lorie, who needed to go to Detroit to retrieve Roy's wife, abandoned there by joy riders. Lorie saw my father's pain, a monumental pain. "We can wait and do this tomorrow," she said, hoping her tone gave the least possible offense. A moment went by with only a shake of his head, and she accepted the fact that the trip would be today.

They drove out Beaver Road, then U.S. 23, where they picked up speed. How quickly could she grab the wheel if he went blank? Only a

few months before he had suffered the first seizure of a weakening heart. Pulling off for gasoline at an exit, my father pumped it himself, then managed to climb back into his pickup. Arriving at the pound for stolen cars, he stayed in his seat, hands braced on the wheel, while Lorie completed the paper work.

The round trip was 290 miles, and altogether they were in traffic seven hours in a slow rain.

While they were still on the road, Diana and I finished our canoe trip. In front of the farmhouse, the grandchildren were not playing. They ran to us and announced how Grandpa had fallen to the ground. My mother was in the kitchen, busying herself. "The rain, that's why he's late getting back from Detroit," she said to us. She pressed bread dough into loaf pans. "I couldn't stop him from going," she said, "not him."

"I know," I said, squeezing her shoulders.

The grandchildren began to yell. My father's truck was in the driveway. With tottering baby steps, he worked his way up the front porch and then to the bedroom. He lay down, still refusing to concede what was evident to everyone – that he must go to a hospital. "Nope," he said. "A little rest, I'll be as good as new."

At last my sister Sandra shooed us out of the room and, talking alone with my father, said something that got him on his feet and back into his truck. He let me drive, but he would not let me assist him into the truck or, at the Bay Osteopathic Hospital, out again, pushing aside also, with a veined hand, an orderly who held out a wheelchair. "I don't belong here," my father said foolishly.

All the brown of a lifetime in the sun was gone. He had the false, bleached color of something not alive. A young nurse, who had eased him finally into a wheelchair, wheeled him from the X-ray lab to a bed. He stood and lifted a leg to get in. "Hold it, stand right there!" a doctor fairly shouted. "I don't want you moving by yourself." The doctor held up a film from the X-ray machine. "It appears you have fifteen fractured vertebrae, Mr. Kohn."

Fifteen fractures of the bones connecting my father's spine – it was impossible that he could walk. There was talk of a cast from neck to waist. Not until a radiologist overruled the initial reading of the X-ray technicians did anyone realize that twelve of the fractures were already healed. They were from old accidents. My father remembered falling onto his back at least twice before, once in the haymow, another time from a wagon, and in each case he had walked off the pain. "I'd have been fine this time, too," he said, his voice weak now to the point of whispering. "Don't know what all the fuss is about."

The doctors ordered him into a back brace of steel and canvas. You could see them at his bedside, clinical, experienced, familiar with his Germanic streak and dismayed by it. They warned him endlessly of possible

> AT EIGHTEEN,
> MY TIME ON THE FARM CAME TO
> AN END, THAT UNFORGETTABLE
> TIME OF COW MILKING AND
> HAYING AND WOODCUTTING.

ILLUSTRATION BY ROSS MACDONALD

Essay

THE STUNT PILOT

For years he thrilled audiences with his daredevil maneuvers. Then one day he ran out of sky

By ANNIE DILLARD
Illustration by Tomio Nitto

DAVE RAHM LIVED in Bellingham, Washington, north of Seattle. Bellingham, a harbor town, lies between the alpine North Cascade Mountains and the San Juan Islands in Haro Strait above Puget Sound. The latitude is that of Newfoundland. Dave Rahm was a stunt pilot, the air's own genius.

In 1975, with a newcomer's willingness to try anything once, I attended the Bellingham Air Fair. The Bellingham airport was a wide clearing in a forest of tall Douglas firs; its runways suited small planes. It was June. It wasn't even raining; the air was cold and dry. People wearing blue or tan zipped jackets stood loosely on the concrete walkways and runways outside the coffee shop. At that latitude in June, you stayed outside because you could, even most of the night, if you could think up something to do. The sky did not darken until 10:00 or so, and it never got very dark; in strict astronomical terms, the sun never dropped sufficient degrees of arc below the horizon to take you from astro-

Annie Dillard *recently finished a new book,* The Writing Life. *She won the Pulitzer Prize for* Pilgrim at Tinker Creek.

nomical twilight into astronomical night. Your life split open like the day. You tossed your dark winter routines, thought up mad projects, and improvised everything from hour to hour. Being a stunt pilot seemed the most reasonable thing in the world; you could wave your arms in the air all day and all night, and sleep next winter.

I saw from the ground ten stunt pilots; the air show scheduled them one after the other, for an hour of aerobatics. Each pilot took up his or her plane and performed a batch of tricks. They were precise and impressive. They flew upside down, and straightened out; they did barrel rolls, and straightened out; they drilled through dives and spins, and landed gently on a far runway.

For the end of the day, separated from all other performances of every sort, the air show had scheduled a program titled "Dave Rahm." The leaflet said he had flown for King Hussein in Jordan. A tall man in the crowd told me King Hussein had seen Rahm fly on a visit to North America; he had invited him to Jordan to perform at ceremonies. Hussein was a pilot, too. "Hussein thought he was the greatest thing in the world." Rahm was also a geologist who taught at Western Washington University.

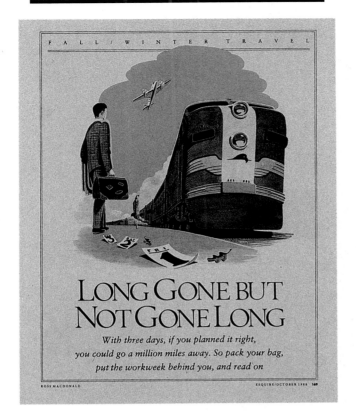

OPPISITE PAGE

TITLE
THE LAST FARMER
ART DIRECTOR
FRED WOODWARD
DESIGNER
JOEL CUYLER
ILLUSTRATOR
**ROSS MacDONALD/
REACTOR**
PUBLICATION
ROLLING STONE
PUBLISHER
**STRAIGHT ARROW
PUBLISHERS INC.**

TITLE
THE STUNT PILOT
ART DIRECTOR
RIP GEORGES
DESIGNER
PAMELA BERRY
ILLUSTRATOR
**TOMIO NITTO/
REACTOR**
PUBLICATION
ESQUIRE
PUBLISHER
HEARST PUBLISHING

TITLE
**LONG GONE BUT
NOT GONE LONG**
ART DIRECTOR
RIP GEORGES
DESIGNER
PAMELA BERRY
ILLUSTRATOR
**ROSS MacDONALD/
REACTOR**
PUBLICATION
ESQUIRE
PUBLISHER
HEARST PUBLISHING

TITLE
GAY AFTER AIDS
ART DIRECTOR
TERESA FERNANDES
EDITOR
MARQ de VILLIERS
DESIGNER
TERESA FERNANDES
ILLUSTRATOR
ALAN E. COBER
PUBLICATION
TORONTO LIFE
PUBLISHER
**KEY PUBLISHERS
CO. LTD.**

STEPHEN JONES

KATHARINE HAMNETT

London's next Wave

FINISHING TOUCHES FROM THE FOGGY CITY'S BRIGHTEST LIGHTS

Stephen Jones, 31, made and sold his designs one by one after graduating from his millinery course in London. His first fall collection, in 1984, was inspired by a trip to Montreal. This fall's line, lightly referred to as "Room Service," features pink satin linings and boudoir luxury: here, the "Cloud 9" swan feather hat.

DOMINO

76

With her first line of prewashed silks, in 1980, Katharine Hamnett, now 40, became a British star. Her political T-shirts made headlines in 1984 (she wore one saying "58% DON'T WANT PERSHING" to meet Margaret Thatcher). Her collection features romantic looks such as this velvet veiled hat and matching velvet cape.

DOMINO

77

JASPER CONRAN

JOHN GALLIANO

Jasper Conran, 28, studied design in London and New York, launching his first collection in 1978. His trademark: daring color and fabric combinations such as pastel chiffons with dark tweeds. Here, a flannel boudoir cap tops off a purple gabardine jacket and pale silk blouse.

DOMINO

78

John Galliano celebrates his 28th birthday this month. His first collection, in 1984, "Afghanistan Repudiates Western Ideals," mixed traditional tailoring with Eastern ethnics. He continues to update classic shapes with his arty, offbeat sense of color and humor, as in this version of the lace-up sevce shoe.

DOMINO

79

They come each year to plant and tend and harvest the produce for our tables, then go back home, a little richer, a little more travelled. But however long they come, they are forever outsiders

THE DIRT WORKERS

BY LINDALEE TRACEY, WITH PHOTOGRAPHY BY TOM SKUDRA

K aterina Banman and her daughter, Net, fumble barefoot down the stairs into the dark, sticky-hot kitchen. It's 4:45 a.m., a mid-July morning in 1988. They are silent except for two or three words whispered in German. The light from the open refrigerator outlines Katerina's puffy face and hunched shoulders. Her tiredness is like a second skin, rubbed raw under her long, sombre cotton dress.

"My mother says she is sorry for this bad place," Net mumbles from behind her broom.

"Sí, sí," Mrs. Banman echoes, offering a shrug as apology.

Inside the unpainted clapboard house, bare boards cover up holes in the walls, and the rooms are scarred with peeling wallpaper. There are no backs to the kitchen chairs, no dressers, no shelves. Clothing is piled in heaps on the floor or hung from nails in the wall. The curtains are tacked to the window frames.

Katerina, her husband, Pieter, and their four children are Mexican Mennonites who have been coming to Canada to work every summer for eight years now. The house is provided free by their employer, Bert De Brouwer, a farmer

GOLD

OPPISITE PAGE

TITLE
LONDON'S NEXT WAVE
ART DIRECTOR
KAREN SIMPSON
DESIGNER
KAREN SIMPSON
PHOTOGRAPHER
JURGEN TELLER
PUBLICATION
DOMINO
PUBLISHER
THE GLOBE AND MAIL

B y eleven we've picked clean whatever cucumbers there are, filling 122 baskets. "I like more pay by the hour than by how many pickles," Pieter sighs

In a good year, the Banmans can earn $20,000 for seven months of stoop work, money that goes back into their farm in Mexico. Practice doesn't make the labor easier. "It always hurts," says fifteen-year-old Net

in Kent County, 290 kilometres west of Toronto. It's the Banmans' second year working for De Brouwer in his cucumber, bean and tomato fields. He will employ about thirty-four workers this season, ten of them from offshore. A quiet, shy man with rosy Dutch cheeks, De Brouwer says he couldn't do without the foreigners: "They say you gotta grow yer own labor, but I only got two kids. And only one of them's interested in farm work."

In the last twenty years, the farm population of Ontario has decreased by forty-five per cent. Farmers are depending less on their families and more on paid labor. But the small wages don't attract as many students or the large Québécois families that once did the planting, hoeing and picking. The ones who do come often leave mid-season for better-paying work. In 1987, of the 1,664 Canadians contracted to work in Kent County, twenty-four per cent quit.

Every year, Ontario produces $500 million worth of fruits and vegetables, and we spend almost fifty per cent of our food budgets on these items, consuming an average of 500 pounds per person per year. Farmers desperately need stoop workers to get the crops to our tables, and increasingly they're turning to offshore laborers—in 1983, Ontario farmers hired 4,500 seasonal workers; by 1988, the number was up to 8,000. The workers come from Jamaica, Mexico, Trinidad and Tobago, Barbados and dot islands in the Caribbean, with Jamaica supplying almost half of the total.

B egun in 1966, the federally incorporated Foreign Seasonal Agricultural Workers Program allows workers into Canada for up to eight months, although the average contract is fifteen weeks. The participating farmers must cover airfare and supply housing. Some of the laborers are asked for by name; they come each year to the same farm and are almost part of the family. When they go back home they are a little richer, a little more travelled, returning

SILVER

TITLE
THE DIRT WORKERS
ART DIRECTOR
TERESA FERNANDES
EDITOR
MARQ de VILLIERS
DESIGNER
TERESA FERNANDES
PHOTOGRAPHER
TOM SKUDRA
PUBLICATION
TORONTO LIFE
PUBLISHER
**KEY PUBLISHERS
CO. LTD.**

Wish You Were Here

Sea belles by the Sea Shore

PHOTOGRAPHS BY KOTO BOLOFO

A BEAUTIFUL DAY for BEACH COMBING. Two-piece tank suit with high-rise bottoms, Romeo Gigli. One-piece suit with squared-off legs, Dolce & Gabbana. Bathing cap with flowers, Spectera.

WE'RE NEVER GOING HOME. Fringed two-piece, Dolce & Gabbana. Crossed-back one-piece with lapels, Claude Montana. Oliver Peoples sunglasses.

A

SILVER

OPPISITE PAGE

TITLE
WISH YOU WERE HERE
ART DIRECTOR
KAREN SIMPSON
DESIGNER
KAREN SIMPSON
PHOTOGRAPHER
KOTO BOLOFO
PUBLICATION
DOMINO
PUBLISHER
THE GLOBE AND MAIL

STAN WATTS

TRUCK DRIVER, CANADIAN CARTAGE

Watts has hauled everything from steel to groceries on every major highway that feeds into Toronto, as well as on all major downtown streets, for fifteen years. He currently drives a 10,000-pound, eighteen-wheel tractor trailer—one of the biggest rigs on the road (it can haul as much as 60,000 pounds). Traffic volume and congestion, illegally parked cars (Watts has had to go from door-to-door in search of drivers to remove their vehicles so he can make a delivery) and narrow intersections, roads and alleys (Watts has backed his rig into alleys that are so narrow he can't wedge a finger between the side mirror and the wall) make truck driving in Toronto, he says, "so frustrating you could scream sometimes." As well, inadequate docking facilities mean that drivers often have to wait in line for hours to make deliveries—which ties up traffic and ultimately adds costs to merchandise.

Apart from the city's physical restrictions (roads were designed before eighteen-wheelers were even conceived of), Watts, like many others, cites driver discourtesy as a major headache. Watts says drivers often fail to let trucks into traffic—both downtown and on freeways—or cut them off, forcing them to gear down through fifteen to twenty gears (depending on how fast they were going). "It

takes ages to build up your speed again," he says, "which slows down traffic."

A TRUCK DRIVER'S SOLUTIONS
◇ Ban parking on all major downtown business streets from 7 to 9 a.m.;
◇ Restrict parking on all major downtown business streets to one side only;
◇ To decrease traffic congestion and increase the number of people using car pools, restrict one lane on the Gardiner Expressway, the Don Valley Parkway and highways 401 and 427 to cars with three or more passengers between 7 and 9 a.m. and 4 and 6 p.m.;
◇ Increase the number of traffic police so rules and regulations can be better enforced;
◇ Extend downtown shipping and receiving hours from 4 to 8 p.m. to avoid competing with rush-hour traffic;
◇ To crack down on freeway speeding and dangerous lane changes, give Department of Transportation drivers authority to use radar and issue speeding tickets;
◇ Build no-exit express lanes (a skyway?) for Highway 401 from Dixie Road to Markham Road (where traffic clogs up during rush hour).

CHRIS WATSON

VAN DRIVER, PUROLATOR

A ten-year veteran of downtown driving, Watson says, "Toronto's not growing bigger, it's getting taller," and the resulting increase in traffic has left parking for commercial vehicles—especially couriers—high and dry. Watson says there's simply no space left on the streets. Thus couriers are forced to park illegally, or to park blocks away from their destinations. In the early morning, between 7 and 9:30 a.m., the tow-away zones make their lives even more difficult.

A COURIER'S SOLUTIONS
◇ Between 6 and 7 a.m. restrict the downtown core to commercial traffic only so that couriers and trucks can get

a head start on deliveries (and exit before rush hour begins);
◇ Implement one or two commercial-vehicle-only unloading zones for each major block within the downtown core;
◇ To encourage more people to leave their cars at home and make greater use of car pools, insurance companies should offer lower rates to car-pool passengers and drivers;
◇ Ensure all downtown buildings have street numbers clearly posted. Traffic is often backed up by drivers—both commercial and commuter—who slow down while searching for their specific destinations.

A

SILVER

TITLE
ROADS SCHOLARS
ART DIRECTOR
**TERESA FERNANDES/
MARTHA WEAVER**
EDITOR
MARQ de VILLIERS
DESIGNER
MARTHA WEAVER
PHOTOGRAPHER
RUSSELL MONK
PUBLICATION
TORONTO LIFE
PUBLISHER
**KEY PUBLISHERS
CO. LTD.**

PAT CURRAN

BUS DRIVER, TTC

Since 1974 Curran has driven buses on most major routes within the Metro area. Unlike many others interviewed for this article, Curran does not cite driver discourtesy as a problem. "Nine out of ten drivers are more than ready to let me in," he says. "I'm constantly opening my window and waving my thanks." However, Curran is less positive about traffic congestion—parked cars, clogged roads and intersections double the time of his bus runs, back up buses along his routes and, in his opinion, discourage commuters from leaving their cars at home and taking the TTC: "Who wants to wait twenty minutes in the rain for a bus?"

A BUS DRIVER'S SOLUTIONS
◇ Prohibit right-hand turns at all major intersections (including Avenue Road and Bloor, Yonge and Eglinton, Yonge and Finch, Bathurst and Eglinton, Bathurst and Bloor, Steeles and Bayview) between 4 and 6 p.m. (Cars turning right at major intersections, says Curran, constitute one of the biggest tie-ups for buses, @hich have to remain in right-hand lanes to make their stops.);
◇ Introduce more bus and taxi lanes during rush hours—

for example, on Steeles Avenue West and Eglinton Avenue West, and all major downtown streets—enabling traffic to move more quickly and attracting more people to the TTC. (The bus lanes that already exist along Eglinton between Bayview and Brentcliffe and along Allen Road are "fantastic," says Curran.);
◇ Introduce—and strictly enforce—more tow-away zones between 4 and 6 p.m. Many commercial vehicles disregard the zones, so that buses, which have to pull to the curb and back out again frequently, become blocked;
◇ Extend the cutoff on parking meters to 9:30 during morning rush hour. ("As soon as meters are used, you've lost a lane of traffic, and rush hour now extends to 9:30 a.m.," says Curran.);
◇ Since pedestrians can clog up major intersections just as much as cars do, introduce the following light system at all major downtown intersections to enable greater numbers of pedestrians to cross at once: at an intersection, don't give pedestrians the "Walk" sign when there is a green light for cars. Instead, have a third light setting: red in all directions, which allows pedestrians to walk through the intersection in any way they choose.

RUSS HOLDEN

TRAFFIC REPORTER, CFTR-AM RADIO

Five days a week, from his Cessna 172 Skyhawk, Holden watches the traffic tie-ups that occur from Oshawa west to the Burlington Skyway and from the lakeshore north to the top of Highway 404. While too many cars and not enough roads are usually given as the source of traffic problems, Holden cites driver discourtesy and sloppiness as the worst offenders. For eleven years now, Holden has seen it all: tailgating, slowing down—even stopping—on acceleration ramps, backing up on expressways to get on to collector lanes, backing along exit ramps to avoid slow traffic. . . . Sadly, says Holden, these traffic infractions are no longer the exception. He points to ignorance of proper expressway driving techniques as a particular problem.

A TRAFFIC REPORTER'S SOLUTIONS
◇ Issue limited-access licences for freeway driving (highways 400, 401 and 427, Queen Elizabeth Way, Don Val-

ley Parkway) to drivers who have passed special tests;
◇ Retest all drivers every five years to ensure they know the rules of the road and are handling their cars safely and defensively;
◇ To attract businesses and workers (and consequently traffic) away from the downtown core, grant businesses and builders tax breaks to construct in Toronto's outlying civic centres;
◇ To decrease the traffic congestion that will inevitably result from events at SkyDome, limit afternoon games to weekends only and restrict weekday games to evenings to avoid the rush hour;
◇ Complete road extensions that have already been proposed—including Front Street West to the Gardiner Expressway, the Leslie Street extension, the Scarborough Expressway, the 400 extension south to Humber Bay, the Crosstown Expressway across Eglinton into Scarborough.

*I*TALIAN RENAISSANCE

*The rebirth
of a notion: that
comfortable
daywear should
also take
your breath away*

PHOTOGRAPHS BY GIOVANNI GASTEL

DOMINO

92

WEBBED FEAT.
SYBILLA WEAVES A WARM
SPELL WITH A SEASIDE-INSPIRED
SHAWL STUDDED WITH
SHELLFISH IN COTTON AND
HEMP, *OPPOSITE*, AND
A FISH-SCALES CROPPED-TOP,
HIGH-WAISTED PANTS
AND FLOPPY STRAW HAT, *ABOVE*.

93

NIGHT HEAT.
GIANNI VERSACE PAIRS GENTLY
PLEATED SILK JERSEY PANTS
WITH A SNUG JEWELLED CAMISOLE
AND A LEMON YELLOW
SPENCER JACKET FOR EVENING
BREEZES. AS ALWAYS, HIS
DETAILS ARE MEMORABLE: THE
BLACK SUEDE BELT WITH YELLOW
TASSLE OR THE EASTERN-
INFLUENCED SILVER CUFF, *OPPOSITE*.

100   DOMINO   DOMINO   101

THE DRESSER

When Holt Renfrew's Krystyne Griffin makes a fashion statement, Toronto is all ears

BY JOHN FITZGERALD

Lofty, leggy and lean, Krystyne Griffin looked saucily *jeune fille* in a black Yves Saint Laurent mini-skirt as she scooted across Bay Street on an autumn afternoon. Griffin had just left Yorkville's Il Posto restaurant and was on her way back to Holt Renfrew, where she reigns theatrically as director of the store's image-rich designer boutiques. By the time she'd swept, diva-style, past the doorman at Holt's Bloor Street entrance, her short progress had garnered a wolf whistle, and a stranger had come up to ask if she was a movie star.

The incidents were a sweet salute to the Polish-born, Paris-trained Griffin, who at 48 is considered by the inter- *continued on page 56*

PHOTOGRAPHY · BY
JOY · VON · TIEDEMAN

46 JANUARY 1989 TORONTO

A
SILVER

OPPISITE PAGE

TITLE
ITALIAN RENAISSANCE
ART DIRECTOR
KAREN SIMPSON
DESIGNER
KAREN SIMPSON
PHOTOGRAPHER
GIOVANNI GASTEL
PUBLICATION
DOMINO
PUBLISHER
THE GLOBE AND MAIL

A
SILVER

TITLE
THE DRESSER
ART DIRECTOR
LINDSAY BEAUDRY
EDITOR
JOHN FITZGERALD
DESIGNER
FERNANDA PISANI
PHOTOGRAPHER
JOY VON TIEDEMAN
PUBLICATION
TORONTO
PUBLISHER
THE GLOBE AND MAIL

A
SILVER

TITLE
RUMOURS OF MORE
ART DIRECTOR
THERESE SHECHTER
EDITOR
SARAH MURDOCH
PHOTOGRAPHER
CHRIS NICHOLLS
PUBLICATION
THE FINANCIAL TIMES OF CANADA
PUBLISHER
JOHN MacFARLANE/ THE FINANCIAL TIMES OF CANADA

MAY 1, 1989 · FINANCIAL TIMES OF CANADA · 23

Farley Mowat believes progress will swallow his patch of small-town Ontario: "This area will vanish out of time." And when it does, he promises, "So will I."

TITLE
JEWELS OF THE NILE
ART DIRECTOR
B.T. GILLEN
EDITOR
KAREN HANLEY
DESIGNER
B.T. GILLEN
PHOTOGRAPHER
**RON WATTS/
FIRST LIGHT**
PUBLICATION
PRIVILEGE
PUBLISHER
AIRMEDIA
PHOTO DIRECTOR
LISA BURROUGHS

JEWELS OF THE NILE

*To cruise its mystical
waters is to plumb the depths
of ancient civilization*

BY • PAR JEREMY FERGUSON

The Nile begins in the melting snows of the peaks of Central Africa. Finally, it undulates—a shimmering, glimmering blue ribbon between tan deserts—out to the Mediterranean at Alexandria. At almost 7,000 kilometres it is the longest river in the world. Because it flows north, the Egyptians, who must be the most easygoing people in the Arab world, have an excuse to befuddle strangers by saying "up south" and "down north." This is but a minor hint of the river's limitless surprises.

Egypt exudes history at every turn of its great river, the Nile. Its temples, which honor the great pharaohs, are flush with the mysteries of the ancient culture

L'histoire nous attend à chaque méandre du grand fleuve d'Egypte, le Nil. Les temples construits en l'honneur des pharaons sont imprégnés des mystères de l'antique culture

Le ruban bleu miroitant du Nil prend sa source dans les neiges fondantes des sommets d'Afrique centrale pour se jeter dans la Méditerranée, à Alexandrie, après bien des détours dans l'ocre des déserts. C'est le plus long fleuve du globe: il fait près de 7 000 km. Comme il coule en direction nord, on ne s'étonnera pas trop si les Égyptiens, sans doute les gens les plus faciles à vivre du monde arabe, brouillent les idées des étrangers en disant qu'ils montent vers le sud et descendent vers le nord.

EN DESCENDANT LE NIL

*Croisant sur ses eaux mythiques,
l'auteur sonde les profondeurs d'une
antique civilisation*

PHOTOS • RON WATTS/FIRST LIGHT

JEWELS OF THE NILE

The Nile Valley is really an oasis, only 19 kilometres across at its widest, unfurled along the river banks. The rest is uninhabitable desert. In this oasis sits an awesome majesty of ruins, and yet these wonders—the Pyramids, the Sphinx, the Temples of Karnak and Luxor, and the Valley of the Kings—seem no greater than the river itself.

Life on the Nile does not seem to have altered much over the centuries. Here are villages of mud huts with thatched roofs, inhabited by peasants (*fellahin*) and surrounded by the age-old menagerie of camels and donkeys, sheep and goats. Water buffalo tread circles on tiny plots, blindfolded to deter dizziness before the plough. At the river's edge, women swathed in black wash clothing, and boys swim naked. River traffic is mostly small cruise ships and *feluccas*—single-masted craft whose oversized triangular sails are mothlike in the peachy hues of dusk.

Close to 80 cruise ships ply the Nile. Most do a five-day stretch between Aswân and Luxor. But I wanted more of the river than that, and found, under the auspices of Lindblad Travel, a 10-day cruise from Aswân all the way to Cairo, almost the full length of Egypt. The ship was the M.S. *Neptune*, touted as the most luxurious floating hotel on the river. It is a sleek and spotless cruiser accommodating up to 104 passengers in spacious quarters, with a handsomely appointed restaurant and genteel touches like tea and pastries at sunset, heralded by a beaming Nubian with a dinner gong.

Our group assembled in Cairo, which, with a population of more than five million, is the largest city in Egypt

Ramses II, the great narcissist of Egypt, built the Abu Simbel temple and dedicated it to himself. His modern-day successors, such as this camel driver, carry on the traditions of ancestors

Ramsès II, le grand narcissique d'Egypte, fit construire le temple d'Abu Simbel en son honneur. Ses successeurs d'aujourd'hui, tel ce meneur de chameau, perpétuent les traditions de leurs ancêtres

EN DESCENDANT LE NIL

Étalée le long de ses rives, la vallée du Nil, de 19 km seulement dans sa plus grande largeur, est une véritable oasis. Le reste est un désert inhabitable. Dans cette oasis se dressent une quantité incroyable de ruines majestueuses et pourtant, ces merveilles—les pyramides, le sphynx, les temples de Karnak et de Louxor ainsi que la vallée des Rois—n'ont pas plus de grandeur que le grand fleuve lui-même.

La vie le long du Nil ne semble pas avoir beaucoup changé au cours des siècles. On y trouve des villages tout en huttes de terre à toit de chaume, habités de paysans (les *fellahin*) et entourés par une ménagerie séculaire: chameaux et ânes, moutons et chèvres. Les yeux bandés pour ne pas attraper le vertige devant la charrue, des arnis labourent de minuscules champs en tournant en rond. Sur le bord du fleuve, des femmes vêtues de noir lavent le linge pendant que les jeunes garçons nagent nus. Ce sont surtout de petits navires de croisière qui circulent sur le Nil, et des felouques, bateaux à un mât dont les immenses voiles triangulaires font l'effet d'insectes dans les couleurs roses du crépuscule.

Près de 80 navires de croisière arpentent le fleuve. La plupart font le trajet de cinq jours entre Assouan et Louxor, mais comme je voulais en découvrir plus, j'ai trouvé, sous les auspices de Lindblad Travel, une croisière de 10 jours entre Assouan et le Caire, c'est-à-dire sur presque toute la longueur de

TITLE
POLI GRAPHS
ART DIRECTOR
EVELYN STOYNOFF
EDITOR
KAREN HANLEY
DESIGNER
AUDREY GOTO/
EVELYN STOYNOFF
PHOTOGRAPHER
GAIL HARVEY
PUBLICATION
ENROUTE
CLIENT
AIR CANADA
PUBLISHER
AIRMEDIA
PHOTO DIRECTOR
LISA BURROUGHS

While so many in the profession of photography search for the readily available and obvious photo opportunity, the best look first for the irony, just as the best magazine writers look beyond the pro forma interview for a sense of the real person who would hide behind these masks.... There is often more told in a single photo than in a parliamentary session of Hansard or in the histories of the men and women attracted to public life.

Adapted from the introduction to *Poli-graphs*
Text by Roy MacGregor
Published by Deneau Publishers

PHOTOS · GAIL HARVEY

Adaptation de l'introduction de *Poli-graphs*
Texte de Roy MacGregor
Publié par Deneau Publishers

Alors qu'en photographie, tant de gens de métier sont en quête de clichés faciles et évidents, l'élite recherche d'abord l'ironie, de même que les meilleurs rédacteurs essaient de trouver, au-delà du curriculum vitae et de l'entrevue, l'homme ou la femme qui se cachent derrière ces masques… On en dit souvent plus dans une seule photo que dans une session parlementaire du *Hansard* ou dans la biographie de ces personnes étranges qu'attire la vie publique.

MARGARET THATCHER
OTTAWA, ONTARIO, 1981

POLI-GRAPHS

"I don't campaign. I just visit with people."
"Je ne fais pas de campagne, je me borne à rendre visite aux gens."

JOHN DIEFENBAKER
CAMBRIDGE, ONTARIO, 1977

"I'm getting totally fed up listening
to these things...I signed the deal.
The deal is no sellout for Canada.
It's a hell of a deal for Canada."

"J'en ai assez d'écouter tout ça...
J'ai conclu l'accord. Ce n'est
pas une trahison pour le Canada,
mais une merveilleuse affaire."

MICHAEL WILSON
TORONTO, ONTARIO, 1988

TITLE
DREAMLAND
ART DIRECTOR
STEVE HALL
EDITOR
KENN JACOBS
PHOTOGRAPHER
YURI DOJC
PUBLICATION
INTERNATIONAL PHOTOGRAPHY
PUBLISHER
EASTMAN KODAK CO.

YURI DOJC
CANADA

(Above) Illustration for a 1988 calendar produced by CBS Records Canada, "The Power of Music." Designers: Dela Kilian and Brian Moore.
(Right) Personal photograph of a rock musician by the Czech-born Dojc, a commercial photographer in Toronto.
Both photos: KODAK High Speed Infrared Film

TITLE
OH, TO GOLF IN BRITAIN
ART DIRECTOR
NADIA MARYNIAK
EDITOR
JACK McIVER
DESIGNER
NADIA MARYNIAK
PHOTOGRAPHER
FRANK HERHOLDT
PUBLICATION
DESTINATIONS
PUBLISHER
THE GLOBE AND MAIL

ALTHOUGH YOU HAVE TO VIRTUALLY INHERIT MEMBERSHIP TO BELONG TO THE VERY SNOOTY ST. ANDREW'S GOLF CLUB, THE COURSE, THE WORLD'S OLDEST, IS OPEN TO THE PUBLIC.

OH, TO GOLF IN BRITAIN

When it comes to the wild and wacky world of golf in the British Isles, very little is obvious. Somehow, though, it all makes sense

S P O R T

There's no telling what the British will do when it comes to playing golf. At the Littlestone Golf Club in Kent they insist only two balls be in play at a time. Then there's the Royal Worlington and Newmarket Golf Club, longtime home to the golf team at Cambridge University. It's only nine holes, only one cart is available and on some holes golfers must hit their tee shots over the previous green. And players get around in 75 minutes or so. The very idea – playing golf quickly and walking.

Golf in the British Isles is different. It's old, for one thing. Many courses haven't been changed in years. The lay of the land dictated the course, heavy earth-moving equipment wasn't available and course designers didn't study landscape architecture. Hence the tee shots over the greens at Royal Worlington. Hence double greens as large as football fields at the Old Course in St. An-

drews, Scotland. Hence a shot from the beach on the last hole at the Waterville Golf Links in southwest Ireland, where the seashore is part of the course. Golf in the British Isles is natural golf, not much changed from centuries ago when players first whacked a ball from point A to point B across open country by the sea, along valleys, between dunes and toward greens situated in hollows created by the action of the wind on the shifting terrain.

Consider the Old Course, that mecca for golfers. It's a narrow strip of treeless, featureless plain. Bleak is the word. Slammin' Sammy Snead wondered what all the fuss was about when he first came upon what looked like a moonscape. It looked nothing like the manicured green, green grass of home. He learned about the ragged rupture known as Hell Bunker that crosses the 14th fairway. He had to find a way around it, which often meant

BY LORNE RUBENSTEIN

JUNE 1989 11

Barking up the right tree

Thanks to farsighted publishing smarts, Canada's most important dog magazine is doing swimmingly at 100.
By Sue Fisher

Ten-week-old Fred-E. Gumby is the closest thing to a controversy to gambol through the doors of *Dogs In Canada* magazine in decades. Straining madly on his leash, whining plaintively through his trendy Shar-Pei wrinkles, the puppy has arrived at the offices of the magazine to meet the people who are going to make him a star. Bending down to greet him, publisher Elizabeth Dunn coos, "Aren't you beautiful!"

Atta boy! Third in popularity after the German shepherd and the poodle, the retriever is the breed that put the dog in the paddle.

CITY & COUNTRY HOME
CUISINE

CHAMPAGNE
AND OYSTERS

Soul mates. A marriage made in heaven. And the rarity of them, the exotic tang. Not for every day, these sensual specimens, products of years of coddling and patient waiting. How brief, by comparison, our enjoyment of them, but how rich as well. Oysters and champagne. Pleasures of the palate have to do with more than satisfying hunger or slaking thirst.

RECIPES BY ELIZABETH BAIRD

PHOTOGRAPHY BERT BELL

TITLE
BARKING UP THE RIGHT TREE
ART DIRECTOR
ROD DELLA VEDOVA
EDITOR
MALCOLM PARRY
DESIGNER
KELLY de REGT/ SARAH BRITNELL
CREATIVE DIR.
ROD DELLA VEDOVA
PHOTOGRAPHER
SKIP DEAN
PUBLICATION
VISTA
PUBLISHER
VISTA PUBLICATIONS

TITLE
CHAMPAGNE & OYSTERS
ART DIRECTOR
MARIAN MUSTARD
EDITOR
ANITA DRAYCOTT
PHOTOGRAPHER
BERT BELL
PUBLICATION
CITY & COUNTRY HOME
PUBLISHER
MACLEAN HUNTER LIMITED

PARADISE FOUND

Sleepwear and Sheer Makeup, Pure and Simple

Satin V-neck gown, Nadine Stuart. Right, silk chemise, Christine. Subtle color: Almay's Autumn Leaves eyes, Warmed Russet blush and Coral Embers lips.

PHOTOGRAPHS BY GEORGE WHITESIDE

96

· PARADISE FOUND ·

Men's-style silk pajamas, Adagio. Makeup now is spare, elegant: translucent colors, matte lips, pale cheeks. Eyes are lined with rich kohls or left appealingly bare. Ultima II's runway collection.

100

TRAVEL

"LA PUBLICITE," EXPLAINED THE COUNT DE MALET ROQUEFORT IN THE ELEGANT FORE-COURT OF HIS ANCIENT AND MUCH TOUTED CHATEAU IN SAINT EMILION, "IS VERY IMPORTANT"

HIGH TIME IN THE MEDOC

Throughout the Médoc the Bordelais grow agitated as they contemplate their only nightmare: bottle after bottle of Château Yamaha or Château Mitsubishi

BY GEORGE GALT

At the beginning of lunch with a château owner in Bordeaux this year, my host asked about my political preferences and then, before I could answer, told me his.

"We do not like the Socialists," he said. Mitterrand had just won the French presidential election.

"We *detest* them," said his wife.

Looking around the dining room at the plush floral curtains, the waxed antiques, and the crystal decanter still half full of the 1966 claret we'd been served, I wouldn't have expected this house to be a breeding ground for French leftists. The Bordeaux business people I met viewed Mitterrand as cunning and unreliable. Property owners weren't interpreting Mitterrand's failure to gain a clear majority in the French national assembly as any kind of safety net.

I asked my host to explain why he disliked the president so much.

"Because we are not Marxists!" he ex-claimed in French, wagging a finger. "You know what will result? Paralysis! France will be ungovernable!"

"Surely you're beyond danger, though," I replied. "He'd never nationalize the wine industry." This was beside the point, but if you're in Bordeaux with a grape-grower and want to avoid a diatribe on politics, shift the subject to wine. In a matter of seconds the future of the Fifth Republic no longer held our attention, and we were onto my host's favourite subject: *vin rouge*. Praising its manifold merits in a long speech, he paused several times to repeat: "*Le vin rouge ne fait que de bien*."

Maybe this is true, but most adults born in Canada were reared, as I was, in the knowledge that drinking wine was naughty and would do you no good. Some of us went on to fulfil the prophecy. With the help of *vin rouge* I once very nearly acquired a criminal record. (A judge who perhaps

● TRAVEL

THE BEST RED BORDEAUX ARE NOW BEYOND MOST PEOPLE'S MEANS. CHATEAU LAFITE'S HIGH PRICES HAVE HELPED PAY FOR A SPEC-

pers and done every blade. "It's quite nice, don't you think?" We wheeled around the pond. A sound man was hovering nearby, holding a boom over our heads. The film crew waved us out of the shadow of a towering cedar. We had begun to hear the story of "a very important" archaeological dig that had exposed an ancient mosaic floor. The film, the tree, the dig, his Canadian audience, all this together seemed to bamboozle the count.

"I was saying . . . ah . . . my family . . . this tree . . . ah, the mosaic! But the mosaic was not here, you understand. It was on my property but some distance away. Shall I tell you about the tree? The mosaic was from the third or fourth century. Roman. But the tree!" He looked alarmed, as if he had forgotten his lines. But he recovered.

"The first of my family to occupy the property planted this, a 400-year-old cedar of Lebanon. Before that" — he looked off into the middle distance again — "the men of my family were warriors."

I asked if there were other family members involved in the estate as is often the case in Bordeaux.

"My only sister inherited another property." He straightened his tie, apparently conscious of the camera. "It's a pity she sold it. But she doesn't have quite the same feel for the soil that I do." It was difficult to imagine the count actually sticking his hand into the dirt.

We walked back for the ritual *dégustation* (usually the sampling of a very young wine) and entered the fourteenth-century kitchen next to the oldest part of the house.

It was a small, low room with a concave ceiling. In one of the stone walls, a microwave oven had been installed. Against another wall stood a table with a tray of glasses and two bottles on it. The count poured us samples of his 1986 vintage. Château la Gaffelière is judged by some to be second in Saint Emilion only to Château Cheval Blanc, the greatest of this *appellation*'s reds, but these are wines that require at least a decade and often longer to mature. What you experience after only two years is something like a right hook to the palate — *kapow*: a rough, bitter, oak-barrel-and-raw-grape-skin taste, and you don't want to swallow too much of this stuff unless you're ready with your headache pills. But I had been reading my wine book and knew 1986 was regarded in the trade as an

exceptionally promising year for the Bordeaux reds.

"This wine shows unusual promise," I said solemnly, and the count agreed, saying it would be *très grand*.

To understand the attitudes of people like Léo de Malet Roquefort, you have to consider the relationship of the Bordelais to real estate. Vineyard proprietors may feel in their hearts an allegiance to liberty, equality, and fraternity, but they certainly don't want any egalitarian system of land ownership. Soil is the single most important ingredient in the raising of grapes and hence in the making of wine, and a vigneron who has developed or upheld a high reputation for his château has therefore a special commitment to his land. He will almost never sell it. "*Le sol, c'est moi*," a vigneron could

truthfully say, and most of the well-known Bordeaux vineyards leave the hands of a family only when complications arise with succession: too little money for taxes, too many heirs, or feuding cousins.

The sale of any large vineyard is always hot gossip in Bordeaux, and even more so in the light of recent events. Jean Miailhe, for example, a jolly man who was managing Château Citran for other members of his family when I met him six years ago, is no longer there, though he has kept three chateaux of his own. I was surprised to learn that the Miailhe family, which has prospered in the wine trade for generations, had sold a property, but not half so surprised as some of the Bordelais. For them the shock is compounded by the origin of the buyers: *les japonais*.

It's fine to talk about *les japonais* as manufacturers of cameras and VCRs. It's even fine that the Japanese have used their new wealth to become major buyers of the most expensive Bordeaux labels. (Japan imported 5.3-million bottles of Bordeaux wine last year, an increase of forty-one per cent over 1986.) It's not fine in the eyes of the Bordelais, on the other hand, that wealthy Japanese interests have begun to acquire French estates. In Bordeaux, the Japanese are regarded as unsophisticated parvenus, and they are making some of their new neighbours uneasy. Several landowners expressed to me their indignation that Japan's leading distillery had bought Château Lagrange, a respected vineyard in the Saint-Julien area. They were even more aggrieved that the new owners were assaulting the ancient French landscape with a Japanese garden.

It is hard to have sympathy for the Bordelais on this score. In fact, I quite like the idea of being able to buy a bottle of Château Yamaha or Château Mitsubishi, though I concede such labels might not have widespread appeal. In matters of wine the French can be insufferably pompous and chauvinistic, so it pleases me to imagine a grave *sommelier* having to explain the virtues of Château Yamaha — its delicate taste and good legs. (This term refers to the streaks of glycerin on a glass of wine you've just swirled and always leaves me wondering why the *sommelier* doesn't go one step farther and tell me when a wine has *belles festes* — a nice ass.)

The Bordelais may secretly wish they could confine the influence of Japan to the motifs on their Art-Nouveau antiques, but I heard no one complaining about the prosperity conferred by the surge of wine sales to Tokyo. Jaguars, Mercedeses, and BMWs are a common sight on the country roads of Bordeaux these days, and many properties

TRAVEL ●

are undergoing costly renovations. The most spectacular recent building project has been the underground rotunda at Château Lafite Rothschild. Designed by the widely admired Italian architect, Ricardo Bofill, Lafite's new *cave* is supported by a circle of columns that echo the lines of a wine barrel. The concrete pillars and walls have been so highly polished that a hand passed in pitch darkness along their cool surfaces could easily mistake them for marble. Designed for the elaborate ceremonies of wine making, the rotunda is a monument

Large and well-known vineyards would leave the hands of an owner only if complications had arisen: too little money for taxes, for example, or too many feuding heirs

to the outrageous sums of money people are willing to pay for this wine.

Standing by one of the polished pillars, Lafite's cellar master poured glasses of his 1986 vintage. I doubt I'll taste it again. Given the recent trend, it could be selling for $1,000 a bottle before I die, and a great many of those bottles will be ageing in Japan. As Lafite's cellar master greeted us, he showed me a list of the people he'd met that week. One of several Japanese had been "the chef in the hotel where M. Eric de Rothschild stays in Tokyo." Is it possible that even Lafite might be purchased by the Japanese? Not likely. The property was nationalized briefly after its owner was guillotined in 1794, but soon reverted to private hands. It has been owned by the Rothschilds for 120 years. The Japanese will, I imagine, chip away at Bordeaux real estate, and the xenophobic tittle-tattle will continue in Bordeaux salons, but the French are much too sure of their place in the world really to fear being dislodged. As one vigneron said to me, a little immodestly I thought, "Any peasant anywhere can make red wine. But only our soil and our hands can produce the best."

TACULAR NEW CELLAR WITH POLISHED PILLARS

OPPISITE PAGE

TITLE
PARADISE FOUND
ART DIRECTOR
KAREN SIMPSON
DESIGNER
KAREN SIMPSON
PHOTOGRAPHER
GEORGE WHITESIDE
PUBLICATION
DOMINO
PUBLISHER
THE GLOBE AND MAIL

TITLE
HIGH TIMES IN THE MEDOC
ART DIRECTOR
BRUCE RAMSAY
EDITOR
GEORGE GALT
PHOTOGRAPHER
RICHARD BURBRIDGE
PUBLICATION
SATURDAY NIGHT
PUBLISHER
HOLLINGER PUBLICATIONS INC.

GOLD · RUSH

*What's new under
the sun? Eight easy pieces, paired
with pure gold*

◆

PHOTOGRAPHS BY PHILLIP DIXON

The sarong, here,
white silk with gold embroidery,
Norma Kamali, silk bandeau
top, Katharine Hamnett.
Gold sandals, Donna Karan, rings,
Robert Lee Morris.

DOMINO

The dress,
opposite page, in silk crepe
with halter top and full skirt,
Anne Klein, earrings,
van der Straeten, belt, Jill Stuart,
sling-back shoes, Manolo
Blahnik, the evening jacket, this page,
with gold buttons over silk
sarong, Norma Kamali, men's clothes,
left to right, mock
crewneck and pants, Basco by Lance Karesh,
mock turtleneck, Bill Robinson,
pants, Sabato Russo
turtleneck, polo by Ralph Lauren,
pants, Ronaldus Shamask.

DOMINO

IS THE CITY THAT WORKS STILL WORKING?

HOOKERS

Street Fight

In the war between the

homeowners and the hookers,

is the real issue propriety

or property values?

VALERIE SCOTT
OF CORP:
"EVER SINCE I
WAS FIVE
I DREAMED OF
GETTING INTO
THE SEX
INDUSTRY"

LAST DECEMBER 10, A DRAMA WAS enacted on an elegant residential street in Cabbagetown. Wearing white sweatshirts emblazoned with a red circle and oblique line slashed across the graphic image of a hooker bending to solicit a john in a car, a handful of neighbors took to the pavements. Except for their sweatshirts and the missionary gleam in their eyes, they looked like any group of upwardly mobile Torontonians you might see in a movie lineup on a Saturday night. Armed with cameras and coming on like a preppy lynch mob, they confronted a chunky, confused-looking prostitute.

"Go away. Go do what you do on someone else's street," one man snarled in disgust. The prostitute stood her ground. With a whaddaya-wanna-make-of-it tone she replied, "I'm a hooker and I work Ontario Street."

"You're suffering. You're abused by pimps," came a sermon, but its recipient remained unmoved. Then, in hysterical tones, another voice shouted: "We're sick of you. You've lowered our property values. You have no idea what you're doing to the people who have spent hundreds of thousands of dollars to live on this street."

"I live here," the exasperated woman spluttered, although when grilled as to where, she could only hurl invective. Finally, she spewed venomously: "Buddy, I've lived in this area for twenty-six years. What made this *your* fucking area?"

There are a few ironies bound up in the downtown hooker wars, and the Ontario Street standoff throws them into high relief. What we have here is a clash in which the real issues have been obscured. They've been obscured because the adversaries aren't acknowledging what those issues are. What the Cabbagetown residents will admit about street soliciting is that it is a nuisance. What they won't say is that it offends their moral sensibilities and threatens their property values. This is not the first time outraged citizens have agitated to make prostitutes go away, but it is the first time that there may be nowhere else in town for them to go. What's going on, then, is a turf war. The street, a pricey chunk of real estate, is up for grabs. But

BY WENDY DENNIS

Photography by Nigel Dickson

NOVEMBER 1988 TORONTO LIFE 85

OPPISITE PAGE

TITLE
GOLD RUSH
ART DIRECTOR
KAREN SIMPSON
DESIGNER
KAREN SIMPSON
PHOTOGRAPHER
PHILLIP DIXON
PUBLICATION
DOMINO
PUBLISHER
THE GLOBE AND MAIL

IS THE CITY THAT WORKS STILL WORKING?

something else is also up for grabs, something that in the mêlée hardly anybody seems to be noticing. At stake is the future of a city. A city that, in altering its priorities and pumping its sense of community to the highest bidder, is in grave danger of losing its innocence.

There was a time when downtowners viewed prostitution as part of the donnée of urban life. If you chose to live downtown, you chose also to tolerate, maybe even cherish, as part of the texture of everyday experience, the loony-tunes and schlock vendors and roving packs of spiky-haired toughs who storm-trooped along Yonge. If streetwalkers belonged to that sometimes seamy world, so be it.

Since the early 1970s, a confluence of forces has conspired to radically disrupt this harmony. With the push to revitalize the downtown core, Cabbagetown's flops and rooming houses gradually vanished, transformed by the white-painters and, later, the sandblasters, who kept tenants to make the mortgage. As real estate prices spiralled, however, a more affluent group, many of them suburban refugees, moved in, grandly upgrading properties and squeezing out those tenants who once had called the neighbourhood their own. Property values leaped to the point where some houses on prime streets were turning over for close to half a million dollars. Not only had the houses been transformed; so too, in some cases, had the sensibilities of their owners. With a significant investment to protect, some residents no longer viewed hookers as part of the local color.

Parallel to those developments were others. In 1977, in the wake of citizen outrage at the murder of shoeshine boy Emanuel Jaques, and increasingly eager to attract more tourist dollars, civic officials padlocked body-rub parlors and cleaned up Yonge Street. Displaced from Yonge, some of the hookers began to move eastward to Church Street, although certain corners, like Jarvis and Gloucester, Isabella and Huntley, had been active hooker turf long before. When Church Street began to sprout smart cafés in the early eighties, the hookers migrated eastward again, off familiar territory and onto neighboring streets where they began doing deals under the noses of residents.

Barry Smith is a lawyer with a let's-skip-the-pleasantries manner who, along with his wife, Judy, bought a house on Cabbagetown's Ontario Street during the real estate boom of 1981. Smith was born and raised in Toronto, but had spent the previous ten years living on a twenty-five-acre property in the bucolic environs of Stouffville. Their two daughters having grown, the Smiths decided to return to the city. It was the charm of the downtown core, with its movie houses, theatres and lively multicultural enclaves, that seduced them back. Other than what Smith describes as a "few drunks" in the neighborhood, Ontario Street seemed the ideal place to locate.

In 1984, a year prior to the passage of Bill C-49, the country's current antisoliciting law, Barry Smith wrote the first of many letters to his alderman. It said that "prostitutes and other undesirable characters" had "begun" to appear in his neighborhood. In fact, Barry Smith's neighborhood had for decades been in the part of town known as Track 1 (an area bordered by Church, Parliament, Isabella and Dundas streets), which was a stroll for the city's hookers and a nesting ground for many of its hoodlums and vagrants. Nevertheless, Smith was not alone in complaining that these unsavory elements were beginning to clash with the scenery. Soon Smith and several hundred other like-minded citizens met with the police, who saw Bill C-49 as a law with more enforcement clout than the legislation it was replacing. So Smith and his cohorts registered politicians to support it, and in December 1985, Bill C-49 was passed. What Smith soon realized was that despite what he saw as "this lovely piece of legislation," the problem seemed to be getting worse.

So, to get the powers-that-be once again, in the summer of 1987 the South of Carlton Community Association, headed by Smith, made a conscious decision to attract press, gambling that the media would lick their chops over a gamy story. Soon *Globe, Star* and *Sun* readers learned that Cabbagetown residents were being greeted, after a hard day's work, by hookers and johns thrashing about on their patios. Tales emerged of streets clogged with the bumper-to-bumper traffic of cruising johns and suburban gawkers, and of residents who practically had to don hip boots to get through the debris of dildos, syringes and used condoms piling up on their properties. An October 25, 1987, *Sunday Star* piece, alliteratively headlined "Hookers haunt homes along The Track," described a scenario in which residents had become prisoners in their own homes, children could no longer play outside and pimps roamed the streets with baseball bats. The situation seemed so alarming and grim it was as if, without anybody else having noticed, Cabbagetown had become the Bronx, and only Charles Bronson could set things right.

By November, the South of Carlton Community Association had swung into Phase 2 of its crusade to win the media's sympathy and the mayor's attention. The group began what Barry Smith prefers now to refer to as neighborhood "street walks." He is somewhat touchy on this subject since some observers, including certain members of the press, have described these as vigilante tactics. In any event, wearing their sweatshirts, a small group of residents would cruise Ontario and Seaton streets three or four nights weekly and, according to Smith, "politely ask the girls to move"; over three months, he says there was only the December 10 confrontation. If they were standing on a street corner, "the girls" would then tell the residents that they were no longer on the residents' turf. Barry Smith's tone turns incredulous at the notion that the hookers would think they had the right to share the public domain of a street corner.

On a cold Saturday afternoon at the end of that month, about 200 residents sweatshirted up again, blocked traffic at the corner of Ontario and Carlton streets, milled about eating hot dogs that were being cooked on the terrace of Melanie's res-

FRONTLINERS LIKE LAURIE EDMISTON (ABOVE) SYMPATHIZE WITH SANDRA JACKSON AND BARRY SMITH, WHO ARE TROUBLED BY HOOKERS IN THEIR NEIGHBORHOOD, BUT THE SOCIAL WORKERS SAY A LEGAL CRACKDOWN WOULD ONLY WORK AGAINST KIDS TRYING TO BEAT THE STREET

SANDRA JACKSON AND BARRY SMITH

TITLE
STREET FIGHT
ART DIRECTOR
**TERESA FERNANDES/
MARTHA WEAVER**
EDITOR
MARQ DE VILLIERS
DESIGNER
MARTHA WEAVER
PHOTOGRAPHER
NIGEL DICKSON
PUBLICATION
TORONTO LIFE
PUBLISHER
**KEY PUBLISHERS
CO. LTD.**

TITLE
TUNNEL OF LIGHT
ART DIRECTOR
JIM IRELAND
EDITOR
JOCELYN LAURENCE
DESIGNER
JIM IRELAND
PHOTOGRAPHER
ANGELA GRAUERHOLZ
PUBLICATION
CANADIAN ART
PUBLISHER
**KEY PUBLISHERS
CO. LTD.**

A CANADIAN
ART PORTFOLIO
TUNNEL OF LIGHT NEW WORK BY ANGELA GRAUERHOLZ
TEXT BY CHANTAL PONTBRIAND

"Clouds and their relationship to the rest of the world, and clouds for themselves, interested me, and clouds which were most difficult to photograph — nearly impossible... I wanted to photograph clouds to find out what I had learned in 40 years about photography. Through clouds to put down my philosophy of life — to show that my photographs were not due to subject matter — not to special trees, or faces, or interiors, to special privileges, clouds were there for everyone — no tax as yet on them — free."
WINDOW (1988), CIBACHROME, 49¼" x 65"

SOFA (1988), CIBACHROME, 49¼" x 65"

CLOUDS (1988), CIBACHROME, 49¼" x 65"

ALLYSON CLAY
These works come from a show I did last year in Vancouver called *Lure*, in which four small paintings were juxtaposed with four texts. Each text was a description of how to make a painting, interrupted by personal dialogue on different issues. I found I wasn't comfortable with traditional, pure abstraction so I tried to find ways of combining the abstract with text. It's like adding narrative back—first taking it out, then adding it back in.

TITLE
THE DEFINITIVE EYE
ART DIRECTOR
JIM IRELAND
EDITOR
JOCELYN LAURENCE
DESIGNER
JIM IRELAND
PHOTOGRAPHER
ARNAUD MAGGS
PUBLICATION
CANADIAN ART
PUBLISHER
**KEY PUBLISHERS
CO. LTD.**

TITLE
FAMILY TIES
ART DIRECTOR
THERESE SHECHTER
EDITOR
SARAH MURDOCH
PHOTOGRAPHER
EDWARD GAJDEL
PUBLICATION
**THE FINANCIAL TIMES
OF CANADA**
PUBLISHER
**JOHN MacFARLANE/
THE FINANCIAL TIMES
OF CANADA**

TITLE
DIGITAL NEWS I
ART DIRECTOR
ARTHUR NIEMI
DESIGNER
**MARK KOUDYS/
ARTHUR NIEMI**
ILLUSTRATOR
GENE GREIF
TYPOGRAPHER
ATLANTA ART & DESIGN
AGENCY
**DDB NEEDHAM
WORLDWIDE
ADVERTISING INC.**
DESIGN FIRM
ATLANTA ART & DESIGN
PUBLICATION
DIGITAL NEWS
PUBLISHER
DIGITAL NEWS

THE TAXI INDUSTRY TAKES A GIANT STEP FORWARD

It's the method that's been used to dispatch taxicabs for almost 40 years. Soon, however, the conveyor belt that delivers hand-written cab requests from the telephone operator to the dispatcher may be a thing of the past. Traditionally resistant to change, the taxi industry is taking a giant step into computerization. ● Today, rather than hand-writing a note, call takers input cab requests into a computer terminal. When a call comes in, they key in the passenger address and destination on the screen. They then send it to the main computer, which directs it to the cab nearest the pick-up point. Parcels and account passengers are noted on the screen as well. ● The driver of the selected cab receives the fare on his Mobile Data Terminal. If he decides to accept it, he presses a button on the terminal. Details of the fare are then displayed on the terminal, which is bolted to the dashboard of the cab. If he's just picked up a passenger who has hailed him, he can refuse the fare. ● Any fare that a driver refuses is sent to the next cab that is closest to the pick-up point. The computer locates cars as they move through predetermined areas of the city. Each cab company that uses the system has divided the city in its own manner, into the number of areas that makes sense in terms of physical size and amount of business. ● "It (the computerized system) works better than I thought," says Bruce E. Bell, president of

the Diamond Taxicab Association of Toronto. Diamond is one of the largest companies in the city with over 450 cabs. Its system was installed in August, 1986. ● A major benefit, according to Bell, is the elimination of dispatcher favoritism toward particular drivers, since the computer makes the choice, based on proximity to pickup point. And since only one driver at a time learns of a fare, there's no more 'scooping', the practice of a driver hearing a fare being given to another driver and beating the assigned car to the customer. ● Both drivers and customers appreciate the computerized system, says Bell, because it offers many advantages. "Not only is it quieter, infor-

mation about available fares is getting to the cabs faster and cabs are reaching customers more quickly than before."

CO-OP Cabs General Manager, Joe Hadhavney is looking for cost-efficiency. A co-operative of cabs in Toronto, CO-OP installed its system earlier this year. Hadavney believes the system will keep his head office costs at the same level for many years. He doesn't have to hire new staff because current telephone operators are the new call takers.

The system also means less storage space is needed for records. "We record every transaction and keep it in one-tenth of the space we used to need," says Bruce Bell of Diamond Cabs.

Greater speed and efficiency have resulted in an increase in the number of fares the com-

panies can handle. In its first year of operation with the computer system, Diamond experienced an 18 percent increase in calls. This means both companies and the drivers benefit.

CO-OP and Diamond use the Gandalf Mobile Data Terminal. Gandalf provides the terminals mounted in the cabs, the software, maintenance and service. Gandalf created the Computer Dispatch Systems division to handle increasing call for its service.

"We see it as a profitable area for us," says John Seymour, Engineering Development Manager of Gandalf's Computer Dispatch Systems. To date, Gandalf has installed thousands of terminals in cabs in Ottawa, Hamilton, Calgary, Orlando and Anaheim.

The main computer, which is used to handle the service, must have a quick response time and be able to handle many bits of data at the same time. Gandalf uses Digital's MicroVAX II computer for the dispatch systems. "It's a superior product and we get tremendous maintenance and service from Digital," says John Seymour of Gandalf.

The MicroVAX II computer is a low-end model in Digital's VAX line of computers. It features virtual memory, 32-bit computing power and software capability across all VAX systems. And it stands less than 25 inches tall.

Concludes Bruce Bell of Diamond, "Any company not considering computerization for its cabs will be left out of the race." ●

DOWN TO EARTH SOLUTIONS FOR
A SPACE-AGE COMPANY

After a hard day's work, a fisherman in a tiny Newfoundland outport switches on the TV to catch his favorite show on an Edmonton station. ● That same evening, a British Columbia logger watches a sitcom on a channel from Detroit. ● And millions of Canadians across the land, even in the most out of the way places, are also tuned to radio and television broadcasts emanating from hundreds, even thousands of miles away, thanks to the miracle of satellite technology and the pioneering efforts of one farsighted company – Cancom. ● Cancom, short for Canadian Satellite Communications Inc. is dedicated to the application of satellite technology to solve communications problems created by geography. Originally established in 1981 with a mandate to provide broadcast signals to remote and underserved regions of Canada, Cancom has grown into a formidable force in the satellite industry. ● "The original idea behind Cancom came from a Yukon broadcaster named Rolf Hougen," says Rob Lockwood, Cancom's Director of

Information Services. "He believed that all Canadians, regardless of where they lived, should have access to a wide variety of television and radio signals. Satellite technology provided the practical means of achieving his goal."

What began as Hougen's dream has become a world-leading reality, as the Mississauga, Ontario company now beams television and radio signals to over 1.8 million Canadian households in 1,300 communities coast to coast.

But success didn't come easily. "Because Cancom was the first company in the world to try to reach small, remote communities with broadcast signals using satellites, we didn't have a model to follow," says Sheelagh Whittaker, Cancom's Senior Vice-President and Chief Financial Officer. "This meant we had to use trial and error nearly every step of the way, and innovate whenever we ran into a roadblock."

As a result of Cancom's pioneering and innovative approach, the company has been able to make cable television service economical for communities as small as 50 homes. Five years ago, the smallest community that could be served profitably was about 500 homes. Cancom has also played a major role in making single-home satellite systems (the dishes so popular in the countryside) affordable.

Cancom's innovative spirit has led the company beyond its original mandate and motivated it to create new services to take advantage of some of its unutilized satellite resources. Today, Cancom provides one-way and two-way interactive data transmission for a growing number of business customers - transmitting news and photos for Canadian Press, radio features for broadcast news and stock trading information for the Toronto Stock Exchange.

Its flexibility and willingness to try new ventures has helped Cancom grow from a single service business in 1984 to a multiple services company today. Its 110 employees now deliver a wide range of satellite audio, video and data communications services to a diversity of customers across the country. In fact, Cancom is the fastest growing public company in Canada, with sales leaping by over 3,000 percent between 1982 and 1986.

A Digital Computing Solution
This kind of growth and Cancom's enthusiasm for new ventures could have been held back by

the company's computing capacity. "We're doing things all the time, starting new applications and opening new businesses," Whittaker says. "Our computer system must be able to adapt to patterns which are hard to predict. It can't hold us back from entering new markets. It has to be ready when we are."

That wasn't possible with Cancom's previous systems. "We'd no sooner get nicely ensconced on a computer than we'd find it was rapidly becoming too small," Whittaker says. "And every change of machine, every upgrade had a major effect on the way we ran on a day-to-day basis."

Cancom relies on its computer system to provide a constant stream of accurate, timely financial information, handle all of the company's corporate accounting, and perform intensive sales and market analyses. "Each time our business lurched upward, the resulting jump in our computing needs was very large, very disruptive and hard to accommodate," Lockwood says.

Seeking to establish a computing environment that could expand as they expanded, Cancom turned to Digital Equipment of Canada. "We went to Digital for help," says Whittaker, "and they supplied it by the ton. All of a very good help."

Digital began by conducting an in-depth analysis of Cancom's system and network needs, and recommending a cost-effective solution. "We thought we needed something quite large, like a VAX 8800 or 8650 computer," Lockwood says. "To our pleasant surprise, Digital specified a cluster of three MicroVAX II systems that was about half the size and cost."

Creating The Right Environment
Digital also provided a number of crucial services. Because Cancom was moving to new offices, Digital recommended its DECsite services to plan, design and construct a new computer facility which could meet the company's long-term system requirements. Digital also provided Network Physical Design and Network Installation Management to make sure Cancom's network needs were met right from the start.

What had to be created was a complete computing environment. "Digital helped us design how big the machine environment had to be, which then led us to how big the room had to be," Lockwood says. "They came back to us with a design that was less costly, more efficient and

TORONTO REGION

8 Mayor Lorna Jackson touts the Town of Vaughan as a single-family community where tenants are not wanted and condo owners are barely tolerated. The average selling price for a new home in Vaughan in 1987 was $267,000. In the past five years, more than 2,000 acres have been developed here for the construction of about 15,000 houses—which means densities lower than in Rosedale.

7 Mississauga, the giant of Toronto suburbs with 423,000 residents, provides both housing and work opportunities, but not in a rationalized way: as many Mississauga residents commute to work in Metro Toronto every day as Metro residents commute to jobs in Mississauga. Why this great waste of fuel and time in cross-commuting? The employees of Mississauga factories can't afford to live there; to buy a Mississauga house, you need a job in a downtown banking tower.

6 Thornhill was once a real village, with a centre on Yonge Street south of Highway 7, where a handful of its old buildings can still be found. But regional government needed boundaries close to Yonge Street, so Vaughan took the western half, Markham the eastern. The dominant characteristic of suburban planning values—the urge to subvert or destroy the past—has overcome Thornhill.

The raw figures for regional growth are quite astounding: from a population of one million in 1976 to 1.28 million in 1981 and an estimated 1.7 million now. Most of this growth has been in York and Peel regions. Within ten years more people will live in the regions than within Metro Toronto itself, and by the end of the century it's estimated that the regional population will be 2.3 million, for a 4.5-million total in the Toronto urban area, or almost half the population of the province.

5 GO Transit is the lifeline of the regional commuter but it is a quite modest operation, carrying only 100,000 riders each weekday—compared to the TTC's 1.9-million daily riders. The cost isn't modest, though: the public's subsidy to GO Transit last year was $190 million, or about $6 per rider. Sounds a bit tough, but Toronto would be much healthier if GO didn't make it easier for suburbanites to rely on downtown for work and entertainment.

1 Only a kitschy shopping strip remains of what was once Markham. Since when was the word "town" meant to imply an area where 130,000 people live in suburban houses sprawling over almost seventy-seven square kilometres?

When people think of planning, they think of downtown streets and how to shoehorn in another couple of houses or how to save an old building. But the significant planning decisions are being made outside Metro Toronto. Rarely does anyone cast a critical eye on these shenanigans, and we can see too well the sad results. In September Queen's Park appointed a deputy minister for the greater Toronto area. Yet another level of government could produce paralysis or allow the space-wasting suburban style to swamp the older, denser city form, basically killing the goose that laid the golden egg. Hardheaded co-ordination is what's needed, and that will require a plan for the region as radical as the Toronto Centred Region Plan, and the political will to stick to it.

METRO TORONTO

2 The province owns 25,000 acres in North Pickering adjacent to 17,000 acres of the former Pickering airport assembly owned by the federal government. It may become the site of a new community eschewing the suburban style. Current thinking seems to favor fifteen units per acre rather than the traditional seven, permitting the community of 90,000 a distinctly urban feel with corner stores, townhouses and small apartment buildings, mixed uses, and a transit system that pays its own way. Seaton, as it will likely be called, could bring to an end our forty-year love affair with the suburb.

3 Thank goodness for the regional fringe—without it, where would we dump our garbage? As both the Pickering and Maple sites are rapidly filled, Metro faces the ultimate crunch: how to live with our own waste. The most likely escape will be the discovery of gravel pits close to rail lines even farther out. Commuters can be shipped in while garbage is shipped out.

4 Remember the Parkway Belt? It was to be a luxuriant green buffer between the urban area and the countryside. By the late 1970s it had been downgraded to a servicing corridor for hydro lines, piped services and new roads. Now the original vision has given way to factory sites, housing developments and, soon, the long-touted Highway 407.

CITY HALL

Power Play

The NDP is out to change the Guards at city hall by taking over the reform movement

IT WAS ON A DECEMBER NIGHT sixteen years ago that Toronto voters handed several members of the Old Guard on city council the pink slip. Their replacements were to be a menagerie of reformers who, with their supporters, flocked to city hall for a spontaneous shindig that very night, as if taking over the building was a declaration that the days of unbridled development were over.

It didn't work out that way. The reform movement, easy to label but harder to define, never fulfilled its vision of the new Toronto. It wasn't long before city hall again became a comfortable place for the developers to do business. Every few years, however, the industry's self-interest gets the better of it and its opponents cash in. That's what happened in 1972, and some think that may be what will happen again this November 14.

It will be an odd election in any case. Though city council has been described as being made up of a mayor and twenty-two aldermen who want to be mayor, the current chief has stared down pretenders to his throne. Even those

aldermen who say Art Eggleton is as bland as melba toast consider him a savvy politician who knows how to play hardball. That's why on election day his only opponents are likely to be the usual cast of kooks, clowns and cranks.

A municipal election without a mayoralty race is about as thrilling as watching the Oilers without Gretzky. Only three of every ten of your neighbors are going to vote at the best of times, and this year's campaign is being conducted under the shadow of an imminent federal election. There will likely be no shindig and few pink slips.

So why pay attention? Because the failures of the reform movement in the past have made the New Democratic Party untrusting. Instead of fighting elections as part of an informal coalition, the party is dedicated to dominating city hall on its own. For now it will be satisfied to command a significant minority of seats. The longer-term goal is to elect a mayor and a majority of councillors in 1991. The NDP, the only political party openly operating as a caucus at the municipal level, is touting itself as the official opposition to what an official party doc-

BY TOM HAWTHORN

Illustration by Simon Ng

A

SILVER

TITLE
ARE WE SCREWING UP?
ART DIRECTOR
TERESA FERNANDES
EDITOR
MARQ de VILLIERS
DESIGNER
**TERESA FERNANDES/
MARTHA WEAVER**
PHOTOGRAPHER
**NANCY SHANOFF/
NIGEL DICKSON/
EDWARD GAJDEL/
RUSSELL MONK/
DOUG FORSTER**
ILLUSTRATOR
**ALAN COBER/
SANDRA DIONISI/
NORMAND COUSINEAU/
SIMON NG/
ANTHONY RUSSO/
SUE COE/
NICHOLAS VITACCO**
PUBLICATION
TORONTO LIFE
PUBLISHER
**KEY PUBLISHERS
CO. LTD.**

TITLE
DIGITAL NEWS II
ART DIRECTOR
ARTHUR NIEMI
DESIGNER
**MARK KOUDYS/
ARTHUR NIEMI**
ILLUSTRATOR
MICK WIGGINS
TYPOGRAPHER
ATLANTA ART & DESIGN
AGENCY
**DDB NEEDHAM
WORLDWIDE
ADVERTISING INC.**
DESIGN FIRM
**ATLANTA ART
& DESIGN INC.**
PUBLICATION
DIGITAL NEWS
PUBLISHER
DIGITAL NEWS

UNE FENÊTRE SUR LE FUTUR
POUR LES RÉSEAUX D'ENTREPRISE

Des possibilités incroyables sont actuellement offertes sur le marché des solutions d'ordinateurs de bureau. Digital entend bien en tirer parti et devenir le fournisseur numéro un dans ce domaine, car nous savons que ce sera une solution informatique très recherchée dans les années 90. Le marché de l'ordinateur de bureau devrait compter pour plus de 40 % des recettes totales

en informatique dans le monde entier en 1991, soit presque 60 milliards de dollars.

Une stratégie gagnante

Depuis ses débuts, Digital a créé des outils permettant à ses clients de travailler intelligemment et efficacement. En 1978, Ken Olsen, président de Digital Equipment Corporation, a déclaré :

« Nous avons toujours cru que les ordinateurs devaient être des outils pour les personnes qui sont tributaires de l'information pour effectuer leur travail. C'est pourquoi au fil des ans, nous avons conçu des systèmes interactifs pouvant être installés là où il faut. La tendance actuelle vers une utilisation accrue de systèmes interactifs répartis confirme l'approche que nous avions adoptée. »

Dix ans plus tard, c'est toujours vrai. Notre conception de l'informatique ne change pas ; si ce n'est qu'elle évolue dans son application. Aujourd'hui, l'informatique de bureau nous apparaît comme la suite logique de cette évolution.

Puisque l'information est devenue un atout précieux pour devancer ses concurrents le professionnel doit pouvoir accéder facilement et rapidement aux données, les analyser et prendre les décisions et les mesures qui s'imposent.

Toutefois, l'information nécessaire est souvent stockée dans différents systèmes, et prend diverses formes : texte, graphiques, images, feuilles de calcul électroniques ou types de documents particuliers à une profession.

Avec les outils couramment utilisés, on se heurte à deux problèmes de taille :

• La surcharge d'information : On reçoit tellement d'information qu'il devient impossible de retrouver ce dont on a réellement besoin.

• Les encombrements : On sait que les données requises existent, mais on ne dispose pas des outils nécessaires pour les retrouver et les transférer à son ordinateur de bureau.

Pour résoudre ces problèmes urgents, il faut un cadre de gestion d'information qui :

• facilite les communications internes, peu importe le matériel utilisé ;

• permette aux utilisateurs d'accéder, à partir de leur bureau, à l'information essentielle à leur travail, sous quelque forme que ce soit ;

• augmente la productivité des employés, des équipes et des services ;

• augmente la productivité de l'entreprise, même dans les rapports avec les fournisseurs et les clients.

AUJOURD'HUI

« Pour la première fois, un géant de l'industrie nous offre le meilleur rapport performances/prix. »

MARC SHULMAN

UBS SECURITIES

Pour Digital, la meilleure solution possible était d'intégrer à l'échelle de l'entreprise des systèmes de divers fournisseurs, des applications très évoluées et des renseignements présentés sous des formes variées, et de créer ainsi un cadre informatique uniforme, qui fournirait obligatoirement à l'utilisateur :

• l'accès direct à des outils de pointe et la possibilité d'étendre les solutions disponibles en tenant compte des investissements effectués ;

• des solutions adaptées aux styles informatiques que les utilisateurs préfèrent.

Pour élaborer sa stratégie gagnante, Digital a tenu compte de plusieurs éléments :

• Aux utilisateurs qui se servent du traitement de texte, de la messagerie et du chiffrier, elle offre des terminaux de pointe.

• Pour ceux qui désirent des ordinateurs personnels conformes aux normes de l'industrie, Digital a créé une nouvelle famille d'ordinateurs personnels.

• Pour satisfaire les clients qui requièrent des postes de travail UNIX rapides, on a lancé de nouvelles machines ULTRIX mettant à profit la technologie RISC.

• Aux clients qui désirent un système articulé autour de VMS, on offre une gamme étendue de postes de travail VAXstation.

• En outre, Digital relie l'utilisateur au réseau de l'entreprise, grâce à des réseaux locaux et à des services d'intégration d'applications.

Et c'est ainsi qu'est née la stratégie d'informatique de bureau de Digital qui fournit aux clients les meilleurs outils qui soient pour effectuer leur travail. C'est simple et logique.

Pour le choix : le matériel

Les terminaux Beaucoup d'utilisateurs choisissent encore le terminal comme ordinateur de

---

M. Fournier recherchait
la technologie idéale...
celle qui permettrait
d'entrer le texte anglais
à un bout et de recevoir
le texte français à
l'autre bout.

l'informaticien Larry Rogers, ont réalisé deux choses importantes. Tout d'abord, pour qu'un tel projet réussisse, la traduction devait être entièrement automatique. Il existe un certain nombre de systèmes de traduction - interactifs - sur le marché. Ces progiciels fonctionnent un peu à la manière d'un thésaurus : on entre un mot ou une expression anglais au clavier et le système propose divers équivalents français à l'écran. Le choix d'un équivalent est laissé au traducteur, qui doit naviguer dans le texte tout au long du processus (une tâche fastidieuse).

« Ce n'était vraiment pas la bonne solution en termes d'uniformité, de rapidité et de qualité technique de la traduction - raconte M. Fournier, qui recherchait la technologie idéale...celle qui permettrait d'entrer le texte anglais à un bout et de recevoir le texte français à l'autre bout.

En outre, si une telle technologie était créée, elle profiterait à des dizaines d'entreprises, au Canada et en Amérique du Nord. »

MM. Fournier et Rogers ont finalement aperçu une lueur au bout du tunnel. Doté de matériel valant plus de 2 millions de dollars, Lexi-tech s'est attaquée à la tâche en août dernier avec une équipe de 46 personnes, dont 16 traducteurs techniques très qualifiés, soit une des plus fortes concentrations d'experts en traduction à l'intérieur de l'appareil gouvernemental.

Selon Ron Fournier, plusieurs entreprises du Canada et des États-Unis se sont montrées intéressées.

« Les clients veulent un service complet ... un point de chute unique où les documents sous toutes leurs formes sont traités et retournés prêts à la copie ou à l'impression. »

Voici comment Lexi-tech allie la technique de l'édition à celle de la traduction machine.

1. Lexi-tech reçoit les originaux anglais sous toutes sortes de formats.

« À l'aide de lecteurs optiques, nous entrons en machine les documents sur papier, et nos ordinateurs acceptent plus de 30 formats de traitement de textes sur disquettes, sur bandes ou sur disques compacts » explique Larry Rogers, maintenant directeur de l'exploitation et du développement chez Lexi-tech.

2. On crée ensuite des feuilles de style conformes aux exigences du client : style de caractère, largeur des colonnes, taille et position des en-têtes. Le texte anglais est formaté automatiquement suivant ces paramètres.

3. On dépouille ensuite le texte anglais pour identifier tous les mots inconnus du logiciel de traduction. L'équipe de traduction fait les ajouts nécessaires au dictionnaire, après quoi le processus de traduction automatique est engagé.

4. Le premier texte traduit est exact à 80 %. En outre, les délais de production sont raccourcis car les versions anglaise et française sont automatiquement formatées et donc prêtes pour la copie ou l'impression.

L'exactitude de la traduction dépend du lexique.

« Notre dictionnaire compte plus de 70 000 termes et expressions techniques approuvés par l'OTAN, le ministère de la Défense nationale et diverses entreprises du domaine de la haute technologie, déclare Larry Rogers. C'est le noyau du système. »

« Nous possédons le plus gros dictionnaire technique privé en Amérique du Nord et sa taille augmente encore très rapidement. »

5. Les graphiques originaux sont balayés et numérisés par un processeur pouvant traiter des feuilles de 40 po sur 19 pi. Tout le texte des graphiques est transféré électroniquement, traduit dans un fichier distinct et réintégré dans le produit final.

Au cœur du système résident deux progiciels : le programme d'édition d'Interleaf Canada Inc. et le système de traduction de LOGOS Canada.

« LOGOS ne tournant que sur IBM, nous avons installé un système 9370/60, explique Larry Rogers. Par contre, le progiciel Interleaf tourne sur divers systèmes. Nous en avons étudié trois avant de choisir une plate-forme de Digital Equipment Corporation composée de trois VAXstation 3600. »

Dix-neuf postes de travail de Digital sont reliés à la plate-forme. Des VAXstation 3000 servent à la saisie des données, au traitement des graphiques, ainsi qu'à la gestion, à la mise en forme et à l'assemblage des documents. Les traducteurs disposent de 11 VAXstation 2000 pour dialoguer avec le système LOGOS et lancer les travaux d'impression au laser.

L'intégration des systèmes s'effectue au moyen de réseau Local Area VAXcluster de Digital.

« C'est en partie pour ses compétences en réseautage que nous avons choisi Digital, confie Larry Rogers. Elle offre les services qu'il nous faut, et l'architecture du matériel nous permet de prendre de l'expansion sans problème. Bref, Digital offrait la solution idéale. »

Ron Fournier voit grand. « Nous avons investi beaucoup d'argent - plus de 4 millions de dollars

en frais d'exploitation la première année - pour concrétiser une très bonne idée. Nous avons un produit unique en Amérique du Nord. »

« Après quelques mois d'exploitation, il semble que notre confiance du début soit pleinement justifiée. La réponse est excellente et nous comptons tripler nos effectifs dans les 36 prochains mois. »

Ron Fournier prévoit que de nombreux traducteurs techniques proviendront de la région de Moncton. « L'université de Moncton est en mesure de former ces futurs spécialistes; nous mettons actuellement sur pied un programme conjoint et envisageons de collaborer à la recherche et le partage des installations. »

David Booth aussi voit grand. Représentant

de Digital à Moncton et responsable du dossier Lexi-tech, c'est lui qui répondra aux besoins de l'entreprise (environ 66 postes de travail et du matériel de soutien), au cours des 3 prochaines années.

David Booth est très heureux de collaborer avec Lexi-tech, qui a emménagé dans un immeuble nouvellement rénové. Construit en 1882, il servait à l'origine de fabrique de biscuits. « Mon père y a travaillé pendant 30 ans pour la compagnie Marven et je venais de temps à autre lorsque j'étais petit. »

« À cette époque, c'étaient les biscuits qui attiraient à cet endroit. Aujourd'hui, qui sait, les murs en ont peut-être conservé l'odeur. » ●

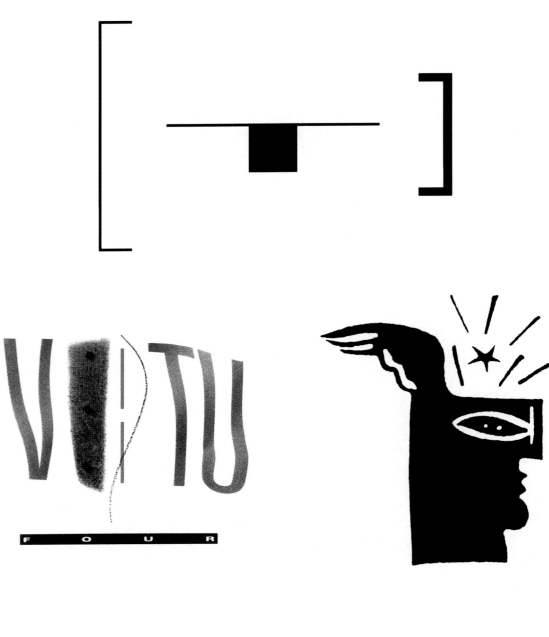

C I T Y C E N T R E

G O L D

TITLE
**TUDHOPE
ASSOCIATES INC.**
ART DIRECTOR
WILLIAM LAM
DESIGNER
TODD RICHARDS
CREATIVE DIR.
**BEV TUDHOPE/
IAN TUDHOPE**
DESIGN FIRM
**TUDHOPE
ASSOCIATES INC.**
CLIENT
**TUDHOPE
ASSOCIATES INC.**

S I L V E R

TITLE
VIRTU
ART DIRECTOR
DEL TERRELONGE
DESIGNER
DEL TERRELONGE
DESIGN FIRM
**TERRELONGE
DESIGN INC.**
CLIENT
FORUM AND FUNCTION
PRINTER
**ADELAIDE PRINTING
LTD.**

S I L V E R

TITLE
MENTAL ART & DESIGN
ART DIRECTOR
**JOE BIAFORE/
JILL CHEN**
DESIGNER
JOE BIAFORE
ILLUSTRATOR
JOE BIAFORE
DESIGN FIRM
MENTAL ART & DESIGN

TITLE
**MISSISSAUGA CITY
CENTRE**
ART DIRECTOR
WILL NOVOSEDLIK
DESIGNER
FIONA PINTO
CREATIVE DIR.
BOB RUSSELL
TYPOGRAPHER
CANADIAN COMPOSITION
DESIGN FIRM
**BOULEVARD
COMMUNICATIONS LTD.**
CLIENT
**MISSISSAUGA CITY
CENTRE
MARKETING GROUP**

TITLE
**SILVERSIDE COMPUTER
SYSTEMS INC.**
ART DIRECTOR
**JOHN TAYLOR/
ROBBIE SPRULES**
DESIGNER
IVAN NOVOTNY
DESIGN FIRM
TAYLOR/SPRULES
CLIENT
**SILVERSIDE COMPUTER
SYSTEMS INC.**

TITLE
ROLL-O-VERT
ART DIRECTOR
**DITI KATONA/
JOHN PYLYPCZAK**
DESIGNER
JOHN PYLYPCZAK
TYPOGRAPHER
CANADIAN COMPOSITION
DESIGN FIRM
CONCRETE
CLIENT
ROLLAND INC.

TITLE
**FOUNTAINHEAD
PICTURES INC.**
ART DIRECTOR
**ELIAHU BARR/
GAETANO LEO**
DESIGNER
GAETANO LEO
DESIGN FIRM
**BARR ASSOCIATES
DESIGNERS**
CLIENT
**FOUNTAINHEAD
PICTURES INC.**

TITLE
ENVIROFRIENDLY LOGO
ART DIRECTOR
TED LARSON
DESIGNER
TED LARSON
DESIGN FIRM
**OASIS CREATIVE
GROUP INC.**
CLIENT
ENVIRONMENT CANADA

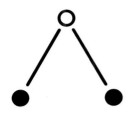

A N D E R S O N   P U B L I C   R E L A T I O N S

TITLE
ANDERSON PUBLIC RELATIONS
ART DIRECTOR
CATHERINE HAUGHTON
DESIGNER
BOB WHELLER
CREATIVE DIR.
CATHERINE HAUGHTON
ILLUSTRATOR
BOB WHELLER
TYPOGRAPHER
COOPER & BEATTY
DESIGN FIRM
HAUGHTON BRAZEAU DESIGN ASSOCIATES LIMITED
CLIENT
ANDERSON PUBLIC RELATIONS

TITLE
R & G OFFICE PRODUCTS
ART DIRECTOR
ROBERT HYLAND
DESIGNER
SUSANNE SCHWARZE
DESIGN FIRM
ROBERT HYLAND DESIGN AND ASSOCIATES
CLIENT
R & G OFFICE PRODUCTS

TITLE
CANADIAN MASTERS
ART DIRECTOR
DAVID SHELLY
DESIGNER
DAVID SHELLY
ILLUSTRATOR
DAVID SHELLY
DESIGN FIRM
GRAPHISPHERE INC.
CLIENT
CANADIAN MASTERS INC.

TITLE
MERLETTO
ART DIRECTOR
AMANDA FINN
DESIGNER
AMANDA FINN
TYPOGRAPHER
TECHNIPROCESS
DESIGN FIRM
LAWRENCE FINN & ASSOCIATES LTD.
CLIENT
MERLETTO

SILVER

TITLE
SISTEMALUX
ART DIRECTOR
MALCOLM WADDELL
DESIGNER
PETER SCOTT
TYPOGRAPHER
CANADIAN COMPOSITION
DESIGN FIRM
ESKIND WADDELL
CLIENT
SISTEMALUX

SILVER

TITLE
**LAURIE LAFRANCE
ILLUSTRATION**
DESIGNER
DON ZACHAROPOULOS
ILLUSTRATOR
LAURIE LAFRANCE
CLIENT
**LAURIE LAFRANCE
ILLUSTRATION**

TITLE
MARTIN/MARYETTA INC.
ART DIRECTOR
MARYETTA MARTIN
DESIGNER
MARYETTA MARTIN
ILLUSTRATOR
DOUG MARTIN
DESIGN FIRM
MARTIN/MARYETTA INC.
CLIENT
MARTIN/MARYETTA INC.

TITLE
**TUDHOPE
ASSOCIATES INC.**
ART DIRECTOR
WILLIAM LAM
DESIGNER
TODD RICHARDS
CREATIVE DIR.
**BEV TUDHOPE/
IAN TUDHOPE**
DESIGN FIRM
**TUDHOPE
ASSOCIATES INC.**
CLIENT
**TUDHOPE
ASSOCIATES INC.**
PRINTER
**M.C. CHARTERS
& CO. LTD./
GRAFO PRINTING**

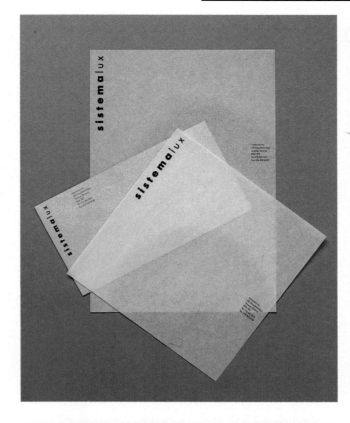

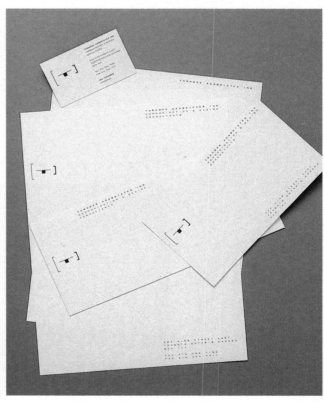

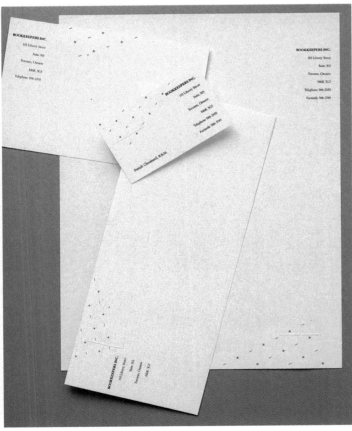

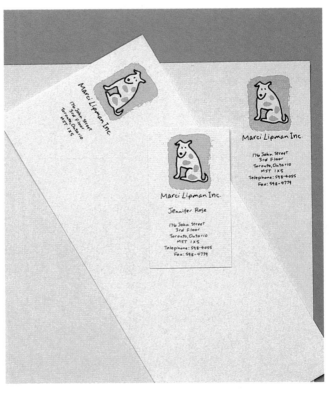

TITLE
ROBINS SHARPE
ART DIRECTOR
CARMEN DUNJKO
DESIGNER
CLARE MERIDEW
TYPOGRAPHER
**PAUL WALKER/
CANADIAN COMPOSITION**
DESIGN FIRM
**CARMEN DUNJKO
ASSOCIATES**
CLIENT
**ROBINS SHARPE
ASSOCIATES LTD.**

TITLE
ACORN
ART DIRECTOR
WILL NOVOSEDLIK
DESIGNER
MICHAEL STOKELY
CREATIVE DIR.
BOB RUSSELL
TYPOGRAPHER
CANADIAN COMPOSITION
DESIGN FIRM
**BOULEVARD
COMMUNICATIONS LTD.**
CLIENT
**ACORN ILLUSTRATION
& ART**
HANDLETTERING
IAN BRIGNELL

TITLE
BOOKKEEPERS INC.
DESIGNER
JOHN BRYSON
TYPOGRAPHER
M & H TYPOGRAPHY
DESIGN FIRM
DESIGN FORCE INC.
CLIENT
BOOKKEEPERS

TITLE
MARCI LIPMAN
ART DIRECTOR
JILL CHEN
DESIGNER
JILL CHEN
ILLUSTRATOR
JILL CHEN
TYPOGRAPHER
JILL CHEN
DESIGN FIRM
**CARMEN DUNJKO
ASSOCIATES**
CLIENT
MARCI LIPMAN INC.

TITLE
ALICIA TYSON
ART DIRECTOR
ALICIA TYSON
DESIGNER
ALICIA TYSON
DESIGN FIRM
A TYSON DESIGN
CLIENT
A TYSON DESIGN

TITLE
JOEL BENARD
ART DIRECTOR
PAUL HASLIP
DESIGNER
PAUL HASLIP
DESIGN FIRM
**HYNES, HASLIP
& PARTNERS INC.**
CLIENT
JOEL BENARD

TITLE
MENTAL ART & DESIGN
ART DIRECTOR
**JOE BIAFORE/
JILL CHEN**
DESIGNER
**JOE BIAFORE/
JILL CHEN**
ILLUSTRATOR
JOE BIAFORE
TYPOGRAPHER
**CANADIAN
COMPOSITION INC.**
DESIGN FIRM
MENTAL ART & DESIGN
PRINTING
C.J. GRAPHICS INC.

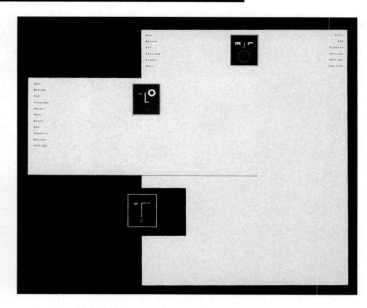

A

S I L V E R

TITLE
POWER
DESIGNER
RICK CARTY
CREATIVE DIR.
BOB RUSSELL
ILLUSTRATOR
RICK CARTY
DESIGN FIRM
**BOULEVARD
COMMUNICATIONS LTD.**
CLIENT
BATA LIMITED

TITLE
**1325 AVENUE
OF THE AMERICAS
LEASING BROCHURE**
DESIGNER
YIN HOSKINS
CREATIVE DIR.
IAN TUDHOPE
DESIGN FIRM
**TUDHOPE
ASSOCIATES INC.**
CLIENT
**EDWARD J. MINSKOFF
EQUITIES**
PRINTER
**ARTHURS-JONES
LITHOGRAPHING LTD.**
FILM SEPARATIONS
EMPRESS GRAPHICS INC.

TITLE
DIRECTIONS '89
ART DIRECTOR
DIANNE EASTMAN
WRITER
IAN MIRLIN
CREATIVE DIR.
BRIAN HARROD
PHOTOGRAPHER
TIM SAUNDERS
TYPOGRAPHER
**THE COMPOSING ROOM
AT COOPER & BEATTY**
AGENCY
HARROD & MIRLIN
CLIENT
**THE ART DIRECTORS
CLUB OF TORONTO**
FILM/PRINTING
**HERZIG SOMERVILLE
LIMITED**
PRODUCTION
JACK WAGA
PAPER
**WARREN PAPER/
GRAPHIC PAPERS**

THE LIMITED EDITION "FESTIVAL" T-SHIRT

BY JEFF JACKSON FOR CLUB MONACO

$12⁰⁰

WITH ANY CLUB MONACO FRAGRANCE PURCHASE

T-shirt without fragrance purchase: $22.00

TITLE
CLUB MONACO T-SHIRT PROMOTION
ART DIRECTOR
LOUIS FISHAUF
ILLUSTRATOR
JEFF JACKSON/ REACTOR
DESIGN FIRM
REACTOR ART & DESIGN
CLIENT
CLUB MONACO

THE LIMITED EDITION "L'AMOUR" T-SHIRT

BY JEFF JACKSON FOR CLUB MONACO

$16⁰⁰
CARD INCLUDED

WITH ANY CLUB MONACO FRAGRANCE PURCHASE

TITLE
VALENTINE
ART DIRECTOR
LOUIS FISHAUF
ILLUSTRATOR
JEFF JACKSON/ REACTOR
DESIGN FIRM
REACTOR ART & DESIGN
CLIENT
CLUB MONACO

1988 AND BEYOND

CONTINUING GROWTH

Ontario continues the strong growth in electricity consumption that began following the recession of the early 1980s. Over the past five years, consumption has risen an average of 5 per cent a year. In 1988, electricity consumption rose by 6.5 per cent, reflecting continued strong growth in the provincial economy.

During 1988, a total of 135.1 billion kilowatt-hours was consumed by our primary customers and secondary customers outside the Province. This is 5.0 per cent higher than in 1987, and 2.2 per cent above our forecast. Peak demand for power in 1988 was 23 million kilowatts, 12.1 per cent higher than the 1987 peak.

Hydro's exports of power in 1988 amounted to 5 billion kilowatt-hours, a decrease from the 1987 level of 6.5 billion kilowatt-hours. These exports, primarily to the American market, continued to benefit Ontario power consumers by generating net revenues of $45 million.

MEETING OUR CUSTOMERS' NEEDS

Hydro relies on three kinds of generation: hydraulic generation from our rivers; thermal generation fuelled by coal and oil; and nuclear generation using natural uranium as the fuel. Most of our customers' constant daily power needs are supplied from hydraulic and nuclear power stations. Since people use more electricity around breakfast time and again around dinnertime, there are peak periods of the day when we need to increase the supply of power quickly. Coal-fuelled and oil-fuelled stations are more expensive to operate but their greater flexibility makes them suited to meeting peak demand periods.

ADDING VALUE TO SERVICE

Hydro has been acutely aware of change in industry and in society through the 1980s, with heightened public concern about the impact of our operations on the environment, and the energy system for the next decade. We have responded to these public views in our planning and programs. Our 1987 annual report dealt with lowering the environmental impact of our operations. In 1988, we emphasized how we were responding to the changing needs and values of our customers through expanded service. 1988 was marked by the growing need of our customers for more expertise in energy efficiency and technical innovation. The onus is on Hydro to listen and come to terms with these new demands.

MAJOR ACCOMPLISHMENTS IN 1988

Planning Strategy Reviewed — At the end of 1987, Hydro submitted its Demand/Supply Planning Strategy to the Ontario Government. It guides our planning for tomorrow's electrical energy system to the turn of the century. The strategy was reviewed during 1988 by the Select Committee on Energy of the Ontario Legislature, which gave us an opportunity to present our understanding of what Ontarians expect from us. As more than just a good electricity company, we must deal with social, economic and environmental factors, as well as technical considerations, in making decisions.

We are trying to maximize gain by influencing the way our customers use electricity, and by making electricity do more for the dollar in demand management programs that will play a major role for Ontario in the 1990s and beyond. We have set a target of 4,500 megawatts — equal to the electricity needs of Metropolitan Toronto — to be achieved through demand management and energy efficiency measures by the year 2000.

AVERAGE PRICE BY
GENERATION
Cents per kW.h

■ Fossil
■ Nuclear
■ Hydraulic

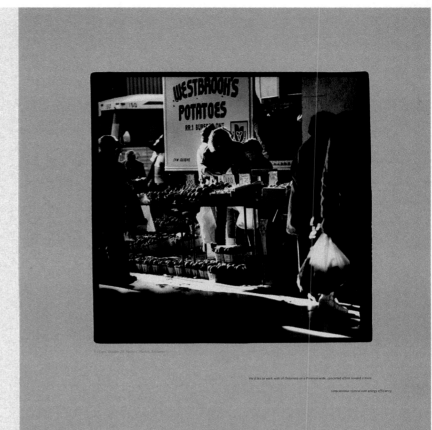

We'd like to work with all Ontarians on a Province-wide, concerted effort toward a more

comprehensive control over energy efficiency.

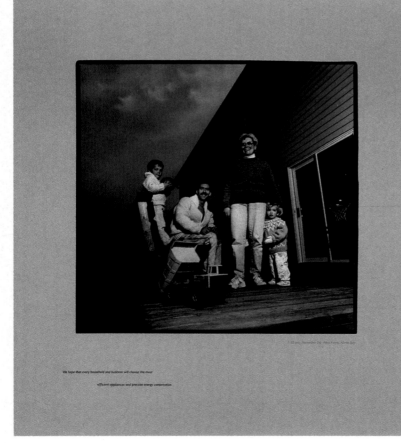

We hope that every household and business will change the most

efficient appliances and practise energy conservation.

In the years ahead, we will continually test new approaches and new methods of limiting our impact on the environment. We accept the urgency of global environmental problems and the need for international and local initiatives toward sustainable development.

Waste Management Program Inside Hydro — Inside Ontario Hydro, we are launching a waste management program in all our offices and plants across the Province to recycle paper and to reduce or eliminate the use of environmentally harmful products, such as styrofoam cups containing chlorofluorocarbons (CFCs).

ENERGY MANAGEMENT

It is more important than ever that we consult with our customers so that we can better manage our energy needs in the decade ahead. To reflect this emphasis, the Marketing Branch was renamed the Energy Management Branch in 1988, with the Vice-President reporting directly to the President.

Energy Management Branch shows our customers how they can save electricity and money by using electricity more wisely, as well as how new electrotechnologies can contribute to productivity, quality, and a better environment. Our approach to increasing the efficiency of the electrical energy system falls into three basic areas.

Information-Based Conservation — Our customers tell us that they are interested in receiving energy savings tips — from advice on residential weather-stripping or insulation to energy efficient commercial lighting or industrial motors. By providing printed information, trade-shows, home energy audits and billing analysis, we will help our customers use electricity more efficiently. We estimate that positive response will result in savings of about 1,500 megawatts over the next decade. In 1988, we expanded our special information days for industrial customers.

Conservation Incentives — The second area, incentive-driven conservation and efficiency improvements, takes a more active approach, requiring utility leadership and customer participation. A number of programs have been launched in 1988 toward saving 2,000 megawatts by the year 2000. The programs range from incentives to use high efficiency electric motors to installing energy monitoring systems in 12 representative industries. Other programs launched in 1988 include more efficient streetlighting, and promoting energy efficiency in the design of new buildings.

Lower Price for Time of Use — The third way to get the most from our resources is load shifting. Many large power users are willing and able to shift some of their energy-intensive workload to off-peak hours. Some customers, for example, can shift high energy usage processes to the nighttime, when rates are lower. This reduces the high peak in demand during the daytime, and results in cost savings that can be passed on to our customers. An example is the thermal cool storage system, in which water is chilled at night and used during the day for air-conditioning in commercial buildings. There are 87 municipal utilities opting for time-of-use rates when they begin in 1989.

The targets for load shifting is 1,000 megawatts by the year 2000. Combined with the targets for information and incentive-based conservation, that makes a total of 4,500 megawatts of power that won't have to be produced by our generating stations.

Energy management is a megaproject in itself, but will cost significantly less than a new generating station. Deferring the need to expand our generation system through conservation will also lower the environmental impact of our operations.

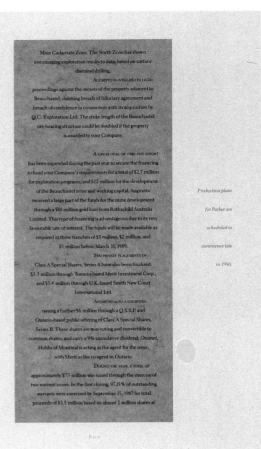

GOLD

OPPISITE PAGE

TITLE
ONTARIO HYDRO
ART DIRECTOR
PHILIP BRAZEAU
WRITER
VIRGINIA PREWITT
DESIGNER
DERWYN GOODALL
CREATIVE DIR.
PHILIP BRAZEAU
PHOTOGRAPHER
PAUL ORENSTEIN
ILLUSTRATOR
CLANCY GIBSON
TYPOGRAPHER
COOPER & BEATTY
DESIGN FIRM
**HAUGHTON BRAZEAU
DESIGN ASSOCIATES
LIMITED**
CLIENT
ONTARIO HYDRO

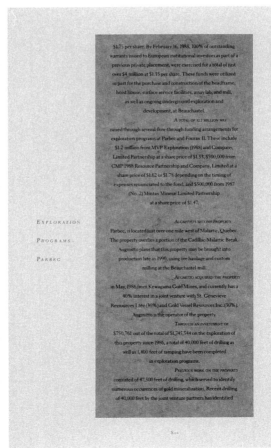

TITLE
**AUGMITTO
EXPLORATIONS 1988**
ART DIRECTOR
DALE HENDERSON
DESIGNER
MARIE POON
PHOTOGRAPHER
DEBORAH SAMUEL
DESIGN FIRM
HENDERSON & COMPANY
CLIENT
**AUGMITTO
EXPLORATIONS LTD.**

Growing Up

An increasing number of children are growing up with the YMCA as a lively and important part of their earliest development. The figures below indicate the scope and scale of our activities.

To the Y, the important aspect of growth in these program areas is the lifelong benefits enjoyed by the children through high quality attention. Beyond touching the lives of 28,000 children, Y programs such as Day Camp treated them as individual people and as members of a group.

Confidence in children's security enables their parents to be more productive at work or to cope with homelife under trying circumstances. In view of the community's ever-increasing demand for Child Care, we are committed to our long-term strategic decision to support the quality of family life and to responding to this area of need.

Many parents find themselves turning to the Y for help in unpredictable circumstances. Because the Y believes that wellness is a necessity rather than a luxury, it assists them through programs, subsidies or both to reduce stress, and to regain the fitness and self-confidence to put their lives back together.

The Y continuously adapts to social realities through refinements and innovations. We implemented an improved reporting system last year to provide Child Care parents with the kind of information they wanted. A unique training program has been developed for all Child Care staff so that they can effectively incorporate parent feedback into the program. Through parent and child enrichment, separately and together, YMCA programs helped youngsters build foundations for adolescence and a healthy community.

Children in YMCA Programs

	1987-88	1986-87	percent increase (decrease)
Day Camps	16,790	16,021	5
Child Care	7,445	7,726	(4)
Membership–Fitness, Health & Recreation	3,198	2,584	24
Resident Camp (Camp Pine Crest)	804	762	6
Total	28,237	27,093	4

Staying Well

Opportunities for children to achieve their potential are inseparable from the well-being of the people closest to, and around them. All adult YMCA programs promoting spiritual, mental and physical health operate without barriers to access.

In Fitness, Health & Recreation family memberships rose last year by 31%. The benefits of Y participation increase through personal interaction with family members, work and volunteer associates, neighbours and friends. This spill-over into the home, the workplace and back to the Y itself, is the kind of holistic experience which enhances the individual's well-being.

Many volunteers begin their activities at the Y when they are establishing their careers. It is a natural balance that is part of staying well. Our triangular logo refers to the spirit, mind and body, but could easily symbolize the partnership between volunteers, users and the Y itself.

Last year, Career Planning and Development assisted 900 people returning to the workforce. ASK!, our information and referral service in South Etobicoke, expanded operations to include a used clothing depot, income tax and form-filling and an emergency assistance food bank providing a 2-3 day food supply to between 150 and 230 households per month. With the help of over 50 volunteers, ASK! handled 15,000 inquiries from people in all walks of life, many unexpectedly in short-term desperate situations.

From the two Adult Protective Service Workers who co-ordinate programs enabling 50-80 developmentally handicapped adults to live independently, to the two new program centres due to open next year in Mississauga and Scarborough, the YMCA performs a responsive and dynamic role in the continuing well-being of the community.

Adults and Families in YMCA Programs

	1987-88	1986-87	percent increase (decrease)
Membership–Fitness, Health & Recreation Adult Members	16,221	15,386	5
Membership–Fitness, Health & Recreation Family Members	6,805	5,209	31
Career Planning and Development	900	874	3
Membership–Parent and Child Enrichment	1,766	535	330
Portugese Referral Services	103	NA	—
Adult Protective Service Participants	115	98	17
Korean Programs	1,400	1,200	17
Enrichment Courses	14,765	18,043	(18)
Total	42,075	41,345	2

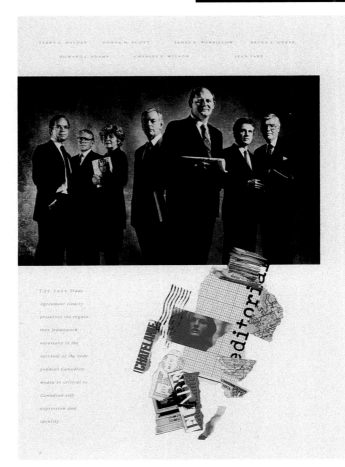

TERRY L. MALDEN DONNA M. SCOTT JAMES K. WARRILLOW BRUCE L. DRANE

HOWARD J. ADAMS CHARLES F. WILSON JEAN PARÉ

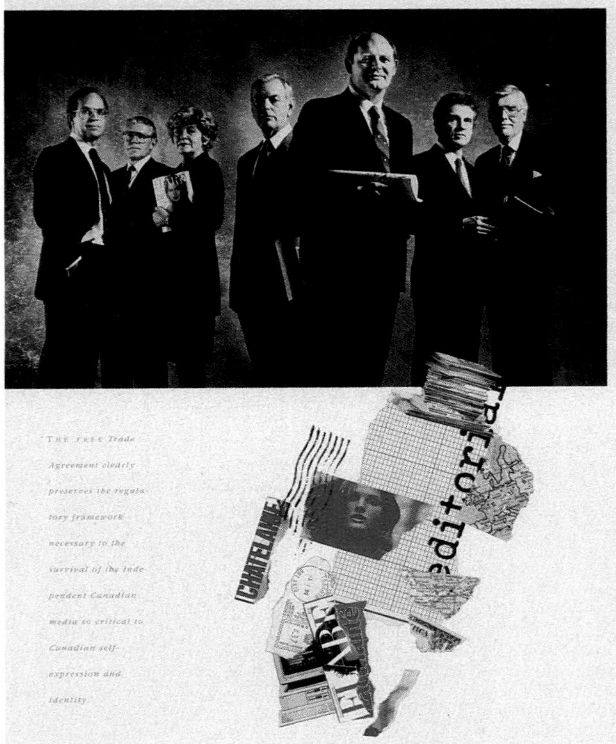

"THE FREE Trade Agreement clearly preserves the regulatory framework necessary to the survival of the independent Canadian media so critical to Canadian self-expression and identity."

8

PERIODICALS

CANADIAN PUBLISHING

Maclean Hunter leads in the publishing of Canadian business and consumer magazines. The Canadian Periodical Publishing Division, under its president, James K. Warrillow, is responsible for many of the leading consumer titles in both French and English Canada, more than 90 publications serving major industries across the country. Operations are based in four publishing centres in Vancouver, Calgary, Toronto, and Montreal to serve a total circulation of nearly 4 million.

1988 was a year of milestones, several of our major titles celebrating important anniversaries. The division saw revenues grow by 9.5% over 1987 levels, an encouraging result given the increasingly competitive climate in magazine publishing in Canada. A series of price increases for coated stock, however, could not be offset by increased advertising recovery rates; consequently margins were below last year's level.

The federal Department of Communications announced increases of between 7 and 12% for Second Class postal rates, which became effective in January of 1989.

Management of the division was further strengthened in 1988 by the addition of Terry L. Malden as Executive Vice-President. The division is well on its way to operating as an autonomous entity within the parent company.

The 1988 Free Trade Agreement with the United States will maintain the current healthy environment for publishing in Canada. However, the publishing operations will feel the effect in 1989 of the government ban on tobacco advertising, a dangerous precedent of infringement upon the freedom of commercial speech.

Consumer Magazines

The leading women's magazine in Canada, Chatelaine, marked 1988 with a new logo and a redesign for its 60th year. Chatelaine and Châtelaine, in Quebec, enjoyed strong growth. Both titles carried record numbers of advertising pages, recording increases of 19% for Chatelaine and 24% for Châtelaine. Despite these gains, our consumer titles felt the effect of paper prices, which reduced margins.

City & Country Home once again led all magazines measured by the Print Measurement Bureau in readers per copy (more than eight adults per copy). The magazine achieved international recognition by winning the prestigious International Association of Printing House Craftsmen Award for printing excellence. In 1989 a new upscale men's supplement, Stature, will be launched.

New Mother and Mère Nouvelle, our digest-size parents' books, saw revenue growth of more than 20% over 1987. Plans are underway for ancillary products to build upon this very successful franchise.

Flare

Flare, Canada's fashion magazine, recorded a 9% increase in revenues over the previous year. These results are encouraging in view of the increased competition in the fashion magazine category. In 1988 Flare won a Judy Award from the Ontario Fashion Exhibitors Association, for excellence in fashion coverage by a Canadian magazine. Flare will celebrate its tenth anniversary with its September issue in 1989.

Maclean's

1988 was a banner year for Maclean's magazine, Canada's national newsweekly. Maclean's marked its tenth anniversary as a newsweekly in September with a complete redesign, which has met with an enthusiastic response from readers and advertisers. 1988 also saw the opening of Maclean's Moscow Bureau, an important editorial resource that will broaden international coverage for Maclean's 2½ million weekly readers across Canada and worldwide.

Maclean's 1988 revenues surpassed last year's levels by more than 17%, buoyed by the highly successful Calgary Winter Games issue. Profits also surpassed those of 1987. In 1989 Maclean's will look for ways to replace tobacco advertising revenue, which has been a significant contributor.

Business Publications

With more than 90 titles serving industries across the country, Maclean Hunter is the largest publisher of business publications in Canada. 1988 was a year of change for the division. Several unprofitable titles were sold or discontinued as part of a continuing program to streamline our business publishing activities and improve performance. A number of new publications were launched to exploit market niches, while other publications were repositioned to better serve changing reader and advertiser needs.

1988 revenues for the division as a whole were slightly ahead of 1987 levels. The medical publications had a particularly strong year, as did publications serving the resource sector.

Quebec Publications

Our Quebec titles enjoyed another strong year in 1988. L'Actualité, which published its 150th issue in February 1989, had revenues grow by more than 10% over 1987. The addition of Le Bulletin des Agriculteurs, the largest French-language farm publication in Canada, helped bring both revenues and profits above 1987 levels for the group overall. Le Bulletin was redesigned during its first year as part of the Quebec publications division. L'Actualité Médicale, a tabloid for the medical profession published 44 times a year, also enjoyed strong revenues and profits.

Special Interest Publications

The five titles making up our Special Interest Publications group serve outdoor enthusiasts across Canada. Significant product improvements were undertaken in 1988, with the redesign of both Canadian Yachting and BC Outdoors. This, coupled with an aggressive pricing strategy on both advertising and circulation for all titles, should improve the group's results in 1989.

9

SILVER

OPPISITE PAGE

TITLE
YMCA OF METROPOLITAN TORONTO
ART DIRECTOR
MICHEL VIAU
WRITER
LORNE VINEBERG
DESIGNER
MONICA KESSLER
PHOTOGRAPHER
TOM SKUDRA
TYPOGRAPHER
COOPER & BEATTY
DESIGN FIRM
OVE DESIGN TORONTO LTD.
CLIENT
THE YMCA OF METROPOLITAN TORONTO

J. DOUGLAS CREIGHTON

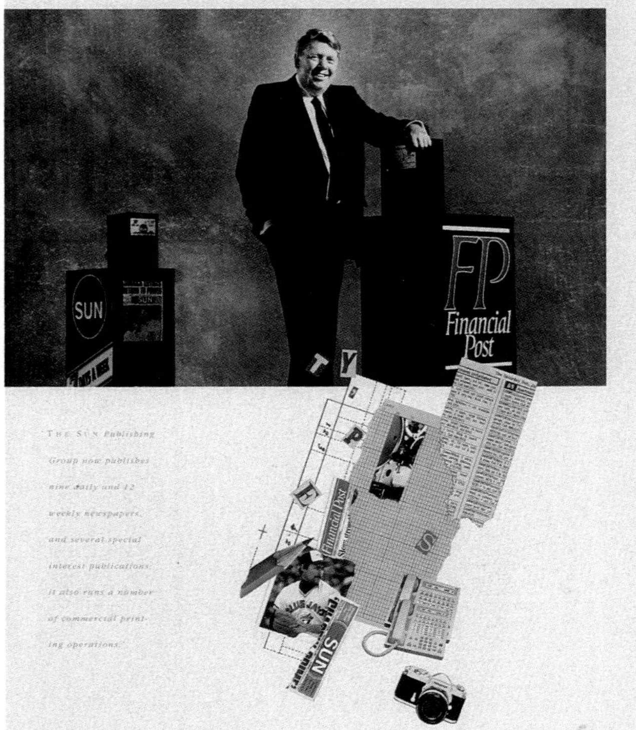

"THE SUN Publishing Group now publishes nine daily and 12 weekly newspapers, and several special interest publications. It also runs a number of commercial printing operations."

14

NEWSPAPERS

Maclean Hunter has a 62% interest in Toronto Sun Publishing, up from 58% as a result of its purchase of common shares in January 1988, together with treasury shares received as proceeds from the sale of The Financial Post to The Toronto Sun.

The "hands-off" management agreement that has limited our involvement in The Toronto Sun's affairs since 1982 remains in effect. The agreement gives Maclean Hunter two seats on the board of directors and certain veto rights over major capital expenditures and dilution of equity.

The following report was prepared by Douglas Creighton, President and Chief Executive Officer of The Toronto Sun Publishing Corporation.

The face of the Sun organization changed substantially in 1988. Our goal was to ensure that its soul did not.

About a year ago, after we sold the Houston Post, the Sun organization consisted of our daily newspapers in Toronto, Edmonton and Calgary. Since that time, however, we have greatly expanded:

* we purchased the Financial Post and turned it into a national daily newspaper;
* we purchased the Sunday Herald in Ottawa and started the daily Ottawa Sun;
* we became a partner in the SkyDome with resulting involvement in tours, travel, printing and publishing;
* we purchased 60% of Bowes Publishers, increased to 85% in early March 1989;
* we purchased Comprint Inc., a Washington, D.C., area commercial printing operation.

All this means that the Sun organization now publishes nine dailies and 12 weeklies. Our staff of 1,600 in early 1988 has increased to over 2,200 employees across Canada and the United States. Our goal is to maintain the camaraderie and employee involvement that the Sun has enjoyed in its 18 year history. I believe we have managed to do this.

In 1988, the Toronto Sun sold more newspapers and more advertising and, therefore, posted record earnings. The western economy impaired the performance of the Edmonton and Calgary Sun newspapers, but they remained profitable with increasing market share.

NEWSPAPERS		
(millions)	**1988**	1987
Revenue	**$278.2**	$213.3
Operating income	**$ 25.9**	$ 35.0
	Canada	**United States**
Employees	2,115	118
	Monday to Friday	**Sunday**
Circulation (Financial Post and Sun newspapers)	511,952	954,268

Bowes Publishers, under the leadership of Chairman Jim Bowes, also had record earnings in 1988. At year end, Jim Bowes relinquished the title of Chief Executive Officer to President Ken Kirkpatrick. Bowes publishes four dailies – The Daily Herald-Tribune in Grande Prairie, Alberta; Fort McMurray TODAY in Fort McMurray, Alberta; the Kenora Miner and News in Kenora, Ontario; and The Daily Graphic in Portage La Prairie, Manitoba; twelve weeklies – The Peace River Record-Gazette in Peace River, Alberta; the Hinton Parklander in Hinton, Alberta; the Fort Saskatchewan Record in Fort Saskatchewan, Alberta; the Wetaskiwin Times-Advertiser in Wetaskiwin, Alberta; The Camrose Canadian in Camrose, Alberta; the Western News-Advertiser in Penticton, British Columbia; the Sherwood Park News in Sherwood Park, Alberta; the Ontario Farmer in London, Ontario, which publishes an eastern and western edition; the Strathroy Age-Dispatch in Strathroy, Ontario; The Herald Leader Press in Portage La Prairie, Manitoba; the Western Weekend of Penticton in Penticton, British Columbia; and the Leamington Shopper in Leamington, Ontario; as well as three magazines – the Ontario Dairy Farmer (quarterly); the London Business (monthly); and the Ontario Hog Farmer (quarterly); all published in London, Ontario.

Comprint, our wholly owned commercial printing business in Washington which was purchased in August 1988, also contributed profits to the Company in the last quarter of 1988. Comprint is in the process of adding press equipment and by the Fall of 1989 will have more than doubled its press capacity.

Turning the Financial Post into a daily was and is a significant challenge but, despite a more costly start-up than projected, the Sun and its partners at the Financial Times of London and Hollinger are extremely pleased with the progress made.

At the time of writing, Financial Post daily circulation is over 70,000, while the weekend paper is selling over 220,000. Home delivery will begin in Ottawa and Montreal in the Spring of 1989, and the Post is projected to reach 100,000 daily circulation in the Fall of 1989. Losses, however, will continue through 1989.

The Ottawa Sun faces severe competition, but circulation is gaining steadily and the product has been generally accepted. Once again, however, the paper is not expected to reach profitability in 1989.

In Toronto, the Sun is in the midst of a major 240,000 square foot expansion which, with additional press equipment, will cost $58 million by the time it is completed in the Spring of 1990. This addition will dramatically increase our printing and colour capacity, and will move the Financial Post employees into the Sun building.

The dreams we had in 1971 continue to be realized. The Sun is truly the little paper that grew. Our loyal employees have seen to that.

15

TITLE
MACLEAN HUNTER
ART DIRECTOR
SCOTT TAYLOR/ PAUL CAMPBELL
DESIGNER
PAUL CAMPBELL/ BEN KUNZ
PHOTOGRAPHER
ED GAJDEL
ILLUSTRATOR
ROGER HILL
TYPOGRAPHER
YORKVILLE PRESS/ COOPER & BEATTY, LIMITED
DESIGN FIRM
TAYLOR & BROWNING DESIGN ASSOCIATES
CLIENT
MACLEAN HUNTER LIMITED

TITLE
CAMCO INC.
ART DIRECTOR
**DITI KATONA/
JOHN PYLYPCZAK**
DESIGNER
DITI KATONA
PHOTOGRAPHER
RON BAXTER SMITH
DESIGN FIRM
CONCRETE
CLIENT
CAMCO INC.

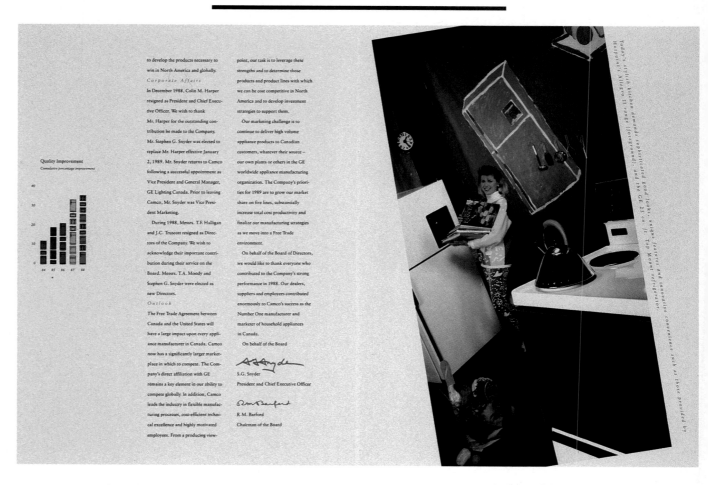

Quality Improvement
Cumulative percentage improvement

to develop the products necessary to win in North America and globally.

Corporate Affairs

In December 1988, Colin M. Harper resigned as President and Chief Executive Officer. We wish to thank Mr. Harper for the outstanding contribution he made to the Company. Mr. Stephen G. Snyder was elected to replace Mr. Harper effective January 2, 1989. Mr. Snyder returns to Camco following a successful appointment as Vice President and General Manager, GE Lighting Canada. Prior to leaving Camco, Mr. Snyder was Vice President Marketing.

During 1988, Messrs. T.F. Halligan and J.C. Truscott resigned as Directors of the Company. We wish to acknowledge their important contribution during their service on the Board. Messrs. T.A. Moody and Stephen G. Snyder were elected as new Directors.

Outlook

The Free Trade Agreement between Canada and the United States will have a large impact upon every appliance manufacturer in Canada. Camco now has a significantly larger marketplace in which to compete. The Company's direct affiliation with GE remains a key element in our ability to compete globally. In addition, Camco leads the industry in flexible manufacturing processes, cost-efficient technical excellence and highly motivated employees. From a producing viewpoint, our task is to leverage these strengths and to determine those products and product lines with which we can be cost competitive in North America and to develop investment strategies to support them.

Our marketing challenge is to continue to deliver high volume appliance products to Canadian customers, whatever their source – our own plants or others in the GE worldwide appliance manufacturing organization. The Company's priorities for 1989 are to grow our market share on five lines, substantially increase total cost productivity and finalize our manufacturing strategies as we move into a Free Trade environment.

On behalf of the Board of Directors, we would like to thank everyone who contributed to the Company's strong performance in 1988. Our dealers, suppliers and employees contributed enormously to Camco's success as the Number One manufacturer and marketer of household appliances in Canada.

On behalf of the Board

S.G. Snyder
S.G. Snyder
President and Chief Executive Officer

R.M. Barford
R.M. Barford
Chairman of the Board

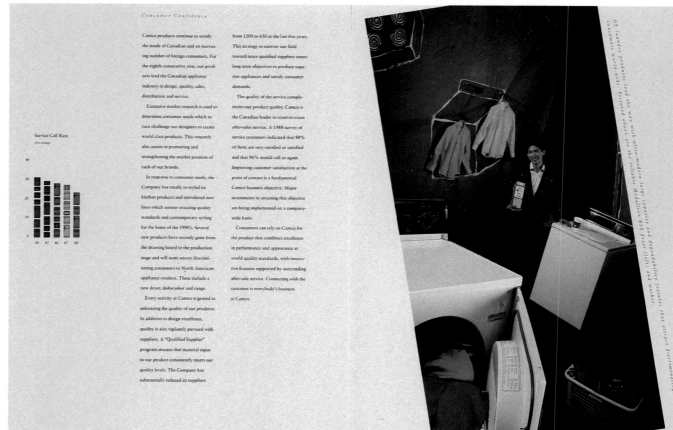

Service Call Rate
per cent

Consumer Confidence

Camco products continue to satisfy the needs of Canadian and an increasing number of foreign consumers. For the eighth consecutive year, our products lead the Canadian appliance industry in design, quality, sales, distribution and service.

Extensive market research is used to determine consumer needs which in turn challenges our designers to create world class products. This research also assists in promoting and strengthening the market position of each of our brands.

In response to consumer needs, the Company has totally re-styled its kitchen products and introduced new lines which answer exacting quality standards and contemporary styling for the home of the 1990's. Several new products have recently gone from the drawing board to the production stage and will soon attract discriminating consumers to North American appliance retailers. These include a new dryer, dishwasher and range.

Every activity at Camco is geared to enhancing the quality of our products. In addition to design excellence, quality is also vigilantly pursued with suppliers. A "Qualified Supplier" program ensures that material input to our product consistently meets our quality levels. The Company has substantially reduced its suppliers from 1200 to 650 in the last five years. This strategy to narrow our field toward more qualified suppliers meets long term objectives to produce superior appliances and satisfy consumer demands.

The quality of the service complements our product quality. Camco is the Canadian leader in coast-to-coast after-sales service. A 1988 survey of service customers indicated that 88% of them are very satisfied or satisfied and that 96% would call us again. Improving customer satisfaction at the point of contact is a fundamental Camco business objective. Major investments in attaining this objective are being implemented on a company-wide basis.

Consumers can rely on Camco for the product that combines excellence in performance and appearance at world quality standards, with innovative features supported by outstanding after-sale service. Connecting with the customer is everybody's business at Camco.

TITLE
**THE FIRST MERCANTILE
CURRENCY FUND, INC.**
ART DIRECTOR
**DITI KATONA/
JOHN PYLYPCZAK**
DESIGNER
DITI KATONA
PHOTOGRAPHER
RON BAXTER SMITH
DESIGN FIRM
CONCRETE
CLIENT
**THE FIRST MERCANTILE
CURRENCY FUND, INC.**

Albert D. Friedberg, Adviser, Maximilian Solomon, President.

Ensuing Feng, Secretary/Treasurer.

D.A. Smith, Clarkson Gordon; Michael St. B. Harrison, Director, Chairman of the Audit Committee.

ALBERT D. FRIEDBERG

Albert D. Friedberg is Director-General Partner of Friedberg Mercantile Group (the Fund's Broker) and Chairman of FCMI Financial Corporation (the parent of the Fund's Adviser). The following commentary is adapted from an interview with Mr. Friedberg in the November, 1988, issue of Barron's, a weekly financial newspaper published in the United States by Dow Jones & Company.

Despite widespread views to the contrary, we believe the path of least resistance for the U.S. dollar at this time is clearly upward.

The most frequently cited reason for a bearish view of the U.S. dollar is the persistent U.S. trade deficit. Currently, the deficit appears to be running at a rate of about U.S.$132 billion a year, a large figure, but down significantly from what it has been in the past few years. Many analysts expect it to rise again during 1989, perhaps to U.S.$150 billion. No doubt, such a trend would put pressure on the American dollar, but we believe this reaction is based on mistaken assumptions.

Some analysts maintain that a U.S. dollar value of about 100 Japanese yen (a 25% drop from current levels) would wipe out the U.S. trade deficit. This is very unlikely to be true. As the experience of the past year has shown, the deficit simply does not respond significantly to changes in the U.S. dollar's value. There is

sufficient flexibility in the prices of major goods imported by the U.S. to offset much of the effect of a devaluation, and only limited capacity in the rest of the world to absorb a major surge in U.S. exports. It is therefore by no means certain that a 25% drop in the U.S. dollar's value would have the predicted effect on the U.S. trade balance.

The key factor affecting the U.S. balance of trade is not the value of the U.S. dollar, but the differential between the rate of growth in the U.S. economy and the economies of the rest of the world. When the U.S. is growing faster than the rest of the world, U.S. imports rise, and exports do not keep pace, so the trade deficit widens. On the other hand, if U.S. growth slows down and the rest of the world picks up, U.S. exports rise faster than imports, and the deficit narrows. That is what happened during most of last year, when growth in Europe accelerated, and U.S. exports surged, reducing the gap with imports.

But a more fundamental question concerns the presumed necessity of eliminating the U.S. trade deficit in the first place. We believe that even if the deficit were to rise as high as U.S.$150 billion, it would be quite sustainable, because it would still be shrinking in relation to the U.S. gross national product. Besides,

SILVER

TITLE
MINTZ & PARTNERS
ART DIRECTOR
PAUL HODGSON/
BRIAN TSANG
DESIGNER
PAUL HODGSON/
BRIAN TSANG
ILLUSTRATOR
MICK WIGGINS/
TOMIO NITTO/
PAULA MUNCK/
ROSS MacDONALD
DESIGN FIRM
THE SPENCER FRANCEY
GROUP
CLIENT
MINTZ & PARTNERS

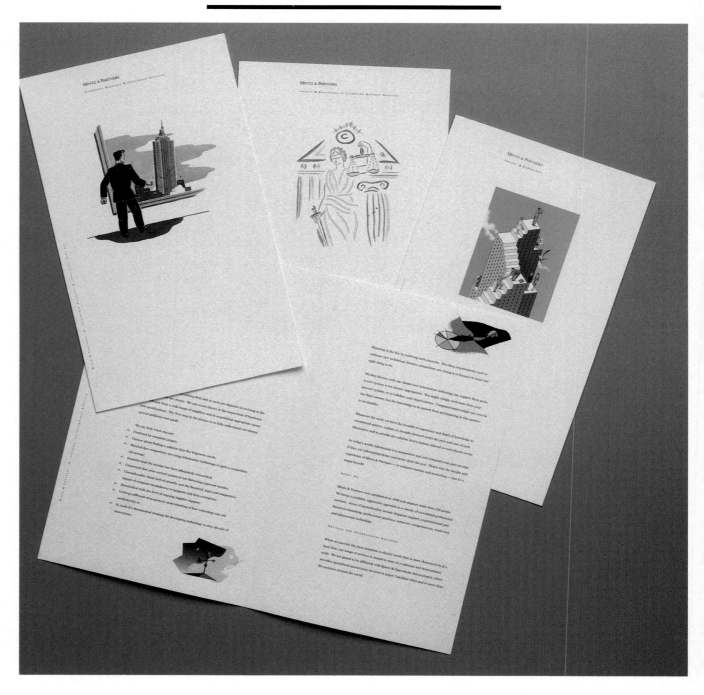

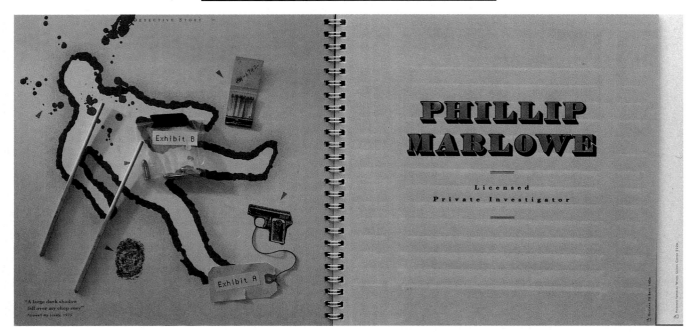

SILVER

TITLE
HOLLYWOOD PULP
WRITER
HELEN BATTERSBY
DESIGNER
JENNIFER COGHILL
CREATIVE DIR.
JEANNETTE HANNA
PHOTOGRAPHER
**BARBARA COLE/
SEE SPOT RUN**
ILLUSTRATOR
**M. CONSTABLE/
S. BATTERSBY/
B. HAMBLY/P. MUNCK/
B. BLITT**
DESIGN FIRM
**THE SPENCER FRANCEY
GROUP**
CLIENT
INTER CITY PAPERS

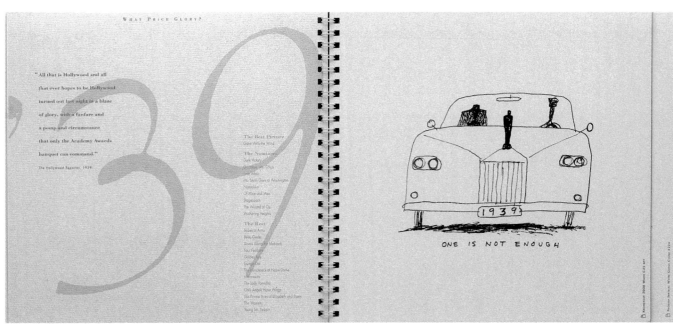

SILVER

TITLE
THE BIKE
ART DIRECTOR
DEL TERRELONGE
DESIGNER
DEL TERRELONGE
PHOTOGRAPHER
RON BAXTER SMITH
TYPOGRAPHER
LIND GRAPHICS
DESIGN FIRM
**TERRELONGE
DESIGN INC.**
CLIENT
**RON BAXTER SMITH
PHOTOGRAPHER LTD.**
PRINTER
**ARTHURS-JONES
LITHOGRAPHING INC.**

TITLE
TANDEM
ART DIRECTOR
**PAUL HODGSON/
BARBARA WOOLLEY**
WRITER
HELEN BATTERSBY
DESIGNER
BARBARA WOOLLEY
CREATIVE DIR.
PAUL HODGSON
PHOTOGRAPHER
JOHN MASTROMONACO
DESIGN FIRM
**THE SPENCER FRANCEY
GROUP**
CLIENT
**TANDEM
INTERNATIONAL INC.**

"I'm probably their greatest outside salesperson – I've sent plenty of business their way. There are other people out there, but I think they're head and shoulders above the competition. I just feel that way."

*General Manager,
Commercial Products and
Services Company*

"As former line managers, we know what our clients are facing." – *Gord Crowson, Senior Consultant*
"We work with our clients to figure out what makes their business tick ... and, more importantly,
what buttons will make it tick louder, faster, and longer." – *Cynthia Kirkland, Senior Consultant*

How do we get into Private Banking and do it right? A large *financial institution* asked us for a complete strategy for Private Banking. Working closely with our client, a thorough business plan was developed, consisting of: a clear positioning for the program; a profile of passive and active investor types; relationship pricing strategy; a private banker training program; and a unique marketing approach for their affluent prospects. We also contributed to facilities-design criteria and developed a financial model that demonstrated profitability in different scenarios. Our work produced a comprehensive blueprint to guide the institution toward maximum profit return with this new service.

As an outsider, how do I crack the Canadian Market? A *U.S. packaged goods company* with a limited organization in Canada relied on us to determine the business direction for the Canadian subsidiary. The business plan centered around a major new product introduction and involved product development, package design, marketing positioning and plans, consumer and trade research and hands-on follow-up to ensure full implementation in the Canadian market.

How do we effectively avert one of the biggest disasters in our industry? When this national association approached us for assistance, an isolated problem in product quality had exploded into a major public relations crisis. Consumer and trade research helped dimensionalize the problem. Within six months, our successful management of a $2-million, multi-facetted marketing campaign helped boost consumer confidence sufficiently to return consumption of the product to pre-crisis levels. Over $235,000 worth of free editorial space appeared in various media; over 30,000 trade personnel were exposed to the message; over 3.7 million recipes were distributed to consumers and 1 million pieces of supportive display materials were requested by the foodservice and retail trade.

"We help sales forces raise their standards and perform with confidence at a higher level."

*Jack McKann
Partner*

Management Development

How can we increase our sales with our major accounts in such a competitive and demanding environment? This has been a common need of many clients, especially within the consumer *packaged goods* industry. In response to this need we developed a state-of-the-art account management system and training program, "The Strategic Management of Key Accounts." Through a rigorous series of classroom workshops, business planning assignments and on-the-job coaching by our training consultants, we have helped over 40 client companies significantly increase their impact and results with major accounts. This program has been so impactful that clients regularly attend refresher sessions to keep abreast of the latest advancements in our approach.

How can our new OTC salesforce develop the skills to be successful in the retail drug trade? This is a new challenge for many *pharmaceutical companies* expanding into the OTC market. We have helped several clients develop an appreciation for how to do business within the retail environment, beginning with an understanding of the key factors for success at the retail store and head office levels. From selling skills for territory representatives to coaching and business planning skills for district managers, we have developed comprehensive training programs to help both OTC and pharmaceutical salesforces increase their success in meeting the OTC challenge.

How do I ensure that my Marketing Managers bring a focussed, strategic approach to Marketing Planning? Over the years, we've helped clients in the *consumer packaged goods, retailing, pharmaceutical* and *service industries* increase the effectiveness of their people and plans through specialized marketing training and development programs. Our Marketing Planning Process provides a logical, step-by-step approach to business planning – from analyzing business situations to formulating action plans. Through a combination of seminars, worksessions and individual counselling, we teach our process by applying it to the client's own brands. This gives participants a clear and powerful understanding of its application and relevance to their business. Our planning approach has become the gold standard for hundreds of marketers and is used by clients around the world.

"We are inspired by confident, aggressive clients who seek our help in strengthening the skills of their people to manage the future."

*Jean-Marie Dubois
Partner*

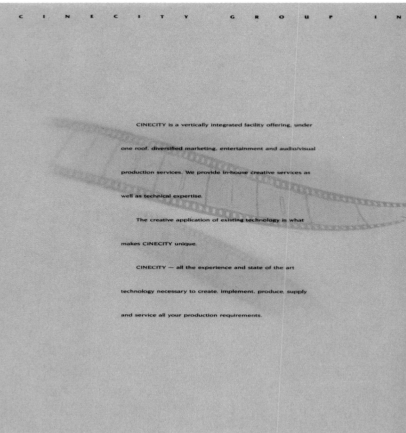

CINECITY GROUP IN

CINECITY is a vertically integrated facility offering, under one roof, diversified marketing, entertainment and audio/visual production services. We provide in-house creative services as well as technical expertise.

The creative application of existing technology is what makes CINECITY unique.

CINECITY — all the experience and state of the art technology necessary to create, implement, produce, supply and service all your production requirements.

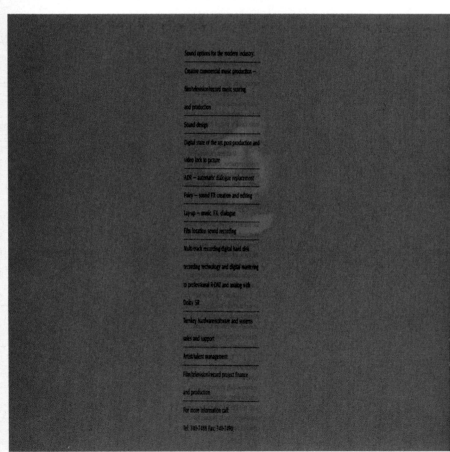

Sound options for the modern industry.

Creative commercial music production — film/television/record music scoring and production

Sound design

Digital state of the art post-production and video lock to picture

ADR — automatic dialogue replacement

Foley — sound FX creation and editing

Lay-up — music, FX, dialogue

Film location sound recording

Multi-track recording/digital hard disk recording technology and digital mastering to professional R-DAT and analog with Dolby SR

Turnkey hardware/software and systems sales and support

Artist/talent management

Film/television/record project finance and production

For more information call:

Tel: 740-7498 Fax: 740-7499

OPPISITE PAGE

TITLE
CINECITY
ART DIRECTOR
DEL TERRELONGE
WRITER
ANIA SZADO
DESIGNER
DEL TERRELONGE
PHOTOGRAPHER
DAVID WHITTAKER
TYPOGRAPHER
LIND GRAPHICS
DESIGN FIRM
TERRELONGE DESIGN INC.
CLIENT
CINECITY GROUP INC.
PRINTER
ARTHURS-JONES LITHOGRAPHING INC.

TITLE
SUPREME BROCHURE
ART DIRECTOR
PAUL BROWNING/ PAUL CAMPBELL
WRITER
TONY LEIGHTON
DESIGNER
PAUL CAMPBELL
PHOTOGRAPHER
SEE SPOT RUN
ILLUSTRATOR
BARRY BLITT/ JAMIE BENNETT/ MAURICE VELLEKOOP/ HENRIK DRESCHER
TYPOGRAPHER
COOPER & BEATTY, LIMITED
DESIGN FIRM
TAYLOR & BROWNING DESIGN ASSOCIATES
CLIENT
GRAPHIC PAPERS

TITLE
CANARY WHARF
ART DIRECTOR
**SIMHA FORDSHAM/
JONAS TSE**
WRITER
**MIKE BENNETT/
WARREN DUNFORD**
DESIGNER
**LISA VIGEON/
LIZ deGREY**
ILLUSTRATOR
**CARLOS DINIZ/
MAGGI CASH**
DESIGN FIRM
**OLYMPIA & YORK
DEVELOPMENTS LIMITED**
CLIENT
**CANARY WHARF, LONDON,
ENGLAND**
COMPUTER GRAPHICS
LISA VIGEON

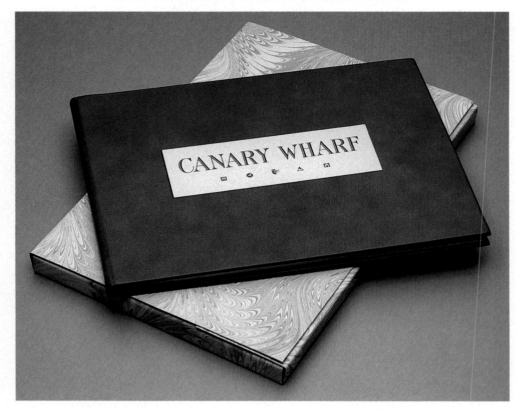

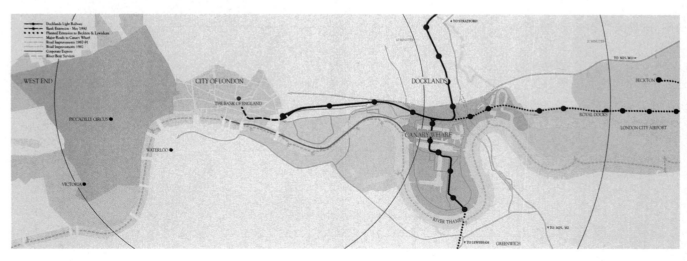

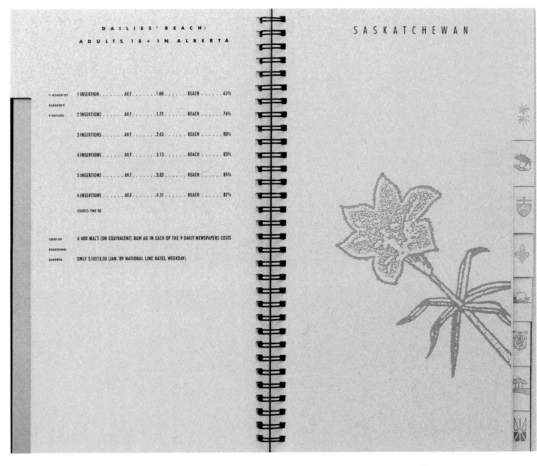

DAILIES' REACH: ADULTS 18+ IN ALBERTA

SASKATCHEWAN

% REACH OF ALBERTA'S 9 DAILIES

1 INSERTION	AV.F.	1.00	REACH	65%
2 INSERTIONS	AV.F.	1.72	REACH	76%
3 INSERTIONS	AV.F.	2.43	REACH	80%
4 INSERTIONS	AV.F.	3.13	REACH	83%
5 INSERTIONS	AV.F.	3.82	REACH	85%
6 INSERTIONS	AV.F.	4.51	REACH	87%

SOURCE: PMB '88

COST OF REACHING ALBERTA

A 600 MAL'S (OR EQUIVALENT) B&W AD IN EACH OF THE 9 DAILY NEWSPAPERS COSTS ONLY $10213.50 (JAN. '89 NATIONAL LINE RATES, WEEKDAY)

1989 DAILY NEWSPAPERS IN ONTARIO

REGULAR FEATURES/SECTIONS

TITLE
NMB 1989
ART DIRECTOR
VICTORIA BIRTA
CREATIVE DIR.
DUNCAN D. BRUCE
DESIGN FIRM
MICHAEL PETERS GROUP
CLIENT
NEWSPAPER MARKETING BUREAU

TITLE
CRINION ASSOCIATES
DESIGNER
ADAMS & ASSOCIATES DESIGN CONSULTANTS INC.
CLIENT
CRINION ASSOCIATES
PRINTER
C.J. GRAPHICS INC. PRINTERS & LITHOGRAPHERS

TITLE
QUESS
ART DIRECTOR
ROBERT VOSBERGH
DESIGNER
PAUL SYCH/ REACTOR
ILLUSTRATOR
JEFF JACKSON/ REACTOR
AGENCY
VOSBURGH & ASSOCIATES
CLIENT
QUESS

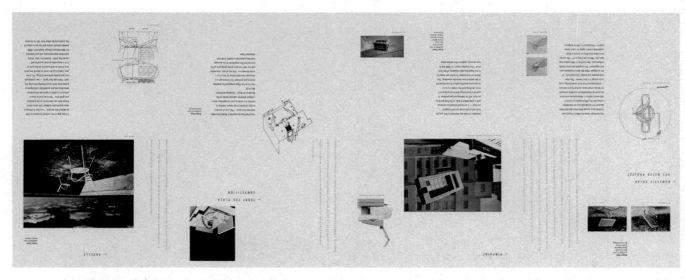

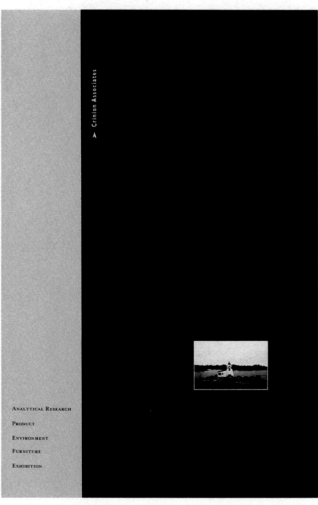

SPRING 1989 SUMMER

REACTOR ARTWEAR, TORONTO CANADA TEL (416) 362 1913

THE BIG IDEA

DESIGNER ● LOUIS FISHAUF
COLORS ● BLACK, RED, WHITE
SHIRT COLOR ● HEATHER GREY
BODY STYLE ● SHORT SLEEVE T

ALL DESIGNS © REACTOR ART & DESIGN

MUMBO JUMBO

ARTIST ● JAMIE BENNETT
COLORS ● SIX COLORS
SHIRT COLOR ● BLACK
BODY STYLE ● SHORT SLEEVE T

ALL DESIGNS © REACTOR ART & DESIGN

FEBRUARY 1989 FEVRIER 1989 SEBBRAIO 1989 FEBRUARY 1989 FEVRIER 1989 SEBBRAIO 1989

GOLD

TITLE
DESIGN FOR THE REAL WORLD
ART DIRECTOR
LOUIS FISHAUF
DESIGNER
STEPHANIE POWER
DESIGN FIRM
REACTOR ART & DESIGN
CLIENT
REACTOR ARTWEAR

SILVER

TITLE
**PHOTOGRAPHS
JANE CORKIN GALLERY**
ART DIRECTOR
JILL CHEN
DESIGNER
**JILL CHEN/
JOE BIAFORE**
TYPOGRAPHER
CANADIAN COMPOSITION
DESIGN FIRM
**CARMEN DUNJKO
ASSOCIATES**
CLIENT
JANE CORKIN GALLERY

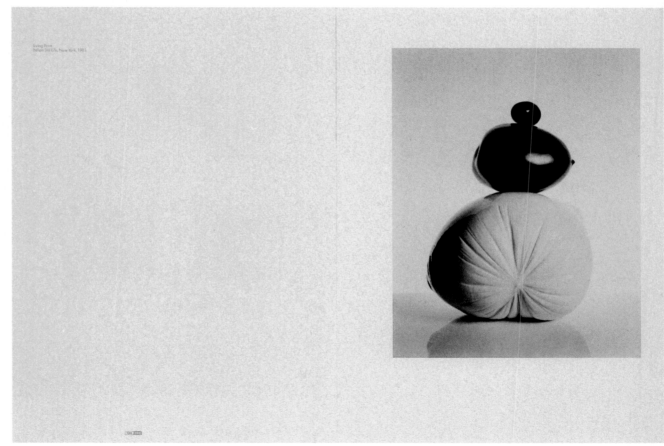

SILVER

TITLE
EAST MEETS WEST IN DESIGN
ART DIRECTOR
DEL TERRELONGE
WRITER
ANNEKE van WAESBERGHE
DESIGNER
DEL TERRELONGE
PHOTOGRAPHER
SHIN SUGINO
TYPOGRAPHER
LIND GRAPHICS
DESIGN FIRM
TERRELONGE DESIGN INC.
CLIENT
EAST MEETS WEST CULTURAL INTERNATIONAL
PRINTER
ARTHURS-JONES LITHOGRAPHING INC.

TITLE
DADA IN COLOGNE
ART DIRECTOR
KEVIN CONNOLLY
DESIGNER
KEVIN CONNOLLY
TYPOGRAPHER
LINOTEXT INC.
DESIGN FIRM
**ART GALLERY OF
ONTARIO PUBLICATION
AND DESIGN
DEPARTMENT**
CLIENT
**ART GALLERY OF
ONTARIO**

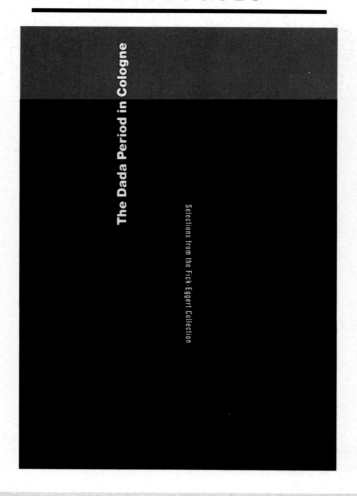

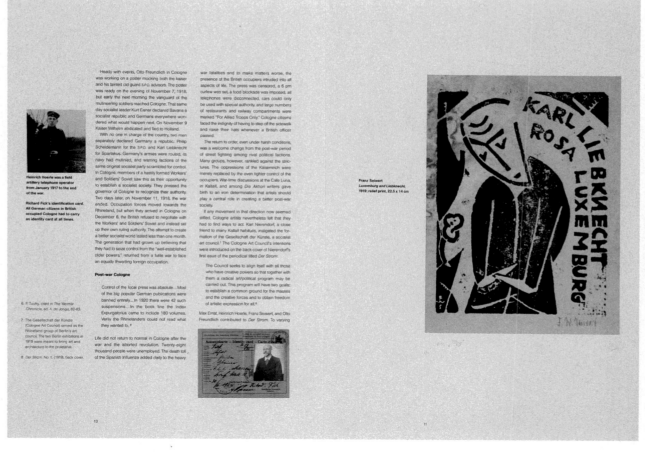

TITLE
WHENEVER THE WIND IS HIGH
ART DIRECTOR
LORRAINE TUSON
WRITER
CARL BRAUN/ PAULA S. GOEPFERT
DESIGNER
LORRAINE TUSON
ILLUSTRATOR
GARY KELLEY
PUBLISHER
NELSON CANADA

TITLE
SOMETHING FURRY, ROUGH AND WILD
ART DIRECTOR
LORRAINE TUSON
WRITER
CARL BRAUN/ PAULA S. GEOPFERT
DESIGNER
LORRAINE TUSON
ILLUSTRATOR
NORMAND COUSINEAU
PUBLISHER
NELSON CANADA

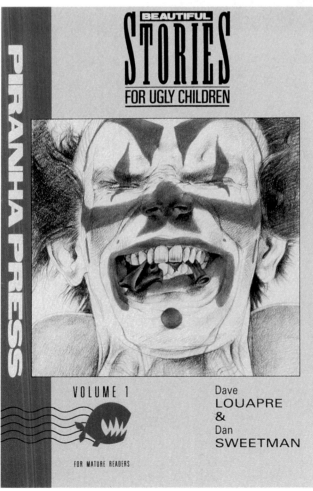

TITLE
BEAUTIFUL STORIES...
ART DIRECTOR
DEAN MOTTER
WRITER
DAVE LOUAPRE
EDITOR
MARK NEVELOW
DESIGNER
VERA LITYNSKY/ JENNIFER PROUD
CREATIVE DIR.
RICHARD BRUNING
ILLUSTRATOR
DAN SWEETMAN
DESIGN FIRM
MAIN ARTERY INC.
CLIENT
PIRANHA PRESS
PUBLISHER
DC COMICS INC.

TITLE
MY SUMMER BOOK
ART DIRECTOR
WYCLIFFE SMITH
EDITOR
THE EDITORS OF OWL MAGAZINE
DESIGNER
WYCLIFFE SMITH
ILLUSTRATOR
ANDREW PLEWES
TYPOGRAPHER
WYCLIFFE SMITH
PUBLISHER
GREEY DE PENCIER BOOKS
EDITORIAL DIRECTOR
SHEBA MELAND

TITLE
THREE WAY MIRROR
ART DIRECTOR
LORRAINE TUSON
EDITOR
JAMES A. MacNEILL
DESIGNER
ROB McPHAIL
ILLUSTRATOR
SANDRA DIONISI
PUBLISHER
NELSON CANADA

TITLE
GEOGRAPHY
ART DIRECTOR
KLAUS UHLIG
DESIGNER
IRINA KHVALOVA
TYPOGRAPHER
Q COMPOSITION INC.
DESIGN FIRM
**KLAUS UHLIG
DESIGNGROUP INC.**
CLIENT
**MINISTRY OF
EDUCATION,
PUBLISHING AND
CREATIVE SERVICES**
PUBLISHER
**QUEEN'S PRINTER
FOR ONTARIO**
WRITER
**CENTER FOR SECONDARY
AND ADULT EDUCATION**

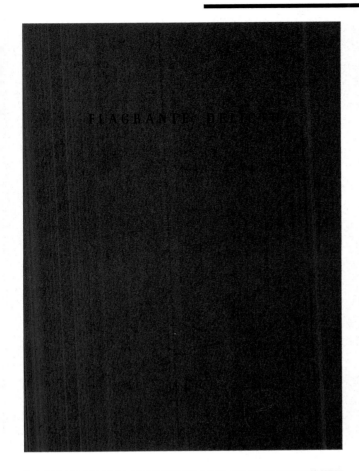

A
GOLD

TITLE
FLAGRANTE DELICTO
ART DIRECTOR
DITI KATONA
WRITER
HENRIK DRESCHER
DESIGNER
DITI KATONA
ILLUSTRATOR
HENRIK DRESCHER
DESIGN FIRM
REACTOR ART & DESIGN
PUBLISHER
REACTOR PUBLISHING

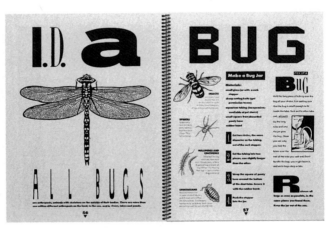

A
SILVER

TITLE
MY SUMMER BOOK
ART DIRECTOR
WYCLIFFE SMITH
EDITOR
**THE EDITORS OF OWL
MAGAZINE**
DESIGNER
**WYCLIFFE SMITH/
JULIE COLANTONIO**
ILLUSTRATOR
**ANDREW PLEWES/
SAM SISCO**
PUBLISHER
**GREEY DE PENCIER
BOOKS**
PRODUCTION EDITOR
LYN THOMAS

SILVER

TITLE
MANNING COOKIES
DESIGNER
DIANE MELLOR
CREATIVE DIR.
BOB RUSSELL
DESIGN FIRM
**BOULEVARD
COMMUNICATIONS LTD.**
CLIENT
PRIMO FOODS LTD.

TITLE
GRENVILLE MUSE
ART DIRECTOR
CARMEN DUNJKO
WRITER
ELLIOT COLLINS
DESIGNER
JOE BIAFORE
ILLUSTRATOR
JOE BIAFORE
TYPOGRAPHER
COOPER & BEATTY
DESIGN FIRM
**CARMEN DUNJKO
ASSOCIATES**
CLIENT
**GRENVILLE PRINTING
& MANAGEMENT LTD.**

TITLE
**BALDERSON CHEESE
PACKAGING**
ART DIRECTOR
SCOTT TAYLOR
DESIGNER
**JOE DRVARIC/
BEN KUNZ**
TYPOGRAPHER
**COOPER & BEATTY,
LIMITED**
DESIGN FIRM
**TAYLOR & BROWNING
DESIGN ASSOCIATES**
CLIENT
AULT FOODS LTD.

TITLE
SPIRIT COOLERS
DESIGNER
DAWN LAMBERT
CREATIVE DIR.
BOB RUSSELL
TYPOGRAPHER
TECHNI PROCESS
DESIGN FIRM
**BOULEVARD
COMMUNICATIONS LTD.**
CLIENT
CHATEAU GAI WINES
HANDLETTERING
KAREN CHEESEMAN

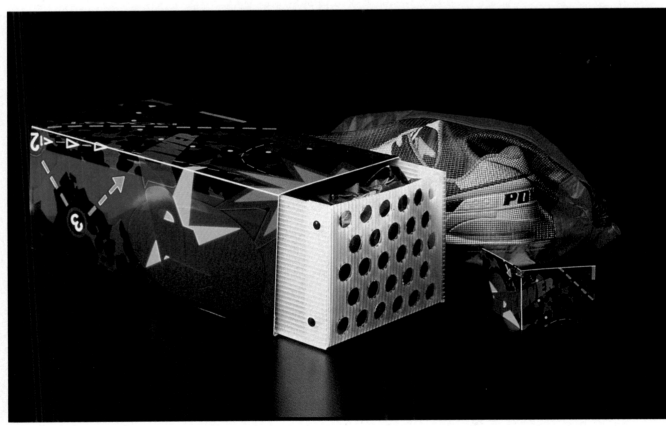

TITLE
POWER
DESIGNER
RICK CARTY
CREATIVE DIR.
BOB RUSSELL
ILLUSTRATOR
RICK CARTY
DESIGN FIRM
**BOULEVARD
COMMUNICATIONS**
CLIENT
BATA LIMITED

GOLD

TITLE
PORTRAITS
DESIGNER
**PAUL HODGSON/
GARY TAUGHER**
PHOTOGRAPHER
RALPH NEWTON
DESIGN FIRM
**THE SPENCER FRANCEY
GROUP**
CLIENT
RALPH NEWTON
PRINTER
C.J. GRAPHICS

SILVER

TITLE
THE BIKE
DESIGNER
DEL TERRELONGE
PHOTOGRAPHER
RON BAXTER SMITH
DESIGN FIRM
TERRELONGE DESIGN
CLIENT
**RON BAXTER SMITH
PHOTOGRAPHER LTD.**

TITLE
T-SHIRT
WRITER
CHRIS ATACK
DESIGNER
PETER COATES
CREATIVE DIR.
PETER COATES
ILLUSTRATOR
GARY ALPHONSO
AGENCY
ATACK/COATES
CLIENT
ATACK/COATES

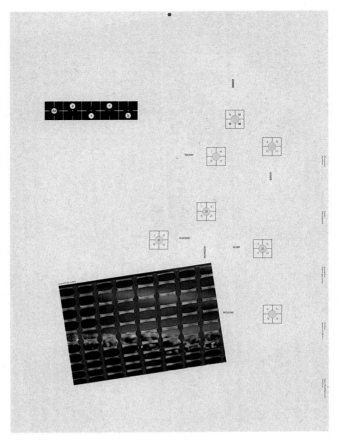

TITLE
**ESKIND WADDELL
CALENDAR**
ART DIRECTOR
MALCOLM WADDELL
DESIGNER
**MALCOLM WADDELL/
PETER SCOTT/
MERCEDES ROTHWELL/
ROSLYN ESKIND/
GLENDA RISSMAN/
DAGMAR NEUDORF**
PHOTOGRAPHER
JAY MAISEL
TYPOGRAPHER
COOPER & BEATTY
DESIGN FIRM
ESKIND WADDELL
CLIENT
**JAY MAISEL/
ESKIND WADDELL/
GRAPHIC SPECIALTIES/
MacKINNON-MONCUR/
MEAD PAPER**

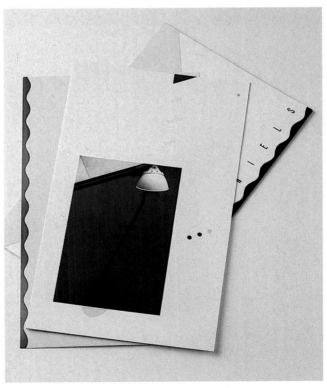

TITLE
BRENT DANIELS
ART DIRECTOR
**JON VOPNI/
SANDRA PARSONS**
WRITER
LARRY HICOCK
DESIGNER
**JON VOPNI/
HENRY ZALUSKI**
PHOTOGRAPHER
BRENT DANIELS
TYPOGRAPHER
M & H TYPOGRAPHY
DESIGN FIRM
**VOPNI & PARSONS
DESIGN LIMITED**
CLIENT
BRENT DANIELS

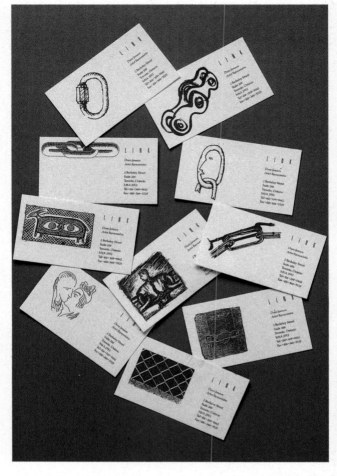

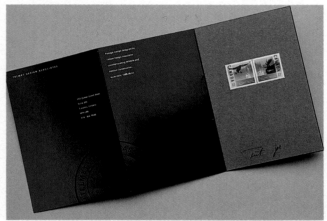

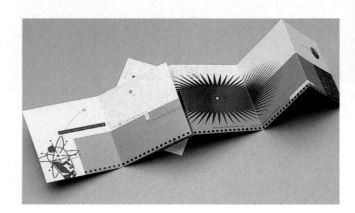

Whether we're printing black and white stationery or a four-colour annual report, we care about your presentation. We know that you need it clean and fast. Adelaide Printing has several locations, to ensure that we remain fully equipped to meet your needs. Call us for free pickup and delivery.

Printing on a Heidelberg MO: from 11″ × 17″ to 19″ × 25½″ and from 16 lb. to 24 pt. in weight.

Copying on 8½″ × 11″ up to 11″ × 17″

Duplicating from 3½″ × 4¼″ up to 11″ × 17″ and from 16 lb. paper to 130 m. cover.

Finishing Collating/Stapling (top left-hand corner or saddlestaple)/Cerlox Binding/Padding/Folding/ Trimming/Drilling (1, 2 or 3 holes)/Wire-O Binding/Snap Binding/Grip Tite Plastic Clamps/ Laminating

10

rigł

4

TITLE
THE PRINTED PAGE
ART DIRECTOR
DEL TERRELONGE
WRITER
ANIA SZADO
DESIGNER
DEL TERRELONGE
PHOTOGRAPHER
DAVID WHITTAKER
TYPOGRAPHER
LIND GRAPHICS
DESIGN FIRM
**TERRELONGE
DESIGN INC.**
CLIENT
**ADELAIDE
PRINTING LTD.**
PRINTER
**ADELAIDE
PRINTING LTD.**

TITLE
CENTARA BROCHURE
ART DIRECTOR
**SCOTT TAYLOR/
JOE DRVARIC**
DESIGNER
JOE DRVARIC
PHOTOGRAPHER
DIDIER DORVAL
ILLUSTRATOR
SIMON NG
TYPOGRAPHER
**COOPER & BEATTY,
LIMITED**
DESIGN FIRM
**TAYLOR & BROWNING
DESIGN ASSOCIATES**
CLIENT
CENTARA CORPORATION

TITLE
SUPREME BROCHURE
ART DIRECTOR
**PAUL BROWNING/
PAUL CAMPBELL**
WRITER
TONY LEIGHTON
DESIGNER
PAUL CAMPBELL
PHOTOGRAPHER
SEE SPOT RUN
ILLUSTRATOR
**BARRY BLITT/
HENRIK DRESCHER**
TYPOGRAPHER
**COOPER & BEATTY,
LIMITED**
DESIGN FIRM
**TAYLOR & BROWNING
DESIGN ASSOCIATES**
CLIENT
GRAPHIC PAPERS

TITLE
**HONEYWELL LIMITED
1988 ANNUAL REPORT**
ART DIRECTOR
MICHEL VIAU
DESIGNER
MONICA KESSLER
PHOTOGRAPHER
ANDREW McKIM
ILLUSTRATOR
JOE FLEMING
DESIGN FIRM
**OVE DESIGN
TORONTO LTD.**
CLIENT
HONEYWELL LIMITED

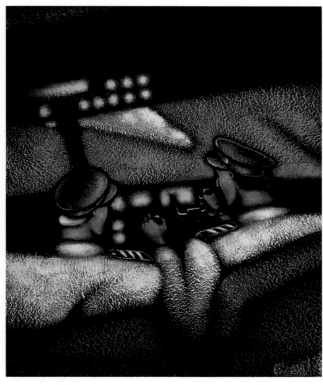

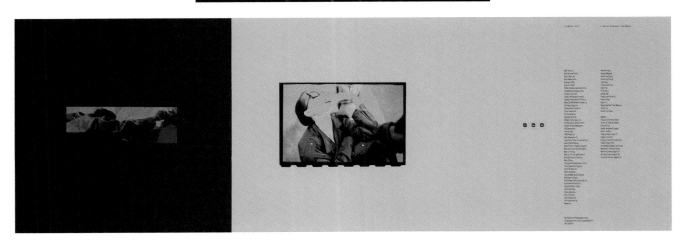

A
G O L D

TITLE
THE BIKE
DESIGNER
DEL TERRELONGE
PHOTOGRAPHER
RON BAXTER SMITH
DESIGN FIRM
**TERRELONGE
DESIGN INC.**
CLIENT
**RON BAXTER SMITH
PHOTOGRAPHER LTD.**

TITLE
THE PRINTED PAGE
ART DIRECTOR
DEL TERRELONGE
DESIGNER
DEL TERRELONGE
PHOTOGRAPHER
DAVID WHITTAKER
TYPOGRAPHER
LIND GRAPHICS
DESIGN FIRM
**TERRELONGE
DESIGN INC.**
CLIENT
**ADELAIDE
PRINTING LTD.**
PRINTER
**ADELAIDE
PRINTING LTD.**

SILVER

TITLE
**EAST MEETS WEST
IN DESIGN**
ART DIRECTOR
DEL TERRELONGE
WRITER
ANNEKE van WAESBERGHE
DESIGNER
DEL TERRELONGE
PHOTOGRAPHER
SHIN SUGINO
TYPOGRAPHER
LIND GRAPHICS
DESIGN FIRM
TERRELONGE DESIGN INC.
CLIENT
**EAST MEETS WEST
CULTURAL
INTERNATIONAL INC.**
PRINTER
**ARTHURS-JONES
LITHOGRAPHING INC.**

TITLE
DIRECTIONS '89
ART DIRECTOR
DIANNE EASTMAN
WRITER
IAN MIRLIN
CREATIVE DIR.
BRIAN HARROD
PHOTOGRAPHER
TIM SAUNDERS
TYPOGRAPHER
THE COMPOSING ROOM
CLIENT
**THE ART DIRECTORS
CLUB OF TORONTO**
FILM/PRINTING
**HERZIG SOMERVILLE
LIMITED**
PRODUCTION
JACK WAGA
PAPER
**WARREN PAPER/
GRAPHIC PAPERS**

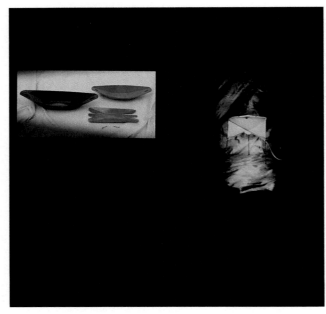

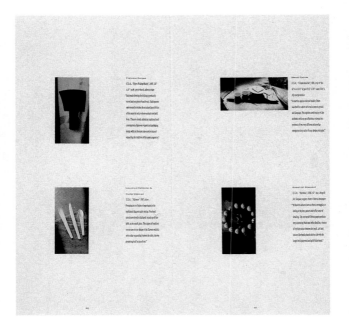

REACTOR ARTWEAR   51 CAMDEN STREET   TORONTO CANADA   TEL (416) 362 1913

FREEDOM TO READ WEEK
FEBRUARY 17·24 1989

FREEDOM OF EXPRESSION COMMITTEE, BOOK & PERIODICAL DEVELOPMENT COUNCIL   34 ROSS STREET TORONTO ONTARIO M5T 1Z9 · (416) 595·9967

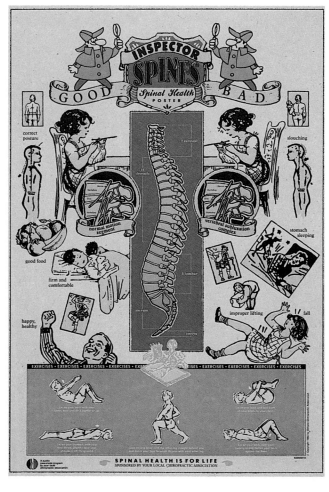

S I L V E R

TITLE
**DESIGN FOR THE REAL
WORLD**
ART DIRECTOR
LOUIS FISHAUF
DESIGNER
**LOUIS FISHAUF/
STEPHANIE POWER**
DESIGN FIRM
REACTOR ART & DESIGN
CLIENT
REACTOR ARTWEAR

S I L V E R

TITLE
**FREEDOM TO READ
WEEK**
ART DIRECTOR
DAVID WYMAN
DESIGNER
DAVID WYMAN
CREATIVE DIR.
DAVID WYMAN
ILLUSTRATOR
DAVID CHESTNUTT
TYPOGRAPHER
M & H TYPOGRAPHY
DESIGN FIRM
DAVID WYMAN DESIGN
CLIENT
**BOOK AND PERIODICAL
DEVELOPMENT COUNCIL**

TITLE
POWER
ART DIRECTOR
RICK CARTY
DESIGNER
RICK CARTY
CREATIVE DIR.
BOB RUSSELL
ILLUSTRATOR
RICK CARTY
DESIGN FIRM
**BOULEVARD
COMMUNICATIONS LTD.**
CLIENT
BATA LIMITED

TITLE
**INSPECTOR SPINE'S
HEALTH POSTER**
ART DIRECTOR
**GLENN TORRESAN/
MICHEL ROULEAU**
DESIGNER
MICHEL ROULEAU
CREATIVE DIR.
MICHEL ROULEAU
ILLUSTRATOR
MICHEL ROULEAU
TYPOGRAPHER
**HANGAR 13/
DAVID BERMAN**
DESIGN FIRM
HANGAR 13
CLIENT
**ONTARIO CHIROPRACTIC
ASSOCIATION**

TITLE
**TUDHOPE ASSSOCIATES
INC. MOVING
ANNOUNCEMENT**
ART DIRECTOR
WILLIAM LAM
DESIGNER
TODD RICHARDS
CREATIVE DIR.
**BEV TUDHOPE/
IAN TUDHOPE**
PHOTOGRAPHER
**DIANA NETHERCOTT,
THE GLOBE & MAIL,
TORONTO**
DESIGN FIRM
**TUDHOPE
ASSOCIATES INC.**
PRINTER
**CAMPBELL
GRAPHICS INC.**
FILM SEPARATIONS
EMPRESS GRAPHICS INC.

TITLE
NEW YORK'S ANNUAL...
WRITER
ED CLEARY
DESIGNER
ED CLEARY
TYPOGRAPHER
**THE COMPOSING ROOM
AT COOPER & BEATTY**
CLIENT
COOPER & BEATTY

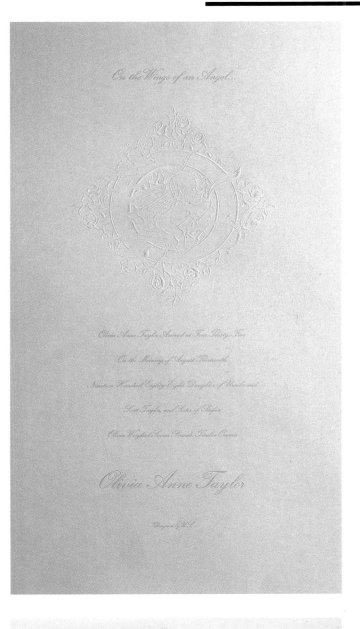

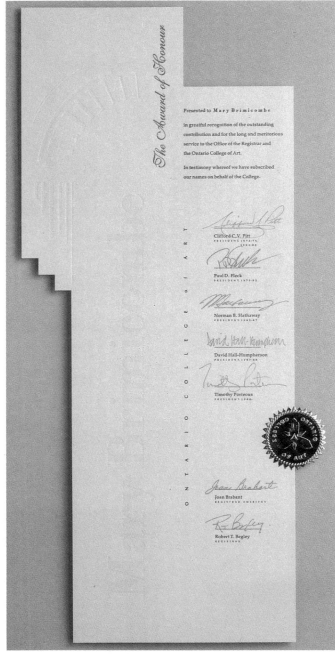

SILVER

TITLE
OLIVIA TAYLOR BIRTH ANNOUNCEMENT
ART DIRECTOR
SCOTT TAYLOR/ URSULA KAISER
WRITER
HELEN BATTERSBY
DESIGNER
PETER BAKER
ILLUSTRATOR
BILL RUSSELL
TYPOGRAPHER
COOPER & BEATTY, LIMITED, PETER BAKER
DESIGN FIRM
TAYLOR & BROWNING DESIGN ASSOCIATES
CLIENT
SCOTT, URSULA, STEFAN TAYLOR
PRINTER
M.C. CHARTERS CO. LTD./ LUNAR CAUSTIC PRESS

SILVER

TITLE
HONORARY AWARD
ART DIRECTOR
KLAUS UHLIG
DESIGNER
IRINA KHVALOVA
TYPOGRAPHER
CROCKER BRYANT INC.
DESIGN FIRM
KLAUS UHLIG DESIGNGROUP INC.
CLIENT
ROBERT T. BEGLEY
PUBLISHER
ONTARIO COLLEGE OF ART
LETTERPRESS
LUNAR CAUSTIC PRESS

SILVER

TITLE
TUDHOPE ASSOCIATES INC. CHRISTMAS RECIPE BOOK
ART DIRECTOR
WILLIAM LAM
DESIGNER
PEGGY PANSEGRAU
CREATIVE DIR.
BEV TUDHOPE/ IAN TUDHOPE
DESIGN FIRM
TUDHOPE ASSOCIATES INC.
CLIENT
TUDHOPE ASSOCIATES INC.
PRINTER
LUNAR CAUSTIC PRESS

TITLE
**GUIDE TO SIGNS,
SYMBOLS & COLOURS**
DESIGNER
JOHN GRANT
TYPOGRAPHER
**COOPER & BEATTY,
LIMITED**
DESIGN FIRM
GRANT DESIGN LTD.
CLIENT
ABITIBI-PRICE

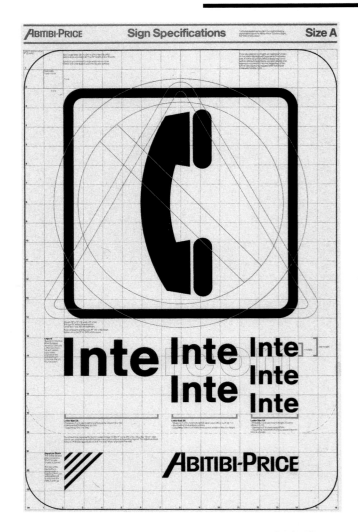

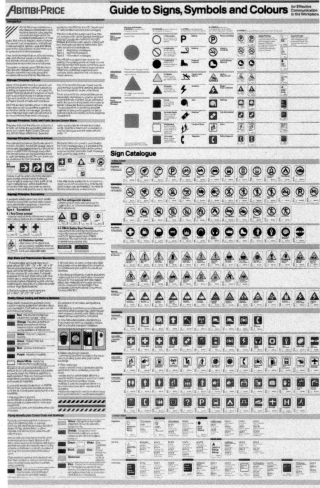

TITLE
**TUDHOPE ASSOCIATES
INC. OPENING PARTY
INVITATION**
DESIGNER
TODD RICHARDS
CREATIVE DIR.
**BEV TUDHOPE/
IAN TUDHOPE**
DESIGN FIRM
**TUDHOPE
ASSOCIATES INC.**
CLIENT
**TUDHOPE
ASSOCIATES INC.**
PRINTER
**ARTHURS-JONES
LITHOGRAPHING LTD.**
FILM SEPARATION
EMPRESS GRAPHICS INC.

TITLE
**ROBERT HYLAND
DESIGN & ASSOCIATES
CHRISTMAS CARD**
ART DIRECTOR
ROBERT HYLAND
DESIGNER
SUSANNE SCHWARZE
ILLUSTRATOR
SUSANNE SCHWARZE
DESIGN FIRM
**ROBERT HYLAND DESIGN
AND ASSOCIATES**

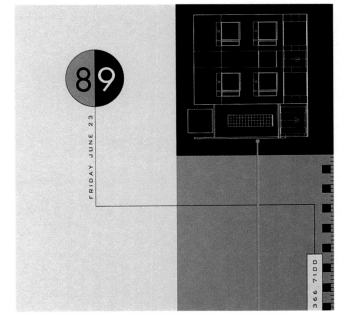

TITLE
**BUTTERFLY HEARTS/
BEACH BLANKET BINGO/
LOBSTER WATCHING/
HOT DOG/
GIRL ON BIKE T-SHIRTS**
ART DIRECTOR
JILL CHEN
DESIGNER
JILL CHEN
ILLUSTRATOR
JILL CHEN
TYPOGRAPHER
JILL CHEN
DESIGN FIRM
**CARMEN DUNJKO
ASSOCIATES**
CLIENT
MARCI LIPMAN INC.

TITLE
DIVER
DESIGNER
JOE BIAFORE
ILLUSTRATOR
JOE BIAFORE
TYPOGRAPHER
JILL CHEN
DESIGN FIRM
**CARMEN DUNJKO
ASSOCIATES**
CLIENT
MARCI LIPMAN INC.

TITLE
MERMAID
ART DIRECTOR
JOE BIAFORE
DESIGNER
**JOE BIAFORE/
JILL CHEN**
ILLUSTRATOR
JOE BIAFORE
TYPOGRAPHER
JILL CHEN
DESIGN FIRM
MENTAL ART & DESIGN
CLIENT
THE SIGNATURE SHOP

TITLE
**THE BODY SHOP 1989
CALENDAR**
ART DIRECTOR
SHARI SPIER
DESIGNER
SHARI SPIER
ILLUSTRATOR
**JAMIE BENNETT/
JEFF JACKSON/
PAULA MUNCK/
REACTOR**
TYPOGRAPHER
CANADIAN COMPOSITION
AGENCY
STRATEGIC OBJECTIVES
DESIGN FIRM
REACTOR ART & DESIGN
CLIENT
THE BODY SHOP

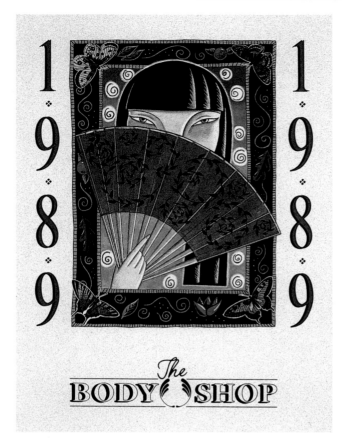

TITLE
**SEASONS GREETINGS
1988 (TANGRAM)**
ART DIRECTOR
KLAUS UHLIG
DESIGNER
IRINA KHVALOVA
DESIGN FIRM
**KLAUS UHLIG
DESIGNGROUP INC.**
PRINTER
**MacKINNON-
MONCUR LTD.**

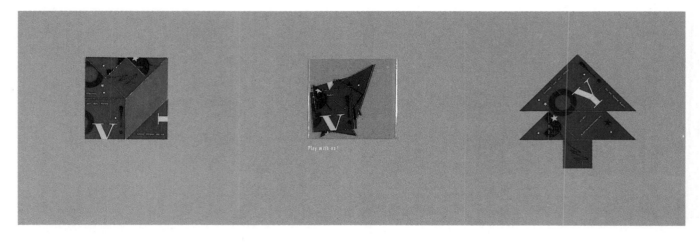

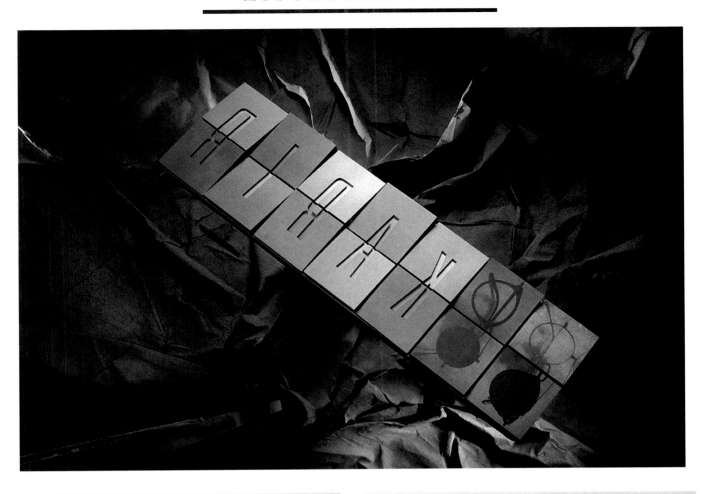

TITLE
KARIR SIGNAGE
ART DIRECTOR
DEL TERRELONGE
DESIGNER
**DEL TERRELONGE/
LESLIE SMITH**
TYPOGRAPHER
LIND GRAPHICS
DESIGN FIRM
**TERRELONGE
DESIGN INC.**
CLIENT
KARIR
FABRICATOR
KING PRODUCTS

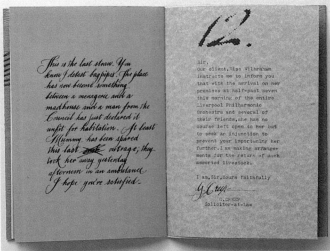

TITLE
CHRISTMAS BOOK
ART DIRECTOR
DENNIS GODDARD
WRITER
NUKNOWW
DESIGNER
DENNIS GODDARD
TYPOGRAPHER
DENNIS GODDARD
DESIGN FIRM
**GRAPHIC
DIRECTIONS INC.**

TITLE
BATA - SUMMER
ART DIRECTOR
LOUIS FISHAUF
ILLUSTRATOR
**PAULA MUNCK/
REACTOR**
CLIENT
BATA

TITLE
BATA - CHRISTMAS
ART DIRECTOR
LOUIS FISHAUF
ILLUSTRATOR
**JEFF JACKSON/
REACTOR**
CLIENT
BATA

3

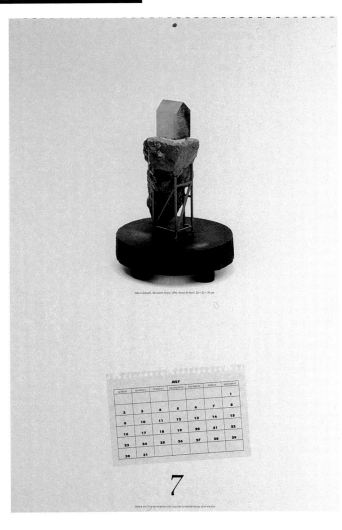

7

TITLE
1989 ART GIFT CALENDAR
DESIGNER
**NELSON VIGNEAULT/
BARBARA SAWCHUK**
PHOTOGRAPHER
NELSON VIGNEAULT
TYPOGRAPHER
PAPERWORDS
DESIGN FIRM
THINKDESIGN LTD.
CLIENT
**CALGARY
CONTEMPORARY ARTS
SOCIETY**
ELECTRONIC IMAGING
COLOUR FOUR
PRINTER
**PAPERWORKS PRESS
LIMITED**

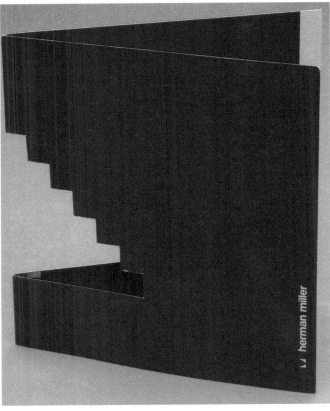

TITLE
SEASON'S GREETINGS
ART DIRECTOR
TIIT TELMET
DESIGNER
**NIGEL SKINNER/
TIIT TELMET**
DESIGN FIRM
**TELMET DESIGN
ASSOCIATES**
CLIENT
**HERMAN MILLER
CANADA, INC.**
PRINTER
**ARTHURS-JONES
LITHOGRAPHING LTD.**

INDEX

INDEX

MEMBERS LIST

Lori Abrams
Charles Abrams
David Adams
Charles Adorjan
Harry Agensky
Leonard Aguanno
Jim Allen
David Allen
Larry Anas
Shigeshi Aoki
Stuart Ash
Roland Aubert
Walter Augustowitsch
Lawrence Ayliffe

Nadia Bailey
Ulrike Balke
Inacio Barata
George Bayne
Doug Beatty
Ann Beatty
Lindsay Beaudry
Terry Bell
Bert Bell
Jay Belmore
Ulrike Bender
Nina Berkson
Joe Biafore
Richard Billinghurst
Kevin Bird
Yolanda Biron
Baiba Black
Stephen Boake
Bruce Bond
Marilyn Bouma–Pyper
Ken Boyd
Bill Boyko
Donna Braggins
Keith Branscombe
Katherine Brown
Jim Brown
Dennis Bruce
Duncan Bruce
Ken Burgin
Robert Burns
Lisa Burroughs

Paul Cade
Silvio Calcagno
Gail Campbell
Jim Carpenter
Gary Carr
Susan Casey
Dario Catana
Barry Chemel
Jill Chen
Michael Chortyk
Ozzie Ciliberti
David Clark
Keith Clarridge
Ed Cleary
Richard Clewes
Peter Coates
Cate Cochran
Jim Cochrane
Dean Coldham
Jai Cole
Kathryn Cole
Philip Congreves
Gerry Cooper
Heather Cooper
John Cormier
Gorette Costa
Chris Crofton
Dianne Croteau
John Cruickshank
Michael Crunkhorn
Mark Cryns

Boris Damast
Janice Davidson
Stanley Davidson
Robert Davidson
Rick Davis
Jack Dawkins
Peter Day
Michael Day
Skip Dean
Yvonne Delaney
Kasper deLine
Michael Dempsey
Stephen Denvir
Kelly Michele deRegt
Lou DiFelice
Theo Dimson
Randy Diplock

Peter Dixon
Yuri Dojc
Jim Donoahue
Christine Downs
Vivian Ducas
Claude Dumoulin
Carmen Dunjko
Philip Dunk
Bill Durnan

Michael Edwards
Bruce English
Peter Enneson
Roslyn Eskind

Robin Fennell
Teresa Fernandes
Martin Finesilver
Jayne Finn
Vic Finucci
Louis Fishauf
Michael Fog
Tim Forbes
Bob Fortier
Pamela Fulford
Kevin Fullarton
Aviva Furman

B.J. Galbraith
John Gallaugher
Paul Ganyon
Alan Gee
Gerald George
Danny Giangualano
Scott Gibbs
Bernadette Gillen
Bob Glynn
Dennis Goddard
Nestor Golets
Audrey Goto
Robbie Goulden
Heidi Graf
Jack Graham
John Grant
Micheal Gregg
Anne Grieve
Gayle Grin

Remzi Hacioglu
Barb Hambly
Bob Hambly
Brett Hamilton
Georges Haroutiun
Julia Harris
Roger Harris
James Harrison
David Heath
Dale Henderson
Robert Herrera
Mr. D Hickman
Jim Hickman
Christine Higdon
Wayne Hilinski
Keith Hillmer
Michael Hollett
Allan Holman
Peter Holmes
Marlene Hore
David How
Thomas Howlett
Paul Hurren
Robert Hyland

Terry Iles
Janice Ivory

Richard Jacobson
Bill James
Anna Janes
Paul Jarsky
Elaine Jewell

Ursula Kaiser
Dennis Kane
Diti Katona
Dieter Kaufmann
Allan Kazmer
Arnold Kelly
Syd Kessler
Dela Kilian
David Kinoshita
Judy Kiyonaga
Cindy Knowles
Tanya Kochnke
Michael Kohn
Diane Kolev
Christa Kroboth

Larry Kuzoff
Bill Kyles

Gerry L'Orange
J.P. LaCroix
Francis Lai
Wes Laing
John Di Lallo
Derek Lamarque
Peter Land
Peter Lanyon
Ted Larson
Jocelyn Laurence
Ed Lea
Raymond Lee
Chris Lee
Tiffany Leger
Nancy Leung
Michael Levy
Robert M. Lewis
Vera Litynsky
Jean Lucdenat

Brad MacIver
Alex Macleod
Fiona MacRae
Vera Maidan
Dennis Maison
Richard Male
Darcy Maloney
Jay Mandarino
Steve Manley
Judy Margolis
Julie Markle
Bill Martin
David Martin
Jose Martucci
Carolyn Martyn
Allen Massey
Maria Mastromarco
Georg Mauerhoff
Emilio Mazzonna
Stephen McLachlan
Michael McLaughlin
Donald McLean
Lisa Miller
Bryan Mills
Frank Moniz
Barry Montgomery
Timothey Morley
Dean Motter
Susan Mui
Lorraine Munro
Shawn Murenbeeld
Maria Murray
Marian Mustard
Steve Mykolyn

Rodney Nash
Julie Nasmith
Arthur Niemi
Vincent Noguchi
Dale Norrie

Dermot O'Brien
Suzanne O'Callaghan
Tim O'Connell
Terrence O'Malley
Peter Oliver
Mary Opper
John Ormsby

Rick Padulo
Derrick Pao
Liz Pardal
Sandra Parsons
Gregory Peek
Dan Peppler
William Perry
George Phair
Ingrid Pill
Catherine Pike
Fernanda Pisani
Barry Platt
Kerry Plumley
Laura Pollard
Gary Prouk
John Pylypczak

Michael Rafelson
Tim Raleigh
Raj Rama
Robert Ramsay
Keith Ravenscroft
Mario Remillard
Mehbs Remtulla
Sue Reynolds

Lisa Richards
Bruce Richardson
Debra Richman
Ingrid Riets
Geoffrey Roche
Beverley Rockett
Ross Rodgers
Ken Rodmell
Rudi Rodrigues
Jim Ronson
Gabrielle Rosen
Philip Rostron
Michel Rouleau

Marcy Sagel
Gerald Schoenhoff
Marie Sequens
Nancy Shanoff
Ivor Sharp
David Sharpe
Therese Shechter
Martin Shewchuck
Lisa Shimotakahara
George Simhoni
Karen Simpson
Marilyn Sing
Chuck Slawich
Geoff Smith
Nelson Smith
Ron Baxter Smith
Wycliffe Smith
John Speakman
Michel St.Jean
Kirk Alexander Stephens
Russell Steventon
Rod Stothers
Evelyn Stoynoff
Jean-Jacques Streliski
Nina Stultz
Leslie Styles
Philip Sung

Tiit Telmet
Del Terrelonge
Frank Teskey
Mark Tharme
John Thompson
Ebbe Thomsen
Derek Timmerman
Chris Tivey
Les Trevor
Kent Turcotte
Lorraine Tuson

Klaus Uhlig
Philip Unger

Derek Vanlint
Rod Della Vedova
John Vennare
Richard Verdiccio
Michel Viau
Mike Visser
Frank Viva
Dale Vokey
Jon Vopni
Diane Vrchovnik

Paul Walker
H.E. Wallis
George Walton
Darren Warner
Edie Wawrychuck
Martha Weaver
Raymond van der Wegen
Cheung Wei-Lieh
Oscar Weis
Vaughn Whelan
Robert White
Arnold Wicht
Jim Wideman
Michael Wilde
Elizabeth Williams
Pamela Wimbush
Larry Wolf
Don Wong
Bruce Wrighte
Spencer Wynn

Jackie Young
Carol Young
Eric Young

Richard Zemnicks
Rose Zgodzinski
Vern Zimmerman